AA001965

Second Workshop on Universal Dependencies (UDW 2018)

Brussels, Belgium
1 November 2018

ISBN: 978-1-5108-7428-2

Printed from e-media with permission by:

Curran Associates, Inc.
57 Morehouse Lane
Red Hook, NY 12571

Some format issues inherent in the e-media version may also appear in this print version.

Copyright© (2018) by the Association for Computational Linguistics
All rights reserved.

Printed by Curran Associates, Inc. (2019)

For permission requests, please contact the Association for Computational Linguistics
at the address below.

Association for Computational Linguistics
209 N. Eighth Street
Stroudsburg, Pennsylvania 18360

Phone: 1-570-476-8006
Fax: 1-570-476-0860

acl@aclweb.org

Additional copies of this publication are available from:

Curran Associates, Inc.
57 Morehouse Lane
Red Hook, NY 12571 USA
Phone: 845-758-0400
Fax: 845-758-2633
Email: curran@proceedings.com
Web: www.proceedings.com

EMNLP 2018

Second Workshop on Universal Dependencies (UDW 2018)

Proceedings of the Workshop

November 1, 2018
Brussels, Belgium

Sponsored by:

©2018 The Association for Computational Linguistics

Order copies of this and other ACL proceedings from:

Association for Computational Linguistics (ACL)
209 N. Eighth Street
Stroudsburg, PA 18360
USA
Tel: +1-570-476-8006
Fax: +1-570-476-0860
acl@aclweb.org

Preface

These proceedings include the program and papers that are presented at the second workshop on Universal Dependencies, held in conjunction with EMNLP in Brussels (Belgium) on November 1, 2018.

Universal Dependencies (UD) is a framework for cross-linguistically consistent treebank annotation that has so far been applied to over 70 languages (http://universaldependencies.org/). The framework is aiming to capture similarities as well as idiosyncrasies among typologically different languages (e.g., morphologically rich languages, pro-drop languages, and languages featuring clitic doubling). The goal in developing UD was not only to support comparative evaluation and cross-lingual learning but also to facilitate multilingual natural language processing and enable comparative linguistic studies.

After a successful first UD workshop at NoDaLiDa in Gothenburg last year, we decided to continue to bring together researchers working on UD, to reflect on the theory and practice of UD, its use in research and development, and its future goals and challenges.

We received 39 submissions of which 26 were accepted. Submissions covered several topics: some papers describe treebank conversion or creation, while others target specific linguistic constructions and which analysis to adopt, sometimes with critiques of the choices made in UD; some papers exploit UD resources for cross-linguistic and psycholinguistic analysis, or for parsing, and others discuss the relation of UD to different frameworks.

We are honored to have two invited speakers: Barbara Plank (Computer Science Department, IT University of Copenhagen), with a talk on "Learning χ^2 – Natural Language Processing Across Languages and Domains", and Dag Haug (Department of Philosophy, Classics, History of Arts and Ideas, University of Oslo), speaking about "Glue semantics for UD". Our invited speakers target different aspects of UD in their work: Barbara Plank's talk is an instance of how UD facilitates cross-lingual learning and transfer for NLP components, whereas Dag Haug will address how UD and semantic formalisms can intersect.

We are grateful to the program committee, who worked hard and on a tight schedule to review the submissions and provided authors with valuable feedback. We thank Google, Inc. for its sponsorship which made it possible to feature two invited talks. We also want to thank Jan Hajic for giving us the impetus to put together and submit a workshop proposal to the ACL workshops, Sampo Pyysalo for his invaluable help with the website and prompt reactions as always, and Joakim Nivre for his constant support and helpful suggestions on the workshop organization.

We wish all participants a productive workshop!

Marie-Catherine de Marneffe, Teresa Lynn and Sebastian Schuster

Workshop Co-Chairs:

Marie-Catherine de Marneffe, The Ohio State University, USA
Teresa Lynn, Dublin City University, Ireland
Sebastian Schuster, Stanford University, USA

Organizers:

Joakim Nivre, Uppsala Univeristy, Sweden
Filip Ginter, University of Turku, Finland
Yoav Goldberg, Bar Ilan University, Israel
Jan Hajic, Charles University in Prague, Czech Republic
Sampo Pyysalo, University of Cambridge, UK
Reut Tsarfaty, Open University of Israel, Israel
Francis Tyers, Higher School of Economics, Moscow, Russia
Dan Zeman, Charles University in Prague, Czech Republic

Program Committee:

Željko Agić, IT University of Copenhagen, Denmark
Marie Candito, Université Paris Diderot, France
Giuseppe Celano, University of Leipzig, Germany
Çağrı Çöltekin, Tübingen, Germany
Miryam de Lhoneux, Uppsala University, Sweden
Tim Dozat, Stanford University, USA
Kaja Dobrovoljc, University of Ljubljana, Slovenia
Jennifer Foster, Dublin City University, Ireland
Kim Gerdes, Sorbonne nouvelle Paris 3, France
Koldo Gojenola, Euskal Herriko Unibertsitatea, Spain
Sylvain Kahane, Université Paris Ouest - Nanterre, France
Natalia Kotsyba, Polish Academy of Sciences, Poland
John Lee, City University of Hong Kong, Hong Kong
Alessandro Lenci, University of Pisa, Italy
Christopher D. Manning, Stanford University, USA
Héctor Martínez Alonso INRIA - Paris 7, France
Ryan McDonald, Google, UK
Simonetta Montemagni, CNR, Italy
Lilja Ovrelid, University of Oslo, Norway
Martin Popel, Charles University, Czech Republic
Peng Qi, Stanford University, USA
Siva Reddy, Stanford University, USA
Rudolf Rosa, Charles University in Prague, Czech Republic
Petya Osenova, Bulgarian Academy of Sciences, Bulgaria
Tanja Samardžić, University of Zurich, Switzerland
Nathan Schneider, Georgetown University, USA
Djamé Seddah, INRIA/ Université Paris 4 La Sorbonne, France
Maria Simi, Università di Pisa, Italy
Zdeněk Žabokrtský, Charles University in Prague, Czech Republic
Amir Zeldes, Georgetown University, USA

Invited Speakers:

Barbara Plank, IT University of Copenhagen, Denmark
Dag Haug, University of Oslo, Norway

Table of Contents

Assessing the Impact of Incremental Error Detection and Correction. A Case Study on the Italian Universal Dependency Treebank
Chiara Alzetta, Felice Dell'Orletta, Simonetta Montemagni, Maria Simi and Giulia Venturi 1

Using Universal Dependencies in cross-linguistic complexity research
Aleksandrs Berdicevskis, Çağrı Çöltekin, Katharina Ehret, Kilu von Prince, Daniel Ross, Bill Thompson, Chunxiao Yan, Vera Demberg, Gary Lupyan, Taraka Rama and Christian Bentz 8

Expletives in Universal Dependency Treebanks
Gosse Bouma, Jan Hajic, Dag Haug, Joakim Nivre, Per Erik Solberg and Lilja Øvrelid 18

Challenges in Converting the Index Thomisticus Treebank into Universal Dependencies
Flavio Massimiliano Cecchini, Marco Passarotti, Paola Marongiu and Daniel Zeman 27

Er ... well, it matters, right? On the role of data representations in spoken language dependency parsing
Kaja Dobrovoljc and Matej Martinc 37

Mind the Gap: Data Enrichment in Dependency Parsing of Elliptical Constructions
Kira Droganova, Filip Ginter, Jenna Kanerva and Daniel Zeman 47

Integration complexity and the order of cosisters
William Dyer 55

SUD or Surface-Syntactic Universal Dependencies: An annotation scheme near-isomorphic to UD
Kim Gerdes, Bruno Guillaume, Sylvain Kahane and Guy Perrier 66

Coordinate Structures in Universal Dependencies for Head-final Languages
Hiroshi Kanayama, Na-Rae Han, Masayuki Asahara, Jena D. Hwang, Yusuke Miyao, Jinho D. Choi and Yuji Matsumoto 75

Investigating NP-Chunking with Universal Dependencies for English
Ophélie Lacroix 85

Marrying Universal Dependencies and Universal Morphology
Arya D. McCarthy, Miikka Silfverberg, Ryan Cotterell, Mans Hulden and David Yarowsky 91

Enhancing Universal Dependency Treebanks: A Case Study
Joakim Nivre, Paola Marongiu, Filip Ginter, Jenna Kanerva, Simonetta Montemagni, Sebastian Schuster and Maria Simi 102

Enhancing Universal Dependencies for Korean
Youngbin Noh, Jiyoon Han, Tae Hwan Oh and Hansaem Kim 108

UD-Japanese BCCWJ: Universal Dependencies Annotation for the Balanced Corpus of Contemporary Written Japanese
Mai Omura and Masayuki Asahara 117

The First Komi-Zyrian Universal Dependencies Treebanks
Niko Partanen, Rogier Blokland, KyungTae Lim, Thierry Poibeau and Michael Rießler 126

The Hebrew Universal Dependency Treebank: Past Present and Future
Shoval Sade, Amit Seker and Reut Tsarfaty 133

Multi-source synthetic treebank creation for improved cross-lingual dependency parsing
Francis Tyers, Mariya Sheyanova, Aleksandra Martynova, Pavel Stepachev and Konstantin Vinogorodskiy 144

Toward Universal Dependencies for Shipibo-Konibo
Alonso Vásquez, Renzo Ego Aguirre, Candy Angulo, John Miller, Claudia Villanueva, Željko Agić, Roberto Zariquiey and Arturo Oncevay 151

Transition-based Parsing with Lighter Feed-Forward Networks
David Vilares and Carlos Gómez-Rodríguez 162

Extended and Enhanced Polish Dependency Bank in Universal Dependencies Format
Alina Wróblewska 173

Approximate Dynamic Oracle for Dependency Parsing with Reinforcement Learning
Xiang Yu, Ngoc Thang Vu and Jonas Kuhn 183

The Coptic Universal Dependency Treebank
Amir Zeldes and Mitchell Abrams 192

Workshop Program

Thursday, November 1, 2018

9:00–10:30   **Opening, Invited Talk & Oral Presentations 1**

9:00–9:10   *Opening*

9:10–10:00   *Invited Talk: Glue semantics for UD*
Dag Haug

10:00–10:15   *Using Universal Dependencies in cross-linguistic complexity research*
Aleksandrs Berdicevskis, Çağrı Çöltekin, Katharina Ehret, Kilu von Prince, Daniel Ross, Bill Thompson, Chunxiao Yan, Vera Demberg, Gary Lupyan, Taraka Rama and Christian Bentz

10:15–10:30   *Integration complexity and the order of cosisters*
William Dyer

10:30–11:00   **Coffee Break**

11:00–12:30   **Poster Session**

From LFG to Enhanced Universal Dependencies (in LFG 2018 and LAW-MWE-CxG-2018)
Adam Przepiórkowski and Agnieszka Patejuk

Approximate Dynamic Oracle for Dependency Parsing with Reinforcement Learning
Xiang Yu, Ngoc Thang Vu and Jonas Kuhn

Transition-based Parsing with Lighter Feed-Forward Networks
David Vilares and Carlos Gómez-Rodríguez

UD-Japanese BCCWJ: Universal Dependencies Annotation for the Balanced Corpus of Contemporary Written Japanese
Mai Omura and Masayuki Asahara

Challenges in Converting the Index Thomisticus Treebank into Universal Dependencies
Flavio Massimiliano Cecchini, Marco Passarotti, Paola Marongiu and Daniel Zeman

Thursday, November 1, 2018 (continued)

Investigating NP-Chunking with Universal Dependencies for English
Ophélie Lacroix

Extended and Enhanced Polish Dependency Bank in Universal Dependencies Format
Alina Wróblewska

Mind the Gap: Data Enrichment in Dependency Parsing of Elliptical Constructions
Kira Droganova, Filip Ginter, Jenna Kanerva and Daniel Zeman

The Coptic Universal Dependency Treebank
Amir Zeldes and Mitchell Abrams

Parsing Japanese Tweets into Universal Dependencies (non-archival submission)
Hayate Iso, Kaoru Ito, Hiroyuki Nagai, Taro Okahisa and Eiji Aramaki

Toward Universal Dependencies for Shipibo-Konibo
Alonso Vásquez, Renzo Ego Aguirre, Candy Angulo, John Miller, Claudia Villanueva, Željko Agić, Roberto Zariquiey and Arturo Oncevay

All Roads Lead to UD: Converting Stanford and Penn Parses to English Universal Dependencies with Multilayer Annotations (in LAW-MWE-CxG-2018)
Siyao Peng and Amir Zeldes

The First Komi-Zyrian Universal Dependencies Treebanks
Niko Partanen, Rogier Blokland, KyungTae Lim, Thierry Poibeau and Michael Rießler

The Hebrew Universal Dependency Treebank: Past Present and Future
Shoval Sade, Amit Seker and Reut Tsarfaty

Enhancing Universal Dependencies for Korean
Youngbin Noh, Jiyoon Han, Tae Hwan Oh and Hansaem Kim

Multi-source synthetic treebank creation for improved cross-lingual dependency parsing
Francis Tyers, Mariya Sheyanova, Aleksandra Martynova, Pavel Stepachev and Konstantin Vinogorodskiy

Thursday, November 1, 2018 (continued)

12:30–14:00   **Lunch Break**

14:00–15:35   **Invited Talk & Oral Presentations 2**

14:00–14:50   *Invited Talk: Learning X^2 – Natural Language Processing Across Languages and Domains*
Barbara Plank

14:50–15:05   *Er ... well, it matters, right? On the role of data representations in spoken language dependency parsing*
Kaja Dobrovoljc and Matej Martinc

15:05–15:20   *Assessing the Impact of Incremental Error Detection and Correction. A Case Study on the Italian Universal Dependency Treebank*
Chiara Alzetta, Felice Dell'Orletta, Simonetta Montemagni, Maria Simi and Giulia Venturi

15:20–15:35   *Enhancing Universal Dependency Treebanks: A Case Study*
Joakim Nivre, Paola Marongiu, Filip Ginter, Jenna Kanerva, Simonetta Montemagni, Sebastian Schuster and Maria Simi

15:35–16:00   **Coffee Break**

16:00–17:30   **Oral Presentations 3 & Closing**

16:00–16:15   *Marrying Universal Dependencies and Universal Morphology*
Arya D. McCarthy, Miikka Silfverberg, Ryan Cotterell, Mans Hulden and David Yarowsky

16:15–16:30   *Arguments and Adjuncts in Universal Dependencies* (in Coling 2018)
Adam Przepiórkowski and Agnieszka Patejuk

16:30–16:45   *Expletives in Universal Dependency Treebanks*
Gosse Bouma, Jan Hajic, Dag Haug, Joakim Nivre, Per Erik Solberg and Lilja Øvrelid

16:45–17:00   *Coordinate Structures in Universal Dependencies for Head-final Languages*
Hiroshi Kanayama, Na-Rae Han, Masayuki Asahara, Jena D. Hwang, Yusuke Miyao, Jinho D. Choi and Yuji Matsumoto

17:00–17:15   *SUD or Surface-Syntactic Universal Dependencies: An annotation scheme near-isomorphic to UD*
Kim Gerdes, Bruno Guillaume, Sylvain Kahane and Guy Perrier

17:15–17:30   *Concluding Remarks*

Invited Talk: Dag Haug, University of Oslo

Glue semantics for UD

The success of the Universal Dependencies initiative has spurned interest in deriving semantic structures from UD trees. The challenge is to do this while relying as little as possible on language-specific, typically lexical resources that are not available for many of the 60 languages for which there are UD treebanks. In this talk I outline an approach to this problem that builds on techniques developed for LFG + Glue. There are several motivations for this: First, LFG's f-structures track the same aspect of syntactic structure as UD dependency trees. Second, the particular version of dependency grammar that UD embodies has inherited much from LFG via the Stanford Dependencies and the PARC dependencies. Third, unlike many other approaches, LFG + Glue does not assume a one-to-one mapping from syntactic to semantic structures but instead develops a syntax-semantics interface that can map a single syntactic structure to several meaning representations, i.e. the syntax underspecifies the semantics, which is useful when dealing with the lack of information one often encounters in UD trees. In the talk, I will present the theoretical background for UD + Glue and discuss some issues that arose in the development of a proof of concept implementation of the framework.

Bio

Dag Haug is professor of classics and linguistics at the University of Oslo. He has worked extensively in theoretical syntax (mainly Lexical-Functional Grammar) and formal semantics. He has also led various treebanking efforts for ancient languages, which among other things have resulted in the UD treebanks for Ancient Greek, Latin, Old Church Slavonic and Gothic.

Invited Talk: Barbara Plank, IT University of Copenhagen

Learning X^2 – Natural Language Processing Across Languages and Domains

How can we build Natural Language Processing models for new domains and new languages? In this talk I will survey some recent advances to address this challenge, from multi-task learning, data selection, cross-lingual transfer to learning models under distant supervision from disparate sources, and outline open challenges. The talk will focus on two target applications: part-of-speech tagging and dependency parsing.

Bio

Barbara Plank is associate professor at ITU (IT University of Copenhagen), Denmark. She holds a BSc and MSc in Computer Science and received her PhD in Computational Linguistics in 2011. Originally from South Tyrol, Italy, she worked and lived in the Netherlands, Italy and Denmark. Barbara is interested in robust language technology, in particular cross-domain and cross-language learning, learning under annotation bias, and generally, semi-supervised and weakly-supervised machine learning for a broad range of NLP applications, including syntactic parsing, author profiling, opinion mining and information and relation extraction.

Assessing the Impact of Incremental Error Detection and Correction.
A Case Study on the Italian Universal Dependency Treebank

Chiara Alzetta*, Felice Dell'Orletta°, Simonetta Montemagni°, Maria Simi•, Giulia Venturi°
*Università degli Studi di Genova
°Istituto di Linguistica Computazionale "Antonio Zampolli" (ILC-CNR), Pisa
ItaliaNLP Lab - *www.italianlp.it*
•Dipartimento di Informatica, Università di Pisa
`chiara.alzetta@edu.unige.it,`
`{felice.dellorletta,simonetta.montemagni,giulia.venturi}@ilc.cnr.it`
`simi@di.unipi.it`

Abstract

Detection and correction of errors and inconsistencies in "gold treebanks" are becoming more and more central topics of corpus annotation. The paper illustrates a new incremental method for enhancing treebanks, with particular emphasis on the extension of error patterns across different textual genres and registers. Impact and role of corrections have been assessed in a dependency parsing experiment carried out with four different parsers, whose results are promising. For both evaluation datasets, the performance of parsers increases, in terms of the standard LAS and UAS measures and of a more focused measure taking into account only relations involved in error patterns, and at the level of individual dependencies.

1 Introduction

Over the last years, many approaches to detect errors and inconsistencies in treebanks have been devised (Dickinson, 2015). They can be categorized in two main groups, depending on whether the proposed quality check procedure relies on heuristic patterns (Dickinson and Meurers, 2003, 2005; Boyd et al., 2008) or on statistical methods (Ambati et al., 2011). More recently, the Universal Dependencies (UD) initiative (Nivre, 2015) has yielded a renewed interest as shown by the methods and tools introduced by de Marneffe et al. (2017); Alzetta et al. (2018); Wisniewski (2018). A number of reasons prompted the importance of these methods: they can be useful to check the internal coherence of the newly created treebanks with respect to other treebanks created for a same language or to the annotation guidelines. The risk of inconsistencies or errors is considerable if we consider that 70% of the released UD treebanks originate from a conversion process and only 29% of them has been manually revised after automatic

conversion. In this paper, we extend the method proposed by Alzetta et al. (2018) for error detection and correction in "gold treebanks" and we evaluate its impact on parsing results.

2 Incremental Approach to Error Detection

Detection of annotation errors is often depicted as a two–stage static process, which consists in finding errors in a corpus and correcting them. Dickinson and Tufis (2017) provide a broader view of the task of improving the annotation of corpora, referred to as *iterative enhancement*: "iterative enhancement encompasses techniques that can be iterated, improving the resource with every pass". Surveyed methods for iterative enhancement are applied to both corpora with (mostly) completed annotation and corpora with in–progress annotation. In our opinion, the strategy of iterative enhancement is particularly relevant in the construction of treebanks which result from the conversion of pre-existing resources, as it is more often the case, and/or whose annotation scheme is continuously evolving e.g. to accommodate new linguistic phenomena or to increase cross-lingual consistency, as it happens in the Universal Dependencies (UD) initiative[1]. In this paper, the error detection method proposed by Alzetta et al. (2018) is incrementally extended to deal with other corpus sections from other domains and registers: this can be seen as a first step of an iterative enhancement approach, which represents one of the currently explored lines of research.

Alzetta et al. (2018) proposed an original error detection and correction method which represents the starting point for the case study reported in this paper. The method, tested against the Italian Universal Dependency Treebank (henceforth IUDT)

---

[1] http://universaldependencies.org/

Proceedings of the Second Workshop on Universal Dependencies (UDW 2018), pages 1–7
Brussels, Belgium, November 1, 2018. ©2018 Association for Computational Linguistics

(Bosco et al., 2013), mainly targets systematic errors, which represent potentially "dangerous" relations providing systematic but misleading evidence to a parser. Note that with systematic errors we refer here to both real errors as well as annotation inconsistencies internal to the treebank, whose origin can be traced back to different annotation guidelines underlying the source treebanks, or that are connected with substantial changes in the annotation guidelines (e.g. from version 1.4 to 2.0).

This error detection methodology is based on an algorithm, LISCA (*LInguiStically–driven Selection of Correct Arcs*) (Dell'Orletta et al., 2013), originally developed to measure the reliability of automatically produced dependency relations that are ranked from correct to *anomalous* ones, with the latter potentially including incorrect ones. The process is carried out through the following steps:

- LISCA collects statistics about a wide range of linguistic features extracted from a large reference corpus of automatically parsed sentences. These features are both *local*, corresponding to the characteristics of the syntactic arc considered (e.g. the linear distance in terms of tokens between a dependent d and its syntactic head h), and *global*, locating the considered arc within the overall syntactic structure, with respect to both hierarchical structure and linear ordering of words (e.g. the number of "siblings" and "children" nodes of d, recurring respectively to its right or left in the linear order of the sentence; the distance from the root node, the closer and furthest leaf node);

- collected statistics are used to assign a *quality* score to each arc contained in a target corpus (e.g. a treebank). To avoid possible interferences in detecting anomalies which are due to the variety of language taken into account rather than erroneous annotations, both reference and target corpora should belong to the same textual genre or register. On the basis of the assigned score, arcs are ranked by decreasing quality scores;

- the resulting ranking of arcs in the target corpus is partitioned into 10 groups of equivalent size. Starting from the assumption that *anomalous* annotations (i.e. dependencies which together with their context occurrence are deviant from the "linguistic norm" computed by

LISCA on the basis of the evidence acquired from the reference corpus) concentrate in the bottom groups of the ranking, the manual search of error patterns is restricted to the last groups. Detected anomalous annotations include both *systematic* and *random* errors. Systematic errors, formalized as *error patterns*, are looked for in the whole target corpus, matching contexts are manually revised and, if needed, corrected.

The methodology was tested against the newspaper section of the Italian Universal Dependency Treebank (henceforth IUDT–news), which is composed by 10,891 sentences, for a total of 154,784 tokens. In this paper, the error detection and correction method depicted above is extended to other sections of the IUDT treebank, containing texts belonging to different genres (namely, legal and encyclopedic texts).

3 Incremental Enhancement of IUDT

The incremental error detection strategy depicted in Section 2 was used to improve IUDT version 2.0 (officially released in March 2017). IUDT 2.0 is the result of an automatic conversion process from the previous version (IUDT 1.4), which was needed because of major changes in the annotation guidelines for specific constructions and new dependencies in the Universal Dependencies (UD) tagset[2]. In spite of the fact that this process was followed by a manual revision targeting specific constructions, the resulting treebank needed a quality check in order to guarantee homogeneity and coherence to the resource: it is a widely acknowledged fact that automatic conversion may cause internal inconsistencies, typically corresponding to systematic errors.

The first step of this revision process is described in Alzetta et al. (2018), which led to IUDT version 2.1, released in November 2017. At this stage, 0.51% dependency relations of IUDT–news were modified (789 arcs): among them, 286 arcs (36.01%) turned out to be random errors, while 503 (63.99%) represent systematic errors.

For the latest published version of IUDT (i.e. 2.2, released in July 2018), error patterns identified in IUDT–news were matched against the other sections of IUDT, which contain legal texts and Wikipedia pages. Although error patterns were acquired from IUDT–news, their occurrence in the

---

[2]http://universaldependencies.org/v2/summary.html

other two sections of the treebank turned out to be equivalent. In particular, modified arcs corresponding to systematic errors are 0.36% in IUDT–news, 0.34% in IUDT–Wikipedia and 0.35% in IUDT–legal, for a total amount of 1028 deprels, 525 of which were modified in the passage from version 2.0 to version 2.1. This result proves the effectiveness of the methodology: despite of the fact that error patterns were retrieved in a significantly limited search space of the news section of the treebank (covering about 25% of the total number of arcs in IUDT–news), they turned out to be general enough to be valid for the other language registers represented by the other IUDT sub–corpora.

Version 2.2 of IUDT has been further improved: the result is IUDT version 2.3, still unpublished. In this version, residual cases instantiating error patterns were corrected and instances of one of the six error patterns (concerned with nonfinite verbal constructions functioning as nominals) were reported to the original annotation, since we observed that the proposed annotation was no longer convincing on the basis of some of the new instances that were found.

Overall, from IUDT version 2.0 to 2.3, a total of 2,237 dependency relations was modified: 50.91% of them (corresponding to 1,139 arcs) represented systematic errors, while 49.08% (i.e. 1,098 arcs) contained non–pattern errors. Among the latter, 25.77% are random errors (286 arcs), while 74.22% are structural errors (i.e. 815 erroneous non-projective arcs).

4 Experiments

In order to test the impact of the result of our incremental treebank enhancement approach, we compared the dependency parsing results achieved using IUDT versions 2.0 vs 2.3 for training.

4.1 Experimental Setup

Data. Although the overall size of IUDT changed across the 2.0 and 2.3 versions, we used two equivalent training sets of 265,554 tokens to train the parsers, containing exactly the same texts but different annotations. For both sets of experiments, parser performances were tested against a dev(elopment) set of 10,490 tokens and a test set of 7,545 tokens, differing again at the annotation level only. **Parsers.** Four different parsers were selected for the experiments, differing at the level of the used parsing algorithm. The configurations of the parsers were kept the same across all experiments.

DeSR MLP is a transition-based parser that uses a Multi-Layer Perceptron (Attardi, 2006; Attardi et al., 2009), selected as representative of transition-based parsers. The best configuration for UD, which uses a rich set of features including third order ones and a graph score, is described in Attardi et al. (2015). We trained it on 300 hidden variables, with a learning rate of 0.01, and early stopping when validation accuracy reaches 99.5%.

TurboParser (Martins et al., 2013) is a graph-based parser that uses third-order feature models and a specialized accelerated dual decomposition algorithm for making non-projective parsing computationally feasible. It was used in configuration "full", enabling all third-order features.

Mate is a graph-based parser that uses passive aggressive perceptron and exploits a rich feature set (Bohnet, 2010). Among the configurable parameters, we set to 25 the numbers of iterations. *Mate* was used in the pure graph version.

UDPipe is a trainable pipeline for tokenization, tagging, lemmatization and dependency parsing (Straka and Straková, 2017). The transition-based parser provided with the pipeline is based on a non-recurrent neural network, with just one hidden layer, with locally normalized scores. We used the parser in the basic configuration provided for the CoNLL 2017 Shared Task on Dependency Parsing.

Evaluation Metrics. The performance of parsers was assessed in terms of the standard evaluation metrics of dependency parsing, i.e. *Labeled Attachment Score* (LAS) and *Unlabeled Attachment Score* (UAS). To assess the impact of the correction of systematic errors, we devised a new metric inspired by the *Content-word Labeled Attachment Score* (CLAS) introduced for the CoNLL 2017 Shared Task (Zeman and al., 2017). Similarly to CLAS, the new metric focuses on a selection of dependencies: whereas CLAS focuses on relations between content words only, our metric is computed by only considering those dependencies directly or indirectly involved in the pattern–based error correction process. Table 2 reports the list of UD dependencies involved in error patterns: it includes both modified and modifying dependencies occurring in the rewriting rules formalizing error patterns. Henceforth, we will refer to this metric as *Selected Labeled Attachment Score* (SLAS).

4.2 Parsing Results

The experiments were carried out to assess the impact on parsing of the corrections in the IUDT version 2.3 with respect to version 2.0. Table 1 reports the results of the four parsers in terms of LAS, UAS and SLAS achieved against the IUDT *dev* and *test* sets of the corresponding releases (2.0 vs 2.3). It can be noticed that all parsers improve their performance when trained on version 2.3, against both the *test set* and the *dev set*. The only exception is represented by UDPipe for which a slightly LAS decrease is recorded for the *dev set*, i.e. -0.12%; note, however, that for the same *dev set* UAS increases (+0.12%). The average improvement for LAS and UAS measures is higher for the *test set* than for the *dev set*: +0.38% vs +0.17% for LAS, and +0.35% vs +0.23% for UAS. The higher improvement is obtained by UDPipe (+0.91% LAS, +0.69% UAS) on the *test set*.

Besides standard measures such as LAS and UAS, we devised an additional evaluation measure aimed at investigating the impact of the pattern–based error correction, SLAS, described in Section 4.1. As it can be seen in Table 1, for all parsers the gain in terms of SLAS is significantly higher: the average improvement for the *test set* and the *dev set* is +0.57% and +0.47% respectively. It is also interesting to note that the SLAS values for the two data sets are much closer than in the case of LAS and UAS, suggesting that the higher difference recorded for the general LAS and UAS measures possibly originates in other relations types and corrections (we are currently investigating this hypothesis). This result shows that SLAS is able to intercept the higher accuracy in the prediction of dependency types involved in the error patterns.

To better assess the impact of pattern–based error correction we focused on individual dependencies involved in the error patterns, both modified and modifying ones. This analysis is restricted to the output of the MATE parser, for which a lower average SLAS improvement is recorded (0.34). For both *dev* and *test* sets versions 2.0 and 2.3, Table 2 reports, for each relation type, the number of occurrences in the gold dataset (column "gold"), the number of correct predictions by the parser (column "correct") and the number of predicted dependencies, including erroneous ones (column "sys"). For this dependency subset, an overall re-

duction of the number of errors can be observed for both evaluation sets. The picture is more articulated if we consider individual dependencies. For most of them, both precision and recall increase from version 2.0 to 2.3. There are however few exceptions: e.g. in the 2.3 version, the number of errors is slightly higher for the *aux* relation in both *dev* and *test* datasets (+4 and +1 respectively), or the *acl* relation in the *dev set* (+3).

Table 3 reports, for the same set of relations, the recorded F-measure (F1), accounting for both precision and recall achieved by the MATE parser for individual dependencies: interesting differences can be noted at the level of the distribution of F1 values in column "Diff", where positive values refer to a gain. Out of the 14 selected dependencies, a F1 gain is reported for 10 relations in the *dev set*, and for 8 in the *test set*. Typically, a gain in F1 corresponds to a reduction in the number of errors. Consider, for example, the *cc* dependency involved in a head identification error pattern (`conj head`), where in specific constructions a coordinating conjunction was erroneously headed by the first conjunct (coordination head) rather than by the second one (this follows from a change in the UD guidelines from version 1.4 to 2.0): in this case, F1 increases for both evaluation datasets (+1.55 and +2.77) and errors decrease (-5 and -6). However, it is not always the case that a decrease of the F1 value is accompanied by a higher number of errors for the same relation. Consider, for example, the *acl* relation for which F1 decreases significantly in version 2.3 of both *dev* and *test* datasets (-6.97 and -4.59). The *acl* relation is involved in a labeling error pattern (`acl4amod`), where adjectival modifiers of nouns (*amod*) were originally annotated as clausal modifiers. Whereas in the *dev set 2.3* the F1 value for *acl* decreases and the number of errors increase, in the *test set 2.3* we observe a decrease in F1 (-4.59%) accompanied by a reduction of the number of errors (-1). The latter case combines apparently contrasting facts: note, however, that the loss in F1 is also influenced by the reduction of *acl* occurrences, some of which were transformed into *amod* in version 2.3.

Last but not least, we carried out the same type of evaluation on the subset of sentences in the development dataset which contain at least one instance of the error patterns: we call it *Pattern Corpus*. For this subset the values of LAS, UAS and

	DeSR MLP			MATE			TurboParser			UDPipe		
	LAS	UAS	SLAS	LAS	UAS	SLAS	LAS	UAS	SLAS	LAS	UAS	SLAS
Dev 2.0	87.89	91.18	81.10	90.73	92.95	85.82	89.83	92.72	84.10	**87.02**	90.14	79.11
Dev 2.3	**87.92**	**91.23**	**81.48**	**90.99**	**93.28**	**86.28**	**90.34**	**93.14**	**84.98**	86.90	**90.26**	**79.25**
Diff.	0.03	0.05	0.38	0.26	0.33	0.46	0.51	0.42	0.88	-0.12	0.12	0.14
Test 2.0	89.00	91.99	82.59	91.13	93.25	86.08	90.39	93.33	84.78	87.21	90.38	79.66
Test 2.3	**89.16**	**92.07**	**83.14**	**91.41**	**93.70**	**86.30**	**90.54**	**93.49**	**85.00**	**88.12**	**91.07**	**80.95**
Diff.	0.16	0.08	0.55	0.28	0.45	0.22	0.15	0.16	0.22	0.91	0.69	1.29

Table 1: Evaluation of the parsers against the IUDT test and development sets version 2.0 and 2.3.

deprel	IUDT 2.0						IUDT 2.3					
	Development			Test			Development			Test		
	gold	correct	sys	gold	correct	sys	gold	correct	sys	gold	correct	sys
acl	151	118	146	83	71	86	115	83	114	71	56	70
acl:relcl	137	106	131	100	77	100	137	112	138	101	80	100
amod	637	606	636	455	439	455	667	641	669	460	445	464
aux	218	208	229	172	162	167	217	206	231	172	159	165
aux:pass	78	69	84	69	64	74	79	71	85	69	63	76
cc	325	305	323	217	194	217	326	311	324	217	200	217
ccomp	62	43	61	29	19	32	62	46	63	30	19	27
conj	372	289	403	253	175	251	370	281	394	257	178	252
cop	126	100	117	85	79	87	126	101	113	85	80	89
nmod	977	828	986	710	612	723	976	827	976	705	615	725
obj	412	372	438	275	247	291	413	374	433	275	247	288
obl	678	541	640	523	427	504	681	551	648	523	425	503
obl:agent	43	39	46	39	36	38	43	40	45	39	36	39
xcomp	92	73	84	58	39	47	96	73	86	62	43	53
TOTAL	4308	3697	4324	3068	2641	3072	4308	3717	4319	3066	2646	3068

Table 2: Statistics of individual dependencies involved in an *error pattern* in the test and development sets of IUDT 2.0 and 2.3 (*gold*). *sys* refers to the number of predicted dependencies by the MATE parser and *correct* to the correct predictions.

deprel	Development			Test		
	F1 2.0	F1 2.3	Diff	F1 2.0	F1 2.3	Diff
acl	**79.46**	72.49	-6.97	**84.02**	79.43	-4.59
acl:relcl	79.11	**81.45**	2.35	77.00	**79.60**	2.60
amod	95.20	**95.95**	0.75	**96.48**	96.32	-0.16
aux	**93.06**	91.97	-1.10	**95.58**	94.36	-1.22
aux:pass	85.18	**86.58**	1.40	**89.51**	86.89	-2.62
cc	94.14	**95.69**	1.55	89.40	**92.17**	2.77
ccomp	69.92	**73.60**	3.68	62.30	**66.66**	4.37
conj	**74.58**	73.56	-1.02	69.44	**69.94**	0.49
cop	82.31	**84.52**	2.21	91.86	**91.96**	0.10
nmod	84.36	**84.73**	0.37	85.42	**86.01**	0.60
obj	87.53	**88.42**	0.89	87.28	**87.74**	0.46
obl	82.09	**82.92**	0.83	**83.15**	82.84	-0.31
obl:agent	87.64	**90.91**	3.27	**93.51**	92.31	-1.20
xcomp	**82.95**	80.22	-2.74	74.29	**74.78**	0.49

Table 3: F1 scores and differences for a selection of individual dependencies involved in error patterns by the MATE parser trained on IUDT 2.0 and 2.3.

SLAS for the MATE parser are much higher, ranging between 98.17 and 98.93 for the Pattern corpus 2.0, and between 98.58 and 99.38 for the Pattern corpus 2.3. The gain is in line with what reported in Table 1 for MATE, higher for what concerns LAS (+0.36) and UAS (+0.45), and slightly lower for SLAS (+0.41). Trends similar to the full evaluation datasets are reported also for the dependency-based analysis, which shows however higher F1 values.

5 Conclusion

In this paper, the treebank enhancement method proposed by Alzetta et al. (2018) was further extended and the annotation quality of the resulting treebank was assessed in a parsing experiment carried out with IUDT version 2.0 vs 2.3.

Error patterns identified in the news section of the IUDT treebank were looked for in the other IUDT sections, representative of other domains and language registers. Interestingly, however, error patters acquired from IUDT-news turned out to be characterized by a similar distribution across different treebank sections, which demonstrates their generality.

The resulting treebank was used to train and test four different parsers with the final aim of assessing quality and consistency of the annotation. Achieved results are promising: for both evaluation datasets all parsers show a performance increase (with a minor exception only), in terms of the standard LAS and UAS as well as of the more focused SLAS measure. A dependency-based analysis was also carried out for the relations involved in error patterns: for most of them, a more or less significant gain in the F-measure is reported.

Current developments include: i) extension of the incremental treebank enhancement method by iterating the basic steps reported in the paper to identify new error patterns in the other treebank subsections using LISCA; ii) extension of the incremental treebank enhancement method to other UD treebanks for different languages; iii) extension of the treebank enhancement method to identify and correct random errors.

Acknowledgements

We thank the two anonymous reviewers whose comments and suggestions helped us to improve and clarify the submitted version of the paper. The work reported in the paper was partially supported by the 2–year project (2016-2018) *Smart News, Social sensing for breaking news*, funded by Regione Toscana (BANDO FAR-FAS 2014).

References

C. Alzetta, F. Dell'Orletta, S. Montemagni, and G. Venturi. 2018. Dangerous relations in dependency treebanks. In *Proceedings of 16th International Workshop on Treebanks and Linguistic Theories (TLT16)*, pages 201–210, Prague, Czech Republic.

B. R. Ambati, R. Agarwal, M. Gupta, S. Husain, and D. M. Sharma. 2011. Error Detection for Treebank Validation. In *Proceedings of 9th International Workshop on Asian Language Resources (ALR)*.

Giuseppe Attardi. 2006. Experiments with a multilanguage non-projective dependency parser. In *Proceedings of the Tenth Conference on Computational Natural Language Learning*, CoNLL-X '06, pages 166–170, Stroudsburg, PA, USA. Association for Computational Linguistics.

Giuseppe Attardi, Felice Dell'Orletta, Maria Simi, and Joseph Turian. 2009. Accurate dependency parsing with a stacked multilayer perceptron. In *Proceeding of Evalita 2009*, LNCS. Springer.

Giuseppe Attardi, Simone Saletti, and Maria Simi. 2015. Evolution of italian treebank and dependency parsing towards universal dependencies. In *Proceedings of the Second Italian Conference on Computational Linguistics*, CLIC-it 2015, pages 23–30, Torino, Italy. Accademia University Press/Open Editions.

Bernd Bohnet. 2010. Very high accuracy and fast dependency parsing is not a contradiction. In *Proceedings of the 23rd International Conference on Computational Linguistics*, COLING '10, pages 89–97, Stroudsburg, PA, USA. Association for Computational Linguistics.

C. Bosco, S. Montemagni, and M. Simi. 2013. Converting Italian Treebanks: Towards an Italian Stanford Dependency Treebank. In *Proceedings of the ACL Linguistic Annotation Workshop & Interoperability with Discourse*, Sofia, Bulgaria.

A. Boyd, M. Dickinson, and W. D. Meurers. 2008. On Detecting Errors in Dependency Treebanks. *Research on Language & Computation*, 6(2):113–137.

F. Dell'Orletta, G. Venturi, and S. Montemagni. 2013. Linguistically-driven Selection of Correct Arcs for Dependency Parsing. *Computaciòn y Sistemas*, 2:125–136.

M. Dickinson. 2015. Detection of Annotation Errors in Corpora. *Language and Linguistics Compass*, 9(3):119–138.

M. Dickinson and W. D. Meurers. 2003. Detecting Inconsistencies in Treebank. In *Proceedings of the Second Workshop on Treebanks and Linguistic Theories (TLT 2003)*.

M. Dickinson and W. D. Meurers. 2005. Detecting Errors in Discontinuous Structural Annotation. In *Proceedings of the 43rd Annual Meeting of the ACL*, pages 322–329.

M. Dickinson and D. Tufis. 2017. Iterative enhancement. In *Handbook of Linguistic Annotation*, pages 257–276. Springer, Berlin, Germany.

M.C. de Marneffe, M. Grioni, J. Kanerva, and F. Ginter. 2017. Assessing the Annotation Consistency of the Universal Dependencies Corpora. In *Proceedings of the 4th International Conference on Dependency Linguistics (Depling 2007)*, pages 108–115, Pisa, Italy.

A. Martins, M. Almeida, and N. A. Smith. 2013. "turning on the turbo: Fast third-order non-projective turbo parsers". In *Annual Meeting of the Association for Computational Linguistics - ACL*, volume -, pages 617–622.

J. Nivre. 2015. Towards a Universal Grammar for Natural Language Processing. In *Computational Linguistics and Intelligent Text Processing - Proceedings of the 16th International Conference, CICLing 2015, Part I*, pages 3–16, Cairo, Egypt.

Milan Straka and Jana Straková. 2017. Tokenizing, pos tagging, lemmatizing and parsing ud 2.0 with udpipe. In *Proceedings of the CoNLL 2017 Shared Task: Multilingual Parsing from Raw Text to Universal Dependencies*, pages 88–99, Vancouver, Canada. Association for Computational Linguistics.

G. Wisniewski. 2018. Errator: a tool to help detect annotation errors in the universal dependencies project. In *Proceedings of the Eleventh International Conference on Language Resources and Evaluation (LREC 2018)*, pages 4489–4493, Miyazaki, Japan.

D. Zeman and al. 2017. CoNLL 2017 shared task: Multilingual parsing from raw text to universal dependencies. In *Proceedings of the CoNLL 2017 Shared Task: Multilingual Parsing from Raw Text to Universal Dependencies*, pages 1–19, Vancouver, Canada.

Using Universal Dependencies in cross-linguistic complexity research

Aleksandrs Berdicevskis[1], Çağrı Çöltekin[2], Katharina Ehret[3], Kilu von Prince[4,5],
Daniel Ross[6], Bill Thompson[7], Chunxiao Yan[8], Vera Demberg[5,9], Gary Lupyan[10],
Taraka Rama[11] and Christian Bentz[2]
[1]Department of Linguistics and Philology, Uppsala University
[2]Department of Linguistics, University of Tübingen
[3]Department of Linguistics, Simon Fraser University
[4]Department of German Studies and Linguistics, Humboldt-Universität
[5]Department of Language Science and Technology, Saarland University
[6]Linguistics Department, University of Illinois at Urbana-Champaign
[7]Department of Psychology, University of California, Berkeley
[8]MoDyCo, Université Paris Nanterre & CNRS
[9]Department of Computer Science, Saarland University
[10]Department of Psychology, University of Wisconsin-Madison
[11]Department of Informatics, University of Oslo
aleksandrs.berdicevskis@lingfil.uu.se

Abstract

We evaluate corpus-based measures of linguistic complexity obtained using Universal Dependencies (UD) treebanks. We propose a method of estimating robustness of the complexity values obtained using a given measure and a given treebank. The results indicate that measures of syntactic complexity might be on average less robust than those of morphological complexity. We also estimate the validity of complexity measures by comparing the results for very similar languages and checking for unexpected differences. We show that some of those differences that arise can be diminished by using parallel treebanks and, more importantly from the practical point of view, by harmonizing the language-specific solutions in the UD annotation.

1 Introduction

Analyses of linguistic complexity are gaining ground in different domains of language sciences, such as sociolinguistic typology (Dahl, 2004; Wray and Grace, 2007; Dale and Lupyan, 2012), language learning (Hudson Kam and Newport, 2009; Perfors, 2012; Kempe and Brooks, 2018), and computational linguistics (Brunato et al., 2016). Here are a few examples of the claims that are being made: creole languages are simpler than "old" languages (McWhorter, 2001); languages with high proportions of non-native speakers tend to simplify morphologically (Trudgill, 2011); morphologically rich languages seem to be more difficult to parse (Nivre et al., 2007).

Ideally, strong claims have to be supported by strong empirical evidence, including quantitative evidence. An important caveat is that complexity is notoriously difficult to define and measure, and that there is currently no consensus about how proposed measures themselves can be evaluated and compared.

To overcome this, the first shared task on measuring linguistic complexity was organized in 2018 at the EVOLANG conference in Torun. Seven teams of researchers contributed overall 34 measures for 37 pre-defined languages (Berdicevskis and Bentz, 2018). All corpus-based measures had to be obtained using Universal Dependencies (UD) 2.1 corpora (Nivre et al., 2017).

The shared task was unusual in several senses. Most saliently, there was no gold standard against which the results could be compared. Such a benchmark will in fact never be available, since we cannot know what the *real* values of the constructs we label "linguistic complexity" are.

In this paper, we attempt to evaluate corpus-based measures of linguistic complexity in the absence of a gold standard. We view this as a small step towards exploring how complexity varies

8

Proceedings of the Second Workshop on Universal Dependencies (UDW 2018), pages 8–17
Brussels, Belgium, November 1, 2018. ©2018 Association for Computational Linguistics

Measure ID	Description	Relevant annotation levels
	Morphological complexity	
CR_TTR	Type-token ratio	T, WS
CR_MSP	Mean size of paradigm, i.e., number of word forms per lemma	T, WS, L
CR_MFE	Entropy of morphological feature set	T, WS, F, L
CR_CFEwm	Entropy (non-predictability) of word forms from their morphological analysis	T, WS, F, L
CR_CFEmw	Entropy (non-predictability) of morphological analysis from word forms	T, WS, F, L
Eh_Morph	Eh_Morph and Eh_Synt are based on Kolmogorov complexity which is approximated with off-the shelf compression programs; combined with various distortion techniques compression algorithms can estimate morphological and syntactic complexity. Eh_Morph is a measure of word form variation. Precisely, the metric conflates to some extent structural word from (ir)regularity (such as, but not limited to, inflectional and derivational structures) and lexical diversity. Thus, texts that exhibit more word form variation count as more morphologically complex.	T, WS
TL_SemDist	TL_SemDist and TL_SemVar are measures of morphosemantic complexity, they describe the amount of semantic work executed by morphology in the corpora, as measured by traversal from lemma to wordform in a vector embedding space induced from lexical co-occurence statistics. TL_SemDist measures the sum of euclidian distances between all unique attested lemma-wordform pairs.	T, WS, L
TL_SemVar	See TL_SemDist. TL_SemVar measures the sum of by-component variance in semantic difference vectors (vectors that result from subtracting lemma vector from word form vector).	T, WS, L
	Syntactic complexity	
CR_POSP	Perplexity (variability) of POS tag bigrams	T, WS, P
Eh_Synt	See Eh_Morph. Eh_Synt is a measure of word order rigidity: texts with maximally rigid word order count as syntactically complex while texts with maximally free word order count as syntactically simple. Eh_Synt relates to syntactic surface patterns and structural word order patterns (rather than syntagmatic relationships).	T, WS
PD_POS_tri	Variability of sequences of three POS tags	T, WS, P
PD_POS_tri_uni	Variability of POS tag sequences without the effect of differences in POS tag sets	T, WS, P
Ro_Dep	Total number of dependency triplets (P, RL, and P of related word). A direct interpretation of the UD corpus data, measuring the variety of syntactic dependencies in the data without regard to frequency.	T, WS, P, ST, RL
YK_avrCW_AT	Average of dependency flux weight combined with dependency length	T, WS, P, ST
YK_maxCW_AT	Maximum value of dependency flux weight combined with dependency length	T, WS, P, ST

Table 1: Complexity measures discussed in this paper. Annotation levels: T = tokenization, WS = word segmentation, L = lemmatization, P = part of speech, F = features, ST = syntactic tree, RL = relation labels. More detailed information can be found in Çöltekin and Rama, 2018 (for measures with the CR prefix), Ehret, 2018 (Eh), von Prince and Demberg, 2018 (PD), Ross, 2018 (Ro), Thompson and Lupyan, 2018 (TL), Yan and Kahane, 2018 (YK).

across languages and identifying important types of variation that relate to intuitive senses of "linguistic complexity". Our results also indicate to what extent UD in its current form can be used for cross-linguistic studies. Finally, we believe that the methods we suggest in this paper may be relevant not only for complexity, but also for other quantifiable typological parameters.

Section 2 describes the shared task and the proposed complexity measures, Section 3 describes the evaluation methods we suggest and the results they yield, Section 4 analyzes whether some of the problems we detect are corpus artefacts and can be eliminated by harmonizing the annotation and/or using the parallel treebanks, Section 5 concludes with a discussion.

2 Data and measures

For the shared task, participants had to measure the complexities of 37 languages (using the "original" UD treebanks, unless indicated otherwise in parentheses): Afrikaans, Arabic, Basque, Bulgarian, Catalan, Chinese, Croatian, Czech, Danish, Greek, Dutch, English, Estonian, Finnish, French, Galician, Hebrew, Hindi, Hungarian, Italian, Latvian, Norwegian-Bokmål, Norwegian-Nynorsk, Persian, Polish, Portuguese, Romanian, Russian (SynTagRus), Serbian, Slovak, Slovenian, Spanish (Ancora), Swedish, Turkish, Ukrainian, Urdu and Vietnamese. Other languages from the UD 2.1 release were not included because they were represented by a treebank which either was too small (less than 40K tokens), or lacked some levels of annotation, or was suspected (according to the information provided by the UD community) to contain many annotation errors. Ancient languages were not included either. In this paper, we also exclude Galician from consideration since it transpired that its annotation was incomplete.

The participants were free to choose which facet of linguistic complexity they wanted to focus on, the only requirement was to provide a clear definition of what is being measured. This is another peculiarity of the shared task: different participants were measuring different (though often related) constructs.

All corpus-based measures had to be applied to the corpora available in UD 2.1, but participants were free to decide which level of annotation (if any) to use. The corpora were obtained by merging together train, dev and test sets provided in the release.

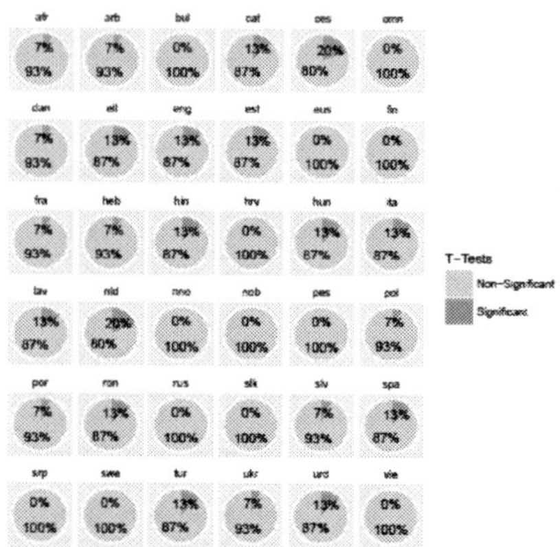

Figure 1: Non-robustness of treebanks.
Languages are denoted by their ISO codes.

From every contribution to the shared task, we selected those UD-based measures that we judged to be most important. Table 1 lists these measures and briefly describes their key properties, including those levels of treebank annotation on which the measures are directly dependent (this information will be important in Section 4). We divide measures into those that gauge morphological complexity and those that gauge syntactic complexity, although these can of course be inter-dependent.

In Appendix A, we provide the complexity rank of each language according to each measure.

It should be noted that all the measures are in fact gauging complexities of treebanks, not complexities of languages. The main assumption of corpus-based approaches is that the former are reasonable approximations of the latter. It can be questioned whether this is actually the case (one obvious problem is that treebanks may not be representative in terms of genre sample), but in this paper we largely abstract away from this question and focus on testing quantitative approaches.

3 Evaluation

We evaluate *robustness* and *validity*. By robustness we mean that two applications of the same measure to the same corpus of the same language should ideally yield the same results. See Section 3.1 for the operationalization of this desideratum and the results.

To test validity, we rely on the following idea: if we take two languages that we know from qualitative typological research to be very similar

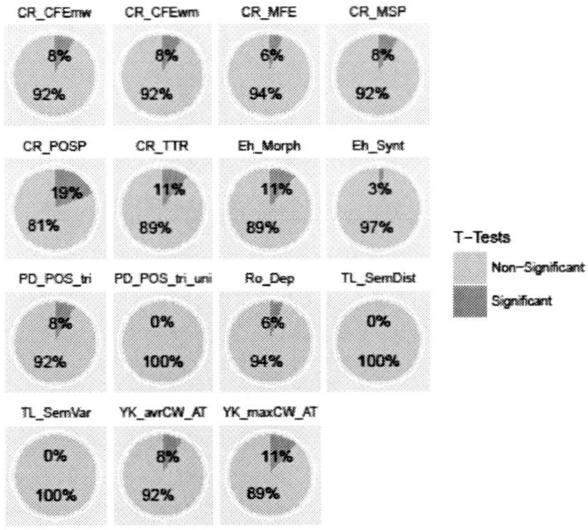

Figure 2: Non-robustness of measures

to each other (it is not sufficient that they are phylogenetically close, though it is probably necessary) and compare their complexities, the difference should on average be lower than if we compare two random languages from our sample. For the purposes of this paper we define *very similar* as 'are often claimed to be variants of the same language'. Three language pairs in our sample potentially meet this criterion: Norwegian-Bokmål and Norwegian-Nynorsk; Serbian and Croatian; Hindi and Urdu. For practical reasons, we focus on the former two in this paper (one important problem with Hindi and Urdu is that vowels are not marked in the Urdu UD treebank, which can strongly affect some of the measures, making the languages seem more different than they actually are). Indeed, while there certainly are differences between Norwegian-Bokmål and Norwegian-Nynorsk and between Serbian and Croatian, they are structurally very close (Sussex and Cubberley, 2006; Faarlund, Lie and Vannebo, 1997) and we would expect their complexities to be relatively similar. See section 3.2 for the operationalization of this desideratum and the results.

See Appendix B for data, detailed results and scripts.

3.1 Evaluating robustness

For every language, we randomly split its treebank into two parts containing the same number of sentences (the sentences are randomly drawn from anywhere in the corpus; if the total number of sentences is odd, then one part contains one extra sentence), then apply the complexity measure of interest to both halves, and repeat the procedure for n iterations ($n = 30$). We want the measure to yield similar results for the two halves, and we test whether it does by performing a paired t-test on the two samples of n measurements each (some of the samples are not normally distributed, but paired t-tests with sample size 30 are considered robust to non-normality, see Boneau, 1960). We also calculate the effect size (Cohen's d, see Kilgarriff, 2005 about the insufficiency of significance testing in corpus linguistics). We consider the difference to be significant and non-negligible if p is lower than 0.10 and the absolute value of d is larger than 0.20. Note that our cutoff point for p is higher than the conventional thresholds for significance (0.05 or 0.01), which in our case means more conservative approach. For d, we use the conventional threshold, below which the effect size is typically considered negligible.

We consider the proportion of cases when the difference is significant and non-negligible a measure of *non-robustness*. See Figure 1 for the non-robustness of treebanks (i.e. the proportion of measures that yielded a significant and non-negligible difference for a given treebank according to the resampling test); see Figure 2 for

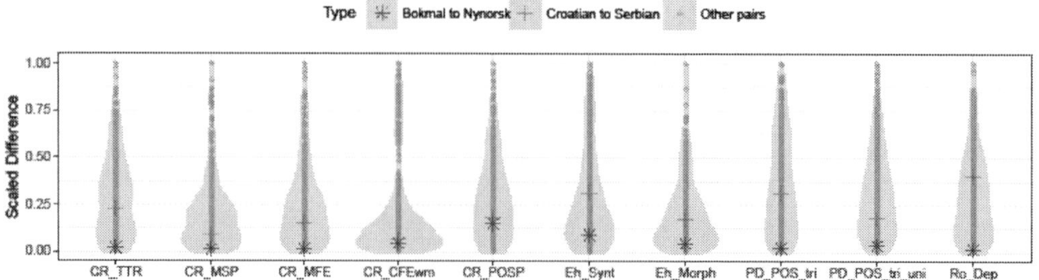

Figure 3: Distributions of pairwise absolute differences between all languages (jittered). Red dots: differences between Serbian and Croatian; blue dots: differences between Norwegian-Bokmål and Norwegian-Nynorsk.

the non-robustness of measures (i.e. the proportion of treebanks for which a given measure yielded a significant and non-negligible difference according to the resampling test).

The Czech and Dutch treebanks are the least robust according to this measure: resampling yields unwanted differences in 20% of all cases, i.e. for three measures out of 15. 12 treebanks exhibit non-robustness for two measures, 9 for one, 13 are fully robust.

It is not entirely clear which factors affect treebank robustness. There is no correlation between non-robustness and treebank size in tokens (Spearman's $r = 0.14$, $S = 6751.6$, $p = 0.43$). It is possible that more heterogeneous treebanks (e.g. those that contain large proportions of both very simple and very complex sentences) should be less robust, but it is difficult to measure heterogeneity. Note also that the differences are small and can be to a large extent random.

As regards measures, CR_POSP is least robust, yielding unwanted differences for seven languages out of 36, while TL_SemDist, TL_SemVar and PD_POS_TRI_UNI are fully robust. Interestingly, the average non-robustness of morphological measures (see Table 1) is 0.067, while that of syntactic is 0.079 (our sample, however, is neither large nor representative enough for any meaningful estimation of significance of this difference). A probable reason is that syntactic measures are likely to require larger corpora. Ross (2018: 28–29), for instance, shows that no UD 2.1 corpus is large enough to provide a precise estimate of RO_DEP. The heterogeneity of the propositional content (i.e. genre) can also affect syntactic

measures (this has been shown for EH_SYNT, see Ehret, 2017).

3.2 Evaluating validity

For every measure, we calculate differences between all possible pairs of languages. Our prediction is that differences between Norwegian-Bokmål and Norwegian-Nynorsk and between Serbian and Croatian will be close to zero or at least lower than average differences. For the purposes of this section, we operationalize *lower than average* as 'lying below the first (25%) quantile of the distribution of the differences'.

The Serbian-Croatian pair does not satisfy this criterion for CR_TTR, CR_MSP, CR_MFE, CR_CFEwm, CR_POSP, EH_SYNT, EH_MORPH, PD_POS_TRI, PD_POS_TRI_UNI and RO_DEP. The Norwegian pair fails the criterion only for CR_POSP.

We plot the distributions of differences for these measures, highlighting the differences between Norwegian-Bokmål and Norwegian-Nynorsk and between Serbian and Croatian (see Figure 3).

It should be noted, however, that the UD corpora are not parallel and that the annotation, while meant to be universal, can in fact be quite different for different languages. In the next section, we explore if these two issues may affect our results.

Issue	Instances	Action taken
nob has feature "Voice" (values: "Pass")	1147	Feature removed
nob has feature "Reflex" (values: "Yes")	1231	Feature removed
Feature "Case" can have value "Gen,Nom" in nob	2	None
Feature "PronType" can have value "Dem,Ind" in nob	1	None

Table 2: Harmonization of the Norwegian-Bokmål (nob) and Norwegian-Nynorsk (nno) treebanks.

Issue	Instances	Action taken
hrv has POS DET (corresponds to PRON in srp)	7278	Changed to PRON
hrv has POS INTJ (used for interjections such as e.g. *hajde* 'come on', which are annotated as AUX in srp)	12	Changed to AUX
hrv has POS X (corresponds most often to ADP in srp, though sometimes to PROPN)	253	Changed to ADP
hrv has POS SYM (used for combinations like *20%*, which in srp are treated as separate tokens: 20 as NUM; % as PUNCT)	117	Changed to NUM
hrv has feature "Gender[psor]" (values: "Fem", "Masc,Neut")	342	Feature removed
hrv has feature "Number[psor]" (values: "Plur", "Sing")	797	Feature removed
hrv has feature "Polarity" (values: "Neg", "Pos")	1161	Feature removed
hrv has feature "Voice" (values: "Act", "Pass")	7594	Feature removed
Feature "Mood" can have value "Cnd" in hrv	772	Value removed
Feature "Mood" can have value "Ind" in hrv	18153	Value removed
Feature "PronType" can have value "Int,Rel" in hrv	3899	Value changed to "Int"
Feature "PronType" can have value "Neg" in hrv	138	Value changed to "Ind"
Feature "Tense" can have value "Imp" in hrv	2	None
Feature "VerbForm" can have value "Conv" in hrv	155	Value removed
Feature "VerbForm" can have value "Fin" in hrv	19143	Value removed
hrv has relation "advmod:emph"	43	Changed to "advmod"
hrv has relation "aux:pass"	998	Changed to "aux"
hrv has relation "csubj:pass"	61	Changed to "csubj"
hrv has relation "dislocated"	8	None
hrv has relation "expl"	12	None
hrv has relation "expl:pv"	2161	Changed to "compound"
hrv has relation "flat:foreign"	115	Changed to "flat"
hrv has relation "nsubj:pass"	1037	Changed to "nsubj"
srp has relation "nummod:gov"	611	Changed to "nummod"
srp has relation "det:numgov"	107	Changed to "det"

Table 3: Harmonization of the Croatian (hrv) and Serbian (srp) treebanks.

4 Harmonization and parallelism

The Norwegian-Bokmål and Norwegian-Nynorsk treebanks are of approximately the same size (310K resp. 301K tokens) and are not parallel. They were, however, converted by the same team from the same resource (Øvrelid and Hohle, 2016). The annotation is very similar, but Norwegian-Bokmål has some additional features. We harmonize the annotation by eliminating the prominent discrepancies (see Table 2). We ignore the discrepancies that concern very few instances and thus are unlikely to affect our results.

The Croatian treebank (Agić and Ljubešić, 2015) has richer annotation than the Serbian one (though Serbian has some features that Croatian is missing) and is much bigger (197K resp. 87K tokens); the Serbian treebank is parallel to a subcorpus of the Croatian treebank (Samardžić et al., 2017). We created three extra versions of the Croatian treebank: Croatian-parallel (the parallel subcorpus with no changes to the annotation); Croatian-harmonized (the whole corpus with the annotation harmonized as described in Table 3);

Measure	Harmonization	Parallelism	Both
CR_TTR	0.000	**-0.887**	**-0.890**
CR_MSP	0.005	**-0.877**	**-0.885**
CR_MFE	**-0.648**	-0.271	**-0.924**
CR_CFEwm	**-0.333**	-0.500	**-0.667**
CR_POSP	**-0.988**	-0.505	**-0.646**
Eh_Synt	0.005	**-0.888**	**-0.872**
Eh_Morph	0.191	0.117	**-0.751**
PD_POS_tri	-0.227	**-0.812**	**-0.985**
PD_POS_tri_uni	0.348	**-0.904**	**-0.574**
Ro_Dep	-0.514	-0.114	-0.605

Table 4: Effects of treebank manipulation on the difference between Croatian and Serbian. Numbers show relative changes of the original difference after the respective manipulation. Bold indicates cases when the new difference lies below the defined threshold, i.e. when the measure passes the validity test.

Croatian-parallel-harmonized (the parallel subcorpus with the annotation harmonized as described in Table 3) and one extra version of the Serbian treebank: Serbian-harmonized.

It should be noted that our harmonization (for both language pairs) is based on comparing the stats.xml file included in the UD releases and the papers describing the treebanks (Øvrelid and Hohle, 2016; Agić and Ljubešić, 2015; Samardžić et al., 2017). If there are any subtle differences that do not transpire from these files and papers (e.g. different lemmatization principles), they are not eliminated by our simple conversion.

Using the harmonized version of Norwegian-Bokmål does not affect the difference for CR_POSP (which is unsurprising, given that the harmonization changed only feature annotation, to which this measure is not sensitive).

For Croatian, we report the effect of the three manipulations in Table 4. Using Croatian-parallel solves the problems with CR_TTR, CR_MSP, EH_SYNT, PD_POS_TRI, PD_POS_TRI_UNI. Using Croatian-harmonized and Serbian-harmonized has an almost inverse effect. It solves the problems with CR_MFE, CR_CFEWM, CR_POSP, but not with any other measures. It does strongly diminish the difference for RO_DEP, though. Finally, using Croatian-parallel-harmonized and Serbian-harmonized turns out to be most efficient. It solves the problems with all the measures apart from RO_DEP, but the difference does become smaller also for this measure. Note that this measure had the biggest original difference (see Section 3.2).

Some numbers are positive, which indicates that the difference increases after the harmonization. Small changes of this kind (e.g. for CR_MSP, EH_SYNT) are most likely random, since many measures are using some kind of random sampling and never yield exactly the same value. The behaviour of EH_MORPH also suggests that the changes are random (this measure cannot be affected by harmonization, so Croatian-harmonized and Croatian-parallel-harmonized should yield similar results). The most surprising result, however, is the big increase of PD_POS_TRI_UNI after harmonization. A possible reason is imperfect harmonization of POS annotation, which introduced additional variability into POS trigrams. Note, however, that the difference for CR_POSP, which is similar to PD_POS_TRI_UNI, was reduced almost to zero by the same manipulation.

It can be argued that these comparisons are not entirely fair. By removing the unreasonable discrepancies between the languages we are focusing on, but not doing that for all language pairs, we may have introduced a certain bias. Nonetheless, our results should still indicate whether the harmonization and parallelization diminish the differences (though they might overestimate their positive effect).

5 Discussion

As mentioned in Section 1, some notion of complexity is often used in linguistic theories and analyses, both as an explanandum and an explanans. A useful visualization of many theories that involve the notion of complexity can be obtained, for instance, through The Causal Hypotheses in Evolutionary Linguistics Database (Roberts, 2018). Obviously, we want to be able to understand such key theoretical notions well and quantify them, if they are quantifiable. To what extent are we able to do this for notions of complexity?

In this paper, we leave aside the question of how well we understand what complexity "really" is and focus on how good we are at quantifying it using corpus-based measures (it should be noted that other types of complexity measures exist, e.g. grammar-based measures, with their own strengths and weaknesses).

Our non-robustness metric shows to what extent a given measure or a given treebank can be trusted. Most often, two equal treebank halves yield virtually the same results. For some treebanks and measures, on the other hand, the proportion of cases in which the differences are significant (and large) is relatively high. Interestingly, measures of syntactic complexity seem to be on average less robust in this sense than measures of morphological complexity. This might indicate that language-internal variation of syntactic complexity is greater than language-internal variation of morphological complexity, and larger corpora are necessary for its reliable estimation. In particular, syntactic complexity may be more sensitive to genres, and heterogeneity of genres across and within corpora may affect robustness. It is hardly possible to test this hypothesis with UD 2.1, since detailed genre metadata are not easily available for most treebanks. Yet another possible explanation is that there is generally less agreement between different conceptualizations of what "syntax" is than what "morphology" is.

Our validity metric shows that closely related languages which should yield minimally divergent results can, in fact, diverge considerably. However, this effect can be diminished by using parallel treebanks and harmonizing the UD annotation. The latter result has practical implications for the UD project. While Universal Dependencies are meant to be universal, in practice language-specific solutions are allowed on all levels. This policy has obvious advantages, but as we show, it can inhibit cross-linguistic comparisons. The differences in Table 2 and Table 3 strongly affect some of our measures, but they do not reflect any real structural differences between languages, merely different decisions adopted by treebank developers. For quantitative typologists, it would be desirable to have a truly harmonized (or at least easily harmonizable) version of UD.

The observation that non-parallelism of treebanks also influences the results has further implications for a corpus-based typology. Since obtaining parallel treebanks even for all current UD languages is hardly feasible, register and genre variation are important confounds to be aware of. Nonetheless, the Norwegian treebanks, while non-parallel, did not pose any problems for most of the measures. Thus, we can hope that if the corpora are sufficiently large and well-balanced, quantitative measures of typological parameters will still yield reliable results despite the non-parallelism. In general, our results allow for some optimism with regards to quantitative typology in general and using UD in particular. However, both measures and resources have to be evaluated and tested before they are used as basis for theoretical claims, especially regarding the interpretability of the computational results.

References

Agić, Željko and Nikola Ljubešić. 2015. Universal Dependencies for Croatian (that Work for Serbian, too). In *Proceedings of the 5th Workshop on Balto-Slavic Natural Language Processing*. Association for Computational Linguistics, pages 1-8. http://www.aclweb.org/anthology/W15-5301

Aleksandrs Berdicevskis and Christian Bentz. 2018. *Proceedings of the First Shared Task on Measuring Language Complexity.*

Boneau, Alan. 1960. The effects of violations of assumptions underlying the *t* test. *Psychological Bulletin* 57(1): 49-64. https://doi.org/10.1037/h0041412

Dominique Brunato, Felice Dell'Orleta, Giulia Venturi, Thomas François, Philippe Blache. 2016. *Proceedings of the Workshop on Computational Linguistics for Linguistic Complexity.* Association for Computational Linguistics. http://www.aclweb.org/anthology/W16-4100

Çağrı Çöltekin and Taraka Rama. 2018. Exploiting universal dependencies treebanks for measuring morphosyntactic complexity. In *Proceedings of the First Shared Task on Measuring Language Complexity*, pages 1-8.

Östen Dahl. 2004. *The growth and maintenance of linguistic complexity.* John Benjamins, Amsterdam, The Netherlands.

Rick Dale and Gary Lupyan. 2012. Understanding the origins of morphological diversity: The linguistic niche hypothesis. *Advances in Complex Systems* 15(3): 1150017 https://doi.org/10.1142/S0219525911500172.

Katharina Ehret. 2017. An information-theoretic approach to language complexity: variation in naturalistic corpora. Ph.D. thesis, University of Freiburg. https://doi.org/10.6094/UNIFR/12243.

Katharina Ehret. 2018. Kolmogorov complexity as a universal measure of language complexity. In *Proceedings of the First Shared Task on Measuring Language Complexity*, pages 8-14.

Jan Terje Faarlund, Svein Lie and Kjell Ivar Vannebo. 1997. *Norsk referansegrammatik*, Universitetsforlaget, Oslo, Norway.

Carla Hudson Kam and Elissa Newport. 2005. Regularizing unpredictable variation: The roles of adult and child learners in language formation and change. *Language Learning and Development* 1(2):151-195. https://doi.org/10.1080/15475441.2005.9684215.

Vera Kempe and Patricia Brooks. 2018. Linking Adult Second Language Learning and Diachronic Change: A Cautionary Note. *Frontiers in Psychology*. https://doi.org/10.3389/fpsyg.2018.00480.

Adam Kilgarriff. 2005. Language is never, ever, ever random. *Corpus Linguistics and Linguistic Theory* 1–2:263-275. https://doi.org/10.1515/cllt.2005.1.2.263.

John McWhorter. 2001. The world's simplest grammars are creole grammars. *Linguistic Typology* 5(2-3):125-166. https://doi.org/10.1515/lity.2001.001.

Joakim Nivre, Johan Hall, Jens Nilsson, Atanas Chanev, Gülşen Eryigit, Sandra Kübler, Svetoslav Marinov and Erwin Marsi. 2007. MaltParser: A language-independent system for data-driven dependency parsing. *Natural Language Engineering* 13(2):95–135. https://doi.org/10.1017/S1351324906004505.

Joakim Nivre, Agić Željko, Lars Ahrenberg et al. 2017. Universal Dependencies 2.1, LINDAT/CLARIN digital library at the Institute of Formal and Applied Linguistics (ÚFAL), Faculty of Mathematics and Physics, Charles University, http://hdl.handle.net/11234/1-2515.

Amy Perfors. 2012. When do memory limitations lead to regularization? An experimental and computational investigation. *Journal of Memory and Language* 67: 486-506. https://doi.org/10.1016/j.jml.2012.07.009.

Øvrelid, Lilja and Petter Hohle. 2016. Universal Dependencies for Norwegian. In *Proceedings of the Tenth International Conference on Language Resources and Evaluation (LREC 2016)*. European Language Resources Association, pages 1579-1585.

Sean Roberts. 2018. Chield: causal hypotheses in evolutionary linguistics database. In *The Evolution of Language: Proceedings of the 12th International Conference (EVOLANGXII)*. https://doi.org/10.12775/3991-1.099.

Kilu von Prince and Vera Demberg. 2018. POS tag perplexity as a measure of syntactic complexity. In In *Proceedings of the First Shared Task on Measuring Language Complexity*, pages 20-25.

Daniel Ross. 2018. Details matter: Problems and possibilities for measuring cross-linguistic complexity. In *Proceedings of the First Shared Task on Measuring Language Complexity*, pages 26-31.

Samardžić, Tanja, Mirjana Starović, Agić Željko and Nikola Ljubešić. 2017. Universal Dependencies for Serbian in Comparison with Croatian and Other Slavic Languages. In *Proceedings of the 6th Workshop on Balto-Slavic Natural Language Processing*. Association for Computational Linguistics, pages 39-44. http://www.aclweb.org/anthology/W17-1407

Roland Sussex and Paul Cubberley. 2006. *The Slavic languages*. Cambridge University Press, Cambridge, UK.

Bill Thompson and Gary Lupyan. 2018. Morphosemantic complexity. In *Proceedings of the First Shared Task on Measuring Language Complexity*, pages 32-37.

Peter Trudgill. 2011. *Sociolinguistic typology: social determinants of linguistic complexity*. Oxford University Press, Oxford, UK.

Alison Wray and George Grace. 2007. The consequences of talking to strangers: Evolutionary corollaries of socio-cultural influences on linguistic form. *Lingua* 117(3):543-578. https://doi.org/10.1016/j.lingua.2005.05.005.

Chunxiao Yan and Sylvain Kahane. 2018. Syntactic complexity combining dependency length and dependency flux weight. In *Proceedings of the First Shared Task on Measuring Language Complexity*, pages 38-43.

A Languages ranked by complexity (descending order)

Language	CR_TTR	CR_MSP	CR_MFE	CR_CFEwm	CR_CFEmw	CR_POSP	Eh_Synt	Eh_Morph	YK_avrCW_AT	YK_maxCW_AT	Ro_Dep	PD_POS_tri	PD_POS_tri_uni	TL_SemDist	TL_SemVar
afr	35	31	26	30	22	26	2	36	7	23	15	29	32	33	33
arb	19	18	23	3	31	20	22	8	3	3	12	31	16	2	2
eus	12	2	14	6	2	23	20	25	16	25	8	13	9	16	16
bul	13	16	11	36	9	22	17	17	33	33	33	24	29	19	19
cat	28	28	28	19	13	30	4	30	10	5	20	28	26	29	29
cmn	17	35	35	8	35	21	32	1	4	6	18	10	3	35	35
hrv	10	9	15	9	27	5	19	22	21	28	2	5	6	15	15
ces	3	14	1	13	26	3	26	12	14	1	9	3	12	17	17
dan	22	27	17	14	16	4	28	7	15	25	22	19	27	28	27
nld	24	32	33	28	4	6	23	18	11	14	3	16	21	31	31
eng	31	30	31	7	5	1	14	15	30	21	1	8	31	34	34
est	8	8	16	26	10	17	36	4	27	23	27	4	10	6	6
fin	1	4	8	35	32	9	31	13	23	4	10	7	5	5	5
fra	18	29	30	20	3	34	10	21	23	11	24	32	34	27	28
ell	30	6	12	4	8	13	5	35	12	19	29	27	28	11	12
heb	29	19	21	15	21	33	34	2	29	29	5	34	33	1	1
hin	33	33	24	2	34	35	7	33	5	18	36	35	20	32	32
hun	15	21	7	23	29	25	9	29	6	16	11	23	11	18	18
ita	26	22	27	31	5	29	11	27	16	6	31	33	36	23	23
lav	11	7	4	27	20	15	21	16	26	27	7	6	8	7	7
nob	23	23	18	25	19	7	25	14	32	29	26	15	25	26	25
nno	25	26	20	16	17	2	18	20	31	20	24	18	23	24	24
pes	32	10	34	32	1	32	13	6	1	6	28	25	2	3	4
pol	5	15	2	11	11	24	35	5	35	34	32	22	22	12	10
por	20	25	32	5	24	19	15	24	13	17	23	30	35	25	26
ron	14	12	13	33	23	18	16	23	16	12	4	14	13	20	20
rus	2	5	10	24	11	16	27	19	28	9	13	2	7	10	11
srp	16	3	22	21	30	11	6	34	22	32	17	20	15	9	9
slk	6	11	3	12	14	8	29	3	36	36	19	9	30	8	8
slv	9	13	9	16	18	10	30	10	25	31	35	12	19	14	13
spa	21	24	25	29	28	27	8	28	9	13	16	26	24	21	22
swe	27	20	19	18	14	14	12	32	20	2	21	21	18	22	21
tur	7	1	6	34	7	28	24	9	8	21	6	11	4	4	3
ukr	4	17	5	10	25	12	33	11	19	9	14	1	14	13	14
urd	34	34	29	1	33	36	1	31	2	15	30	36	17	30	30
vie	36	36	36	22	35	31	3	26	34	35	33	17	1	36	36

B Supplementary material

Data, detailed results and scripts that are necessary to reproduce the findings can be found at
https://sites.google.com/view/sasha-berdicevskis/home/resources/sm-for-udw-2018

Expletives in Universal Dependency Treebanks

Gosse Bouma[*°] **Jan Hajic**[†°] **Dag Haug**[‡°] **Joakim Nivre**[•°] **Per Erik Solberg**[‡°] **Lilja Øvrelid**[*°]

[*]University of Groningen, Centre for Language and Cognition
[†]Charles University in Prague, Faculty of Mathematics and Physics, UFAL
[‡]University of Oslo, Department of Philosophy, Classics, History of Arts and Ideas
[•]Uppsala University, Department of Linguistics and Philology
[*]University of Oslo, Department of Informatics
[°]Center for Advanced Study at the Norwegian Academy of Science and Letters

Abstract

Although treebanks annotated according to the guidelines of Universal Dependencies (UD) now exist for many languages, the goal of annotating the same phenomena in a cross-linguistically consistent fashion is not always met. In this paper, we investigate one phenomenon where we believe such consistency is lacking, namely expletive elements. Such elements occupy a position that is structurally associated with a core argument (or sometimes an oblique dependent), yet are non-referential and semantically void. Many UD treebanks identify at least some elements as expletive, but the range of phenomena differs between treebanks, even for closely related languages, and sometimes even for different treebanks for the same language. In this paper, we present criteria for identifying expletives that are applicable across languages and compatible with the goals of UD, give an overview of expletives as found in current UD treebanks, and present recommendations for the annotation of expletives so that more consistent annotation can be achieved in future releases.

1 Introduction

Universal Dependencies (UD) is a framework for morphosyntactic annotation that aims to provide useful information for downstream NLP applications in a cross-linguistically consistent fashion (Nivre, 2015; Nivre et al., 2016). Many such applications require an analysis of referring expressions. In co-reference resolution, for example, it is important to be able to separate anaphoric uses of pronouns such as *it* from non-referential uses (Boyd et al., 2005; Evans, 2001; Uryupina et al., 2016). Accurate translation of pronouns is another challenging problem, sometimes relying on co-reference resolution, and where one of the choices is to not translate a pronoun at all. The latter situation occurs for instance when translating from a language that has expletives into a language that does not use expletives (Hardmeier et al., 2015; Werlen and Popescu-Belis, 2017). The ParCor co-reference corpus (Guillou et al., 2014) distinguishes between anaphoric, event referential, and pleonastic use of the English pronoun *it*. Loáiciga et al. (2017) train a classifier to predict the different uses of *it* in English using among others syntactic information obtained from an automatic parse of the corpus. Being able to distinguish referential from non-referential noun phrases is potentially important also for tasks like question answering and information extraction.

Applications like these motivate consistent and explicit annotation of expletive elements in treebanks and the UD annotation scheme introduces a dedicated dependency relation (`expl`) to account for these. However, the current UD guidelines are not specific enough to allow expletive elements to be identified systematically in different languages, and the use of the `expl` relation varies considerably both across languages and between different treebanks for the same language. For instance, the manually annotated English treebank uses the `expl` relation for a wide range of constructions, including clausal extraposition, weather verbs, existential *there*, and some idiomatic expressions. By contrast, Dutch, a language in which all these phenomena occur as well, uses `expl` only for extraposed clausal arguments. In this paper, we provide a more precise characterization of the notion of expletives for the purpose of UD treebank annotation, survey the annotation of expletives in existing UD treebanks, and make recommendations to improve consistency in future releases.

2 What is an Expletive?

The UD initiative aims to provide a syntactic annotation scheme that can be applied cross-

Proceedings of the Second Workshop on Universal Dependencies (UDW 2018), pages 18–26
Brussels, Belgium, November 1, 2018. ©2018 Association for Computational Linguistics

linguistically, and that can be used to drive semantic interpretation. At the clause level, it distinguishes between core arguments and oblique dependents of the verb, with core arguments being limited to subjects (nominal and clausal), objects (direct and indirect), and clausal complements (open and closed). Expletives are of interest here, as a consistent distinction between expletives and regular core arguments is important for semantic interpretation but non-trivial to achieve across languages and constructions.

The UD documentation currently states that `expl` is to be used for *expletive or pleonastic nominals, that appear in an argument position of a predicate but which do not themselves satisfy any of the semantic roles of the predicate*. As examples, it mentions English *it* and *there* as used in clausal extrapostion and existential constructions, cases of true clitic doubling in Greek and Bulgarian, and inherent reflexives. Silveira (2016) characterizes `expl` as *a wildcard for any element that has the morphosyntactic properties associated with a particular grammatical function but does not receive a semantic role*.

It is problematic that the UD definition relies on the concept of argument, since UD otherwise abandons the argument/adjunct distinction in favor of the core/oblique distinction. Silveira's account avoids this problem by instead referring to grammatical functions, thus also catering for cases like:

(1)   He will see to *it* that you have a reservation.

However, both definitions appear to be too wide, in that they do not impose any restrictions on the form of the expletive, or require it to be non-referential. It could therefore be argued that the subject of a raising verb, like *Sue* in *Sue appears to be nice*, satisfies the conditions of the definition, since it is a nominal in subject position that does not satisfy a semantic role of the predicate *appear*.

It seems useful, then, to look for a better definition of expletive. Much of the literature in theoretical linguistics is either restricted to specific languages or language families (Platzack, 1987; Bennis, 2010; Cardinaletti, 1997) or to specific constructions (Vikner, 1995; Hazout, 2004). A theory-neutral and general definition can be found in Postal and Pullum (1988):

[T]hey are (i) morphologically identical to pro-forms (in English, two relevant forms are *it*, identical to the third person neuter pronoun, and *there*, identical to the non-proximate locative pro-adverb), (ii) nonreferential (neither anaphoric/cataphoric nor exophoric), and (iii) devoid of any but a vacuous semantic role. As a tentative definition of expletives, we can characterize them as pro-forms (typically third person pronouns or locative pro-adverbs) that occur in core argument positions but are non-referential (and therefore not assigned a semantic role).

Like the UD definition, Postal and Pullum (1988) emphasize the vacuous semantics of expletives, but understand this not just as the lack of semantic role (iii) but also more generally as the absence of reference (ii). Arguably, (ii) entails (iii) and could seem to make it superfluous, but we will see that it can often be easier to test for (iii). The common, pre-theoretic understanding of expletives does not include idiom parts such as *the bucket* in *kick the bucket*, so it is necessary to restrict the concept further. Postal and Pullum (1988) do this by (i), which restricts expletives to be pro-forms. This is a relatively weak constraint on the form of expletives. We will see later that it may be desirable to strengthen this criterion and require expletives to be pro-forms that are selected by the predicate with which it occurs. Such purely formal selection is needed in many cases, since expletives are not interchangeable across constructions – for example, *there rains* is not an acceptable sentence of English. Criteria (ii) and (iii) from the definition of Postal and Pullum (1988) may be hard to apply directly in a UD setting, as UD is a syntactic, not a semantic, annotation framework. On the other hand, many decisions in UD are driven by the need to provide annotations that can serve as input for semantic analysis, and distinguishing between elements that do and do not refer and fill a thematic role therefore seems desirable.

In addition to the definition, Postal and Pullum (1988) provide tests for expletives. Some of these (tough-movement and nominalization) are not easy to apply cross-linguistically, but two of them are, namely absence of coordination and inability to license an emphatic reflexive.

(2)   *It and John rained and carried an umbrella respectively.

(3)   *It itself rained.

The inability to license an emphatic reflexive is probably due to the lack of referentiality. It is less immediately obvious what the absence of coordination diagnoses. One likely interpretation is that sentences like (2) are ungrammatical because the verb selects for a particular syntactic string as its subject. If that is so, form-selection can be considered a defining feature of expletives.

Finally, following Postal and Pullum (1988), we can draw a distinction between expletives that occur in chains and those that do not, where we understand a chain as a relation between an expletive and some other element of the sentence which has the thematic role that would normally be associated with the position of the expletive, for example, the subordinate clause in (4).

(4)   It surprised me that she came.

It is not always possible to realize the other element in the chain in the position of the expletive. For example, the subordinate clause cannot be directly embedded under the preposition in (1).

Whether the expletive participates in a chain or not is relevant for the UD annotation insofar as it is often desirable – for the purposes of semantic interpretation – to give the semantically active element of the chain the "real" dependency label. For example, it is tempting to take the complement clause in (4) as the subject (`csubj` in UD) to stay closer to the semantics, although one is hard pressed to come up with independent syntactic evidence that an element in this position can actually be a subject. This is in line with many descriptive grammar traditions, where the expletive would be called the *formal* subject and the subordinate clause the *logical* subject.

We now review constructions that are regularly analyzed as involving an expletive in the theoretical literature and discuss these in the light of the definition and tests we have established.

2.1 Extraposition of Clausal Arguments

In many languages, verbs selecting a clausal subject or object often allow or require an expletive and place the clausal argument in extraposed position. In some cases, extraposition of the clausal argument is obligatory, as in (5) for English. Note that the clausal argument can be either a subject or an object, and thus the expletive in some cases appears in object position, as in (6). Also note that in so-called raising contexts, the expletive may actually be realized in the structural subject position of a verb governing the verb that selects the clausal argument (7).

(5)   *It* seems that she came (en)

(6)   Hij betreurt *het* dat jullie verliezen (nl)
       He regrets it   that you   lose
       'He regrets that you lose'

(7)   *It* is going to be hard to sell the Dodge (en)

It is fairly straightforward to argue that this construction involves an expletive. Theoretically, *it* could be cataphoric to the following clause and so be referential, but in that case we would expect it to be able to license an emphatic reflexive. However, this is not what we find, as shown in (8-a), which contrasts with (8-b) where the raised subject is a referential pronoun.

(8)   a.   *It seems itself that she came
       b.   It seems itself to be a primary metaphysical principle

But if *it* does not refer cataphorically to the extraposed clause, its form must also be due to the construction in which it appears. This construction therefore fulfills the criteria of an expletive even on the strictest understanding.

2.2 Existential Sentences

Existential (or presentational) sentences are sentences that involve an intransitive verb and a noun phrase that is interpreted as the logical subject of the verb but does not occur in the canonical subject position, which is instead filled by an expletive. There is considerable variation between languages as to which verbs participate in this construction. For instance, while English is quite restrictive and uses this construction mainly with the copula *be*, other languages allow a wider range of verbs including verbs of position and movement, as illustrated in (9)–(11). There is also variation with respect to criteria for classifying the nominal constituent as a subject or object, with diagnostics such as agreement, case, and structural position often giving conflicting results. Some languages, like the Scandinavian languages, restrict the nominal element to indefinite nominals, whereas German for instance also allows for definite nominals in this construction.

(9)   *Det* sitter en katt på mattan (sv)
       it   sits   a cat on the-mat
       'A cat sits on the mat'

(10)   *Es* landet ein Flugzeug (de)
       it lands a   plane
       'A plane lands'

(11)   *Il* nageait quelques personnes (fr)
there swim some people
'Some people are swimming'

Despite the cross-linguistic variation, existential constructions like these are uncontroversial cases of expletive usage. The form of the pronoun(s) is fixed, it cannot refer to the other element of the chain for formal reasons, and no emphatic reflexive is possible.

2.3 Impersonal Constructions

By impersonal constructions we understand constructions where the verb takes a fixed, pronominal, argument in subject position that is not interpreted in semantics. Some of these involve zero-valent verbs, such as weather verbs, which are traditionally assumed to take an expletive subject in Germanic languages, as in Norwegian *regne* 'rain' (12). Others involve verb that also take a semantic argument, such as the French *falloir* in (13).

(12)   *Det* regner (no)
it rains
'It is raining'

(13)   *Il* faut trois nouveaux recrutements (fr)
it needs three new staff-members
'Three new staff members are needed'

Impersonal constructions can also arise when an intransitive verb is passivized (and the normal semantic subject argument therefore suppressed).

(14)   *Es* wird gespielt (de)
It is played
'There is playing'

In all these examples, the pronouns are clearly non-referential, no emphatic reflexive is possible and the form is selected by the construction, so these elements can be classified as expletive.

2.4 Passive Reflexives

In some Romance and Slavic languages, a passive can be formed by adding a reflexive pronoun which does not get a thematic role but rather signals the passive voice.

(15)   dospívá *se* dříve (cs)
mature REFL earlier
'(they/people) mature up earlier'

In Romance languages, as shown by Silveira (2016), these are not only used with a strictly passive meaning, but also with inchoative (anticausative) and medio-passive readings.

(16)   La branche *s'* est cassée
The branch SE is broken
'The branch broke.'

In all of these cases, it is clear that the reflexive element does not receive a semantic role. In (15), *dospívá* 'mature' only takes one semantic argument, and in (16), the intended reading is clearly not that the branch broke itself. We conclude that these elements are expletives according to the definition above. This is in line with the proposal of Silveira (2016).

2.5 Inherent Reflexives

Many languages have verbs that obligatorily select a reflexive pronoun without assigning a semantic role to it:

(17)   Pedro *se* confundiu (pt)
Pedro REFL confused
'Pedro was confused'

(18)   Směje *se* (cs)
laugh REFL
'he/she/it laughs'

There are borderline cases where the verb in question can also take a regular object, but the semantics is subtly different. A typical case are verbs like *wash*. That there are in fact two different interpretations is revealed in Scandinavian by the impossibility of coordination. (19) is grammatical unless *seg* is stressed.

(19)   *Han vasket seg og de andre (no)
He washed REFL and the others
'He washed himself and the others'

From the point of view of our definition, it is clear that inherent reflexives (by definition) do not receive a semantic role. It may be less clear that they are non-referential: after all, they typically agree with the subject and could be taken to be co-referent. It is hard to test for non-referentiality in the absence of any semantic role. In particular, the emphatic reflexive test is not easily applicable, since it may be the subject that antecedes the emphatic reflexive in cases like (20).

(20)   Elle s'est souvenue elle-même
she REFL-is reminded herself
'She herself remembered...'

Inherent reflexives agree with the subject, and thus their form is not determined (only) by the verb. Nevertheless, under the looser understanding of the formal criterion, it is enough that reflexives are

pronominal and thus can be expletives. This is also
the conclusion of Silveira (2016).

2.6 Clitic Doubling

The UD guidelines explicitly mention that "true"
(that is, regularly available) clitic doubling, as in
the Greek example in (21), should be annotated
using the `expl` relation:

(21)   pisteuô oti einai dikaio na to
            I-believe that it-is fair   that this-CLITIC
            anagnôrisoume auto (el)
            we-recognize   this

The clitic *to* merely signals the presence of the full
pronoun object and it can be argued that it is the
latter that receives the thematic role. It is less clear,
however, that *to* is non-referential, hence it is unclear that this is an instance of an expletive. The
alternative is to annotate the clitic as a core argument and use `dislocated` for the full pronoun
(as is done for other cases of doubling in UD).

3 Expletives in UD 2.1 treebanks

We will now present a survey of the usage of the
`expl` relation in current UD treebanks. In particular, we will relate the constructions discussed
in Section 2 to the treebank data. Table 1 gives
an overview of the usage of `expl` and its language specific extensions in the treebanks in UD
v2.1.[1] We find that, out of the 60 languages included in this release, 27 make use of the `expl`
relation, and its use appears to be restricted to European languages. For those languages that have
multiple treebanks, `expl` is not always used in all
treebanks (Finnish, Galician, Latin, Portuguese,
Russian, Spanish). The frequency of `expl` varies
greatly, ranging from less than 1 per 1,000 words
(Catalan, Greek, Latin, Russian, Spanish, Ukra-
nian) to more than 2 per 100 words (Bulgarian,
Polish, Slovak). For most of the languages, there
is a fairly limited set of lemmas that realize the
`expl` relation. Treebanks with higher numbers of
lemmas are those that label inherent reflexives as
`expl` and/or do not always lemmatize systematically. Some treebanks not only use `expl`, but
also the subtypes `expl:pv` (for inherent reflexives), `expl:pass` (for certain passive constructions), and `expl:impers` (for impersonal constructions).

---

[1]The raw counts as well as the script we used to collect the data can be found at `github.com/gossebouma/`
`expletives`

The counts and proportions for specific constructions in Table 1 were computed as follows.
Extraposition covers cases where an expletive co-
occurs with a `csubj` or `ccomp` argument as in
the top row of Figure 1. This construction occurs
frequently in the Germanic treebanks (Dutch, English, German, Norwegian, Swedish), as in (22),
but is also fairly frequent in French treebanks, as
in (23).

(22)   *It* is true that Google has been in acquisi-
          tion mode (en)

(23)   Il est de notre devoir de participer [. . .] (fr)
          it is of our duty to participate [. . .]
          'It is our duty to participate . . . '

Existential constructions can be identified by the
presence of a nominal subject (`nsubj`) as a sibling of the `expl` element, as illustrated in the middle row of Figure 1. Existential constructions are
very widespread and span several language families in the treebank data. They are common in all
Germanic treebanks, as illustrated in (24), but are
also found in Finnish, exemplified in (25), where
these constructions account for half of all expletive occurrences, as well as in several Romance
languages (French, Galician, Italian, Portuguese),
some Slavic languages (Russian and Ukrainian),
and Greek.

(24)   *Es* fehlt ein System umfassender   sozialer
          it lacks a   system comprehensive social
          Sicherung (de)
          security
          'A system of comprehensive social secu-
          rity is lacking'

(25)   *Se* oli paska homma, että Jyrki loppu (fi)
          it was shit thing   that Jyrki end
          'It was a shit thing for Jyrki to end'

For the impersonal constructions discussed in Section 2.3, only a few UD treebanks make use of
an explicit `impers` subtype (Italian, Romanian).
Apart from these, impersonal verbs like *rain* and
French *falloir* prove difficult to identify reliably
across languages using morphosyntactic criteria.
For impersonal passives, on the other hand, there
are morphosyntactic properties that we may employ in our survey. Passives in UD are marked
either morphologically on the verb (by the feature
`Voice=Passive`) or by a passive auxiliary dependent (`aux:pass`) in the case of periphrastic
passive constructions. These two passive constructions are illustrated in the bottom row (left

	Banks	Count	Freq	Lemmas	Extraposed		Existential		Impersonal		Reflexives		Remaining	
Bulgarian		3379	0.021	7	12	0.0	82	0.02	2	0.0	3204	0.95	79	0.02
Catalan		512	0.001	4	0	0.0	0	0.0	0	0.0	512	1.0	0	0.0
Croatian		2173	0.011	11	2	0.0	4	0.0	1	0.0	2161	0.99	5	0.0
Czech	5/5	35929	0.018	4	0	0.0	0	0.0	0	0.0	35929	1.0	0	0.0
Danish		441	0.004	2	8	0.02	10	0.02	62	0.14	0	0.0	361	0.82
Dutch	2/2	459	0.001	5	321	0.7	120	0.26	6	0.01	0	0.0	12	0.03
English	4/4	1221	0.003	6	380	0.31	724	0.59	9	0.01	0	0.0	107	0.09
Finnish	1/3	524	0.003	9	15	0.03	268	0.51	53	0.1	0	0.0	188	0.36
French	5/5	6117	0.005	26	162	0.03	1486	0.24	27	0.0	3378	0.55	1064	0.17
Galician	1/2	288	0.01	6	19	0.07	131	0.45	0	0.0	0	0.0	138	0.48
German	2/2	487	0.003	1	114	0.23	287	0.59	21	0.04	1	0.0	64	0.13
Greek		18	0.000	1	0	0.0	6	0.33	0	0.0	0	0.0	12	0.67
Italian	4/4	4214	0.009	22	107	0.03	1901	0.45	589	0.14	396	0.09	1218	0.29
Latin	1/3	257	0.001	1	0	0.0	0	0.0	0	0.0	257	1.0	0	0.0
Norwegian	3/3	6890	0.01	8	1894	0.27	1758	0.26	374	0.05	0	0.0	2864	0.42
Polish		1708	0.02	1	0	0.0	0	0.0	6	0.0	1702	1.0	0	0.0
Portuguese	2/3	1624	0.003	1	20	0.01	628	0.39	20	0.01	672	0.41	284	0.17
Romanian	2/2	5209	0.002	22	43	0.01	327	0.06	140	0.03	4281	0.82	418	0.08
Russian	2/3	55	0.000	3	6	0.11	42	0.76	1	0.02	0	0.0	6	0.11
Slovak		2841	0.03	3	0	0.0	0	0.0	0	0.0	2841	1.0	0	0.0
Slovenian	2/2	2754	0.02	2	0	0.0	1	0.0	0	0.0	2297	1.0	0	0.0
Spanish	1/3	503	0.001	2	0	0.0	0	0.0	0	0.0	503	1.0	0	0.0
Swedish	3/3	1079	0.005	6	371	0.34	283	0.26	85	0.08	0	0.0	340	0.32
Ukrainian		94	0.001	4	16	0.17	62	0.66	0	0.0	12	0.13	4	0.04
Upper Sorbian		177	0.02	1	0	0.0	0	0.0	1	0.01	176	0.99	0	0.0

Table 1: Use of `expl` in UD v2.1 treebanks. Languages with Count < 10 left out (Arabic, Sanskrit). Freq = average frequency for treebanks containing `expl`. Count and proportion for construction types.

and center) of Figure 1. The quantitative overview in Table 1 shows that impersonal constructions occur mostly in Germanic languages, such as Danish, German, Norwegian and Swedish, illustrated by (26). These are all impersonal passives. We note that both Italian and Romanian also show a high proportion of impersonal verbs, due to the use of `expl:impers` mentioned above and exemplified by (27).

(26) *Det* ble ikke nevnt   hvor omstridt
      it was not mentioned how controversial
      han er (no)
      he is
      'It was not mentioned how controversial he is'

(27) *Si* compredono inoltre i figli   adottivi
      it includes   also   the children adopted
      (it)

'Adopted children are also included'

Both the constructions of passive reflexives and inherent reflexives (Sections 2.4 and 2.5), make use of a reflexive pronoun. Some treebanks distinguish these through subtyping of the `expl` relation, for instance, `expl:pass` and `expl:pv` in the Czech treebanks. This is not, however, the case across languages and since the reflexive passive does not require passive marking on the verb, it

is difficult to distinguish these automatically based on morphosyntactic criteria. In Table 1 we therefore collapse these two construction types (Reflexive). In addition to the `pv` subtype, we further rely on another morphological feature in the treebanks in order to identify inherent reflexives, namely the `Reflex` feature, as illustrated by the Portuguese example in Figure 1 (bottom right).[2] In Table 1 we observe that the distribution of passive and inherent reflexives clearly separates the different treebanks. They are highly frequent in Slavic languages (Bulgarian, Croatian, Czech, Polish, Slovak, Slovenian, Ukrainian and Upper Sorbian). as illustrated by the passive reflexive in (28) and the inherent reflexive in (29). They are also frequent in two of the French treebanks and in Brazilian Portuguese. Interestingly, they are also found in Latin, but only in the treebank based on medieval texts.

(28) O   centrální výrobě   tepla *se* říká,
      about central   production heating it says
      že je nejefektivnější (cs)
      that the most-efficient

<hr>

[2]The final category discussed in section 2 is that of clitic doubling. It is not clear, however, how one could recognize these based on their morphosyntactic analysis in the various treebanks and we therefore exclude them from our empirical study, although a manual analysis confirmed that they exist at least in Bulgarian and Greek.

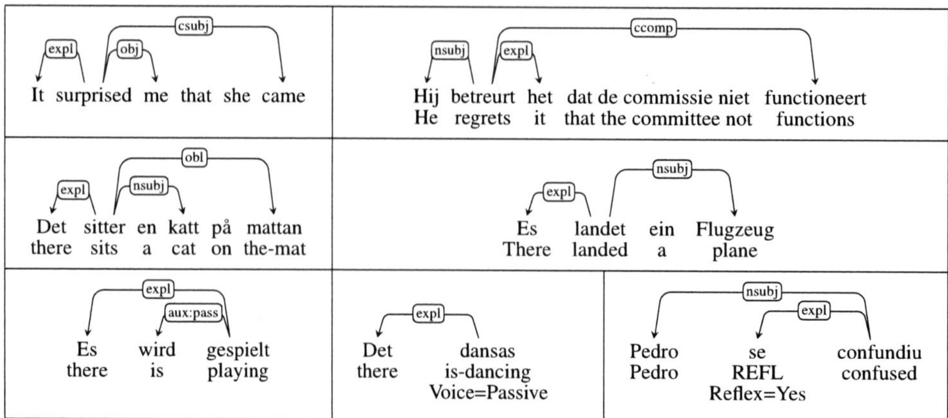

Figure 1: UD analyses of *extraposition* [(4) and (6)] (top), *existentials* [(9) and (10)] (middle), *impersonal constructions* (bottom left and center), and *inherent reflexives* [(17)] (bottom right).

'Central heat production is said to be the most efficient'

(29)　Skozi　steno slišim,　kako *se*
　　　through wall　I-hear-it, how　REFL
　　　zabavajo. (sl)
　　　have-fun
　　　'I hear through the wall how they have fun'

(30)　O deputado *se*　　aproximou (pt)
　　　the deputy　REFL approached
　　　'The deputy approached'

It is clear from the discussion above that all constructions discussed in Section 2 are attested in UD treebanks. Some languages have a substantial number of expl occurrences that are not captured by our heuristics (i.e. the Remaining category in Table 1). In some cases (i.e. Swedish and Norwegian), this is due to an analysis of *cleft* constructions where the pronoun is tagged as expl. It should be noted that the analysis of clefts differs considerably across languages and treebanks, and therefore we did not include it in the empirical overview. Another frequent pattern not captured by our heuristics involves clitics and clitic doubling. This is true especially for the Romance languages, where Italian and Galician have a substantial number of occurrences of expl marked as Clitic not covered by our heuristics. In French, a frequent pattern not captured by our heuristics is the *il y a* construction.

The empirical investigation also makes clear that the analysis of expletives under the current UD scheme suffers from inconsistencies. For inherent reflexives, the treebanks for Croatian, Czech, Polish, Portuguese, Romanian, and Slovak use the subtype expl:pv, while the treebanks for French, Italian and Spanish simply use expl for this purpose. And even though languages like German, Dutch and Swedish do have inherent reflexives, their reflexive arguments are currently annotated as regular objects.

Even in different treebanks for one and the same language, different decisions have sometimes been made, as is clear from the column labeled Banks in Table 1. Of the three treebanks for Spanish, for instance, only Spanish-AnCora uses the expl relation, and of the three Finnish UD treebanks, only Finnish-FTB. In the French treebanks, we observe that the expl relation is employed to capture quite different constructions. For instance, in French-ParTUT, it is used for impersonal subjects (non-referential *il*, whereas the other French treebanks do not employ an expletive analysis for these. We also find that annotation within a single treebank is not always consistent. For instance, whereas the German treebank generally marks *es* in existential constructions with *geben* as expl, the treebank also contains a fair amount of examples with *geben* where es is marked nsubj, despite being clearly expletive.

4　Towards Consistent Annotation of Expletives in UD

Our investigations in the previous section clearly demonstrate that expletives are currently not annotated consistently in UD treebanks. This is partly due to the existence of different descriptive and theoretical traditions and to the fact that many treebanks have been converted from annotation schemes that differ in their treatment of expletives. But the situation has probably been made worse by the lack of detailed guidelines concerning which constructions should be analyzed as involving expletives and how exactly these constructions should be annotated. In this section, we will take a first step towards improving the situation by making specific recommendations on both of these aspects.

Based on the definition and tests taken from Postal and Pullum (1988), we propose that the class of expletives should include non-referential pro-forms involved in the following types of constructions:

1. Extraposition of clausal arguments (Section 2.1)
2. Existential (or presentational) sentences (Section 2.2)
3. Impersonal constructions (including weather verbs and impersonal passives) (Section 2.3)
4. Passive reflexives (Section 2.4)
5. Inherent reflexives (Section 2.5)

For inherent reflexives, the evidence is not quite as clear-cut as for the other categories, but given that the current UD guidelines recommend using `expl` and given that many treebanks already follow these guidelines, it seems most practical to continue to include them in the class of expletives, as recommended by Silveira (2016). By contrast, the arguments for treating clitics in clitic doubling (Section 2.6) as expletives appears weaker, and very few treebanks have implemented this analysis, so we think it may be worth reconsidering their analysis and possibly use `dislocated` for all cases of double realization of core arguments.

The distinction between core arguments and other dependents of a predicate is a cornerstone of the UD approach to syntactic annotation. Expletives challenge this distinction by (mostly) behaving as core arguments syntactically but not semantically. In chain constructions like extraposition and existentials, they compete with the other chain element for the core argument relation. In impersonal constructions and inherent reflexives, they are the sole candidate for that relation. This suggests three possible ways of treating expletives in relation to core arguments:

1. Treat expletives as distinct from core arguments and assign the core argument relation to the other chain element (if present).
2. Treat expletives as core arguments and allow the other chain element (if present) to instantiate the same relation (possibly using subtypes to distinguish the two).
3. Treat expletives as core arguments and forbid the other chain element (if present) to instantiate the same relation.

All three approaches have advantages and drawbacks, but the current UD guidelines clearly favor the first approach, essentially restricting the application of core argument relations to *referential* core arguments. Since this approach is already implemented in a large number of treebanks, albeit to different degrees and with considerable variation, it seems practically preferable to maintain and refine this approach, rather than switching to a radically different scheme. However, in order to make the annotation more informative, we recommend using the following subtypes of the `expl` relation:

1. `expl:chain` for expletives that occur in chain constructions like extraposition of clausal arguments and existential or presentational sentences (Section 2.1–2.2)
2. `expl:impers` for expletive subjects in impersonal constructions, including impersonal verbs and passivized intransitive verbs (Section 2.3)
3. `expl:pass` for reflexive pronouns used to form passives (Section 2.4)
4. `expl:pv` for inherent reflexives, that is, pronouns selected by pronominal verbs (Section 2.5)

The three latter subtypes are already included in the UD guidelines, although it is clear that they are not used in all treebanks that use the `expl` relation. The first subtype, `expl:chain`, is a novel proposal, which would allow us to distinguish constructions where the expletive is dependent on the presence of a referential argument. This subtype could possibly be used also in clitic doubling, if we decide to include these among expletives.

5   Conclusion

Creating consistently annotated treebanks for many languages is potentially of tremendous importance for both NLP and linguistics. While our study of the annotation of expletives in UD shows that this goal has not quite been reached yet, the development of UD has at least made it possible to start investigating these issues on a large scale. Based on a theoretical analysis of expletives and an empirical survey of current UD treebanks, we have proposed a refinement of the annotation guidelines that is well grounded in both theory and data and that will hopefully lead to more consistency. By systematically studying different linguistic phenomena in this way, we can gradually approach the goal of global consistency.

Acknowledgments

We are grateful to two anonymous reviewers for constructive comments on the first version of the paper. Most of the work described in this article was conducted during the authors' stays at the Center for Advanced Study at the Norwegian Academy of Science and Letters.

References

Hans Bennis. 2010. *Gaps and dummies*. Amsterdam University Press.

Adriane Boyd, Whitney Gegg-Harrison, and Donna Byron. 2005. Identifying non-referential it: A machine learning approach incorporating linguistically motivated patterns. In *Proceedings of the ACL Workshop on Feature Engineering for Machine Learning in Natural Language Processing*, FeatureEng '05, pages 40–47, Stroudsburg, PA, USA. Association for Computational Linguistics.

Anna Cardinaletti. 1997. Agreement and control in expletive constructions. *Linguistic Inquiry*, 28(3):521–533.

Richard Evans. 2001. Applying machine learning toward an automatic classification of it. *Literary and linguistic computing*, 16(1):45–58.

Liane Guillou, Christian Hardmeier, Aaron Smith, Jörg Tiedemann, and Bonnie Webber. 2014. Parcor 1.0: A parallel pronoun-coreference corpus to support statistical MT. In *9th International Conference on Language Resources and Evaluation (LREC), May 26-31, 2014, Reykjavik, Iceland*, pages 3191–3198. European Language Resources Association.

Christian Hardmeier, Preslav Nakov, Sara Stymne, Jörg Tiedemann, Yannick Versley, and Mauro Cettolo. 2015. Pronoun-focused MT and cross-lingual pronoun prediction: Findings of the 2015 DiscoMT shared task on pronoun translation. In *Proceedings of the Second Workshop on Discourse in Machine Translation*, pages 1–16.

Ilan Hazout. 2004. The syntax of existential constructions. *Linguistic Inquiry*, 35(3):393–430.

Sharid Loáiciga, Liane Guillou, and Christian Hardmeier. 2017. What is it? disambiguating the different readings of the pronoun 'it'. In *Proceedings of the 2017 Conference on Empirical Methods in Natural Language Processing*, pages 1325–1331.

Joakim Nivre. 2015. Towards a universal grammar for natural language processing. In *International Conference on Intelligent Text Processing and Computational Linguistics*, pages 3–16. Springer.

Joakim Nivre, Marie-Catherine de Marneffe, Filip Ginter, Yoav Goldberg, Jan Hajic, Christopher D Manning, Ryan T McDonald, Slav Petrov, Sampo Pyysalo, Natalia Silveira, et al. 2016. Universal dependencies v1: A multilingual treebank collection. In *10th International Conference on Language Resources and Evaluation (LREC), Portoroz, Slovenia*, pages 1659–1666. European Language Resources Association.

Christer Platzack. 1987. The Scandinavian languages and the null-subject parameter. *Natural Language & Linguistic Theory*, 5(3):377–401.

Paul M Postal and Geoffrey K Pullum. 1988. Expletive noun phrases in subcategorized positions. *Linguistic Inquiry*, 19(4):635–670.

Natalia Silveira. 2016. *Designing Syntactic Representations for NLP: An Empirical Investigation*. Ph.D. thesis, Stanford University, Stanford, CA.

Olga Uryupina, Mijail Kabadjov, and Massimo Poesio. 2016. Detecting non-reference and non-anaphoricity. In Massimo Poesio, Roland Stuckardt, and Yannick Versley, editors, *Anaphora Resolution: Algorithms, Resources, and Applications*, pages 369–392. Springer Berlin Heidelberg, Berlin, Heidelberg.

Sten Vikner. 1995. *Verb movement and expletive subjects in the Germanic languages*. Oxford University Press on Demand.

Lesly Miculicich Werlen and Andrei Popescu-Belis. 2017. Using coreference links to improve Spanish-to-English machine translation. In *Proceedings of the 2nd Workshop on Coreference Resolution Beyond OntoNotes (CORBON 2017)*, pages 30–40.

Challenges in Converting the *Index Thomisticus* Treebank into Universal Dependencies

Flavio Massimiliano Cecchini and **Marco Passarotti**
Università Cattolica del Sacro Cuore, CIRCSE Research Centre
Largo Gemelli 1, 20123 - Milan, Italy
{flavio.cecchini}{marco.passarotti}@unicatt.it

Paola Marongiu
Università degli Studi di Pavia
Corso Strada Nuova 65, 27100 - Pavia, Italy
paola.marongiu01@universitadipavia.it

Daniel Zeman
Charles University in Prague, Institute of Formal and Applied Linguistics
Malostranské náměstí 25, 118 00 - Prague, Czech Republic
zeman@ufal.mff.cuni.cz

Abstract

This paper describes the changes applied to the original process used to convert the *Index Thomisticus* Treebank, a corpus including texts in Medieval Latin by Thomas Aquinas, into the annotation style of Universal Dependencies. The changes are made both to harmonise the Universal Dependencies version of the *Index Thomisticus* Treebank with the two other available Latin treebanks and to fix errors and inconsistencies resulting from the original process. The paper details the treatment of different issues in PoS tagging, lemmatisation and assignment of dependency relations. Finally, it assesses the quality of the new conversion process by providing an evaluation against a gold standard.

1 Introduction

Since release 1.2, Universal Dependencies (UD) (Nivre et al., 2016)[1] has been including treebanks for ancient languages or historical phases of modern ones. In the current release of UD (2.2), there are treebanks for Ancient Greek, Gothic, Latin, Old Church Slavonic, Old French and Sanskrit.

Among these languages, Latin is not only the one provided with most data in UD 2.2 (520K tokens), but also the one with the most treebanks (3). These are PROIEL (Haug and Jøhndal, 2008), which includes the entire New Testament in Latin (the so called *Vulgata* by Jerome) and texts from the Classical era (199K tokens), the Latin Dependency Treebank (LDT) by the Perseus Digital Library (Bamman and Crane, 2006), which collects a small selection of texts by Classical authors (29K tokens), and the *Index Thomisticus* Treebank (IT-TB) (Passarotti, 2011), based on works written in the XIIIth century by Thomas Aquinas (291K tokens).

The greater number of treebanks available for Latin than for other ancient languages reflects the large diachronic (as well as diatopic) span of Latin texts, which are spread across a time frame of more than two millennia and in most areas of what is called Europe today. This aspect is peculiar to Latin, which has represented for a long time a kind of *lingua franca* in Europe. The variety of textual typologies in Latin is thus wide: to name just a few, scientific treaties, literary works, philosophical texts and official documents were mostly written in Latin for centuries all around Europe. Today, this makes it impossible to build a textual corpus that can be sufficiently representative of "Latin", just because there are too many varieties of Latin, which can be even very different from each other.[2]

The three Latin treebanks were all developed before UD came into use and thus have been following a different annotation style. Although they are all dependency-based, only the IT-TB and the LDT have been sharing the same annotation

---

[1] http://universaldependencies.org/

[2] For instance, Ponti and Passarotti (2016) show the dramatic decrease of accuracy rates provided by a dependency parsing pipeline trained on the IT-TB when applied on texts of the Classical era taken from the LDT.

Proceedings of the Second Workshop on Universal Dependencies (UDW 2018), pages 27–36
Brussels, Belgium, November 1, 2018. ©2018 Association for Computational Linguistics

guidelines since the beginning of their respective projects (Bamman et al., 2007), while PROIEL has adopted a slightly different style.[3] The treebanks had been originally converted into the UD style by means of different and independent processes, which led to a number of inconsistencies in treating syntactic constructions as well as in part-of-speech (PoS) tagging and lemmatisation. In order to overcome such situation, a consensus has been achieved between the three projects with the aim of bringing the Latin treebanks closer to each other, establishing fundamental common criteria for both syntactic and morphological annotation.

In particular, so far the IT-TB has been always converted into UD through the same process used for the Prague Dependency Treebank for Czech (PDT) (Hajič et al., 2017), since both treebanks follow the same annotation style; just few modifications were made to cope with issues in PoS tagging.

This paper describes the changes applied to the original process of conversion from the IT-TB into the UD style, both to harmonise the IT-TB with the other Latin treebanks and to fix errors and inconsistencies during conversion. The result of the new conversion process is the UD version of the IT-TB that will be made available in the release 2.3 of UD, scheduled to be published in November 2018.

The paper is organised as follows. Section 2 describes the conversion process, by detailing its two phases, i.e. the so called *harmonisation*, which mostly deals with issues in PoS tagging and lemmatisation (Section 2.1), and the UD *conversion proper*, which is responsible for assigning dependency relations and rearranging the nodes in the syntactic trees to fit the UD annotation style (Section 2.2). Section 3 provides an evaluation of the conversion process. Finally, Section 4 concludes the paper and sketches some future work.

2 Conversion Process

The conversion process is performed via two sets of scripts, both written in Perl language[4] and embedded as modules in TREEX's[5] architecture. They consist of a preparatory *harmonisation* phase

(Section 2.1), followed by the UD *conversion proper* (Section 2.2).

2.1 Harmonisation

Here, with *harmonisation* we mean adjusting a treebank to the PDT annotation style, with regard to the notation of lemmas, PoS and dependency relations. This is the starting point for the current UD conversion proper script (developed as part of the HamleDT project (Rosa et al., 2014)), which in a second phase infers morphological features and intervenes on the structure of the syntactic trees. In our case, harmonisation also includes making the IT-TB adhere to the agreed-upon annotation criteria for the three Latin treebanks, by means of a number of interdependent harmonisation scripts.

In what follows, we describe the most relevant issues that are dealt with during harmonisation of the IT-TB and their treatment in the script.

2.1.1 PoS Tagging of Inflectable Words

The syntactic annotation style of the IT-TB already substantially coincides with the PDT one (with the exception of one *afun*;[6] see Section 2.1.6). Hence, no substantial changes have to be carried out during harmonisation in this respect. However, the IT-TB does not distinguish PoS: instead, it applies a tripartite classification on a morphological basis between (a) nominal inflection, including nouns, adjectives, pronouns and numerals, (b) verbal inflection, including verbs, and (c) no inflection, including conjunctions, prepositions, adverbs and interjections.[7]

This means that, while words belonging to the class of verbal inflection (including also their nominal forms; see Section 2.1.2) can be readily assigned PoS VERB,[8] assigning a PoS to words of the other classes is not straightforward. To this end, we take advantage of the finer morphological classification provided by LEMLAT (Passarotti, 2004), where each inflectable nominal, adjectival and pronominal paradigm is treated differently. This gives us a PoS tagging for inflectable word classes, but not for uninflectable ones. From LEM-

---

[3] http://folk.uio.no/daghaug/syntactic_guidelines.pdf

[4] https://www.perl.org/

[5] TREEX is a modular software system in Perl for Natural Language Processing. It is described in (Popel and Žabokrtský, 2010) and available online at http://ufal.mff.cuni.cz/treex.

[6] *afun* means "*a*nalytical *fun*ction", which is the term used for syntactic labels in the surface syntax ("analytical") layer of annotation in the PDT. The corresponding term in UD is *deprel*, standing for "*depr*el, standing for "*dep*endency *rel*ation".

[7] Actually, the IT-TB also considers a fourth inflectional class to acknowledge the nominal inflections in verbal paradigms, like for instance for participles and gerunds.

[8] UD makes use of the Universal PoS tagset by (Petrov et al.).

LAT we thus obtain three lists of lemmas, respectively for nouns, adjectives and pronouns, which are hard-coded into the Perl script as look-up tables for PoS assignment (lemmas are already provided by the IT-TB annotation).

These lists are manually checked and partly corrected; indeed, some terms that are new to Thomistic Latin, or that have changed PoS or gained a new one in the passage from the Classical to the Medieval era[9] need to be added to their respective list or moved to a different one. This procedure does not resolve lexical ambiguity: for example, *philosophus* 'philosopher; philosophical' can function both as a noun and as an adjective. This ambivalence between noun and adjective can not be solved by look-up tables alone, but requires taking into account the syntactic behaviour of the word in the dependency tree. More precisely, if in the IT-TB the node in question is found to be dependent on another node and has *afun* Atr (attribute)[10] and they agree by case, number and gender, we will label it as an adjective; otherwise, as a noun. The genitive case needs to be excluded from this procedure, as one of its functions is to make a noun the attribute of another noun; e. g., a phrase like *amici philosophi*, where both words are in the genitive case, might be interpreted as 'of the philosophical friend' (noun *amicus* and adjective *philosophus*), 'of the philosopher's friend' (two nouns), or 'of the philosopher friend' (noun and nominal apposition). This ambiguity can not be solved *a priori*, as in the IT-TB all these three constructions yield the same annotation:

... amici philosophi ...

In general, the boundaries between adjectives and nouns are blurred. Thus, in those occurrences where an adjective is not assigned *afun* Atr in the IT-TB, we give it PoS NOUN in UD.

2.1.2 PoS of Verbal Nouns

Words belonging to the verbal inflectional class are always assigned PoS tag VERB, also when nominal forms are concerned (participles, gerunds, gerundives, supines).[11] Since a verbal noun is still able to take complements, the strongest argument in favour of this decision is that in the current version of UD nominals can not govern the same syntactic relations as verbs (e. g. no core/oblique distinction between complements is made). For example, in the sentence from *Summa contra gentiles*, Lib. III, Cap. CXXIX[12]

> *Transgredi autem terminum hunc a iudice positum, non est secundum se malum...*
> 'But to pass over a boundary line set up by a judge is not essentially evil...'

we have *positum* 'set up' (perfect participle of *pono*) acting as a modifier of *terminum* 'boundary line', whose Agent is represented by the prepositional phrase *a iudice* 'by a judge'. Our UD conversion yields:[13]

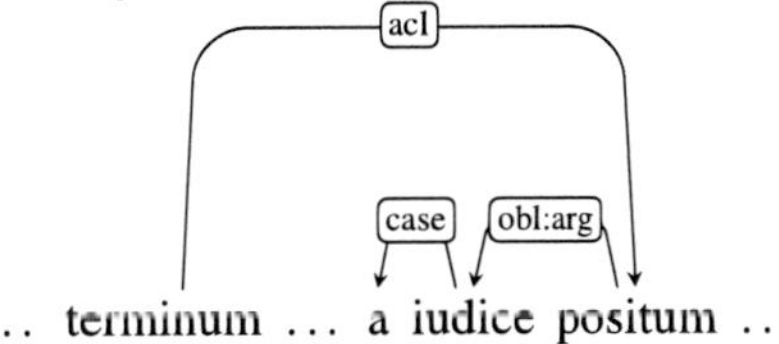

... terminum ... a iudice positum ...

Here, if we were to use amod (adjectival modifier) instead of acl, we would not be able to identify *a iudice* as an agent, and for the corresponding node we should then choose between nmod (noun modifier) and *amod*, both however unsuitable to this context.[14]

In the IT-TB, the only possible identification of a verbal noun as an adjective or another nominal is made at the level of lemmatisation: some occurrences of e. g. *abstractus* 'abstract' (adjective), perfect participle of *abstraho* 'to drag away', are assigned their own adjectival lemma (reported in the look-up table) instead of the verbal one, on the basis of their lexicalisation.

2.1.3 PoS Tagging of Uninflectable Words

Words belonging to uninflectable classes (prepositions, conjunctions, adverbs, interjections) are all

---

[9]E. g. *sanctus* 'saint' was originally only a participial form of the verb *sancio* 'to ratify', but subsequently it was perceived and used also as an independent noun or adjective.

[10]For further details about *afuns*, see the annotation guidelines for PDT's analytical layer at `https://ufal.mff.cuni.cz/pdt2.0/doc/manuals/en/a-layer/html/`.

[11]A practical reference for Latin grammar is (Greenough and Allen, 2006).

[12]Here and thereafter, English translations of excerpts from *Summa contra gentiles* are taken from (Aquinas, 1955–1957). Those from *Scriptum super sententiis* are based on the Italian translation provided by (d'Aquino, 2001).

[13]acl: adjectival clause; obl:arg: oblique argument; case: case-marking element.

[14]The IT-TB is not the only treebank following this approach, another one being the Sanskrit treebank: `http://universaldependencies.org/treebanks/sa_ufal/index.html`.

labeled with a common PoS tag I (for "invariable") in LEMLAT.

To assign a Universal PoS tag to such words, we use a number of *ad hoc* rules relying on the original IT-TB syntactic annotation, where such words are assigned specific *afuns*: AuxC for subordinating conjunctions, AuxZ and AuxY for a closed subset of non-derived adverbs, and Coord for coordinating conjunctions.[15] All those uninflectable words that are not assigned a PoS by these *ad hoc* rules are considered to be non-derived adverbs.

2.1.4 PoS and Lemmas of Derived Adverbs

In the IT-TB, the lemma of a derived adverb is the adjective or the verb from which it is regularly formed. For example, *continue* 'continuously', *continuius* 'more continuously' (comparative) and *continuissime* 'most continuously' (absolute superlative) are all lemmatised under the adjective *continuus*, while the lemma for *abundanter* 'abundantly', *abundantius* 'more abundantly' and *abundantissime* 'most abundantly' is the verb *abundo*, on whose present participle (*abundans*) the adverb is formed. However, in UD Latin treebanks, the lemma of an adverb is defined to be its positive degree. In the examples above, we will thus have lemmas *continue* and *abundanter*.

To assign a PoS to derived adverbs, we exploit the original tagging of the IT-TB, which features a specific morphological tag for the "adverbial case", as this is considered to be part of the nominal inflection (so that e. g. *continue* is the adverbial case of *continuus*).

2.1.5 The Article

Latin does not feature the lexical category of the article, but all modern Romance languages descended from it, like Italian, have developed one. Remarkably, in the IT-TB we find 8 occurrences of the otherwise unattested word *ly*, as in *ly homo* 'the human being'. This is clearly an ancestor of the Italian definite article making its way in the XIIIth-century Latin of Thomas, whose mother tongue was a southern Italian variety. In the IT-TB, *ly* is then the only word receiving PoS DET (determiner); it does not show any inflection.

2.1.6 Verbal Complements

For what concerns the *afun* tagset, the only innovation of the IT-TB with respect to the PDT standard is the *afun* OComp for predicative complements (or secondary predicates), precisely for object complements (the *afun* Pnom being used for subject complements). For example, see *Summa contra gentiles*, Lib. II, Cap. XXXVIII (OComp highlighted):

> ...*posuerunt mundum* **aeternum**.
> '...(they) asserted the world's eternity.'
> lit. '...(they) supposed the world eternal.'

In UD this syntactic relation is represented by assigning the *deprel* xcomp (open clausal complement) to object complements. However, in the original version of the conversion script, OComp was equated to *afun* Obj (direct or indirect object) and as such erroneously translated into UD as *deprel* obj.[16] Since the harmonisation to the PDT style does not accept the OComp *afun*, we have to mark the affected nodes by using a "miscellaneous" field in the XML TREEX file, so that we will be able to treat OComp as a subcase of Obj later during conversion proper. A similar approach is also pursued for appositions (cf. Section 2.2.3).

2.2 UD Conversion Proper

The UD conversion script manages the relabeling of *afuns* into *deprels* and, most importantly, rearranges the dependencies in the tree according to the UD style.

After describing the main differences between the IT-TB and UD annotation styles (2.2.1), in this Section we will focus on two syntactic constructions that we deem to be particularly challenging to tackle while adapting the conversion script to the IT-TB: namely, ellipsis (2.2.2) and apposition (2.2.3).

2.2.1 Differences between IT-TB and UD

The main difference between the IT-TB and UD styles is that in the IT-TB conjunctions, prepositions and copulas govern their phrases, while UD favours dependencies between content words, with function words tending to end up as leaves of the tree.[17] To illustrate this with an example, we consider the following excerpt from *Scriptum super sententiis* (Lib. I, Dist. III, Qu. II, Art. II):

---

[15]AuxY is also assigned to coordinating conjunctions occurring in multiple coordinations (like ...*et*...*et*... '...and...and...').

[16]In the IT-TB, the *afun* Obj is also used for annotating oblique nominals expressing Result, Origin and Target (mostly) with motion verbs. As these are considered to be (non-core) arguments, they are assigned *deprel* obl (oblique nominals) with a specific subtype arg (argument).

[17]The basic principles of UD are explained at http://universaldependencies.org/u/overview/syntax.html.

...quae imperfecta sunt, ut patet in materia et forma...

'...which are imperfect, as it clearly appears in matter and form...'

Here, *sunt* '(they) are' is a copula and *ut* 'as' is a conjunction introducing a subordinate clause. They both govern the predicate of their respective clause in the IT-TB style:[18]

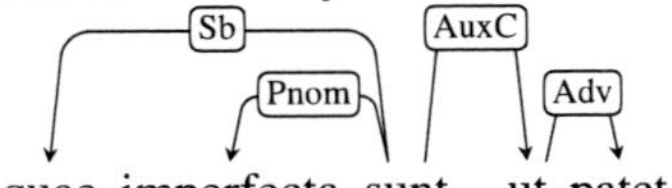

... quae imperfecta sunt , ut patet ...

The same goes for *in* 'in' (preposition) and *et* 'and' (coordinating conjunction):[19]

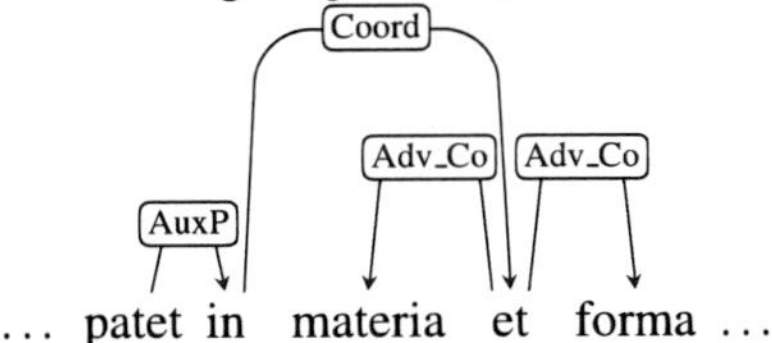

... patet in materia et forma ...

Here, *in* and *et* govern the two conjuncts of the coordinated phrase *in materia et forma*. On the contrary, the UD tree looks as follows:[20]

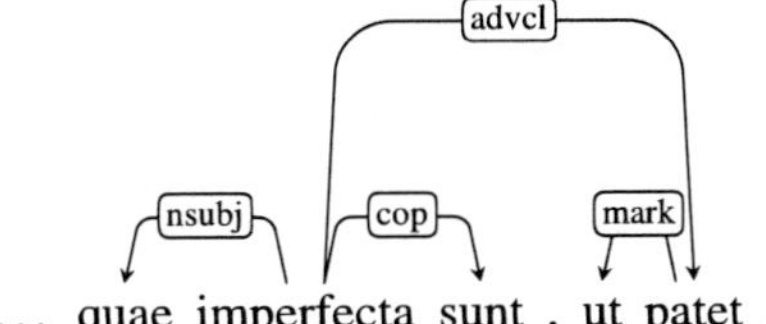

... quae imperfecta sunt , ut patet ...

and

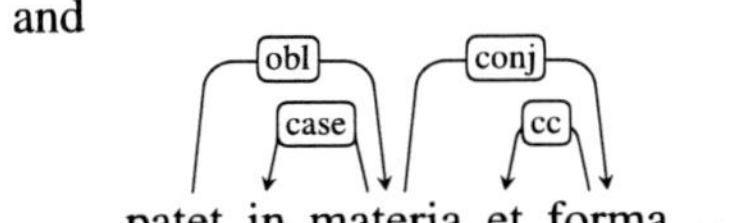

... patet in materia et forma ...

Once a treebank is harmonised into a standard PDT-style form, the UD conversion script acts in two ways: (a) it translates all *afun*s into UD *deprel*s. This translation is not always biunivocal and is handled through a set of rules exploiting both morphological and syntactic annotation: e. g., *afun* Adv can correspond to different *deprel*s, like `advcl` or `advmod` (adverbial modifier); (b)

---

[18] Sb: subject; Pnom: nominal predicate; AuxC: subordinating conjunction; Adv: adverbial.

[19] AuxP: adposition; Coord: coordinating element; Co adscript: member of a coordination.

[20] nsubj: nominal subject; cop: copula; advcl: adverbial clause; mark: marker introducing a finite subordinate clause; obl: oblique nominal (see footnote 17); conj: conjunct; cc: coordinating conjunction. The complete list of *deprel*s and their explanations can be found at `http://universaldependencies.org/u/dep/index.html`.

it rearranges the nodes in the tree. TREEX features a number of specific modules to manage different kinds of constructions, such as coordinations and subordinate clauses. These Perl subroutines are language-independent and make use of the PoS, the morphological features and the *afun*s found in the source data. Thus, even after harmonisation, the basic conversion script is still inadequate to properly handle a language-specific treebank. Therefore, we have to tune the script to better address the specific needs of the IT-TB.

We will illustrate this point with the aid of two constructions: ellipsis and apposition.[21]

2.2.2 Ellipsis

The IT-TB and UD styles treat ellipsis quite differently, in a way that is not directly related to the UD primacy of content words. To clarify this point, we will use the following excerpt from the IT-TB (*Scriptum super sententiis*, Lib. IV, Dist. VII, Qu. I, Art. III):

> *In illis autem sacramentis quae perficiuntur in usu materiae, sicut baptismus [perficitur] in ipsa tinctione...*
>
> 'In those sacraments, however, which are accomplished through the use of matter, like baptism [is accomplished] through the submersion itself...'

The text in square brackets (a verb) is the elided part of the sentence. In the IT-TB, the only recorded ellipses, i. e. constructions for which the *afun* `ExD` (external dependency) is used, are those of verbal elements. On the contrary, nominal ellipses are not explicitly marked in the annotation. Therefore, in the following we will consider verbal ellipses only.

In the IT-TB style, if ellipsis resolution were applied, the comparative clause introduced by *sicut* would look as follows:

... sicut baptismus perficitur in ipsa tinctione

Since the node for *perficitur* is missing, the nodes for *baptismus* and *in* (head of *tinctione*), lacking their governor, become children of their closest

---

[21] Ellipsis and apposition are challenging constructions where different UD teams have faced similar problems and sometimes found different, yet compatible, solutions. Discussion about the treatment of such constructions in different languages can be found in (Aranzabe et al., 2014), (Dobrovoljc and Nivre, 2016), (Pyysalo et al., 2015), (Tandon et al., 2016) and (Zeman, 2015).

ancestor (in this case *sicut* for both) and are assigned *afun* ExD. Since nodes labeled with AuxP, AuxC or Coord can never take the *afun* ExD, this percolates down the tree to the first content word. Here, this happens from *in* to *tinctione*:

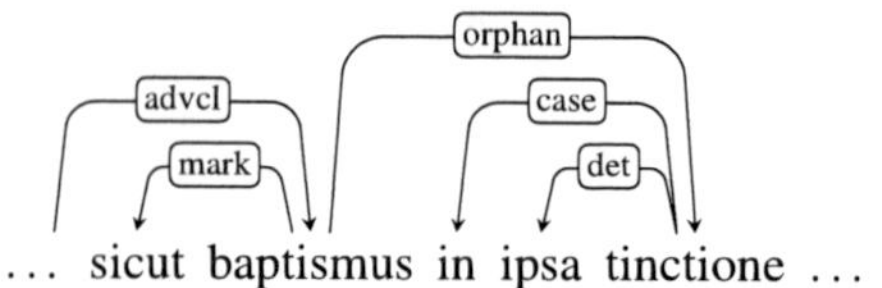

... sicut baptismus in ipsa tinctione ...

In UD a member of the elliptical clause is promoted to clause's head on the basis of its *coreness* value[22] and receives the *deprel* that would have been otherwise assigned to the elided predicate. The remaining nodes of the clause become its children and are assigned the special *deprel* orphan to avoid misleading dependencies.[23]

For elliptical constructions, the task of our conversion script is then to identify one of the ExD siblings in the IT-TB source data as the node to promote to head of the elliptical clause in UD. Following the UD guidelines, we consider a coreness hierarchy that gives precedence to a subject over an object, to an object over an indirect object, to an indirect object over an oblique one, and generally to core complements over peripheral ones. Now, the *afun* ExD obscures such relations. However, we can retrieve this information heuristically, by exploiting the rich Latin morphology (word order being much less meaningful) and cross-checking it with the PoS assigned during harmonisation.

In the example above, the conversion script has to choose the head of the elliptical clause between *baptismus* and *tinctione* (*tinctione* being the content word, and thus the UD head, in its prepositional phrase). Both are nominals (with PoS NOUN assigned by harmonisation), but the fact that *baptismus* is in the nominative case, while *tinctione* is in the ablative (lemma *tinctio*) tells us that the former is most probably the subject of the elliptical clause, while the latter is an oblique complement. Hence, the script promotes *baptismus* and restructures the subtree as follows:

---

[22]See the UD guidelines at http://universaldependencies.org/u/overview/specific-syntax.html#ellipsis.

[23]Again, this does not apply to function words like conjunctions and prepositions, which keep their *deprel*.

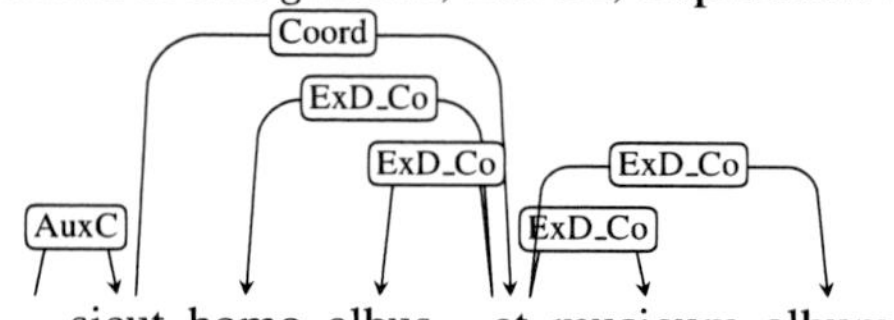

... sicut baptismus in ipsa tinctione ...

Such approach shows some limitations, especially when dealing with coordinating constructions, which are quite tricky when paired with elliptical constructions. Indeed, *a priori* it is not possible to set a hierarchy of the ExD siblings occurring in a coordination, since they all equally depend on one common coordinating element. For example (*Summa contra gentiles*, Lib. III, Cap. LXXIV):

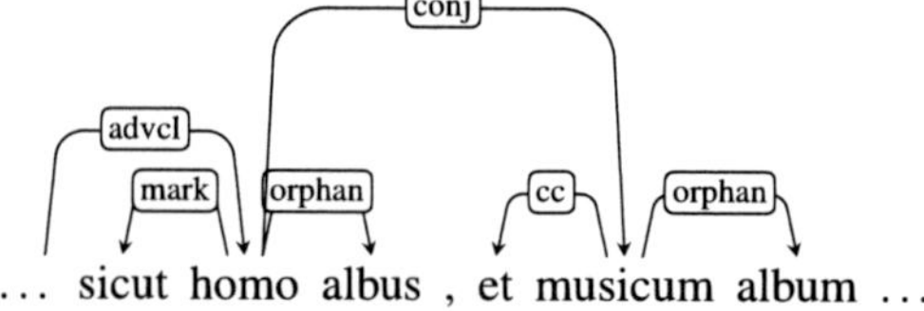

... sicut homo albus , et musicum album ...

This clause means "just like a man [is] white and a musical being [is] white". First, we know that the ExD siblings need to be distributed among the (at least) two members of the coordination, but, in principle, we do not know this distribution: e.g., both *homo albus*/*musicum album* and *homo*/*albus musicum album* might be valid splits.[24] To address this issue, we implement a heuristic approach that takes into account both frequently used separators (like commas and conjunctions) and word order to identify the most probable boundaries between coordination members; in the example above, the two members *homo albus* and *musicum album* are separated by the coordinating conjunction *et*. Second, head promotion for elliptical constructions takes place according to the PoS hierarchy described above: in our example, the nouns *homo* and *musicum* become governors of the adjectives *albus* and *album* respectively, via *deprel* orphan. The resulting UD subtree is the following:[25]

... sicut homo albus , et musicum album ...

As it clearly stands out from the UD subtree above, in such a case our conversion fails. Here, the adjectives are nominal predicates and only their

---

[24]The latter is probably not grammatical, but we are working at a very shallow level here.

[25]cc: coordinating conjunction; conj: conjunct.

copulas (*est*) are missing, so that the correct dependencies should be assigned in the opposite way, with no *deprel* `orphan` involved:

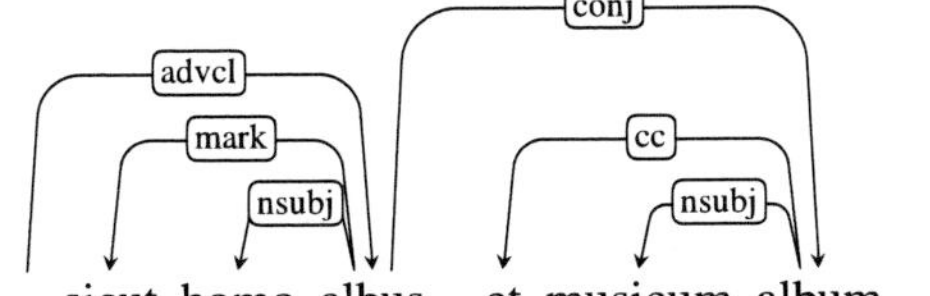

Being aware of such limitations, when treating specific elliptical constructions we print different kinds of warnings at the end of the conversion process to support a subsequent manual revision.

In the previous version of the IT-TB conversion script, ellipsis was not dealt with at all, providing the TREEX modules with no clues about how to interpret such constructions correctly. The way we treat elliptical constructions exemplifies how to take advantage of properties of a language like Latin to address linguistic issues that impact the UD conversion.

A particular case of ellipsis is the omission of the auxiliary verb *sum* 'to be' in the gerundive construction when occurring at the beginning of a sentence, e. g. in a frequent formula of the type *Ad secundum dicendum [est], quod…* 'Secondly, [it has] to be said that…'. According to the IT-TB style, the subtree for this clause looks as follows:

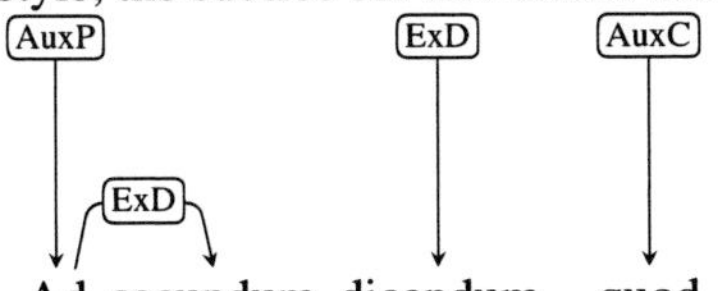

The nodes for *ad*, *dicendum* and *quod* directly depend on the root as a consequence of the missing root node for *est*. The conversion script promotes *dicendum* to the head, as verbs have priority over nominals. The children of *dicendum* are then assigned the correct *deprel* (instead of `orphan`), by using heuristics similar to those to establish coreness hierarchy. In the end, the UD subtree will be:[26]

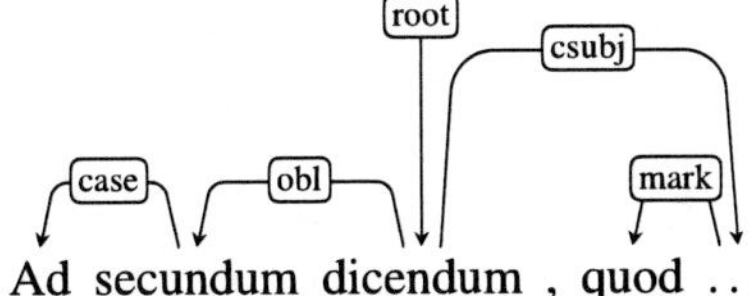

In the UD subtree, the elided node for *est* would be a child of the node for *dicendum* with *deprel*

---

[26] `csubj`: clausal subject.

`aux:pass`. This is a case where an elliptical construction represented in the IT-TB style is not apparent anymore in UD, because the primacy of content words obscures the ellipsis of *est* in the UD subtree.

2.2.3 Apposition

Just like in the PDT style, in the IT-TB an apposition is defined as a binary relation where one phrase or clause is reworded or specified in some way by another following phrase or clause, which is separated from the first one by punctuation or a grammatical element.[27] In the IT-TB, this element is in most cases *scilicet* 'that is, namely', less frequently *sicut* 'as', like in *Summa contra gentiles*, Lib. III, Cap. CXVI:

> …*amor summi boni, scilicet Dei…*
> '…the love of the highest good, namely, God…'

In the IT-TB style, we have:[28]

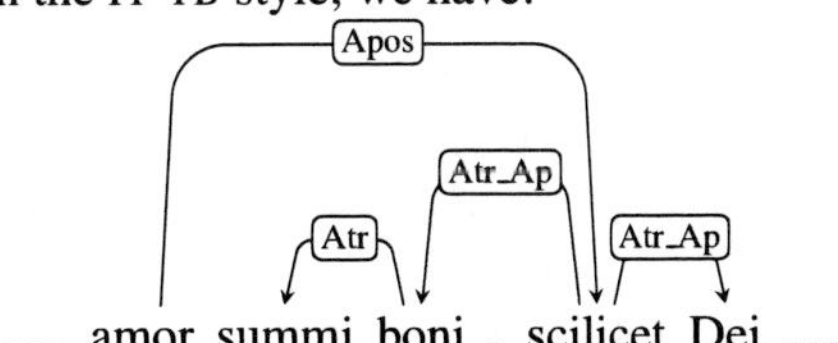

Apposition in this sense can take place for any noun, verb or adverb phrase. However, the definition of the UD *deprel* `appos` is stricter[29] and limited to a noun immediately following another one and specifying it, like in *Moyses, propheta iudaeorum* 'Moses, prophet of the Jews', where *propheta* is assigned *deprel* `appos` and is made dependent on the node for *Moyses*.

This means that we can not translate the IT-TB *afun* Apos directly into the UD *deprel* `appos`, but have to resort to other *deprel*s expressing modifiers, according to their appropriateness. These include `acl`, `nmod`, `amod`, `advmod` (adverbial modifier) and `advcl`. Anyway, according to the definitions of such *deprel*s in the current UD guidelines, none of them is suitable to express (and thus convert) the joint, coordination-like relationship holding between the two members of an apposition as meant in the IT-TB. In particular, the status of *scilicet* remains unclear, as it can neither

---

[27] `https://ufal.mff.cuni.cz/pdt2.0/doc/manuals/en/a-layer/html/ch03s04x12.html`
[28] Apos: Apposition (assigned to the connecting element); Ap adscript: member of an apposition.
[29] `http://universaldependencies.org/u/dep/appos.html`

be considered an adverbial modifier (it introduces, but does not modify the apposition), nor a coordinating conjunction (*deprel* cc).

We address this issue by assigning a specific subtype appos (a) to appositive adverbial modifiers like *scilicet*, (b) to non-nominal appositions and (c) to appositions whose second member does not immediately follow the first one.

Our UD subtree for the example above will look like this:

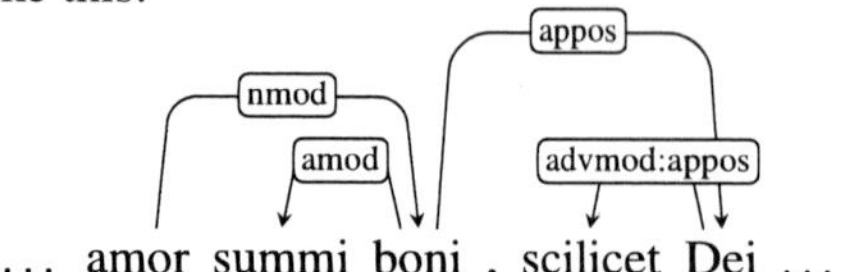

Here we can use the *deprel* appos since the apposition is made of two nominals (*boni*, lemma *bonum*, and *Dei*, lemma *Deus*).

A case of two non-nominals involved in an apposition is the following (*Summa contra gentiles*, Lib. III, Cap. XXV), where the second member of the apposition (*scilicet intelligere deum* 'namely, to understand God') is an attributive clause modifying the pronoun *hoc* 'this' and it is thus assigned *deprel* acl and subtype appos:

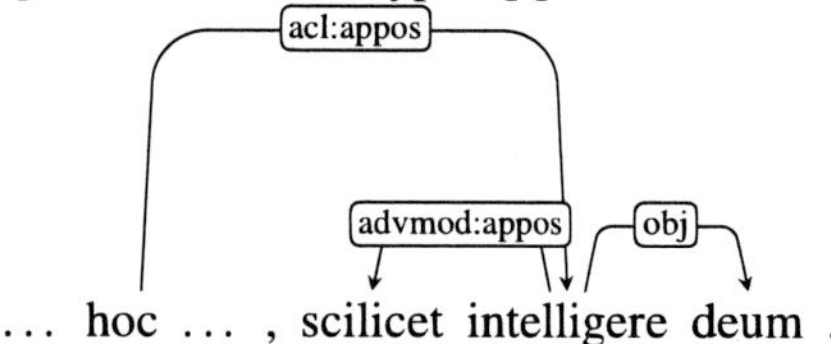

Treating appositions also requires a quite substantial rearrangement of the nodes in an IT-TB subtree prior to the UD conversion proper, including a complex system of cross-references in the Perl script to reconstruct all considered syntactic dependencies, that was completely absent from the original conversion script.

3 Evaluation

We perform an evaluation to assess to what degree our modifications to the IT-TB–UD conversion process impact the quality of the conversion. To this aim, we first build a gold standard that we use as a benchmark for our data.

The 2.2 UD version of the IT-TB includes 21 011 sentences (291K tokens), 17 721 of which pertain to the first three books of *Summa contra gentiles*, the remaining 3 290 being the concordances of the lemma *forma* 'form' from a selection of works of Thomas Aquinas. We randomly extract 994 sen-

	LAS	LA	UAS	PoS	Lemma
Orig.	84.8	87.9	94.2	95.5	95.2
New	97.0	98.0	98.3	98.5	99.8

Table 1: Evaluation of original and new conversion.

tences out of the IT-TB and check that they are balanced and representative of the whole treebank according to a number of topological and annotation parameters.[30] Then, the gold standard is built by manually checking the output of the automatic conversion of these 994 sentences into the UD style and fixing the mistakes.

Finally, we compare the gold standard with (a) the output of our new conversion process and (b) the output of the original conversion process. We compute the rates for the usual evaluation metrics of dependency parsers: LAS (Labeled Attachment Score), LA (Label Accuracy) and UAS (Unlabeled Attachment Score) (Buchholz and Marsi, 2006). Table 1 shows the results together with the accuracy rates for PoS tagging and lemmatisation, as a way to evaluate the harmonisation phase too.

Results reveal a general improvement of the quality of conversion. In particular, there is a substantial increase in LAS, while this is smaller for what concerns UAS. This shows that, while the basic TREEX conversion modules are already capable of addressing well the rearrangement of some subtrees required by the conversion to UD, they nonetheless need and greatly benefit from a language-specific fine-tuning, mainly but not only for what concerns the assignment of *deprel*s.

4 Conclusion

We presented the new conversion process of the *Index Thomisticus* Treebank of Medieval Latin into the Universal Dependencies annotation style. We detailed the changes applied not only to make the IT-TB consistent with the other UD treebanks, but also to harmonise it with the other Latin treebanks available in the UD dataset. This aspect is particularly relevant, because the wide diachronic and diatopic span of Latin language requires to collect (and annotate) several sets of textual data to represent its different varieties. These corpora need to follow a common set of guidelines for annotation so as to enable users to run queries pro-

---

[30]Length of the sentence; depth of trees; cases of elliptical constructions (ExD) and of coordination chains (a Coord governing another Coord); distribution of PoS and *afun*s.

viding results that support research in comparative linguistics, as well as to train stochastic NLP tools.

Beside harmonisation, refining the original conversion process has opened questions concerning the annotation of specific constructions. This is e. g. the case of appositions, where our decision is to use the subtype `appos` to address structures that are not yet considered in the current UD guidelines. We hope that our solution will be helpful also for other treebanks getting through similar problems.

Given the good quality of the conversion, as shown by our evaluation, after publishing the new version of the IT-TB in the release 2.3 of UD, we plan to start working on enriching the treebank with enhanced dependencies.

The current harmonisation and conversion scripts can be downloaded from the Github pages of the TREEX and HamleDT projects.[31]

Acknowledgments

Marco Passarotti gratefully acknowledges the support of the project LiLa (Linking Latin. Building a Knowledge Base of Linguistic Resources for Latin). This project has received funding from the European Research Council (ERC) European Union's Horizon 2020 research and innovation programme under grant agreement No 769994.

References

Thomas Aquinas. 1955–1957. *Summa contra gentiles*. Hanover House, New York, NY, USA. Accessible at https://dhspriory.org/thomas/ ContraGentiles.htm.

S. Tommaso d'Aquino. 2001. *Commento alle sentenze di Pietro Lombardo*. Edizioni Studio Domenicano, Bologna, Italy.

Maria Jesus Aranzabe, Aitziber Atutxa, Kepa Bengoetxea, Arantza Diaz, Iakes Goenaga de Ilarraza, Koldo Gojenola, and Larraitz Uria. 2014. Automatic conversion of the basque dependency treebank to universal dependencies. In *Proceedings of the Fourteenth Workshop on Treebanks an Linguistic Theories (TLT 14)*, pages 233–241, Warszawa, Poland. Polish Academy of Sciences.

David Bamman and Gregory Crane. 2006. The design and use of a Latin dependency treebank. In *Proceedings of the Fifth Workshop on Treebanks and Linguistic Theories (TLT 2006)*, pages 67–78, Prague, Czech Republic. Univerzita Karlova.

David Bamman, Marco Passarotti, Gregory Crane, and Savina Raynaud. 2007. Guidelines for the syntactic annotation of Latin treebanks. *Tufts University Digital Library*.

Sabine Buchholz and Erwin Marsi. 2006. CoNLL-X shared task on multilingual dependency parsing. In *Proceedings of the Tenth Conference on Computational Natural Language Learning (CoNLL-X)*, pages 149–164, New York, USA. Association for Computational Linguistics.

Kaja Dobrovoljc and Joakim Nivre. 2016. The universal dependencies treebank of spoken slovenian. In *Proceedings of the Tenth International Conference on Language Resources and Evaluation (LREC 2016)*, pages 1566–1573, Paris, France. European Language Resources Association (ELRA).

James B Greenough and JH Allen. 2006. *Allen and Greenough's new Latin grammar*. Dover publications, Mineola, NY, USA.

Jan Hajič, Eva Hajičová, Marie Mikulová, and Jiří Mírovský. 2017. Prague Dependency Treebank. In Nancy Ide and James Pustejovsky, editors, *Handbook of Linguistic Annotation*, pages 555–594. Springer, Dordrecht, Netherlands.

Dag TT Haug and Marius Jøhndal. 2008. Creating a parallel treebank of the old Indo-European Bible translations. In *Proceedings of the Second Workshop on Language Technology for Cultural Heritage Data (LaTeCH 2008)*, pages 27–34, Marrakesh, Morocco. European Language Resources Association (ELRA).

Joakim Nivre, Marie-Catherine de Marneffe, Filip Ginter, Yoav Goldberg, Jan Hajič, Christopher Manning, Ryan McDonald, Slav Petrov, Sampo Pyysalo, Natalia Silveira, Reut Tsarfaty, and Daniel Zeman. 2016. Universal Dependencies v1: A multilingual treebank collection. In *Proceedings of the Tenth International Conference on Language Resources and Evaluation (LREC 2016)*, pages 1659–1666, Portorož, Slovenia. European Language Resources Association (ELRA).

Marco Passarotti. 2004. Development and perspectives of the Latin morphological analyser LEMLAT. *Linguistica computazionale*, XX-XXI:397–414.

Marco Passarotti. 2011. Language resources. The state of the art of Latin and the *Index Thomisticus* treebank project. In *Corpus anciens et Bases de données*, number 2 in ALIENTO. Échanges sapientiels en Méditerranée, pages 301–320, Nancy, France. Presses universitaires de Nancy.

Slav Petrov, Dipanjan Das, and Ryan McDonald. A universal part-of-speech tagset. *ArXiv e-prints*. arXiv:1104.2086 at https://arxiv. org/abs/1104.2086.

---

[31] https://github.com/ufal/treex; https://github.com/ufal/hamledt.

Edoardo Maria Ponti and Marco Passarotti. 2016. Differentia compositionem facit. A slower-paced and reliable parser for Latin. In *Proceedings of the Tenth International Conference on Language Resources and Evaluation (LREC 2016)*, pages 683–688, Portorož, Slovenia. European Language Resources Association (ELRA).

Martin Popel and Zdeněk Žabokrtský. 2010. TectoMT: modular NLP framework. In *Advances in Natural Language Processing*, volume 6233 of *Lecture Notes in Computer Science*, pages 293–304, Berlin - Heidelberg, Germany. Springer.

Sampo Pyysalo, Jenna Kanerva, Anna Missilä, Veronika Laippala, and Filip Ginter. 2015. Universal dependencies for finnish. In *Proceedings of the 20th Nordic Conference of Computational Linguistics (Nodalida 2015)*, pages 163–172, Linköping, Sweden. Linköping University Press.

Rudolf Rosa, Jan Mašek, David Mareček, Martin Popel, Daniel Zeman, and Zdeněk Žabokrtský. 2014. HamleDT 2.0: Thirty dependency treebanks Stanfordized. In *Proceedings of the Ninth International Conference on Language Resources and Evaluation (LREC 2014)*, pages 2334–2341, Reykjavík, Iceland. European Language Resources Association (ELRA).

Juhi Tandon, Himani Chaudhry, Riyaz Ahmad Bhat, and Dipti Sharma. 2016. Conversion from paninian karakas to universal dependencies for hindi dependency treebank. In *Proceedings of the 10th Linguistic Annotation Workshop held in conjunction with ACL 2016 (LAW-X 2016)*, pages 141–150, Berlin, Germany. Association for Computational Linguistics.

Daniel Zeman. 2015. Slavic languages in universal dependencies. In *Natural Language Processing, Corpus Linguistics, E-learning (proceedings of SLOVKO 2015)*, pages 151–163, Bratislava, Slovakia. RAM-Verlag.

Er ... well, it matters, right?
On the role of data representations in spoken language dependency parsing

Kaja Dobrovoljc
Jožef Stefan Institute
Ljubljana, Slovenia
`kaja.dobrovoljc@ijs.si`

Matej Martinc
Jožef Stefan Institute
Ljubljana, Slovenia
`matej.martinc@ijs.si`

Abstract

Despite the significant improvement of data-driven dependency parsing systems in recent years, they still achieve a considerably lower performance in parsing spoken language data in comparison to written data. On the example of Spoken Slovenian Treebank, the first spoken data treebank using the UD annotation scheme, we investigate which speech-specific phenomena undermine parsing performance, through a series of training data and treebank modification experiments using two distinct state-of-the-art parsing systems. Our results show that utterance segmentation is the most prominent cause of low parsing performance, both in parsing raw and pre-segmented transcriptions. In addition to shorter utterances, both parsers perform better on normalized transcriptions including basic markers of prosody and excluding disfluencies, discourse markers and fillers. On the other hand, the effects of written training data addition and speech-specific dependency representations largely depend on the parsing system selected.

1 Introduction

With an exponential growth of spoken language data available online on the one hand and the rapid development of systems and techniques for language understanding on the other, spoken language research is gaining increasing prominence. Many syntactically annotated spoken language corpora have been developed in the recent years to benefit the data-driven parsing systems for speech (Hinrichs et al., 2000; van der Wouden et al., 2002; Lacheret et al., 2014; Nivre et al., 2006), including two spoken language treebanks adopting the Universal Dependencies (UD) annotation scheme, aimed at cross-linguistically consistent dependency treebank annotation (Nivre, 2015).

However, in the recent CoNLL 2017 shared task on multilingual parsing from raw text to UD (Zeman et al., 2017), the results achieved on the Spoken Slovenian Treebank (Dobrovoljc and Nivre, 2016) - the only spoken treebank among the 81 participating treebanks - were substantially lower than on other treebanks. This includes the written Slovenian treebank (Dobrovoljc et al., 2017), with a best labeled attachment score difference of more than 30 percentage points between the two treebanks by all of the 33 participating systems.

Given this significant gap in parsing performance between the two modalities, spoken and written language, this paper aims to investigate which speech-specific phenomena influence the poor parsing performance for speech, and to what extent. Specifically, we focus on questions related to data representation in all aspects of the dependency parsing pipeline, by introducing different types of modifications to spoken language transcripts and speech-specific dependency annotations, as well as to the type of data used for spoken language modelling.

This paper is structured as follows. Section 2 addresses the related research on spoken language parsing and Section 3 presents the structure and annotation of the Spoken Slovenian Treebank on which all the experiments were conducted. Section 4 presents the parsing systems used in the experiments (4.1) and the series of SST data modifications to narrow the performance gap between written and spoken treebanks for these systems, involving the training data (4.3.1), speech transcriptions (4.3.2) and UD dependency annotations (4.3.3). Results are presented in Section 5, while conclusions and some directions for further work are addressed in Section 6.

Proceedings of the Second Workshop on Universal Dependencies (UDW 2018), pages 37–46
Brussels, Belgium, November 1, 2018. ©2018 Association for Computational Linguistics

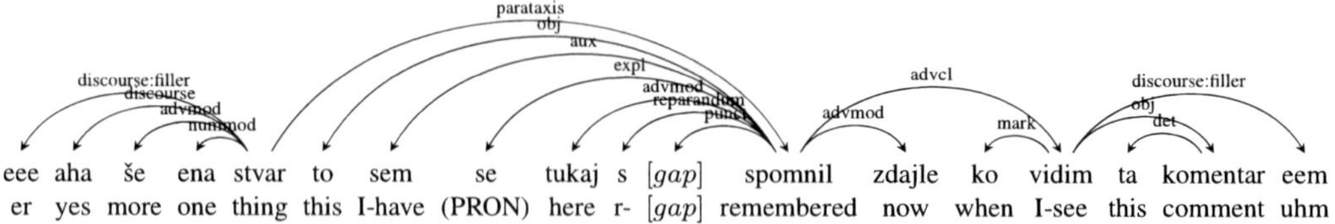

(oh yes one more thing I just r- [gap] remembered this here now that I see this comment)

Figure 1: An example utterance taken from the Spoken Slovenian Treebank.

2 Related work

In line with divergent approaches to syntactic annotation of transcribed spoken data that either aim to capture the syntactic structure involving all uttered lexical phenomena in an utterance, or discard the (variously defined) noisy speech-specific structural particularities on the other, research into parsing spoken language can broadly be categorized in two main groups. On the one side of the spectrum, we find approaches that separate disfluences from parsing. Charniak and Johnson (2001) and Jørgensen (2007), for example, both report a significant increase in parsing the Switchboard section of the Penn Discourse Treebank (Godfrey et al., 1992), if disfluencies are first removed from the data. These two-pass pipeline approaches thus involve a separate task of automatic disfluency detection, one of the fundamental issues in automatic speech recognition (Liu et al., 2006; Lease et al., 2006).

Recently, however, several parsing systems using non-monotonic transition-based algorithms have emerged that enable joint parsing and disfluency detection (Honnibal et al., 2013; Honnibal and Johnson, 2015; Rasooli and Tetreault, 2013), showing that joint treatment of both problems can actually outperform state-of-the-art pipeline approaches (Honnibal and Johnson, 2014). These findings open a promising line of future research for the development of speech-specific parsing systems (Yoshikawa et al., 2016), especially those that also incorporate acoustic information (Kahn et al., 2005; Tran et al., 2017).

Nevertheless, apart from research on speech-specific parsing systems, very little research has been dedicated to other, data-related aspects of spoken language parsing. To our knowledge, with expection of Caines et al. (2017) and Nasr et al. (2014), who investigate the role of different types of training data used for parsing transcripts of speech, there have been no other systematic studies on the role of spoken data representations, such as transcription or annotation conventions, in spoken language parsing.

3 Spoken Slovenian Treebank

The Spoken Slovenian Treebank (Dobrovoljc and Nivre, 2016), which was first released as part of UD v1.3 (under the CC-BY-NC-SA 4.0 licence), is the first syntactically annotated collection of spontaneous speech in Slovenian. It is a sample of the Gos reference corpus of Spoken Slovenian (Zwitter Vitez et al., 2013), a collection of transcribed audio recordings of spontaneous speech in different everyday situations, in both public (TV and radio shows, school lessons, academic lectures etc.) and private settings (work meetings, services, conversations between friends and family etc.).

The SST treebank currently amounts to 29,488 tokens (3,188 utterances), which include both lexical tokens (words) and tokens signalling other types of verbal phenomena, such as filled pauses (fillers) and unfinished words, as well as some basic markers of prosody and extralinguistic speech events. The original segmentation, tokenization and spelling principles described by Verdonik et al. (2013) have also been inherited by SST. Among the two types of Gos transcriptions (pronunciation-based and normalized spelling, both in lowercase only), subsequent manual annotations in SST have been performed on top of normalized transcriptions.

For syntactic annotation of the transcripts, unavailable in Gos, the SST treebank adopted the Universal Dependencies annotation scheme due to its high degree of interoperability across different grammatical frameworks, languages and modalities. In this original application of the UD scheme to spoken language transcripts, several modifications of the scheme were implemented to accommodate the syntactic particularities in speech, either by extending the scope of application of existing universal labels (e.g. using *punct* for labeling markers of prosody) or introducing new speech-specific sub-labels (e.g. *discourse:filler* for annotation of hesitation sounds). In subsequent comparison of the SST treebank with the written SSJ Slovenian UD treebank (Dobrovoljc et al., 2017), Dobrovoljc and Nivre (2016) observed several syntactic differences between the two modalities, as also illustrated in Figure 1.

4 Experiment setup

4.1 Parsing systems and evaluation

To enable system-independent generalizations, two parsing systems were selected, UDPipe 1.2 (Straka and Straková, 2017) and Stanford (Dozat et al., 2017), covering the two most common parsing approaches, transition-based and graph-based parsing (Aho and Ullman, 1972), respectively. UDPipe 1.2 is a trainable pipeline for sentence segmentation, tokenization, POS tagging, lemmatization and dependency parsing. It represents an improved version of the UDPipe 1.1 (used as a baseline system in the CONLL-2017 Shared Task (Zeman et al., 2017)) and finished as the 8th best system out of 33 systems participating in the task.

A single-layer bidirectional GRU network together with a case insensitive dictionary and a set of automatically generated suffix rules are used for sentence segmentation and tokenization. The part of speech tagging module consists of a guesser, which generates several universal part of speech (XPOS), language-specific part of speech (UPOS), and morphological feature list (FEATS) tag triplets for each word according to its last four characters. These are given as an input to an averaged perceptron tagger (Straka et al., 2016) to perform the final disambiguation on the generated tags. Transition-based dependency parser is based on a shallow neural network with one hidden layer and without any recurrent connections, making it one of the fastest parsers in the CONLL-2017 Shared Task. We used the default parameter configuration of ten training iterations and a hidden layer of size 200 for training all the models.

Stanford parser is a neural graph-based parser (McDonald et al., 2005) capable of leveraging word and character based information in order to produce part of speech tags and labeled dependency parses from segmented and tokenized sequences of words. Its architecture is based on a deep biaffine neural dependency parser presented by (Dozat and Manning, 2016), which uses a multilayer bidirectional LSTM network to produce vector representations for each word. These representations are used as an input to a stack of biaffine classifiers capable of producing the most probable UD tree for every sentence and the most probable part of speech tag for every word. The system was ranked first according to all five relevant criteria in the CONLL-2017 Shared Task. Same hyperparameter configuration was used as reported in (Dozat et al., 2017) with every model trained for 30,000 training steps. For the parameters values that were not explicitly mentioned in (Dozat et al., 2017), default values were used.

For both parsers, no additional fine-tuning was performed for any specific data set, in order to minimize the influence of training procedure on the parser's performance for different data preprocessing techniques, especially given that no development data has been released for the small SST treebank.

For evaluation, we used the official CoNLL-ST-2017 evaluation script (Zeman et al., 2017) to calculate the standard labeled attachments score (LAS), i.e. the percentage of nodes with correctly assigned reference to parent node, including the label (type) of relation. For baseline experiments involving parsing of raw transcriptions (see Section 4.2), for which the number of nodes in gold-standard annotation and in the system output might vary, the F_1 LAS score, marking the harmonic mean of precision an recall LAS scores, was used instead.

4.2 Baseline

Prior to experiments involving different data modifications, both parsing systems were evaluated on the written SSJ and spoken SST Slovenian treebanks, released as part of UD version 2.2 (Nivre et al., 2018).[1] The evaluation was performed both for parsing raw text (i.e. automatic tokenization, segmentation, morphological annotation and dependency tree generation) and parsing

---

[1] Note that the SST released as part of UD v2.2 involves a different splitting of utterances into training and test tests as in UD v2.0, which should be taken into account when comparing our results to the results reported in the CoNLL 2017 Shared Task.

	UDPipe			**Stanford**			
	Parsing raw text						
Treebank	Sents	UPOS	UAS	LAS	Sents	UPOS	UAS	LAS
sst	20.35	88.32	52.49	<u>45.47</u>	20.35	93.21	60.35	<u>54.00</u>
ssj	76.49	94.59	79.90	76.32	76.49	96.32	87.50	85.02
ssj_20k	76.42	89.88	71.79	66.40	76.42	94.61	82.60	78.60
	Dependency parsing only						
Treebank	Sents	UPOS	UAS	LAS	Sents	UPOS	UAS	LAS
sst	100	100	74.66	<u>69.13</u>	100	100	77.58	<u>72.52</u>
ssj	100	100	90.16	88.41	100	100	95.63	94.52
ssj_20k	100	100	86.69	84.21	100	100	91.93	89.60

Table 1: UDPipe and Stanford sentence segmentation (Sents), part-of-speech tagging (UPOS), unlabelled (UAS) and labelled attachment (LAS) F_1 scores on the spoken SST and written SSJ Slovenian UD treebanks for parsing raw text, and for parsing texts with gold-standard tokenization, segmentation and tagging information.

gold-standard annotations (i.e. dependency parsing only). For Stanford parser, which only produces tags and dependency labels, the UDPipe tokenization and segmentation output was used as input.

The results displayed in Table 1 (Parsing raw text) confirm the difficulty of parsing spoken language transcriptions, given that both UDPipe and Stanford systems perform significantly worse on the spoken SST treebank in comparison with the written SSJ treebank, with the difference in LAS F_1 score amounting to 30.85 or 31.02 percentage points, respectively. These numbers decrease if we neutralize the important difference in treebank sizes - with 140.670 training set tokens for the written SSJ and 29.488 tokens for the spoken SST - by training the written model on a comparable subset of SSJ training data (20.000 tokens), however, the difference between the two modalities remains evident.

A subsequent comparison of results in dependency parsing only (Table 1, Dependency parsing only) reveals that a large share of parsing mistakes can be attributed to difficulties in lower-level processing, in particular utterance segmentation (with an F_1 score of 20.35),[2] as spoken language parsing performance increases to the (baseline) LAS score of 69.13 and 72.52 for the UDPipe and Stanford parser, respectively. Consequently, the actual difference between written and spoken language

parsing reduces to approximately 15-17 percentage points, if based on the same amount of training data.

In order to prevent the dependency parsing experiments in this paper being influenced by the performance of systems responsible for producing other levels of linguistic annotation, the experiments set out in the continuation of this paper focus on evaluation of gold-standard dependency parsing only.

4.3 Data modifications

Given the observed difference in parsing spoken and written language for both parsing systems, several automated modifications of the data featured in the parsing pipeline have been introduced, to investigate the influence of different factors on spoken language parsing performance.

4.3.1 Modifications of training data type

Although the relationship between written and spoken language has often been portrayed as a domain-specific dichotomy, both modalities form part of the same language continuum, encouraging further investigations of cross-modal model transfers. In the first line of experiments, we thus conducted experiments on evaluation of spoken language parsing by training on spoken (`sst`) and written (`ssj`) data alone, as well as on the combination of both (`sst+ssj`). Given that the transcriptions in the SST treebank are written in lowercase only and do not include any written-like punctuation, two additional models excluding these features were generated for the written treebank (`ssj_lc` and `ssj_no-punct`) to neutralize the differences in writing system conventions

---

[2]Note that the low segmentation score is not specific to UDPipe, but to state-of-the-art parsing systems in general, as none of the 33 systems competing in the CoNLL 2017 Shared Task managed to achieve a significantly better result in SST treebank segmentation: `http://universaldependencies.org/conll17/results-sentences.html`.

for both modalities.

4.3.2 Modifications of speech transcription

The second line of experiments investigates the role of spoken language transcription conventions for the most common speech-specific phenomena, by introducing various automatically converted versions of the SST treebank (both training and testing data).

Spelling: For word form spelling, the original normalized spelling compliant with standard orthography was replaced by pronunciation-based spelling (`sst_pron-spell`), reflecting the regional and colloquial pronunciation variation (e.g. the replacement of the standard pronominal word form *jaz* "I" by pronunciation-based word forms *jz, jaz, jst, jez, jes, ja* etc.).

Segmentation: Inheriting the manual segmentation of the reference Gos corpus, sentences (utterances) in SST correspond to "semantically, syntactically and acoustically delimited units" (Verdonik et al., 2013). As such, the utterance segmentation heavily depends on subjective interpretations of what is the basic functional unit in speech, in line with the multitude of existing segmentation approaches, based on syntax, semantics, prosody, or their various combinations (Degand and Simon, 2009). To evaluate parsing performance for alternative types of segmentation, based on a more objective set of criteria, two additional SST segmentations were created. In the minimally segmented version of the SST treebank (`sst_min-segm`), utterances involving two or more clauses joined by a *parataxis* relation (denoting a loose inter-clausal connections without explicit coordination, subordination, or argument relation) have been split into separate syntactic trees (clauses), as illustrated in the example below (Figure 2).

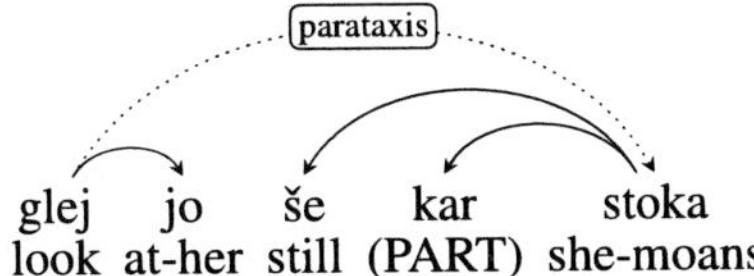

(look at her she's still moaning)

Figure 2: Splitting utterances by *parataxis*.

Vice versa, the maximally segmented SST version (`sst_max-segm`) includes utterances corresponding to entire turns (i.e. units of speech by one speaker), in which neighbouring utterances by

a speaker have been joined into a single syntactic tree via the *parataxis* relation.

Disfluencies: Following the traditional approaches to spoken language processing, the `sst_no-disfl` SST treebank version marks the removal of disfluencies, namely filled pauses, such as *eee, aaa, mmm* (labeled as *discourse:filler*), overridden disfluencies, such as repetitions, substitutions or reformulations (labeled as *reparandum*), and *[gap]* markers, co-occurring with unfinished or incomprehensible speech fragments (Figure 3).

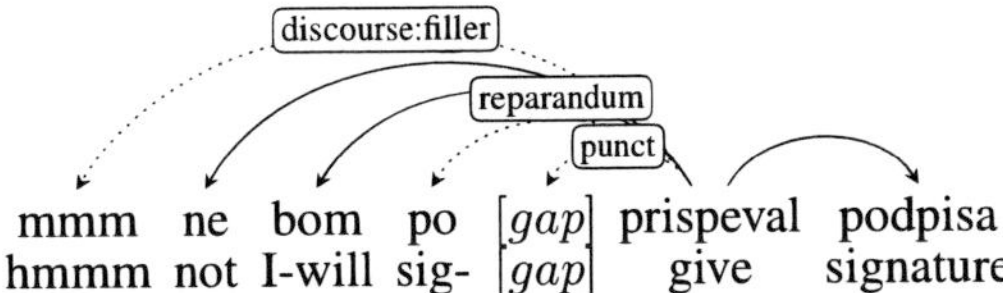

(uhm I will not sig- [gap] give my signature)

Figure 3: Removal of disfluencies.

Similar to structurally 'redundant' phenomena described above, the `sst_no-discourse` version of the SST treebank excludes syntactically peripheral speech-specific lexical phenomena, annotated as *discourse, discourse:filler* or *parataxis:discourse*, such as interjections (*aha* "uh-huh"), response tokens (*ja* "yes"), expressions of politeness (*adijo* "bye"), as well as clausal and non-clausal discourse markers (*no* "well", *mislim* "I think").

Prosody: Although the SST treebank lacks phonetic transcription, some basic prosodic information is provided through specific tokens denoting exclamation or interrogation intonation, silent pauses, non-turn taking speaker interruptions, vocal sounds (e.g. laughing, sighing, yawning) and non-vocal sounds (e.g. applauding, ringing). In contrast to the original SST treebank, in which these nodes were considered as regular nodes of dependency trees (labeled as *punct*), prosodic markers have been excluded from the `sst_no-pros` version of the treebank.

4.3.3 Modifications of UD annotation

Given that the SST treebank was the first spoken treebank to be annotated using the UD annotation scheme, the UD annotation principles for speech-specific phenomena set out in Dobrovoljc and Nivre (2016) have not yet been evaluated within a wider community. To propose potential future improvements of the UD annotation guidelines for spoken language phenomena, the third set of SST modifications involved alternations of selected speech-specific UD representations.

Extensions: The SST treebank introduced five new subtypes of existing UD relations to annotate filled pauses (*discourse:filler*), clausal repairs (*parataxis:restart*), clausal discourse markers (*parataxis:discourse*) and general extenders (*conj:extend*). In the `sst_no-extensions` version of the treebank, these extensions have been replaced by their universal counterparts (i.e. *discourse*, *parataxis* and *conj*).

Head attachment: For syntactic relations, such as *discourse* or *punct*, which are not directly linked to the predicate-driven structure of the sentence, the choice of the head node to which they attach to is not necessarily a straightforward task. The original SST treebank followed the general UD principle of attaching such nodes to the highest node preserving projectivity, typically the head of the most relevant nearby clause or clause argument. To evaluate the impact of such high attachment principle on parsing performance, an alternative robust attachment has been implemented for two categories with the weakest semantic connection to the head, filled pauses (`sst_discourse:filler`) and prosodic markers (`sst_punct`), attaching these nodes to the nearest preceding node instead, regardless of its syntactic role, as illustrated in Figure 4.

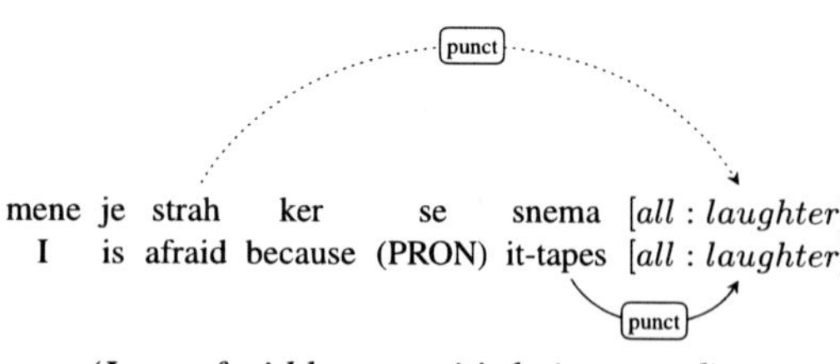

(I am afraid because it's being taped)

Figure 4: Change of head for prosody markers.

For the reparandum relation, which currently denotes a relation between the edited unit (the reparandum) and its repair, the opposite principle was implemented in `sst_reparandum`, by attaching the reparandum to the head of its repair, i.e. to the node it would attach to had it not been for the repair (Figure 5).

Following a similar higher-attachment principle, the *parataxis:restart* relation, used for

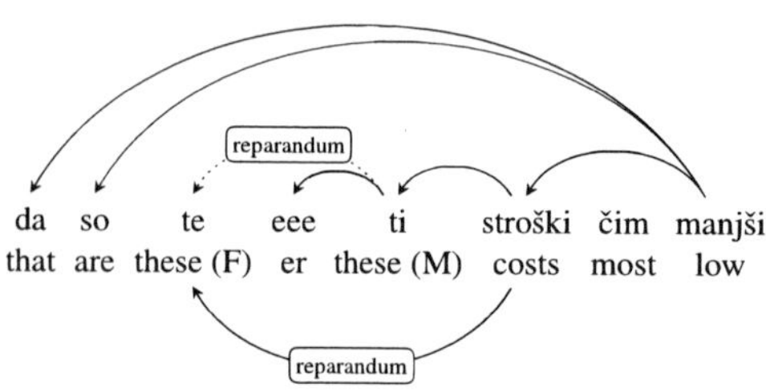

(so that these costs are as low as possible)

Figure 5: Change of head for *reparandum*.

annotation of sentences replacing an abandoned preceding clause, has been modified in `sst_parataxis:restart` so as to span from the root node instead of the more or less randomly positioned head of the unfinished clause.

Clausal discourse markers: In the original SST treebank, clausal discourse markers (e.g. *ne vem* "I don't know", (*a*) *veš* "you know", *glej* "listen") have been labeled as parataxis (specifically, the *parataxis:discourse* extension), in line with other types of sentential parentheticals. Given the distinct distributional characteristics of these expressions (limited list, high frequency) and similar syntactic behaviour to non-clausal discourse markers (no dependents, both peripheral and clause-medial positions), their label has been changed to *discourse* in the `sst_parataxis:discourse` version of the treebank. For multi-word clausal markers, the *fixed* label was also introduced to annotate the internal structure of this highly grammaticized clauses (Figure 6.

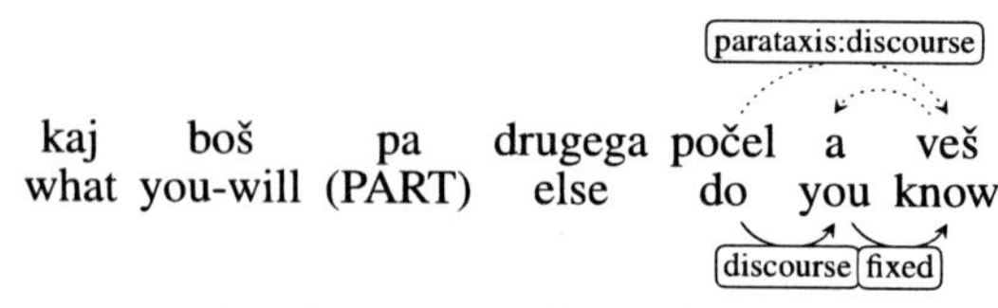

(what else can you do you know)

Figure 6: Change of annotation for clausal discourse markers.

5   Results

Table 2 gives LAS evaluation of both parsing systems for each data modification described in Section 4.3 above, including the baseline results for training and parsing on the original SST treebank

	Model	UDPipe	Stanford
	Training data		
1	sst (= baseline)	69.13	72.52
2	ssj+sst	68.53	**77.38**
3	ssj_no-punct	57.40	62.57
4	ssj	55.76	62.08
5	ssj_lc	55.61	61.99
	Transcriptions		
6	sst_min-segm	**74.89**	**78.31**
7	sst_no-disfl	**71.47**	**74.77**
8	sst_no-discourse	**70.73**	**75.47**
9	sst_no-pros	68.70	71.78
10	sst_pron-spell	67.52	71.64
11	sst_max-segm	63.93	68.13
	Annotations		
12	sst_punct	**71.32**	**73.65**
13	sst_discourse:filler	69.13	**72.85**
14	sst_parataxis:restart	68.53	71.95
15	sst_no-new-ext.	68.45	**73.05**
16	sst_reparandum	68.41	**72.81**
17	sst_parataxis:disc.	68.32	72.35
	Best combination		
18	sst_6-7-8-12	**79.58**	N/A
19	sst_6-7-8-12-15	N/A	**87.35**

Table 2: LAS on the Spoken Slovenian Treebank (sst) for different types of training data, transcription and annotation modifications. Improvements of the baseline are marked in bold.

(see Section 4.2).

When evaluating the impact of different types of training data on the original SST parsing, both parsers give significantly poorer results than the baseline sst model if trained on the written SSJ treebank alone (ssj), which clearly demonstrates the importance of (scarce) spoken language treebanks for spoken language processing. In addition, no significant improvement is gained if the written data is modified so as to exclude punctuation (ssj_no-punct) or perform lowercasing (ssj_lc), which even worsens the results. Somewhat surprisingly, no definite conclusion can be drawn on the joint training model based on both spoken and written data (sst+ssj), as the parsers give significantly different results: while Stanford parser substantially outperforms the baseline result when adding written data to the model (similar to the findings by Caines et al. (2017)), this addition has a negative affect on UD-Pipe. This could be explained by the fact that

global, exhaustive, graph-based parsing systems are more capable of leveraging the richer contextual information gained with a larger train set in comparison with local, greedy, transition-based systems (McDonald and Nivre, 2007).

The results of the second set of experiments, in which LAS was evaluated for different types of spoken language transcriptions, confirm that parsing performance varies with different approaches to transcribing speech-specific phenomena. As expected, both systems achieve significantly better results if parsing is performed on shorter utterances (sst_min-segm). On the other hand, a similar LAS drop-off interval is identified for parsing full speaker turns (sst_max-segm). These results confirm the initial observations in Section 4.2 that speech segmentation is the key bottleneck in the spoken language dependency parsing pipeline. Nevertheless, it is encouraging to observe that even the absence of any internal segmentation of (easily identifiable) speaker turns returns moderate parsing results.

As has already been reported in related work, parsing performance also increases if spoken data is removed of its most prominent syntactic structures, such as disfluencies, discourse markers and fillers. Interestingly, for Stanford parser, the removal of discourse markers (sst_no-discourse) is even more beneficial than the removal of seemingly less predictable false starts, repairs and other disfluencies (sst_no-disfl). On the contrary, the removal of prosody markers (sst_no-pros) damages the baseline results for both parsers, suggesting that the presence of these markers might even contribute to parsing accuracy for certain types of constructions given their punctuation-like function in speech.

As for spelling, the results on the treebank based on pronunciation-based word spelling (sst_pron-spell) support our initial hypothesis that the multiplication of token types damages parser performance, yet not to a great extent. This could be explained by the fact that token pronunciation information can sometimes help with syntactic disambiguation of the word form in context, if a certain word form pronunciation is only associated with a specific syntactic role (e.g. the colloquial pronunciation *tko da* of the discourse connective *tako da* "so that" that does not occur with other syntactic roles of this lexical string).

No definite conclusion can be drawn from the parsing results for different alternations of speech-specific UD annotations, as the results vary by parsing system and by the types of UD modification. While both systems benefit from an alternative attachment of prosodic markers to their nearest preceding token (sst_punct),[3] and prefer the current labeling and attachment principles for clausal repairs (sst_parataxis:restart) and clausal discourse markers (parataxis:discourse), the effect of other changes seems to be system-dependent. What is more, none of the changes in UD representations seem to affect the parsing performance to a great extent, which suggests that the original UD adaptations for speech-specific phenomena, applied to the Spoken Slovenian Treebank, represent a reasonable starting point for future applications of the scheme to spoken language data.

Finally, all transcription and annotation variables that were shown to improve spoken language LAS for each of the parsing systems, have been joined into a single representation, i.e. a treebank with new, syntax-bound utterance segmentation, excluding disfluencies and discourse elements, and a change in prosody-marker-attachment (UD-Pipe), as well as a change in filler-attachment and addition of written parsing model (Stanford).[4] Both UDPipe and Stanford achieved substantially higher LAS scores for their best-fitting combination than the original SST baseline model (sst), i.e. 79.58 and 87.35, respectively, moving the SST parsing performance much closer to the performance achieved on its same-size written counterpart (ssj_20k, Table 1), with the gap narrowing to 4.63 for UDPipe and 2.25 for Stanford. This confirms that the speech-specific phenomena outlined in this paper are indeed the most important phenomena affecting spoken language processing scores. Nevertheless, the remaining gap between

the two modalities encourages further data-based investigations into the complexity of spoken language syntax, which evidently reaches beyond the prototypical structural and pragmatic phenomena set forward in this paper and the literature in general.

6 Conclusion and Future Work

In this paper, we have investigated which speech-specific phenomena are responsible for below optimal parsing performance of state-of-the-art parsing systems. Several experiments on Spoken Slovenian Treebank involving training data and treebank modifications were performed in order to identify and narrow the gap between the performances on spoken and written language data. The results show that besides disfluencies, the most common phenomena addressed in related work, segmentation of clauses without explicit lexical connection is also an important factor in low parsing performance. In addition to that, our results suggest that for graph-based parsing systems, such as Stanford parser, spoken language parsing should be performed by joint modelling of both spoken and written data excluding punctuation.

Other aspects of spoken data representation, such as the choice of spelling, the presence of basic prosodic markers and the syntactic annotation principles seem less crucial for the overall parser performance. It has to be emphasized, however, that the UD annotation modifications set forward in this paper represent only a few selected transformations involving labeling and attachment, whereas many other are also possible, in particular experiments involving enhanced representations (Schuster and Manning, 2016).

These findings suggest several lines of future work. For the SST treebank in particular and spoken language treebanks in general, it is essential to increase the size of annotated data and reconsider the existing transcription and annotation principles to better address the difficulties in spoken language segmentation and disfluency detection. Particularly in relation to the latter, our results should be evaluated against recent speech-specific parsing systems references in Section 2, as well as other state-of-the-art dependency parsers. A promising line of future work has also been suggested in related work on other types of noisy data (Blodgett et al., 2018), employing a variety of cross-domain strategies for improving parsing with little

---

[3]Note that the sst_punct results should be interpreted with caution, as a brief analysis into the *punct*-related parsing errors on the original SST treebank revealed a substantial amount of (incorrect) non-projective attachments of the [*gap*] marker indicating speech fragments. This issue should be resolved in future releases of the SST treebank.

[4]Modifications set out in 13 (sst_discourse:filler) and 16 (sst_reparandum) that have also increased Stanford parser performance, are not applicable to the Stanford best-combination representation, since discourse fillers and repairs have already been removed by modifications set out in 7 (sst_no-disfl) and 8 (sst_no-discourse).

in-domain data.

Our primary direction of future work, however, involves an in-depth evaluation of parsing performance for individual dependency relations, to determine how the modifications presented in this paper affect specific constructions, and to overcome the prevailing approaches to spoken language parsing that tend to over-generalize the syntax of speech.

References

Alfred V. Aho and Jeffrey D. Ullman. 1972. *The Theory of Parsing, Translation, and Compiling.* Prentice-Hall, Inc., Upper Saddle River, NJ, USA.

Su Lin Blodgett, Johnny Wei, and Brendan O'Connor. 2018. Twitter Universal Dependency parsing for African-American and Mainstream American English. In *Proceedings of the 56th Annual Meeting of the Association for Computational Linguistics (Volume 1: Long Papers)*, pages 1415–1425. Association for Computational Linguistics.

Andrew Caines, Michael McCarthy, and Paula Buttery. 2017. Parsing transcripts of speech. In *Proceedings of the Workshop on Speech-Centric Natural Language Processing*, pages 27–36. Association for Computational Linguistics.

Eugene Charniak and Mark Johnson. 2001. Edit detection and parsing for transcribed speech. In *Proceedings of the Second Meeting of the North American Chapter of the Association for Computational Linguistics on Language Technologies*, NAACL '01, pages 1–9, Stroudsburg, PA, USA. Association for Computational Linguistics.

Liesbeth Degand and Anne Catherine Simon. 2009. On identifying basic discourse units in speech: theoretical and empirical issues. *Discours*, 4.

Kaja Dobrovoljc, Tomaz Erjavec, and Simon Krek. 2017. The Universal Dependencies Treebank for Slovenian. In *Proceedings of the 6th Workshop on Balto-Slavic Natural Language Processing, BSNLP@EACL 2017, Valencia, Spain, April 4, 2017*, pages 33–38.

Kaja Dobrovoljc and Joakim Nivre. 2016. The Universal Dependencies Treebank of Spoken Slovenian. In *Proceedings of the Tenth International Conference on Language Resources and Evaluation (LREC 2016)*, Paris, France. European Language Resources Association (ELRA).

Timothy Dozat and Christopher D. Manning. 2016. Deep biaffine attention for neural dependency parsing. *CoRR*, abs/1611.01734.

Timothy Dozat, Peng Qi, and Christopher D. Manning. 2017. Stanford's graph-based neural dependency parser at the CoNLL 2017 Shared Task. In *Proceedings of the CoNLL 2017 Shared Task: Multilingual Parsing from Raw Text to Universal Dependencies*, pages 20–30, Vancouver, Canada. Association for Computational Linguistics.

John J. Godfrey, Edward C. Holliman, and Jane McDaniel. 1992. Switchboard: Telephone speech corpus for research and development. In *Proceedings of the 1992 IEEE International Conference on Acoustics, Speech and Signal Processing - Volume 1*, ICASSP'92, pages 517–520, Washington, DC, USA. IEEE Computer Society.

Erhard W. Hinrichs, Julia Bartels, Yasuhiro Kawata, Valia Kordoni, and Heike Telljohann. 2000. The Tübingen treebanks for spoken German, English, and Japanese. In Wolfgang Wahlster, editor, *Verbmobil: Foundations of Speech-to-Speech Translation*, Artificial Intelligence, pages 550–574. Springer Berlin Heidelberg.

Matthew Honnibal, Yoav Goldberg, and Mark Johnson. 2013. A non-monotonic arc-eager transition system for dependency parsing. In *Proceedings of the Seventeenth Conference on Computational Natural Language Learning*, pages 163–172, Sofia, Bulgaria. Association for Computational Linguistics.

Matthew Honnibal and Mark Johnson. 2014. Joint incremental disfluency detection and dependency parsing. *Transactions of the Association for Computational Linguistics*, 2(1):131–142.

Matthew Honnibal and Mark Johnson. 2015. An improved non-monotonic transition system for dependency parsing. In *Proceedings of the 2015 Conference on Empirical Methods in Natural Language Processing*, pages 1373–1378. Association for Computational Linguistics.

Fredrik Jørgensen. 2007. The effects of disfluency detection in parsing spoken language. In *Proceedings of the 16th Nordic Conference of Computational Linguistics NODALIDA-2007*, pages 240–244.

Jeremy G Kahn, Matthew Lease, Eugene Charniak, Mark Johnson, and Mari Ostendorf. 2005. Effective use of prosody in parsing conversational speech. In *Proceedings of the conference on human language technology and empirical methods in natural language processing*, pages 233–240. Association for Computational Linguistics.

Anne Lacheret, Sylvain Kahane, Julie Beliao, Anne Dister, Kim Gerdes, Jean-Philippe Goldman, Nicolas Obin, Paola Pietrandrea, and Atanas Tchobanov. 2014. Rhapsodie: a prosodic-syntactic treebank for spoken French. In *Proceedings of the Ninth International Conference on Language Resources and Evaluation (LREC'14)*, pages 295–301, Reykjavik, Iceland. European Language Resources Association (ELRA).

Matthew Lease, Mark Johnson, and Eugene Charniak. 2006. Recognizing disfluencies in conversational speech. *IEEE Transactions on Audio, Speech, and Language Processing*, 14(5):1566–1573.

Yang Liu, Elizabeth Shriberg, Andreas Stolcke, Dustin Hillard, Mari Ostendorf, and Mary Harper. 2006. Enriching speech recognition with automatic detection of sentence boundaries and disfluencies. *IEEE Transactions on audio, speech, and language processing*, 14(5):1526–1540.

Ryan McDonald and Joakim Nivre. 2007. Characterizing the errors of data-driven dependency parsing models. In *Proceedings of the 2007 Joint Conference on Empirical Methods in Natural Language Processing and Computational Natural Language Learning (EMNLP-CoNLL)*.

Ryan McDonald, Fernando Pereira, Kiril Ribarov, and Jan Hajič. 2005. Non-projective dependency parsing using spanning tree algorithms. In *Proceedings of the conference on Human Language Technology and Empirical Methods in Natural Language Processing*, pages 523–530. Association for Computational Linguistics.

Alexis Nasr, Frederic Bechet, Benoit Favre, Thierry Bazillon, Jose Deulofeu, and andre Valli. 2014. Automatically enriching spoken corpora with syntactic information for linguistic studies. In *Proceedings of the Ninth International Conference on Language Resources and Evaluation (LREC'14)*, Reykjavik, Iceland. European Language Resources Association (ELRA).

Joakim Nivre. 2015. Towards a universal grammar for natural language processing. In Alexander Gelbukh, editor, *Computational Linguistics and Intelligent Text Processing*, volume 9041 of *Lecture Notes in Computer Science*, pages 3–16. Springer International Publishing.

Joakim Nivre, Jens Nilsson, and Johan Hall. 2006. Talbanken05: A Swedish treebank with phrase structure and dependency annotation. In *Proceedings of the 5th International Conference on Language Resources and Evaluation (LREC)*, pages 1392–1395.

Joakim Nivre et al. 2018. Universal Dependencies 2.2. LINDAT/CLARIN digital library at the Institute of Formal and Applied Linguistics (UFAL), Faculty of Mathematics and Physics, Charles University.

Mohammad Sadegh Rasooli and Joel Tetreault. 2013. Joint parsing and disfluency detection in linear time. In *Proceedings of the 2013 Conference on Empirical Methods in Natural Language Processing*, pages 124–129, Seattle, Washington, USA. Association for Computational Linguistics.

Sebastian Schuster and Christopher D. Manning. 2016. Enhanced english universal dependencies: An improved representation for natural language understanding tasks. In *Proceedings of the Tenth International Conference on Language Resources and Evaluation (LREC 2016)*, Paris, France. European Language Resources Association (ELRA).

Milan Straka, Jan Hajic, and Jana Straková. 2016. Udpipe: Trainable pipeline for processing CoNLL-U files performing tokenization, morphological analysis, POS tagging and parsing. In *Proceedings of the Tenth International Conference on Language Resources and Evaluation (LREC 2016)*, Paris, France. European Language Resources Association (ELRA).

Milan Straka and Jana Straková. 2017. Tokenizing, pos tagging, lemmatizing and parsing UD 2.0 with UDPipe. In *Proceedings of the CoNLL 2017 Shared Task: Multilingual Parsing from Raw Text to Universal Dependencies*, pages 88–99, Vancouver, Canada. Association for Computational Linguistics.

Trang Tran, Shubham Toshniwal, Mohit Bansal, Kevin Gimpel, Karen Livescu, and Mari Ostendorf. 2017. Joint modeling of text and acoustic-prosodic cues for neural parsing. *CoRR*, abs/1704.07287.

Darinka Verdonik, Iztok Kosem, Ana Zwitter Vitez, Simon Krek, and Marko Stabej. 2013. Compilation, transcription and usage of a reference speech corpus: the case of the Slovene corpus GOS. *Language Resources and Evaluation*, 47(4):1031–1048.

Ton van der Wouden, Heleen Hoekstra, Michael Moortgat, Bram Renmans, and Ineke Schuurman. 2002. Syntactic analysis in the Spoken Dutch Corpus (CGN). In *Proceedings of the Third International Conference on Language Resources and Evaluation, LREC 2002, May 29-31, 2002, Las Palmas, Canary Islands, Spain*.

Masashi Yoshikawa, Hiroyuki Shindo, and Yuji Matsumoto. 2016. Joint transition-based dependency parsing and disfluency detection for automatic speech recognition texts. In *Proceedings of the 2016 Conference on Empirical Methods in Natural Language Processing, EMNLP 2016, Austin, Texas, USA, November 1-4, 2016*, pages 1036–1041.

Daniel Zeman et al. 2017. CoNLL 2017 Shared Task: Multilingual parsing from raw text to Universal Dependencies. In *Proceedings of the CoNLL 2017 Shared Task: Multilingual Parsing from Raw Text to Universal Dependencies*, pages 1–19, Vancouver, Canada. Association for Computational Linguistics.

Ana Zwitter Vitez, Jana Zemljarič Miklavčič, Simon Krek, Marko Stabej, and Tomaž Erjavec. 2013. Spoken corpus Gos 1.0. Slovenian language resource repository CLARIN.SI.

Mind the Gap: Data Enrichment in Dependency Parsing of Elliptical Constructions

Kira Droganova[*] Filip Ginter[†] Jenna Kanerva[†] Daniel Zeman[*]

[*]Charles University, Faculty of Mathematics and Physics

[†]University of Turku, Department of Future Technologies

{droganova, zeman}@ufal.mff.cuni.cz

{figint, jmnybl}@utu.fi

Abstract

In this paper, we focus on parsing rare and non-trivial constructions, in particular ellipsis. We report on several experiments in enrichment of training data for this specific construction, evaluated on five languages: Czech, English, Finnish, Russian and Slovak. These data enrichment methods draw upon self-training and tri-training, combined with a stratified sampling method mimicking the structural complexity of the original treebank. In addition, using these same methods, we also demonstrate small improvements over the CoNLL-17 parsing shared task winning system for four of the five languages, not only restricted to the elliptical constructions.

1 Introduction

Dependency parsing of natural language text may seem like a solved problem, at least for resource-rich languages and domains, where state-of-the-art parsers attack or surpass 90% labeled attachment score (LAS) (Zeman et al., 2017). However, certain syntactic phenomena such as coordination and ellipsis are notoriously hard and even state-of-the-art parsers could benefit from better models of these constructions. Our work focuses on one such construction that combines both coordination and ellipsis: *gapping*, an omission of a repeated predicate which can be understood from context (Coppock, 2001). For example, in *Mary won gold and Peter bronze*, the second instance of the verb is omitted, as the meaning is evident from the context. In dependency parsing this creates a situation where the parent node is missing (omitted verb *won*) while its dependents are still present (*Peter* and *bronze*). In the Universal Dependencies annotation scheme (Nivre et al., 2016) gapping constructions are analyzed by promoting one of the orphaned dependents to the position of its missing parent, and connecting all remaining core arguments to that promoted one with the `orphan` relation (see Figure 1). Therefore the dependency parser must learn to predict relations between words that should not usually be connected. Gapping has been studied extensively in theoretical works (Johnson, 2009, 2014; Lakoff and Ross, 1970; Sag, 1976). However, it received almost no attention in NLP works, neither concerned with parsing nor with corpora creation. Among the recent papers, Kummerfeld and Klein (2017) proposed a one-endpoint-crossing graph parser able to recover a range of null elements and trace types, and Schuster (Schuster et al., 2018) proposed two methods to recover elided predicates in sentences with gapping. The aforementioned lack of corpora that would pay attention to gapping, as well as natural relative rarity of gapping, leads to its underrepresentation in training corpora: they do not provide enough examples for the parser to learn gapping. Therefore we investigate methods of enriching the training data with new material from large raw corpora.

The present work consist of two parts. In the first part, we experiment on enriching data in general, without a specific focus on gapping constructions. This part builds upon self-training and tri-training related work known from the literature, but also develops and tests a stratified approach for selecting a structurally balanced subcorpus. In the second part, we focus on elliptical sentences, comparing general enrichment of training data with enrichment using elliptical sentences artificially constructed by removal of a coordinated element.

2 Data

2.1 Languages and treebanks

For the parsing experiments we selected five treebanks from the Universal Dependencies (UD) col-

Proceedings of the Second Workshop on Universal Dependencies (UDW 2018), pages 47–54

Brussels, Belgium, November 1, 2018. ©2018 Association for Computational Linguistics

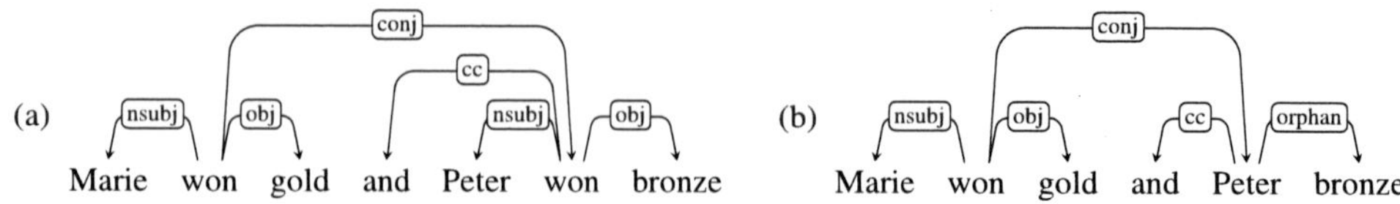

Figure 1: UD representation of a sentence with repeated verb (a), and with an omitted verb in a gapping construction (b).

lection (Nivre et al., 2016). We experiment with the following treebanks: UD_Czech, UD_English, UD_Finnish, UD_Russian-SynTagRus, and UD_Slovak. With the exception of UD_Russian-SynTagRus, all our experiments are based on UD release 2.0. This UD release was used in the CoNLL-17 Shared Task on Multilingual Parsing from Raw Text to Universal Dependencies (Zeman et al., 2017), giving us a point of comparison to the state-of-the-art. For UD_Russian-SynTagRus, we use UD release 2.1, which has a considerably improved annotation of elliptic sentences. For English, which has only a few elliptical sentences in the original treebank, we also utilize in testing a set of elliptical sentences gathered by Schuster et al. (2018).

This selection of data strives to maximize the amount of elliptical constructions present in the treebanks (Droganova and Zeman, 2017), while also covering different modern languages and providing variation. Decisions are based on the work by Droganova and Zeman (2017) who collected statistics on elliptical constructions that are explicitly marked with orphan relation within the UD treebanks. Relatively high number of elliptical constructions within chosen treebanks is the property of the treebanks rather than the languages.

2.2 Additional material

Automatic parses As an additional data source in our parsing experiments, we use the multilingual raw text collection by Ginter et al. (2017). This collection includes web crawl data for 45 languages automatically parsed using the UDPipe parser (Straka and Straková, 2017) trained on the UD version 2.0 treebanks. For Russian, where we use newer version of the treebank, we reparsed the raw data with UDPipe model trained on the corresponding treebank version to agree with the treebank data in use.

As our goal is to use the web crawled data to enrich the official training data in the parsing experiments, we want to ensure the quality of the

automatically parsed data. To achieve this, we apply a method that stands between the standard self-training and tri-training techniques. In self-training, the labeled training data (L) is iteratively enriched with unlabeled data (U) automatically labeled with the same learning system ($L = L + U_l$), whereas in tri-training (Zhou and Li, 2005) there are three different learning systems, A, B and C, and the labeled data for the system A is enriched with instances from U on which the two other systems agree, therefore $L_a = L + (U_b \cap U_c)$. Different variations of these methods have been successfully applied in dependency parsing, for example (McClosky et al., 2006; Søgaard and Rishøj, 2010; Li et al., 2014; Weiss et al., 2015). In this work we use two parsers (A and B) to process the unlabeled crawl data, and then the sentences where these two parsers fully agree are used to enrich the training data for the system A, i.e. $L_a = L + (U_a \cap U_b)$. Therefore the method can be seen as a form of expanded self-training or limited tri-training. A similar technique is successfully used for example by Sagae and Tsujii (2007) in parser domain adaptation and Björkelund et al. (2014) in general parsing.

In our experiments the main parser used in final experiments as well as labeling the crawl data, is the neural graph-based Stanford parser (Dozat et al., 2017), the winning and state-of-the-art system from the CoNLL-17 Shared Task (Zeman et al., 2017). The secondary parser for labeling the crawl data is UDPipe, a neural transition-based parser, as these parses are already provided together with the crawl data. Both of these parsers include their own part-of-speech tagger, which is trained together (but not jointly) with the dependency parser in all our experiments. In the final self-training web crawl datasets we then keep only deduplicated sentences with identical part-of-speech and dependency analyses. All results reported in this paper are measured on gold tokenization, and the parser hyperparameters are those used for these systems in the CoNLL-17

Shared Task.

Artificial treebanks on elliptical constructions
For specifically experimenting on elliptical constructions, we additionally include data from the semi-automatically constructed artificial treebanks by Droganova et al. (2018). These treebanks simulate gapping by removing words in particular coordination constructions, providing data for experimenting with the otherwise very rare construction. For English and Finnish the given datasets are manually curated for grammaticality and fluency, whereas for Czech the quality relies on the rules developed for the process. For Russian and Slovak, which are not part of the original artificial treebank release, we create automatically constructed artificial datasets by running the pipeline developed for the Czech language. Size of the artificial data is shown in Table 1.

	Token	**Sentence**
Czech	50K	2876
English	7.3K	421
Finnish	13K	1000
Russian	87K	5000
Slovak	7.1	564

Table 1: The size of the artificial data

3 Experiments

First, we set out to evaluate the overall quality of the trees in the raw enrichment dataset produced by our self-training variant by parsing and filtering web crawl data. In our baseline experiments we train parsers (Dozat et al., 2017) using purely the new self-training data. From the full self-training dataset we sample datasets comparable to the sizes of the original treebanks to train parsers. These parsers are then evaluated using the original test set of the corresponding treebank. This gives us an overall estimate of the self-training data quality compared to the original treebanks.

3.1 Tree sampling

Predictably, our automatically selected self-training data is biased towards short, simple sentences where the parsers are more likely to agree. Long sentences are in turn often composed of simple coordinated item lists. To rectify this bias, we employ a sampling method which aims to more closely follow the distribution of the original treebank compared to randomly sampling sentences

from the full self-training data. We base the sampling on two features of every tree: the number of tokens, and the number of unique dependency relation types divided by the number of tokens. The latter accounts for tree complexity, as it penalizes trees where the same relation type is repeated too many times, and it specifically allows us to downsample the long coordinated item lists where the ratio drops much lower than average. We of course take into account that a relation type can naturally occur more than once in a sentence, and that it is not ideal to force the ratio close to 1.0. However, as the sampling method tries to mimic the distribution from the original treebank, it should to pick the correct variance while discarding the extremes.

The sampling procedure proceeds as follows: First, we divide the space of the two features, length and complexity, into buckets and estimate from the treebank training data the target distribution, and the expected number of trees to be sampled in each bucket. Then we select from the full self-training dataset the appropriate number of trees into each bucket. Since the web crawl data is heavily skewed, it is not possible to obtain a sufficient number of sampled trees in the exact desired distribution, because many rare length–complexity combinations are heavily underrepresented in the data. We therefore run the sampling procedure in several iterations, until the desired number of trees have been obtained. This results in a distribution closer to, although not necessarily fully matching, the original treebank.

To evaluate the impact of this sampling procedure, we compare it to two baselines. *RandomS* randomly selects the exact same number of sentences as the above-mentioned *Identical* sampling procedure. This results in a dataset which is considerably smaller in terms of tokens, because the web crawl data (on which the two parsers agree) is heavily biased towards short trees. To make sure our evaluation is not affected by simply using less data in terms of tokens, we also provide the *RandomT* baseline, where trees are randomly selected until the same number of tokens is reached as in the *Identical* sample. Here we are able to evaluate the quality of the sampled data, not its bulk.

In Table 2 we see that, as expected, when sampling the same amount of sentences as in the training section of the original treebank, the *RandomS* sampling produces datasets considerably smaller in terms of tokens, whereas *RandomT* results in

Language	Random T	Random S	Identical	TB
Czech	102K/982K	68K/611K	68K/982K	68K/1175K
English	18K/183K	13K/102K	13K/183K	13K/205K
Finnish	17K/144K	12K/92K	12K/144K	12K/163K
Russian	73K/694K	49K/431K	49K/694K	49K/871K
Slovak	11K/83K	8K/58K	8K/83K	8K/81K

Table 2: Training data sizes after each sampling strategy compared to the original treebank training section (TB), sentences/tokens.

datasets considerably larger in terms of trees when the same amount of tokens as in the *RandomS* dataset is sampled. This confirms the assumption that parsers tend to agree on shorter sentences in the web crawl data, introducing the bias towards them. On the other hand, when the same number of sentences is selected as in the *RandomS* sampling and the original treebank, the *Identical* sampling strategy results in dataset much closer to the original treebank in terms of tokens.

Parsing results for the different sampling strategies are shown in Table 3. Except for Slovak, the results follow an intuitively expectable pattern: the sample with the least tokens results in the worst score, and of the two samples with the same number of tokens, the one which follows the treebank distribution receives the better score. Surprisingly, for Slovak the sampling strategy which mimics the treebank distribution receives a score almost 3pp lower than the one with random sampling of the same amount of tokens. A possible explanation is given in the description of the Slovak treebank which mentions that it consists of sentences on which two annotators agreed, and is biased towards short and simple sentences. The data is thus not representative of the language use, possibly causing the effect. Lacking a better explanation for the time being, we also add the *RandomT* sampling dataset into our experiments for Slovak. Overall, the parsing results on the automatically selected data are surprisingly good, lagging only several percent points behind parsers trained on the manually annotated treebanks.

3.2 Enrichment

In this section, we test the overall suitability of the sampled trees as an additional data for parsing. We produce training data composed of the original treebank training section, and a progressively increasing number of sampled trees: 20%, 100%, and 200% (relative to the treebank training data size, i.e. +100% sample doubles the total amount of training data). The parsing results

Language	Random T	Random S	Identical	TB
Czech	88.50%	88.18%	**88.77%**	91.20%
English	83.67%	82.86%	**84.18%**	86.94%
Finnish	82.67%	80.69%	**83.01%**	87.89%
Russian	91.28%	90.85%	**91.49%**	93.35%
Slovak	**85.02%**	83.67%	82.35%	86.04%

Table 3: Results of the baseline parsing experiments, using only automatically collected data, reported in terms of LAS%. Random T: random sample, same amount of tokens as in the Random S samples; Random S: random sample, same amount of sentences as in the original treebanks; Identical: identical sample, imitates the distribution of trees in the original treebanks. For comparison, the TB column shows the LAS of a parser trained on the original treebank training data.

Language	TB	+20%	+100%	+200%
Czech	**91.20%**	91.13%	90.98%	90.72%
English	86.94%	87.32%	**87.43%**	87.29%
Finnish	87.89%	87.83%	88.24%	**88.32%**
Russian	93.35%	**93.38%**	93.22%	93.08%
Slovak	86.04%	87.89%	**88.36%**	**88.36%**
Slovak T	86.04%	88.14%	88.57%	**88.77%**

Table 4: Enriching treebank data with identical sample from automatic data, LAS%. TB: original treebank (baseline experiment; the scores are better than reported in the CoNLL-17 Shared Task because we evaluate on gold segmentation while the shared task systems are evaluated on predicted segmentation); +20% − +200%: size of the identical sample used to enrich the treebank data (with respect to the original treebank size). Slovak T: enriching Slovak treebank with random tokens sample instead of identical.

are shown in Table 4. Positively, for all languages except Czech, we can improve the overall parsing accuracy, for Slovak by as much as 2.7pp, which is a rather non-trivial improvement. In general, the smaller the treebank, the larger the benefit. With the exception of Slovak, the improvements are relatively modest, in the less than half-a-percent range. Nevertheless, since our baseline is the winning parser of the CoNLL-17 Shared Task, these constitute improvements over the current state-of-the-art. Based on these experiments, we can conclude that self-training data extracted from web crawl seem to be suitable material for enriching the training data for parsing, and in next section we continue to test whether the same data and methods can be used to increase occurrences of a rare linguistic construction to make it more learnable for parsers.

3.3 Ellipsis

Our special focus point is that of parsing elliptic constructions. We therefore test whether increasing the number of elliptical sentences in the training data improves the parsing accuracy of these constructions, without sacrificing the overall parsing accuracy. We follow the same data enrichment methods as used above in general domain and proceed to select elliptical sentences (recognized through the `orphan` relation) from the same self-training data automatically produced from web crawl (Section 2.2). We then train parsers using a combination of the ellipsis subset and the original training section for each language. We enrich Czech, Russian and Slovak training data with elliptical sentences, progressively increasing their size by 5%, 10% and 15%. For Finnish, only 5% of elliptical sentences was available in the filtered web crawl data, and for English not a single sentence.

The experiments showed mixed results (Table 5). For Russian and Slovak the accuracy of the dependencies involved in gapping is improved by web crawl enrichment, whereas the results for Czech remained largely the same and Finnish slightly decreased (column *Web crawl*). Unfortunately, for Slovak and Finnish, we cannot draw firm conclusions due to the small number of orphan relations in the test set. For English, even the treebank results are very low: the parser predicts only very few orphan relations (recall 1.71%) and the web crawl data contains no orphans on which the two parsers could agree, thus making it impossible to enrich the data using this method. Clearly, English requires a different strategy, and we will return to it shortly. Positively, none of the languages substantially suffered in terms of overall LAS when adding extra elliptical sentences into the training data. For Slovak, we can even see a significant improvement in overall parsing accuracy, in line with the experiments in Section 3.1. Increasing the proportion of orphan sentences in the training data has the predictable effect of in-

creasing the orphan F-score and decreasing the overall LAS of the parser. These differences are nevertheless only very minor and can only be observed for Czech and Russian which have sufficient number of orphan relation examples in the test set. For Slovak, with 18 examples, we cannot draw any conclusions, and for English and Finnish, there is not a sufficient number of orphan examples in the filtered web crawl data to allow us to vary the proportion.

For all languages, we also experiment with the artificial elliptic sentence dataset of Droganova et al. (2018), described earlier in Section 2.2. For Czech, English and Finnish, the dataset contains semi-automatically produced, and in the case of English and Finnish, also manually validated instances of elliptic sentences. For Slovak and Russian, we replicate the procedure of Droganova et al., sans the manual validation, obtaining artificial orphan datasets for all the five languages under study. Subsequently, we train parsers using a combination of sentences from the artificial treebank and the original training set. The results of this experiments are in Table 5, column *Artificial*. Compared to web crawl, the artificial data results in a lower performance on orphans for Czech, Slovak and Russian, and higher for Finnish, but once again keeping in mind the small size of Finnish and Slovak test set, it is difficult to come to a firm conclusion. Clearly, though, the web crawl data does not perform substantially worse than the artificial data, even though it is gathered fully automatically. A very substantial improvement is achieved on English, where the web crawl data fails to deliver even a single orphan example, whereas the artificial data gains recall of 9.62%.

This offers us an opportunity to once again try to obtain orphan examples for English from the web crawl data, since this time we can train the parsers on the combination of the original treebank and the artificial data, hopefully resulting in parsers which are in fact able to predict at least some orphan relations, which in turn can result in new elliptic sentences from the web crawl data. As seen from Table 5, the artificial data increases the orphan F-score from 3.36% to 17.18% relative to training only on the treebank, and we are therefore able to obtain a parser which is at least by the order of magnitude comparable to the other four languages in parsing accuracy of elliptic constructions. We observe no loss in terms of the over-

Language	All	Treebank				Web crawl +5/+10/+15%				Artificial			
		LAS	O Pre	O Rec	O F	LAS	O Pre	O Rec	O F	LAS	O Pre	O Rec	O F
Czech	418	91.20%	54.84%	56.94%	**55.87%**	91.22% 91.11% 91.06%	48.96% 49.80% 50.19%	61.72% 60.05% 62.68%	54.60% 54.45% 55.74%	91.15%	51.79%	58.85%	55.10%
English	2+466	86.94%	100.00%	1.71%	3.36%	—	—	—	—	**86.95%**	80.36%	9.62%	**17.18%**
Finnish	43	87.89%	66.67%	32.56%	43.75%	87.76%	48.15%	30.23%	37.14%	**88.04%**	54.76%	53.49%	**54.12%**
Russian	138	93.35%	44.57%	29.71%	35.65%	93.50% 93.41% 93.42%	42.86% 38.26% 40.69%	39.13% 41.30% 42.75%	40.91% 39.72% **41.70%**	93.20%	33.14%	40.58%	36.48%
Slovak	18	86.04%	60.00%	16.67%	26.09%	87.90% 87.76% 87.80%	36.36% 33.33% 30.77%	22.22% 16.67% 22.22%	**27.59%** 22.22% 25.81%	87.80%	37.50%	16.67%	23.08%

Table 5: Enriching treebank data with elliptical sentences. All: number of `orphan` labels in the test data; Treebank: original treebank (baseline experiment); Web crawl: Enriching the original treebank with the elliptical sentences extracted from the automatically parsed web crawl data; Artificial: Enriching the original treebank with the artificial ellipsis treebank; LAS, %: overall parsing accuracy; O Prec (orphan precision): number of correct `orphan` nodes divided by the number of all predicted `orphan` nodes; O Rec (orphan recall): number of correct `orphan` nodes divided by the number of gold-standard `orphan` nodes; O F (Orphan F-score): F-measure restricted to the nodes that are labeled as `orphan` : 2PR / (P+R). For English, the orphan P/R/F scores are evaluated on a dataset of the two orphan relations in the original test section, combined with 466 English elliptic sentences of Schuster et al. (2018). The extra sentences are not used in the LAS column, so as to preserve comparability of overall LAS scores across the various runs.

all LAS, demonstrating that it is in fact possible to achieve a substantial improvement in parsing of a rare, non-trivial construction without sacrificing the overall performance.

Using the web data self-training filtering procedure with two parsers trained on the treebank+artificial data, we can now repeat the experiment with enriching parser training data with orphan relations, results of which are shown in Table 6. We test the following models:

- original UD_English v.2.0 treebank;

- original UD_English v.2.0 treebank combined with the artificial sentences;

- original UD_English v.2.0 treebank combined with the artificial sentences and web crawl dataset; size progressively increased by 5%, 10% and 15%. Here we use the original UD_English v.2.0 treebank extended with the artificial sentences to train the models (Section 2.2) that produce the web crawl data for English.

The best orphan F-score of 36%, more than ten times higher compared to using the original treebank, is obtained by enriching the training data with 15% elliptic sentences from the artificial and filtered web data. The orphan F-score of 36% is on par with the other languages and, positively, the overall LAS of the parser remains essentially unchanged — the parser does not sacrifice anything

Model	LAS	O Precision	O Recall	O F-score
Treebank	86.94%	100%	1.71%	3.36%
Artificial	86.95%	80.36%	9.62%	17.18%
Art.+Web 5%	86.72%	86.11%	19.87%	32.29%
Art.+Web 10%	86.68%	78.36%	22.44%	34.88%
Art.+Web 15%	**87.07%**	84.38%	23.08%	**36.24%**

Table 6: Enriching the English treebank data with elliptical sentences. LAS, %: overall parsing accuracy; O Precision (orphan precision): number of correct `orphan` labels divided by the number of all predicted `orphan` nodes; O Recall (orphan recall): number of correct `orphan` labels divided by the number of gold-standard `orphan` nodes; O F-score (orphan F-score): F-measure restricted to the nodes that are labeled as `orphan` : 2PR / (P+R). For English, the orphan P/R/F scores are evaluated on a dataset of the two orphan relations in the original test set, combined with 466 English elliptic sentences of Schuster et al. (2018). The extra sentences are not used in the LAS column, so as to preserve comparability of overall LAS scores across the various runs. This is necessary since elliptic sentences are typically syntactically more complex and would therefore skew overall parser performance evaluation.

in order to gain the improvement on orphan relations. These English results therefore not only explore the influence of the number of elliptical sentences on the parsing accuracy, but also test a method applicable in the case where the treebank does not contain almost any elliptical constructions and results in parsers that only generate the relation very rarely.

4 Conclusions

We have explored several methods of enriching training data for dependency parsers, with a specific focus on rare phenomena such as ellipsis (gapping). This focused enrichment leads to mixed results. On one hand, for several languages we did not obtain a significant improvement of the parsing accuracy of ellipsis, possibly in part owing to the small number of testing examples. On the other hand, though, we have demonstrated that for English ellipsis parsing accuracy can be improved from single digit numbers to performance on par with the other languages. We have also validated the method of constructing artificial elliptical examples as a mean to enrich parser training data. Additionally, we have shown that useful training data can be obtained using web crawl data and a self-training or tri-training style method, even though the two parsers in question differ substantially in their overall performance.

Finally, we have shown that this parser training data enrichment can lead to improvements of general parser accuracy, improving upon the state of the art for all but one language. The improvement was especially notable for Slovak. Czech was the only treebank not benefiting from this additional data, likely owing to the fact that is is an already very large, and homogenous treebank. As part of these experiments, we have introduced and demonstrated the effectiveness of a stratified sampling method which corrects for the skewed distribution of sentences selected in the web filtering experiments.

Acknowledgments

The work was partially supported by the grant 15-10472S of the Czech Science Foundation (GAČR), the GA UK grant 794417, Academy of Finland, and Nokia Foundation. Computational resources were provided by CSC - IT Center for Science, Finland.

References

Anders Björkelund, Özlem Çetinoğlu, Agnieszka Faleńska, Richárd Farkas, Thomas Müller, Wolfgang Seeker, and Zsolt Szántó. 2014. Self-training for Swedish Dependency Parsing – Initial Results and Analysis. In *Proceedings of the Fifth Swedish Language Technology Conference (SLTC 2014)*.

Elizabeth Coppock. 2001. Gapping: In defense of deletion. In *Proceedings of the Chicago Linguistics Society*, volume 37, pages 133–148.

Timothy Dozat, Peng Qi, and Christopher D Manning. 2017. Stanford's Graph-based Neural Dependency Parser at the CoNLL 2017 Shared Task. *Proceedings of the CoNLL 2017 Shared Task: Multilingual Parsing from Raw Text to Universal Dependencies*, pages 20–30.

Kira Droganova and Daniel Zeman. 2017. Elliptic Constructions: Spotting Patterns in UD Treebanks. In *Proceedings of the NoDaLiDa 2017 Workshop on Universal Dependencies (UDW 2017)*, 135, pages 48–57.

Kira Droganova, Daniel Zeman, Jenna Kanerva, and Filip Ginter. 2018. Parse Me if You Can: Artificial Treebanks for Parsing Experiments on Elliptical Constructions. *Proceedings of the 11th International Conference on Language Resources and Evaluation (LREC 2018)*.

Filip Ginter, Jan Hajič, Juhani Luotolahti, Milan Straka, and Daniel Zeman. 2017. CoNLL 2017 Shared Task - Automatically Annotated Raw Texts and Word Embeddings. LINDAT/CLARIN digital library at the Institute of Formal and Applied Linguistics (ÚFAL), Faculty of Mathematics and Physics, Charles University.

Kyle Johnson. 2009. Gapping is not (VP) ellipsis. *Linguistic Inquiry*, 40(2):289–328.

Kyle Johnson. 2014. Gapping.

Jonathan K Kummerfeld and Dan Klein. 2017. Parsing with Traces: An $O(n^4)$ Algorithm and a Structural Representation. *arXiv preprint arXiv:1707.04221*.

George Lakoff and John Robert Ross. 1970. Gapping and the order of constituents. *Progress in linguistics: A collection of papers*, 43:249.

Zhenghua Li, Min Zhang, and Wenliang Chen. 2014. Ambiguity-aware ensemble training for semi-supervised dependency parsing. In *Proceedings of the 52nd Annual Meeting of the Association for Computational Linguistics (Volume 1: Long Papers)*, volume 1, pages 457–467.

David McClosky, Eugene Charniak, and Mark Johnson. 2006. Effective self-training for parsing. In *Proceedings of the main conference on human language technology conference of the North American Chapter of the Association of Computational Linguistics*, pages 152–159. Association for Computational Linguistics.

Joakim Nivre, Marie-Catherine de Marneffe, Filip Ginter, Yoav Goldberg, Jan Hajič, Christopher Manning, Ryan McDonald, Slav Petrov, Sampo Pyysalo, Natalia Silveira, Reut Tsarfaty, and Daniel Zeman. 2016. Universal Dependencies v1: A Multilingual Treebank Collection. In *Proceedings of the 10th International Conference on Language Resources and*

Evaluation (LREC 2016), pages 1659–1666, Portorož, Slovenia.

Ivan Sag. 1976. *Deletion and Logical Form*. MIT. PhD dissertation.

Kenji Sagae and Junichi Tsujii. 2007. Dependency parsing and domain adaptation with LR models and parser ensembles. In *Proceedings of the 2007 Joint Conference on Empirical Methods in Natural Language Processing and Computational Natural Language Learning (EMNLP-CoNLL)*.

Sebastian Schuster, Joakim Nivre, and Christopher D. Manning. 2018. Sentences with Gapping: Parsing and Reconstructing Elided Predicates. In *Proceedings of the 16th Annual Conference of the North American Chapter of the Association for Computational Linguistics: Human Language Technologies (NAACL 2018)*.

Anders Søgaard and Christian Rishøj. 2010. Semi-supervised dependency parsing using generalized tri-training. In *Proceedings of the 23rd International Conference on Computational Linguistics*, pages 1065–1073. Association for Computational Linguistics.

Milan Straka and Jana Straková. 2017. Tokenizing, POS Tagging, Lemmatizing and Parsing UD 2.0 with UDPipe. In *Proceedings of the CoNLL 2017 Shared Task: Multilingual Parsing from Raw Text to Universal Dependencies*, pages 88–99, Vancouver, Canada. Association for Computational Linguistics.

David Weiss, Chris Alberti, Michael Collins, and Slav Petrov. 2015. Structured Training for Neural Network Transition-Based Parsing. In *Proceedings of ACL 2015*, pages 323–333.

Daniel Zeman, Martin Popel, Milan Straka, Jan Hajič, Joakim Nivre, Filip Ginter, Juhani Luotolahti, Sampo Pyysalo, Slav Petrov, Martin Potthast, Francis Tyers, Elena Badmaeva, Memduh Gökrmak, Anna Nedoluzhko, Silvie Cinková, jr. Jan Hajič, Jaroslava Hlaváčová, Václava Kettnerová, Zdeňka Urešová, Jenna Kanerva, Stina Ojala, Anna Missilä, Christopher Manning, Sebastian Schuster, Siva Reddy, Dima Taji, Nizar Habash, Herman Leung, Marie-Catherine de Marneffe, Manuela Sanguinetti, Maria Simi, Hiroshi Kanayama, Valeria de Paiva, Kira Droganova, Héctor Martínez Alonso, Çağr Çöltekin, Umut Sulubacak, Hans Uszkoreit, Vivien Macketanz, Aljoscha Burchardt, Kim Harris, Katrin Marheinecke, Georg Rehm, Tolga Kayadelen, Mohammed Attia, Ali Elkahky, Zhuoran Yu, Emily Pitler, Saran Lertpradit, Michael Mandl, Jesse Kirchner, Hector Fernandez Alcalde, Jana Strnadová, Esha Banerjee, Ruli Manurung, Antonio Stella, Atsuko Shimada, Sookyoung Kwak, Gustavo Mendonça, Tatiana Lando, Rattima Nitisaroj, and Josie Li. 2017. CoNLL 2017 shared task: Multilingual parsing from raw text to universal dependencies. In *Proceedings of the CoNLL 2017 Shared Task: Multilingual Parsing from Raw Text to Universal Dependencies*, pages 1–19, Stroudsburg, PA, USA. Charles University, Association for Computational Linguistics.

Zhi-Hua Zhou and Ming Li. 2005. Tri-training: Exploiting unlabeled data using three classifiers. *IEEE Transactions on knowledge and Data Engineering*, 17(11):1529–1541.

Integration complexity and the order of cosisters

William Dyer
Oracle Corp `william.dyer@oracle.com`

Abstract

The cost of integrating dependent constituents to their heads is thought to involve the distance between dependent and head and the complexity of the integration (Gibson, 1998). The former has been convincingly addressed by Dependency Distance Minimization (DDM) (cf. Liu et al., 2017). The current study addresses the latter by proposing a novel theory of integration complexity derived from the entropy of the probability distribution of a dependent's heads. An analysis of Universal Dependency corpora provides empirical evidence regarding the preferred order of isomorphic cosisters—sister constituents of the same syntactic form on the same side of their head—such as the adjectives in *pretty blue fish*. Integration complexity, alongside DDM, allows for a general theory of constituent order based on integration cost.

1 Introduction

An open question in the field is why certain constituent orders are preferred to their reverse-order variants. For example, why do *pretty blue fish* or *Toni went to the store after eating lunch* seem more felicitous than *blue pretty fish* or *Toni went after eating lunch to the store*? In both sequences, two constituents of the same syntactic type depend on the same head—two 'stacked' adjectives modify *fish* and two prepositional phrases modify *went*. Yet despite their syntactic and truth-conditional equivalence, one order is preferred.

This order preference has often been treated with discrete models for each constituent type. For example, it has been proposed that stacked adjectives follow (1) a general hierarchy based on inherence (Whorf, 1945)—that is, the adjective closest to the head is more inherent to the head—discrimination (Ziff, 1960), intrinsicness (Danks and Glucksberg, 1971), temporariness (Bolinger, 1967; Larson, 2000), or

subjectivity (Scontras et al., 2017); (2) a binary hierarchy based on features such as relative/absolute (Sproat and Shih, 1991), stage-/individual-level (Larson, 1998), or direct/indirect (Cinque, 2010); or (3) a multi-category hierarchy of intensional/subsective/intersective (Kamp and Partee, 1995; Partee, 2007; Truswell, 2009), reinforcer/epithet/descriptor/classifier (Feist, 2012), and perhaps most famously, semantic features such as size/shape/color/nationality (Quirk et al., 1985; Scott, 2002). Similarly, prepositional phrases and adverbials have been held to follow a hierarchy based on manner/place/time (Boisson, 1981; Cinque, 2001) or thematic roles such as evidential/temporal/locative (Schweikert, 2004). While these models may be reasonably accurate—though see Hawkins (2000); Truswell (2009); Kotowski (2016)—they seem to lack external motivation (Cinque, 2010, pp. 122-3) and explanatory power outside their specific constituent types.

A more general approach suggests that certain tendencies—constituents placed closer to their heads than their same-side sisters are more often complements than adjuncts (Culicover and Jackendoff, 2005) and are more likely to be shorter (Behaghel, 1930; Wasow and Arnold, 2003), less complex (Berlage, 2014), or have less grammatical weight (Osborne, 2007)—are the result of larger motivations such as Head Proximity (Rijkhoff, 1986, 2000), Early Immediate Constituents (Hawkins, 2004), or Minimize Domains (Hawkins, 2014). This line of inquiry seeks to explain Behaghel's (1932) observation that syntactic proximity mirrors semantic closeness, either due to iconicity or more recently as an efficiency-based aid to cognitive processing.

The current study sits within this latter approach of appealing to a general principle to motivate a constituent-ordering pattern.

Proceedings of the Second Workshop on Universal Dependencies (UDW 2018), pages 55–65
Brussels, Belgium, November 1, 2018. ©2018 Association for Computational Linguistics

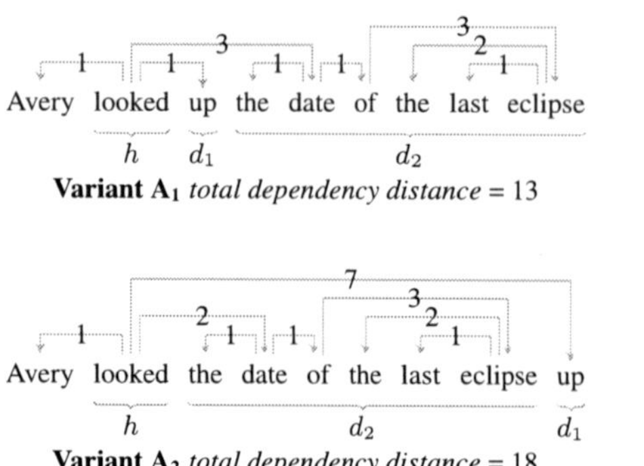

Variant A₁ *total dependency distance* = 13

Variant A₂ *total dependency distance* = 18

Figure 1: DDM variants

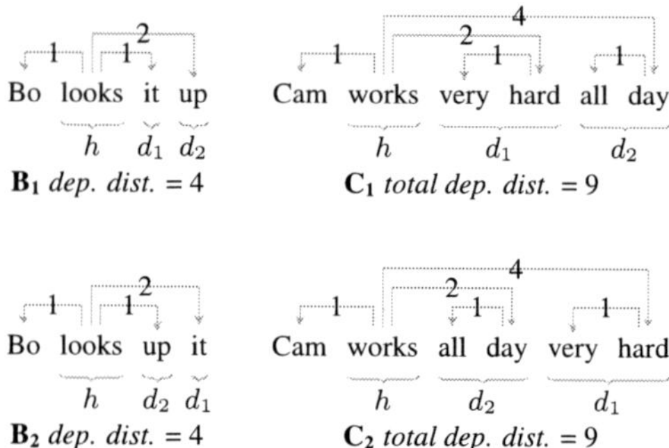

B₁ *dep. dist.* = 4   **C₁** *total dep. dist.* = 9

B₂ *dep. dist.* = 4   **C₂** *total dep. dist.* = 9

Figure 2: Isomorphic cosisters

2 Dependency Distance & Isomorphic Cosisters

Dependency is a relation between words such that each word except the root depends on another word, forming a tree of dependents and heads (Tesnière, 1959; Mel'čuk, 2000). Dependency Distance Minimization[1] (DDM) holds that word orders which minimize the cumulative linear distance between dependents and their heads tend to be preferred to variants with longer total distances, where dependency distance is the count of words intervening between dependent and head (Liu et al., 2017). In Figure 1, for example, the two sentences may be semantically equivalent, but variant A₁ yields a total dependency distance of 13, which is smaller than that of A₂ at 18; thus A₁ is preferred according to DDM. The variants in Figure 1 hinge on whether the particle *up* appears closer to the head *looked* than the longer noun phrase *the date of the last eclipse*. DDM has been shown to be quite widespread, if not universal (Futrell et al., 2015), and rests on solid theoretical and empirical foundations from linguistics (Hudson, 1995), psycholinguistics (Futrell et al., 2017), and mathematics (Ferrer-i Cancho, 2004).

The methodology underlying DDM effectively punishes certain structures, including those in which two sister constituents are placed on the same side of their head—'cosisters' after Osborne (2007)—where the longer cosister appears closest to the head. Variant A₂ in Figure 1 shows such a case. One strategy for avoiding these struc-

tures is to alternate the placement of sister constituents on either side of the head (Temperley, 2008), as in many double-adjective noun phrases in Romance—the Spanish *gran globo rojo* [big balloon red] 'big red balloon'—and single- and multi-word adjective phrases in English, as in *the happy child / the child happy from playing outside.*

Another strategy for minimizing dependency distance is to place shorter cosisters closer to the head, as in Figure 1 variant A₁, in which the shorter dependent cosister d_1 is placed closer to the head h than its longer cosister d_2. Because the two cosisters are of differing length, DDM is able to predict that variant A₁ be preferred to A₂.

However, if the cosisters are of the same length, or more accurately if they have the same form, DDM is unable to explain the preference for one variant over another. Figure 2 shows two such structures, B and C, in which varying whether d_1 or d_2 appears closest to the head h does not yield a different total dependency distance. The cosisters d_i in B have the same structure, as do the cosisters d_i and C: the single-word *it* and *up* in B are single leaf-node dependents with no other internal structure, and the internal structure of *to LA* and *after lunch* is the same in that the first word depends on the second in both cases.

These isomorphic cosisters, or same-side sister constituents that share the same internal syntactic form, are the focus of the current study. In order to motivate a preference for one linear order over another, as in Figure 2 B₁ and C₁ over B₂ and C₂[2] we must appeal to a mechanism other than DDM.

---

[1] This approach is also called Dependency *Length* Minimization (DLM). Liu et al. (2017) suggests that because distance connotes a dynamic state which may vary, while 'length' is a more static feature, 'distance' is preferred. Recent literature (e.g. Ferrer-i Cancho, 2017; Futrell et al., 2017; Ouyang and Jiang, 2017) is converging on 'distance.'

[2] B₂ and C₂ are not necessarily impossible, just disfavored. When asked *Does Cam work very hard in the morning?*, the response *No, Cam works* ALL DAY *very hard*, might be marginally acceptable, especially with focus stress (Rooth, 1992). Adjective order tendencies—BLUE *pretty fish*—are also violable under similar contexts (Matthews, 2014, p. 95).

3   Integration Complexity

The cost of integrating a dependent to its head "consists of two parts: (1) a cost dependent on the complexity of the integration [... and] (2) a distance-based cost" (Gibson, 1998, p. 13). If we accept DDM as the basis for the distance-based cost and a valid motivation for preferred orders among different-length constituents (Futrell et al., 2017), a definition of integration complexity may allow the ordering preference between variant orders of isomorphic cosisters to be addressed.

Many have wrestled with the notion of linguistic complexity (Newmeyer and Preston, 2014) or grammatical weight (Wasow, 1997; Osborne, 2007), though a consensus has yet to emerge. Suggestions often involve number of words or phrase-structure nodes—more words or nodes equates to higher complexity—yet counterexamples to this sort of reasoning are readily found: Chomsky (1975, p. 477) notes that *they brought the man I saw in* is shorter and yet more complex than *they brought all the leaders of the riot in*. Further, isomorphic cosisters cannot be differentiated based on number of words or internal nodes, since the sister constituents in question are equal on both counts. Yet ordering preferences among this type of constituent remain; thus neither length nor syntactic structure can fully account for complexity.

We have an initial clue about relative integration complexity, inherited from the strategy used to minimize dependency distances: the shorter cosister should be placed closer to the head than the longer cosister. By analogy, we expect that the less-complex cosister should likewise be placed closer to the head than the more-complex one. For example, in Figure 2 B and C, we expect both d_1 constituents to have lower integration complexity than their d_2 cosisters; that is, because *looked it up* is preferred to *looked up it*, we infer that *looked* $\rightarrow$ *it* is a less complex integration than *looked* $\rightarrow$ *up*.

A second clue regarding integration complexity comes from nonce words, like *wug* or *tolver*, which seem to maintain order preferences when they appear as heads but not as dependents. For example, while *pretty blue wug* is preferred to *blue pretty wug* when the nonce word is a head, there is no obvious preference between *wuggy tolvic aliens* and *tolvic wuggy aliens*.

Together, these clues allow us to create two inferences: (1) integration complexity is based on a feature of dependents rather than heads, and (2) dependents with lower integration complexity tend to be placed closer to heads than their cosisters.

A plausible feature of dependents, one which could form the basis of integration complexity, is their frequency. However, a simple example shows that this cannot be the case: in *big chartreuse blanket*, the less-frequent adjective *chartreuse* is placed closest to the head, while in *miniscule white blanket* the more-frequent *white* is placed closest the head. Clearly frequency of dependent alone cannot be the force driving integration complexity.

A similar feature is the range of heads that a word can depend on. Ziff (1960) initially proposes that this 'privilege of occurrence' could be the mechanism underlying adjective order, giving the example of *little white house*, in which *little* can depend on a wider range of nouns than can *white*—*little sonnet* for example, but not *white sonnet*—suggesting that the dependent with a more narrow range of possible heads should be placed closest to the head. However, Ziff's counterexample of *intelligent old man*—"*old* has a much greater privilege of occurrence than *intelligent*" (p. 205)—suggests just the opposite, that the dependent with a wider range of heads should be placed closest to the head. Thus similar to raw frequency, the range of possible heads cannot directly define integration complexity.

Futrell et al. (2017) suggest that the mutual information of the dependent-head pair may hold the key to explaining why, "for instance, adjuncts are typically farther from their heads than arguments, if it is the case that adjuncts have lower mutual information with their heads" (p. 2). Mutual information (MI) is one of a series of information-theoretic measures based on Shannon entropy (Shannon, 1948) to gauge how knowing the value of one random variable informs us about another variable (Cover and Thomas, 1991). Pointwise mutual information (PMI) (Bouma, 2009), a version of MI, is frequently used for quantifying the relationship between words (Church and Hanks, 1989). However, PMI requires that the individual frequencies of dependent, head, and dependent-head co-occurrence be known. Nonce words by definition have no frequency, either alone or in co-occurrence with a dependent, so their PMI with a dependent is undefined. It is unclear how an integration complexity based on mutual information could deal with nonce words.

Instead of frequency, 'privilege of occurrence,' or mutual information, it seems plausible that given a dependent word, the relative predictability of its heads should correlate with integration complexity: a dependent whose set of heads is quite small or predictable should be easier to integrate, while a dependent with a wide variety of equally probable heads should be more difficult.

Therefore a measure of integration complexity should be low in the case of a word which depends predictably on very few heads and high when the word's heads are numerous or varied. Entropy (Shannon, 1948) captures this idea mathematically by measuring the 'peakedness' of a probability distribution—the more peaked a distribution, the lower its entropy (Jaynes, 1957)—and is calculated as the logarithm of the probabilities in a distribution, weighted by each probability (Cover and Thomas, 1991), as shown in Equation 1.

$$\mathrm{H}(X) = -\sum_{i=1}^{n} \mathrm{P}(x_i) * \log_b \mathrm{P}(x_i) \qquad (1)$$

A dependent whose heads form a peaked probability distribution is easier to integrate—and therefore has a lower entropy—than a dependent whose heads form a flatter distribution.

In information-theoretic terms, given a dependent with a wide variety of heads of equal probability, we expect a large amount of surprisal or information when the head is determined; this is high entropy. Conversely a dependent with a few very likely heads is expected to yield a small amount of information, captured as low entropy.

However, using the actual head-word lexemes or lemmata in our entropy calculation for dependents is problematic for a subtle reason: it would weight head words equally. Integrating a dependent to a set of heads which are themselves quite similar semantically or distributionally should not yield a large amount of surprisal. One way to more properly weight head words according to their similarity is to use syntactic categories as a basis for the probability distribution. Words of each category—nouns, verbs, adjectives, and so on—are by definition closer to each other functionally and distributionally.

It is the proposal of this paper that by weighting each dependent word by its integration complexity, as measured by the entropy of the probability distribution of the syntactic categories of the word's heads, the order preference between iso-

morphic cosisters can be modeled—specifically that the constituent with a lower integration complexity tends to be placed closer to the head. Further, cosisters with roughly equal integration complexity should not show a particularly strong order tendency, while cosisters with greatly differing integration complexity should have a strong tendency of placing the constituent with lower integration complexity closest to the head.

Formally, let the integration complexity IC of dependent d be the entropy H of the probability distribution of the syntactic categories of the heads of d. Let a head h have two isomorphic dependent constituents d_1 and d_2 appearing on the same linear side of h in the surface realization and with integration complexity $\mathrm{IC}(d_1)$ and $\mathrm{IC}(d_2)$. It is hypothesized that as the difference between the two complexities $|\mathrm{IC}(d_1) - \mathrm{IC}(d_2)|$ increases, the tendency to place the constituent with lower IC closer to the head should also increase.

4 Methodology

The Universal Dependencies (UD) project provides corpora that can be used to both calculate the integration complexity of dependent words and show a preference for one variant order over another. That is, the UD corpora can be used to formulate the probability distribution of the syntactic categories of the heads that a given word tends to depend on—training—as well as the apparent order preference for a pair of cosisters: testing.

Because one goal of Universal Dependencies is to "create cross-linguistically consistent treebank annotation for many languages within a dependency-based lexicalist framework" (Nivre et al., 2016, p. 1659), certain linguistic features are annotated in a somewhat non-intuitive way. Copula and auxiliaries are not treated as the root of a sentence, but instead depend on a predicate or main verb. Further, rather than considering adpositions as the heads of adpositional phrases, as would be common under a phrase-structure framework (cf. Stockwell, 1977), UD treats them as dependents of their associated nouns or verbs. This approach is not without controversy, and there are cross-linguistic arguments, mainly typological, to be made in favor of an adpositional-phrase treatment (Hagège, 2010). Nevertheless, because UD corpora are tagged such that copula, auxiliaries, and adpositions are dependents rather than heads, the current study uses this annotation scheme.

(1) head lemmata of *happy*
afford, always, band, birthday, camper, check, choose, customer (2), enjoy, feel (2), give, go, happy (2), holiday, hour (2), keep, make, need, safe, say (3), tell, walk, year (2)
(2) syntactic categories of lemmata
ADJ (3), ADV, NOUN (8), PROPN (2), VERB (15)
(3) probability distribution of syntactic categories
$3/29$, $1/29$, $8/29$, $2/29$, $15/29$
(4) entropy of probability distribution
1.78 bits

Figure 3: Calculating integration complexity of *happy*

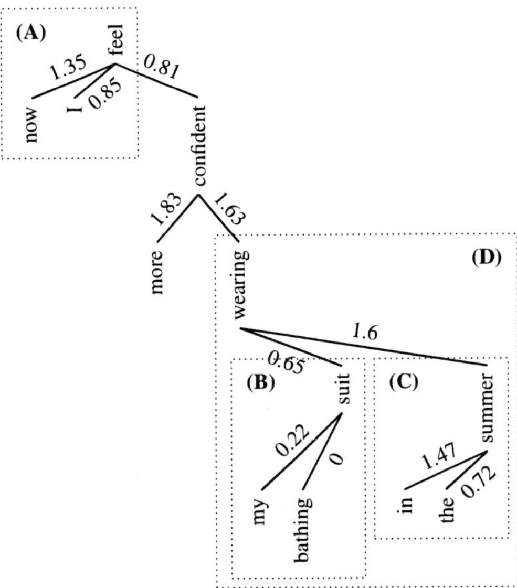

Figure 4: Integration complexity of cosisters

Finally, UD version 2.2 contains multiple corpora for some languages, designed to be applied to various types of analysis. Because the current study requires as full a picture as possible for the syntactic-category tendencies for each dependent word, as well as a sufficient quantity of isomorphic-cosister sequences to test, the largest corpus for each language in the Universal Dependencies will be analyzed here.

4.1 Training

Determining the integration complexity of each dependent is done by finding the probability distribution of the syntactic categories of the heads each word depends on in the UD corpus and calculating the entropy with Equation 1.

For example, Figure 3 shows the entropy calculation for the adjective *happy*. The word appears 29 times in the English-EWT corpus as a dependent on a set of head lemmata (1), with a variety of syntactic categories (2). Those categories form a probability distribution (3) whose entropy, assuming a logarithmic base of 2, is 1.78 bits (4). For comparison, other adjectives have integration complexities such as *little* (1.56 bits), *Italian* (0.76 bits), and *chemical* (0.5 bits).

This process of finding the heads of each dependent, using the heads' syntactic categories to create a probability distribution, and calculating the entropy of that distribution, is repeated for each word in the corpus, thereby determining the integration complexity of all dependents.

4.2 Testing

The UD corpora can also be used to test the hypothesis that the lower-complexity cosister tends to be placed closest to the head. While the order of words as attested in a corpus is not a direct substi-tution for an order preference in all situations, the corpus order does imply that in the specific context of the sentence in the corpus, the attested order is preferred to others. In effect, we are using frequency—the sentence exists at least once in the corpus—as a logistically convenient stand-in for actual order preference (Song, 2012, pp. 14-5).

Figure 4 shows an example sentence from the English-EWT corpus: *now I feel more confident wearing my bathing suit in the summer*. The sentence is annotated according to the UD scheme—notably the preposition *in* is a dependent of the noun *summer*—and lists the integration complexity of each dependent word. For example, the integration complexity of *now* is 1.35 bits, calculated as the entropy of the probability distribution of the syntactic categories of the heads of the adverb *now* in the UD English-EWT corpus.

The sentence contains four instances of isomorphic cosisters and their heads: (A) *now I feel*, where *now* and *I* are cosisters of the same syntactic form—single-leaf nodes with no dependents themselves—which precede their head *feel*; (B) *my bathing suit*, where *my* and *bathing* precede their head *suit*; (C) *in the summer*, where *in* and *the* precede their head *summer*; and (D) *wearing my bathing suit in the summer*, where the multi-word *my bathing suit* and *in the summer* are isomorphic cosisters following their head *wearing*.

In the first case (A), the adverb *now* has an integration complexity of 1.35 bits, while the pronoun

I has 0.85 bits; therefore the lower-complexity cosister, *I*, has been placed closest to the head *feel*. Both (B) *my bathing suit* and (C) *in the summer* also follow this pattern—the lower-complexity *bathing* and *the* are placed closer to their heads than their cosisters *my* and *in*—thereby confirming the hypothesis for these single-word cosisters.

For the multi-word isomorphic cosisters *my bathing suit* and *in the summer*, there are at least two possible strategies. One method is to sum the integration complexity of all nodes, yielding an integration complexity of 0.87 bits for *my bathing suit*—*my* (0.22) + *bathing* (0) + *suit* (0.65)—and a summed complexity of 3.79 bits for *in the summer*: *in* (1.47) + *the* (0.72) + *summer* (1.6).

Another approach is to treat multi-word constituents according to the Dependency Distance Minimization method: a total dependency distance is created by calculating the sum of integration complexity of all words intervening between a dependent and head. This approach yields a total integration complexity of 0.99 bits for *my bathing suit*: (0.22 + 0) for *my ← suit*; (0) for *bathing ← suit*; and (0.65 + 0.22 + 0) for *wearing → suit*.

It is not clear which method is a better representation of the complexity of integrating multi-word constituents for a human parser. Further, given the limited scope of the structures under analysis in this study, it is not clear that one method would result in markedly different outcomes *vis-à-vis* the relative complexity of isomorphic cosisters. For simplicity, the first method of summing the integration complexity of all nodes in a constituent will be used here[3]. Thus for the isomorphic cosisters in Figure 4 (D), the complexity of *my bathing suit* is calculated as 0.87 bits, while that of *in the summer* is 3.79 bits; as such the lower-complexity cosister has been placed closer to the head.

5 Results

Table 1 shows logistic regressions for single- and multi-word isomorphic cosisters. Each language with at least 20 analyzed isomorphic cosisters is listed, along with the specific UD corpus and total number of structures analyzed. The x-axis in each graph shows the difference between the integration complexity of the two cosisters from 0

to 5 bits, and the y-axis shows the probability between 0 and 1 that the lower-complexity cosister has been placed closest to the head.

We see that of the 70 languages analyzed, 61 show a pattern that as the difference between the integration complexity increases, the lower-complexity cosister is more likely to be placed closest to the head. Croatian and Russian show a general preference for placing the less-complex cosister closest to the head, but that preference does not appear to increase as the integration complexities diverge. Japanese is indeterminate showing approximately 50% probability regardless of complexity difference. Six do not follow the hypothesized pattern: Afrikaans, Ancient Greek, Galician, North Sami, Tamil, and Vietnamese seem to prefer that the higher-complexity cosister be placed closest to the head as the difference in integration complexity increases.

There does not seem to be a clear pattern to the set of languages which do not follow the study's hypothesis. Ancient Greek, and North Sami have rich inflectional systems—and resulting 'free' word order —but so do Basque, Estonian, Latin, Old Church Slavonic, and Turkish, which conform to the study's hypothesis.

Nor do language families seem to play a role in these non-conforming languages. Afrikaans and Gothic are outweighed by the many other Germanic languages—Danish, Dutch, English, and so on—which do follow the hypothesis; likewise the conformity of Catalan, French, Italian, Latin, Old French, Portuguese, Romanian, and Spanish to the hypothesized pattern discounts Romance as an explanation for Galician's non-conformity. North Sami is countered by its Uralic cousins of Estonian, Finnish, Hungarian, and Komi Zyrian.

Data sparsity is a possibility—North Sami and Vietnamese both contain fewer than 1,000 structures analyzed—but Ancient Greek and Galician seem to have sufficient data, and other corpora with few structures conform to the hypothesis: Armenian (398), Belarusian (267), and so on.

Instead, a likely cause is noise from language-specific tagging and lemmatization in the UD corpora, amplified by the calculation of integration complexity, especially in multi-word cosisters. However, that noise actually makes the overall success rate—61 of 70, or 87.1% of languages—more impressive, as it suggests that a real structural regularity can be found in the data.

---

[3]Entropy is additive for independent systems (Wehrl, 1978). Because the integration of each dependent to its head is treated as a separate event—the integration of dependent *A* to head *B* is independent the integration of *B* to its head *C*—summing integration complexity should be sound.

Table 1: Results

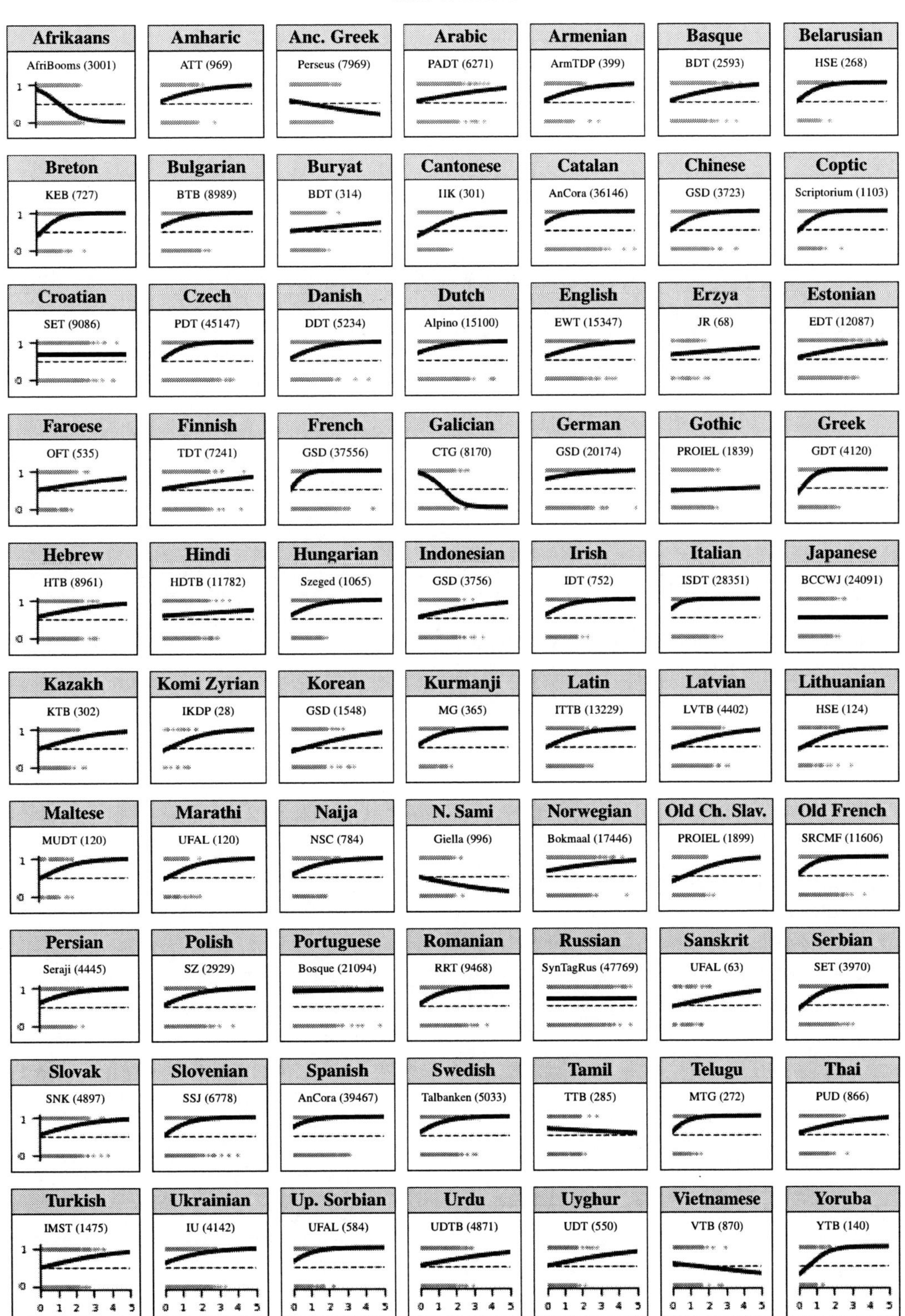

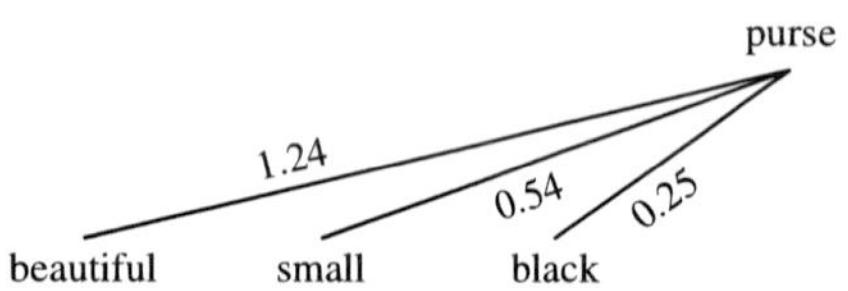

Figure 5: Hierarchical adjective order restrictions

Figure 6: Greenberg's Universal 20

6 Discussion

The findings of this study reveal a widespread cross-linguistic tendency to order isomorphic cosisters such that those placed nearest to the head have the lowest integration complexity (IC). Because this tendency seems to occur across all constituent types, many fine-grained models previously proposed for specific constituent types can be subsumed by an IC approach. Further, by combining IC with DDM, a general theory of constituent ordering based on integration cost begins to take shape.

6.1 Subsuming previous models

Previous constituent-specific models of ordering can be reformulated in terms of the larger insight of ordering based on integration complexity. For example, rather than appeal to an arbitrary adjective-specific hierarchy of features such as subjective comment, size, and color to explain the order of *beautiful small black purse*—preferred to other permutations (Teodorescu, 2006)—the order can be attributed to integration complexity and the pattern that cosisters with lower IC tend to be placed closest to the head. Figure 5 shows the IC of each adjective, and indeed they follow the pattern: *beautiful* (1.24 bits[4]), *small* (0.54 bits), and *black* (0.25 bits).

As to why adjectives of size or color should congregate with regard to their placement around the noun, because the distribution of size- or color-type adjectives is likely quite similar—the set of heads that *black* depends on is presumably similar to the set that *white* or *yellow* depend on as well—their IC is likely much the same. As such, the hierarchy reveals itself as an epiphenomenon resulting from the distributional similarity of classes of adjectives.

Other patterns of noun modifiers also seem to yield to an integration-complexity explanation. In Universal 20, Greenberg (1963) observes that

"When any or all of the items (demonstrative, numeral, and descriptive adjective) precede the noun, they are always in that order. If they follow, the order is either the same or its opposite." Dryer (2009) further refines the formulation based on a set of languages larger than Greenberg's, confirming the prenominal order as near-universal and showing that postnominal orders are vastly more likely to be the mirror order. However, why this pattern might be appears to be an open question.

Adopting an integration-complexity approach, we see in Figure 6 that the IC of the demonstrative *those* (1.67 bits) is larger than than of the numeral *three* (0.89 bits), which is itself larger than the adjective *big* (0.49 bits)[5]. Thus the IC of the noun modifiers[6] in *these three big houses* follows the established pattern that constituents placed closest to the head tend to have lower IC.

Other phenomena, such as heavy noun phrase shift, dative shift or alternation, and particle movement or placement (Gries, 1999; Wasow and Arnold, 2003), largely deal with deviations from the supposedly canonical verb-complement-adjunct order. However, both the canonical order and its deviations can be reformulated as an effect of a strategy based on integration complexity: because both complements and constituents with lower IC tend to be placed closest to the head, complements likely have lower IC than adjuncts. Similarly, deviations tend to occur when the adjunct has a lower IC than the complement.

Integration complexity is the more inclusive mechanism, able to account for preferred orders of adjectives, noun modifiers, and both the canonical order of complements and adjuncts as well as deviations from that order.

---

[5]UD marks demonstratives as "PronType=Dem" and cardinal numerals as "NumType=Card." Descriptive adjectives are not differentiated from modals or intensionals like *possible* or *former* by UD.

[6]There is an ongoing debate over whether demonstratives or determiners in general modify nouns and are therefore part of the noun phrase, or if nouns instead are the dependents of a larger determiner phrase (cf. Szabolsci, 1983; Abney, 1987; Hudson, 2004; Matthews, 2014). The current study follows UD and treats determiners as syntactic dependents of nouns.

---

[4]Here and throughout this section, integration complexity is calculated from the UD-English-EWT corpus.

6.2 Integration Cost

DDM measures the distance between a word and its head as the count of words intervening between the two (Liu et al., 2017). This count quantifies the distance-based cost of integrating dependents to their heads (Gibson, 1998, 2000). By introducing integration complexity as formulated in the current study as a sort of weight for each word, we are able to capture both the distance- and complexity-based parts of the cost of integration. Integration cost is therefore the sum of the integration complexity of a dependent and that of any words intervening between the dependent and its head.

Integration cost as so defined allows us to address another constituent-ordering phenomenon: English adverb placement. For example, Potsdam (1998), citing Jackendoff (1980), suggests that inserting the adverb *probably* into *Sam has been called* is possible in three preverbal positions but disfavored in a fourth. As the examples in Figure 7 show, it may appear clause-initially (S_1); immediately after the subject (S_2); immediately after a modal or finite auxiliary (S_3); but is disfavored immediately after a non-finite auxiliary (S_4).

Figure 7 also shows the integration complexity and cost of each dependent and the total integration cost for each variant. For example, *probably* has a complexity of 1.7 bits and an integration cost of 3.41 bits in S_1—the sum of the integration complexity of *probably* and that of each word intervening between *probably* and *called*: 1.7 (*probably*) + 0.81 (*Sam*) + 0.71 (*has*) + 0.19 (*been*). The total integration cost of S_1 is 6.21 bits, the sum of the cost of integrating each dependent in the sentence.

The total integration cost of the disfavored S_4 is 9.6 bits, higher than the acceptable variants S_1 (6.21), S_2 (7.1), and S_3 (8.09). The unacceptability of S_4 may derive from its higher integration cost.

Integration cost as defined here rests on dependency distance minimization and a pattern of placing isomorphic cosisters with lower integration complexity closest to the head, both of which are evident as widespread structural regularities in corpora, and seems capable of addressing various ordering phenomena previously unexplored or explained by constituent-specific models.

7 Summary

This study addresses the order preference of isomorphic cosisters—pairs of sister constituents of the same syntactic form on the same side of their

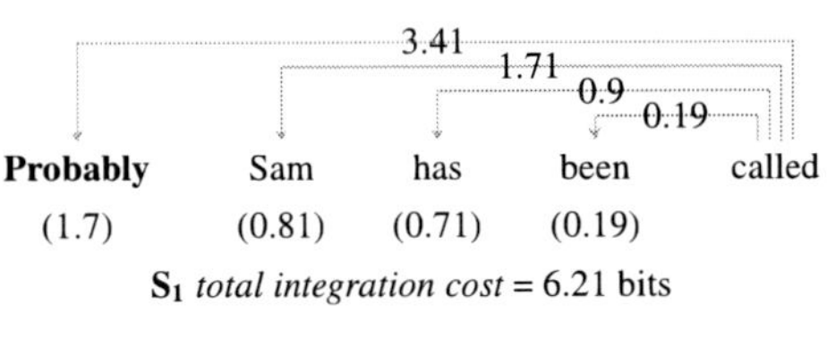

S_1 *total integration cost* = 6.21 bits

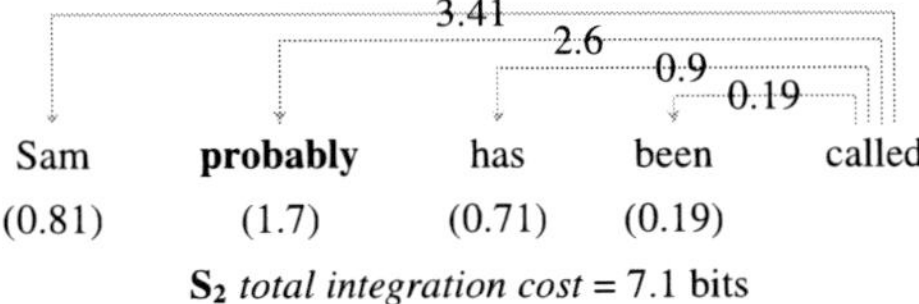

S_2 *total integration cost* = 7.1 bits

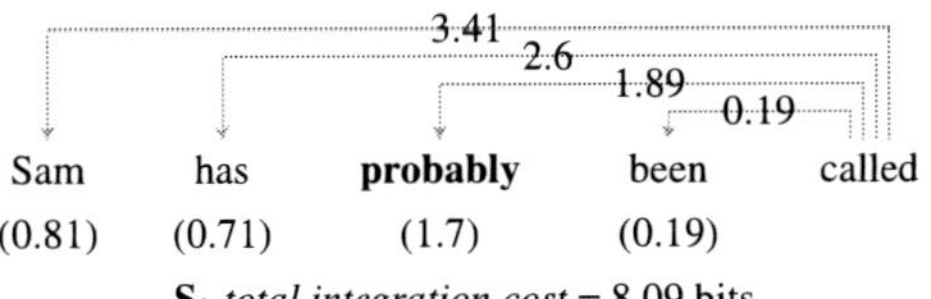

S_3 *total integration cost* = 8.09 bits

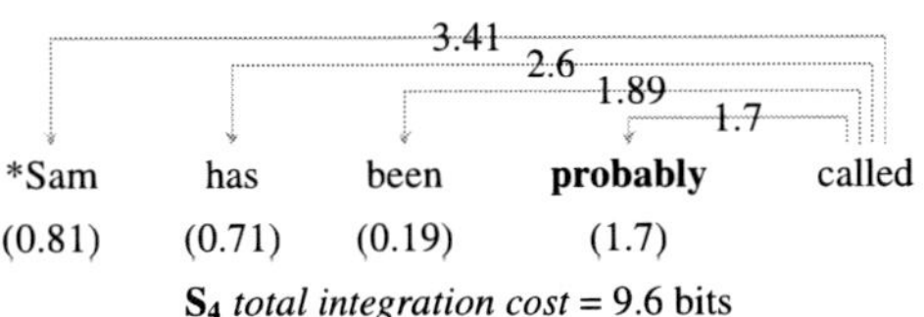

S_4 *total integration cost* = 9.6 bits

Figure 7: Integration cost of adverb placement

head—by building upon the insight that the cost of integrating dependents to their heads derives from the complexity of the integration and the distance between dependent and head (Gibson, 1998, 2000). Adopting methodology from Dependency Distance Minimization, which favors structures where the shorter of two cosisters appears closest to the head, this paper shows that as the integration complexity between two cosisters diverges, the tendency to place the constituent with the lower integration complexity closer to the head increases across most languages analyzed.

As such, this study contributes to the field by (1) providing a novel definition of integration complexity as the entropy of the probability distribution of the syntactic categories of a dependent word's heads; (2) demonstrating with a 70-language analysis that the order of isomorphic cosisters based on integration complexity describes a widespread cross-linguistic structural regularity; and (3) suggesting that many previously proposed constituent-specific ordering models can be subsumed by a more inclusive and externally motivated theory based on integration cost.

References

Steven P. Abney. 1987. *The English noun phrase in its sentential aspect*. Ph.D. thesis, Massachusetts Institute of Technology.

Otto Behaghel. 1930. Von deutscher Wortstellung [On German word order]. *Zeitschrift für Deutschkunde, Jargang 44 der Zeitschrift für deutschen Unterricht*, pages 81–9.

Otto Behaghel. 1932. *Deutsche Syntax eine geschichtliche Darstellung*. Carl Winters Unversitätsbuchhandlung, Heidelberg.

Eva Berlage. 2014. *Noun Phrase Complexity in English*. Cambridge University Press, Cambridge.

Claude Boisson. 1981. Hiérarchie universelle des spécifications de temps, de lieu, et de manière. *Confluents*, 7:69–124.

Dwight Bolinger. 1967. Adjectives in English: Attribution and Predication. *Lingua*, 18:1–34.

Gerlof Bouma. 2009. Normalized (pointwise) mutual information in collocation extraction. *Proceedings of GSCL*, pages 31–40.

Ramon Ferrer-i Cancho. 2004. Euclidean distance between syntactically linked words. *Physical Review E*, 70(056135):1–5.

Ramon Ferrer-i Cancho. 2017. Towards a theory of word order. Comment on" Dependency distance: a new perspective on syntactic patterns in natural language" by Haitao Liu et al. *Physics of Life Reviews*.

Noam Chomsky. 1975. *The Logical Structure of Linguistic Theory*. University of Chicago Press, Chicago. 1955.

Kenneth Ward Church and Patrick Hanks. 1989. Word association norms, mutual information, and lexicography. In *Proceedings of the 27th annual meeting on Association for Computational Linguistics -*, pages 76–83, Vancouver, British Columbia, Canada. Association for Computational Linguistics.

Guglielmo Cinque. 2001. "Restructuring" and functional structure. *University of Venice Working Papers in Linguistics*, 11:45–127.

Guglielmo Cinque. 2010. *The Syntax of Adjectives: A Comparative Study*. The MIT Press, Cambridge, Massachusetts.

T. M. Cover and Joy A. Thomas. 1991. *Elements of information theory*. Wiley series in telecommunications. Wiley, New York.

Peter Culicover and Ray Jackendoff. 2005. *Simpler Syntax*. Oxford linguistics. Oxford University Press.

Joseph H. Danks and Sam Glucksberg. 1971. Psychological scaling of adjective orders. *Journal of Verbal Learning and Verbal Behavior*, 10(1):63–7.

Matthew S. Dryer. 2009. On the order of demonstrative, numeral, adjective, and noun: an alternative to Cinque. In *Conference on theoretical approaches to disharmonic word orders*.

James Murray Feist. 2012. *Premodifiers in English*. Cambridge University Press, Cambridge.

Richard Futrell, Roger Levy, and Edward Gibson. 2017. Generalizing dependency distance. *Physics of Life Reviews*, 21:197–9.

Richard Futrell, Kyle Mahowald, and Edward Gibson. 2015. Large-scale evidence of dependency length minimization in 37 languages. *Proceedings of the National Academy of Sciences*, 112(33):10336–41.

Edward Gibson. 1998. Linguistic complexity: Locality of syntactic dependencies. *Cognition*, 68(1):1–76.

Edward Gibson. 2000. The dependency locality theory: A distance-based theory of linguistic complexity. *Image, language, brain*, pages 95–126.

Joseph Greenberg. 1963. Some universals of grammar with particular reference to the order of meaningful elements. In Joseph Greenberg, editor, *Universals of Grammar*, pages 73–113. MIT Press, Cambridge, Massachusetts.

Stefan T. Gries. 1999. Particle movement: A cognitive and functional approach. *Cognitive Linguistics*, 10(2).

Claude Hagège. 2010. *Adpositions*. Oxford University Press, Oxford.

John A. Hawkins. 2000. The relative order of prepositional phrases in English: Going beyond Manner–Place–Time. *Language variation and change*, 11(03):231–66.

John A. Hawkins. 2004. *Efficiency and Complexity in Grammars*. Oxford University Press, Oxford.

John A. Hawkins. 2014. *Cross-linguistic variation and efficiency*. Oxford University Press, New York.

Richard Hudson. 1995. Measuring syntactic difficulty.

Richard Hudson. 2004. Are determiners heads? *Functions of Language*, 11(1):7–42.

Ray Jackendoff. 1980. *Semantic Interpretation in Generative Grammar*. Studies in linguistics series. MIT Press.

E. T. Jaynes. 1957. Information Theory and Statistical Mechanics. *The Physical Review*, 106(4):620–30.

Hans Kamp and Barbara Partee. 1995. Prototype theory and compositionality. *Cognition*, 57:129–91.

Sven Kotowski. 2016. *Adjectival Modification and Order Restrictions*. De Gruyter, Berlin.

Richard Larson. 1998. Events and modification in nominals. In *Proceedings from Semantics and Linguistic Theory (SALT)*, volume 8, pages 145–68.

Richard Larson. 2000. Temporal modification in nominals. *Handout of paper presented at the International Round Table "The Syntax of Tense and Aspect" Paris, France.*

Haitao Liu, Chunshan Xu, and Junying Liang. 2017. Dependency distance: A new perspective on syntactic patterns in natural languages. *Physics of Life Reviews*, 21:171–93.

Peter Matthews. 2014. *The Positions of Adjectives in English.* Oxford University Press, New York.

Igor Mel'čuk. 2000. Dependency in Linguistic Description.

Frederick Newmeyer and Laurel Preston. 2014. *Measuring Grammatical Complexity.* Oxford University Press, Oxford.

Joakim Nivre, Marie-Catherine de Marneffe, Filip Ginter, Yoav Goldberg, Jan Hajic, Christopher D. Manning, Ryan McDonald, Slav Petrov, Sampo Pyysalo, Natalia Silveira, and others. 2016. Universal dependencies v1: A multilingual treebank collection. In *Proceedings of the 10th International Conference on Language Resources and Evaluation (LREC 2016)*, pages 1659–1666.

Timothy Osborne. 2007. The Weight of Predicates: A Dependency Grammar Analysis of Predicate Weight in German. *Journal of Germanic Linguistics*, 19(01):23–72.

Jinghui Ouyang and Jingyang Jiang. 2017. Can the Probability Distribution of Dependency Distance Measure Language Proficiency of Second Language Learners? *Journal of Quantitative Linguistics*, pages 1–19.

Barbara Partee. 2007. Compositionality and coercion in semantics: The dynamics of adjective meaning. *Cognitive foundations of interpretation*, pages 145–61.

Eric Potsdam. 1998. A Syntax for Adverbs. *Proceedings of the Twenty-seventh Western Conference on Linguistics*, 10:397–411.

Randolph Quirk, Sidney Greenbaum, Geoffrey Leech, and Jan Svartvik. 1985. *A Comprehensive Grammar of Contemporary English.* Longman, London.

Jan Rijkhoff. 1986. Word Order Universals Revisited: The Principle of Head Proximity. *Belgian Journal of Linguistics*, 1:95–125.

Jan Rijkhoff. 2000. When can a language have adjectives? An implicational universal. In Petra Vogel and Bernard Comrie, editors, *Approaches to the Typology of Word Classes*, pages 217–58. Mouton de Gruyter, New York.

Mats Rooth. 1992. A theory of focus interpretation. *Natural language semantics*, 1(1):75–116.

Walter Schweikert. 2004. The order of prepositional phrases. *Working Papers in Linguistics*, 14:195–216.

Gregory Scontras, Judith Degen, and Noah D. Goodman. 2017. Subjectivity Predicts Adjective Ordering Preferences. *Open Mind*, pages 1–14.

Gary-John Scott. 2002. Stacked adjectival modification and the structure of nominal phrases. In *Functional Structure in DP and IP: The Cartography of Syntactic Structures*, volume 1, pages 91–210. Oxford University Press, New York.

Claude Elwood Shannon. 1948. A mathematical theory of communication. *ACM SIGMOBILE Mobile Computing and Communications Review*, 5(1):3–55.

Jae Jung Song. 2012. *Word Order.* Cambridge University Press, New York.

Richard Sproat and Chilin Shih. 1991. The Cross-Linguistic Distribution of Adjective Ordering Restrictions. In Carol Georgopoulos and Roberta Ishihara, editors, *Interdisciplinary Approaches to Language*, pages 565 – 93. Kluwer Academic Publishers, Boston.

Robert Stockwell. 1977. *Foundations of syntactic theory.* Prentice-Hall foundations of modern linguistics series. Prentice-Hall.

Anna Szabolsci. 1983. The possessor that ran away from home. *The Linguistic Review*, 3(1):89–102.

David Temperley. 2008. Dependency-length minimization in natural and artificial languages. *Journal of Quantitative Linguistics*, 15(3):256–82.

Alexandra Teodorescu. 2006. Adjective ordering restrictions revisited. In *Proceedings of the 25th west coast conference on formal linguistics*, pages 399–407. Citeseer.

Lucien Tesnière. 1959. *Éléments de syntaxe structural.* Klincksieck, Paris.

Robert Truswell. 2009. Attributive adjectives and nominal templates. *Linguistic Inquiry*, 40(3):525–33.

Thomas Wasow. 1997. Remarks on grammatical weight. *Language Variation and Change*, 9(01):81–105.

Thomas Wasow and Jennifer Arnold. 2003. Postverbal constituent ordering in English. *Topics in English Linguistics*, 43:119–54.

Alfred Wehrl. 1978. General properties of entropy. *Reviews of Modern Physics*, 50(2):221–60.

Benjamin Lee Whorf. 1945. Grammatical Categories. *Language*, 21(1):1–11.

Paul Ziff. 1960. *Semantic Analysis.* Cornell University Press, Cornell, NY.

SUD or Surface-Syntactic Universal Dependencies:
An annotation scheme near-isomorphic to UD

Kim Gerdes*, Bruno Guillaume[†], Sylvain Kahane[◊], Guy Perrier[†]
*LPP, Sorbonne Nouvelle & CNRS
[†]Loria, Université de Lorraine & CNRS & INRIA, Nancy;
[◊]Modyco, Université Paris Nanterre & CNRS
`kim@gerdes.fr, bruno.guillaume@inria.fr,`
`sylvain@kahane.fr, guy.perrier@loria.fr`

Abstract

This article proposes a surface-syntactic annotation scheme called SUD that is near-isomorphic to the Universal Dependencies (UD) annotation scheme while following distributional criteria for defining the dependency tree structure and the naming of the syntactic functions. Rule-based graph transformation grammars allow for a bi-directional transformation of UD into SUD. The back-and-forth transformation can serve as an error-mining tool to assure the intra-language and inter-language coherence of the UD treebanks.

1 Introduction

Universal Dependencies (UD) is an astonishing collaborative project of dozens of research groups around the world, developing an annotation scheme that is applicable to all languages and proposing treebanks based on that scheme for more than 70 languages from different language families (Nivre et al. 2016). From the start, considerable efforts have been made to avoid an anglocentric scheme, going as far as analyzing English prepositions as case markers. The project is based on an ongoing and constantly evolving collaborative construction of the annotation scheme itself by means of an open online discussion group. The project welcomes and collaborates with enrichment efforts such as the enhanced UD annotation of deep syntax (Schuster & Manning 2016) or the annotation of multi-word expressions (Savary et al. 2015).

Just as any annotation project, UD had to make choices among the different annotation options that commonly reflect opposing goals and downstream applications of the resulting treebanks. UD decided to stick to simple tree structures (compared to graphs with multiple governors) and to favor content words as heads,

which is supposed to maximize "parallelism between languages because content words vary less than function words between languages" (UD Syntax: General Principles page http://universaldependencies.org/u/overview/syntax.html). The goal of "maximizing parallelism between languages" might be of use for parser development of neighboring languages, but reducing language differences makes the resulting treebank by definition less interesting for typological research on syntax. In particular, UD does not account for the hierarchy between functional words and tends to flatten syntactic structures. The content-word-centric annotation is also problematic for the internal cohesion of the treebank (cf. the difficulty of coherently annotating complex prepositions that usually contain a content word, Gerdes & Kahane 2016) and it marks a break with syntactic traditions, where headedness is defined by distributional properties of individual words (Bloomfield 1933), see Section 2.[1]

One of the central advantages of dependency grammar is the clear distinction of category (the POS, i.e. an intrinsic distributional class) and function (i.e. the specific role a word plays towards another word). Sentences such as *She became an architect and proud of it* which have given rise to a considerable amount of scholarly discussions (Sag 2003) because an X-bar based phrase structure analysis requires deciding on the category of the coordinated argument first. UD inherited from the Stanford parser[2] a mixed annotation scheme where relation labels include

---

[1] UD defines headedness indirectly via the category of the word: Content words are heads in UD and content words are usually understood as words belonging to open distributional classes, such as nouns, verbs, adjectives, and adverbs.

[2] The first versions of the Stanford parser were phrase structure based, providing trees that did not include functional information. The dependency output was a conversion from the phrase structure tree where the relations were computed from the category of the constituents (de Marneffe et al. 2006).

Proceedings of the Second Workshop on Universal Dependencies (UDW 2018), pages 66–74
Brussels, Belgium, November 1, 2018. ©2018 Association for Computational Linguistics

categories, as for example *nsubj* where the "n" indicates the category of the dependent. As a consequence of including the POS of the dependent in the relation name, UD has different labels for the same paradigm occupying the same syntactic position. For instance the complement of *consider* can be nominal or clausal as in *I consider this point / to leave / that you leave* and receives three different UD relation labels (*obj/xcomp/ccomp*).

We propose a new surface-syntactic annotation scheme, similar to UD, that we name SUD for *Surface-syntactic Universal Dependencies*. We want dependency links as well as the dependency labels to be defined based on purely syntactic criteria (Mel'čuk 1988), giving dependency structures closer to traditional dependency syntax (Meaning-Text Theory, Mel'čuk 1988; Word Grammar, Hudson 1984, 2007; Prague Dependency Treebank, Hajič et al. 2017) and headed constituency trees in phrase structure grammar (X-bar Syntax, Jackendoff 1977; Penn Treebank, Marcus et al. 1993). We also propose a hierarchy of SUD dependency relations that allows for under-specifications of dependency labeling.

We conceived the SUD scheme as an alternative to UD and not as a competing annotation scheme, which means that the annotation scheme should have the same information content, the information being only expressed another way. Put differently, we looked for an annotation scheme based on distributionial criteria with an elementary conversion going both ways without loss, i.e. an "isomorphic" annotation. Since the principles underlying SUD are different, the isomorphism with UD cannot be perfect. As a result, SUD is near-isomorphic to UD, and we have developed two treebank conversion grammars for the Grew platform (http://grew.fr, Bonfante et al. 2018): UD to SUD and SUD to UD. We will evaluate the differences between a UD treebank and the results of a double-conversion through SUD in Section 4.

SUD treebanks can be obtained by simple conversion from UD treebanks and can be useful for teaching and typological studies. Inversely, annotations can be done directly in SUD, and ultimately converted into UD. SUD annotations are less redundant and more economical than UD annotations. For instance SUD uses a simple *subj* relation because the nominal character of a subject should be indicated only once (as a POS). The distinction between clausal and nominal subjects can be recovered automatically from the POS of the subject and its context, but how this context is taken into account depends on the language.[3]

The conversion tool Grew and the conversion grammars are freely distributed, and we envision to propose the UD treebanks also under the automatically converted SUD scheme on the UD website.[4] This SUD annotation scheme proposal could benefit from future discussions and evolutions of the UD ecosystem.

As a side effect, the double UD→SUD→UD conversion provides a powerful error mining tool for UD treebanks. Trees that are not stable under this conversion very often contain non-standard uses of the UD annotation scheme that deserve special attention.

Section 2 explain what is surface syntax, what are the criteria defining a surface syntactic structure and how such a structure differs from UD trees. Our SUD annotation scheme is introduced in Section 3. The conversion between UD and SUD is presented in Section 4 and evaluated on the whole set of UD treebanks.

2 Surface Syntax

We will present defining criteria for a surface syntactic analysis following Mel'čuk 1988 who proposes three types of criteria: A: When to connect two words? B: Who is the governor in a connection? C: How to classify the dependencies?

2.1 Criteria for structural choices

The basic type A criterion is the stand-alone property or "autonomizability": Two words are connected if they can form a speech turn. For example in the sentence *The little boy talked to Mary* "the boy" or "to Mary" can stand alone with the same meaning, for instance as an answer to a question such as *Who talked to Mary?* or *Who did the little boy talk to?*. Autonomizability is not sufficient to determine a dependency structure as the set of connections does not necessarily form a tree, and we need further structural criteria to decide which links to preserve (Gerdes & Kahane 2011).

For instance, there are no simple criteria to establish a connection between *talk* and *to* or *talk* and *Mary* because both *talk to*, and *talk Mary* are ungrammatical speech turns. This connection can

---

[3] The clausal character of a phrase is more or less explicit depending on the language. If a language allows for clauses without subjects, without subordinating conjunctions, or without verbs, the conversion SUD → UD has to be adapted accordingly. If all three indicators are absent while the clause-noun distinction remains relevant, we would have to rely on an additional feature in SUD in order to obtain a correct transformation.

[4] For the time being, the SUD treebanks are available on https://gitlab.inria.fr/grew/SUD

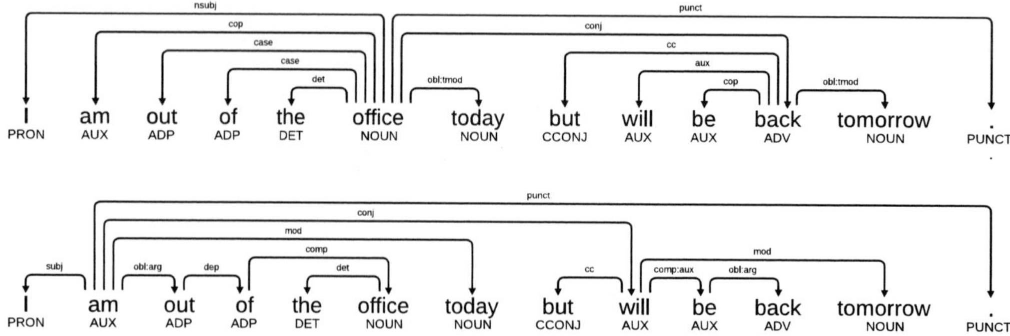

Figure 1: UD and SUD analysis of the same sentence (UD_English-EWT@2.2 email-enronsent38_01-0114)

be established by means of criteria of type B determining who, *to* or *Mary,* is the head of *to Mary*. At this point, UD parts with surface syntax criteria and applies the criterion of "content word as head" whereas surface syntax uses distributional criteria of each individual word. The main criterion is that **the surface syntactic head determines the distribution of the unit**. For instance, *Mary* and *to Mary* have a profoundly different distribution as they can never commute:

Mary slept vs. **To Mary slept.*
The boy talked to Mary vs. **The boy talked Mary.*

This suffices to show that *Mary* is not the head. Although we cannot test whether *to* has the same distribution as *to Mary* because a preposition such as *to* never appears without a noun or a verb, we consider *to* to be the head, a choice that is consistent with most if not all theoretical syntactic frameworks.[5] The same reasoning can be applied to the auxiliary-verb connection such as *has chosen* or the copula-adjective connection such as *is happy*: *chosen* never commutes with *has chosen*.[6]

A less clear case of function words as heads is the case of a conjunct in a coordination: *I invited Bill and Mary*. In most positions, *Mary* and *and Mary* cannot commute (again *and* cannot stand alone and cannot be tested). Here a second distributional criterion can be used: A dependent does not change the distribution of its governor. This shows that *Mary* cannot be considered as a dependent of *and*, because the commutation of *Mary* with units of other POSs (*and red, and is*

sleeping, etc.) completely changes the distribution of the phrase.

Note that the case of the determiner-noun connections is less clear-cut. Both UD and traditional surface syntax (Mel'čuk 1988) chooses the noun as the head although *boy* and *the boy* do not have the same distribution. The DP analysis makes the opposite choice (Hudson 1984, 2007, Abney 1987). For these two controversial cases, we keep the UD analysis with the functional word as a dependent.

As an illustration of the flat UD structures compared to SUD, consider Figure 1 showing the analyses of *I am out of the office today but will be back tomorrow*. The UD tree has depth 3 and a maximum number of 8 dependents per node whereas the SUD tree has depth 5 and only a maximum number of 5 dependents per node. We generalize this observation into a general principle: We believe that the syntactic structure follows the *dependency length minimization principle:* "Languages tend to minimize the surface syntactic dependency length" because this reduces the cognitive load of language processing (Liu 2008, Futrell et al. 2015). We use this argument to attach each conjunct to its closest neighbor conjuncts and to attach shared dependents to the closest conjunct. This gives us a chaining analysis of coordination instead of UD's bouquet analysis.[7] Figure 2 shows an example that illustrates the structural differences for coordination between UD and SUD.

---

[5] The tokenization is quintessential here. If an annotation scheme of a inflectional language decides to separate case markers, such a case marker will become the head of the word (Groß 2011).

[6] If the dependent of an *aux* relation is optional, invariable, and non-verbal, it should be tagged as PART. Then it will not be promoted to the head-position in the UD → SUD conversion.

[7] One of the arguments in favor of a bouquet analysis is to allow the disambiguation of embedded coordinations such as *A and B or C*: For *(A and B) or C, or C* depends on *A*, while for *A and (B or C), or C* depends on *B*. Nevertheless, this disambiguation is partial because in case of a flat coordination such as *A, B, or C*, we see that or *C* also depends on *A* and thus, the bouquet structure cannot distinguish the embedded *(A and B) or C* situation from the flat *A, B, or C* situation.

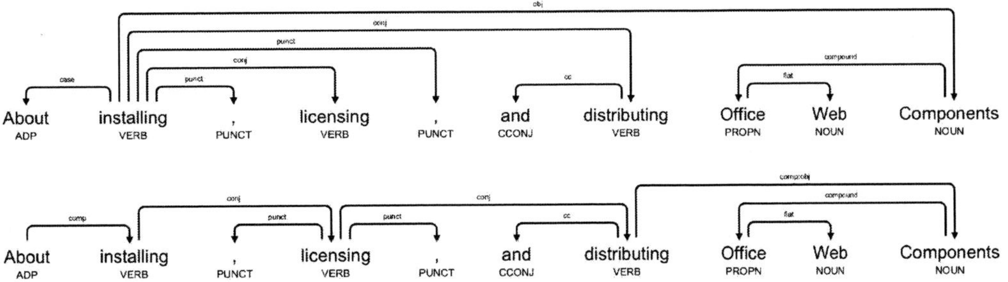

Figure 2: Coordination in UD and in SUD
(UD_English-LinES@2.2 257, comma attachment as in the original treebank).

2.2 Criteria for dependency labels

We need criteria to decide whether two dependencies (in two different sentences) must be labeled by the same relation or not. Our first criterion allows us to decide when the governors are the same: If two dependents occupy the same position, i.e. they are mutually exclusive, they must be connected to their governor by the same relation.[8] This implies that in *This apple is good for you* and *Eating this apple is good for you*, both *this apple* and *eating this apple* must have the same function. Equally, *that apple* and *to eat that apple* have the same function in *I want that apple* and *I want to eat that apple*. This criterion is currently not used in UD (cf. *nsubj* vs. *csubj* for subjects and *obj* vs. *xcomp* for objects).

Our second criterion is used to decide whether a dependent D that appears in two governor-dependent relations in two different sentences should be labeled with the same function: The relations are the same if the paradigms of units that can commute with D in the two positions are roughly the same, semantic constraints apart. As an example of a semantic selectional restriction, we establish the same *subject* positions for "think" and "sink" although the paradigms are not exactly the same: *the boat sinks* vs. *???the boat thinks*.[9] Inversely, the French verbs *parler* 'talk' and *penser* 'think' both have a complement with the preposition *à* 'to', but the pronominalization of these arguments is different: *parler à Mary* 'talk to Mary' → *lui parler* 'speak to her' vs.

penser à Mary 'think of Mary' → *penser à elle* 'think of her'. This could lead us to distinguishing two types of arguments (e.g. "indirect object" vs. "oblique complement").[10]

Two positions only rarely have exactly the same paradigms and constraints, but they can be more or less similar. Thus, the notion of function is not absolute but rather relative, which justifies a hierarchy of functions, thus allowing for choosing between coarser or finer grained analyses.

Although, as we have shown, UD has a tendency to use several relation labels for the same syntactic function, the UD annotation scheme can also combine two syntactic functions into one: For example, all PP dependents of a verb are connected with the same relation *obl* to their governor, conflating prepositional arguments and repeatable modifiers.[11]

3 SUD

With this basis, we have developed an annotation scheme that attempts to remain as close as possible to the UD annotation scheme while obeying to surface-syntactic criteria. The SUD annotation scheme is a surface-syntax annotation

---

[8] The inverse is not a necessary condition: We can decide to group together under one relation label two dependents that can co-occur with the same governor, in particular modifiers of verbs or of nouns, which can be repeated.

[9] Put differently, the set of elements that can occupy *sink*'s subject position and the set of elements that can occupy *think*'s subject position are different. But the two sets are sufficiently similar and the restriction seems to be of semantic nature that we decide not to introduce an "animate-subject" relation and an "inanimate-subject" relation, but to simply use the *subj* function for these verbs' first positions.

[10] A third criterion states that redistribution and agreement constraints for both dependency should be the same. As an example of different redistributions, consider *cost* vs. *win*: *Peter won 100€* can be passivized but not *The book costs 100€*. Accordingly, an annotation scheme can decide to establish two distinct functions (e.g. "direct object" vs "measure complement").

In SUD, we unite all these cases under the function name *comp*, see Section 3.1, therefore not distinguishing "indirect objects" from "oblique complements" or "direct objects" from "measure complements".

[11] Several UD treebanks decided to keep the verbal valency and thus to mark the distinction between prepositional arguments and modifiers, for example by means of *obl:arg* vs. *obl:mod*, such as Arabic, Cantonese, Chinese, Czech, French, Hindi, Polish, Sanskrit, and Slovak. The secondary annotation label of this argument vs. modifier distinction has not yet been unified across languages and some treebanks use *:tmod*, *:npmod*, and *:loc* vs. *:agent* among others.

scheme, which implies in particular that: 1. Contrarily to UD, function words such as adpositions, subordinating conjunctions, auxiliaries, and copulas are heads. 2. Words that are in the same paradigm of commutation (and thus occupy the same syntactic position) have the same function, i.e. they are connected to their governor by the same syntactic relation.

3.1 Structural choices

In a nutshell, UD's *case, mark, aux,* and *cop* dependencies are inverted while other UD dependency directions are preserved. In particular, we kept coordinating conjunctions and determiners as dependents (see Section 2.1).

The directional changes of a relation opens the question of the attachment of the dependents involved in the changes. In UD, function words do not have dependents, but in surface syntax, modifiers of the whole phrase are traditionally attached to the head, which can now be a function word. Put differently, we have to decide which dependents are attached to the function word and which remains on the lexical word. It is generally accepted that the subject is a dependent of the auxiliary or the copula, with whom it agrees in inflectional languages. Highly grammaticalized elements such as negation should go onto the auxiliary whereas arguments should remain on the lexical element. For the sake of simplicity, all modifiers have been attached on the auxiliary in SUD and all arguments except the subject remain on the lexical verb.[12] Conjuncts need special rules to be handled correctly, because sometimes they must be raised (*Mary was sleeping and knew it*) and sometimes not (*Mary was sleeping and snoring*).

3.2 Labeling choices

SUD introduces four new relations: *subj, comp, mod,* and *unknown* and reassign a more specific meaning to the *dep* label. All subjects have the function **subj**, grouping together UD's *nsubj* and *csubj*. All other arguments of adjectives and verbs have the function **comp**, bundling UD's *obj, iobj, xcomp,* and *ccomp; comp* is also used for all complements of function words such as auxiliaries, copulas, adpositions, and subordinating conjunctions, thus replacing UD's *aux, cop, case,* and *mark*. Modifiers have the function **mod** wherever we can clearly distinguish the modifiers

from arguments. If not, we use the **dep** relation to indicate that we cannot.[13] This **dep** relation is particularly useful for PP attachments to nouns but also for UD's *obl* relation if it is not specified further as *obl:arg* or *obl:mod*. If we have the argument-modifier distinction for PP dependents of verbs we classify *obl:arg* as *comp* and *obl:mod* as *mod*. If the nature of the relation cannot be determined, we use the **unknown** label (where UD used the *dep* label), which becomes the hypernym of all SUD relations (Figure 3).

Compared to UD we thus grouped together relation labels whenever the distinction between them is purely categorical, i.e. contingent on the POS of the governor or the dependent. To avoid annotation redundancy, we do not use UD's *acl, advcl, advmod, amod, aux, case, ccomp, cop, csubj, iobj, mark, nmod, nsubj, nummod, obj, obl,* and *xcomp* relations. All other UD relation labels are preserved.

SUD dependency	Corresponding UD dependencies
dep	*acl, amod, nmod, nummod, obl*
comp	*aux, ccomp, iobj, obj, obl:arg, xcomp, cop, mark, case*
mod	*advcl, advmod, obl:mod*
subj	*csubj, nsubj*

Table 1: SUD and corresponding UD relation labels

As a general principle of allowing a varying granularity of dependency relation labels, but also to assure the convertibility with UD, SUD relies heavily on secondary relation labels that are, just like in UD, separated from the main label by a colon: *primary:secondary*. These secondary labels are optional in a simple native SUD annotation but necessary for a full convertibility into UD. On the contrary, the converted SUD uses the distinction between *comp:aux* and *comp:pass* to discriminate the complement of an AUX used as a tense auxiliary and as a passive auxiliary, and it also uses *comp:cop* or *comp:caus* for the conversion of UD's *cop* and *aux:caus*. The UD relations *iobj* and *obl:arg* both give *comp:obl* in SUD, *ccomp* and *obj* give *comp:obj*, and *xcomp* gives *comp:rais* (Table 2).[14]

---

[12] A native SUD annotation might choose to propose more specific rules defining the distribution of modifiers between the function verb and the lexical verb. This has no incidence on the automatically obtained corresponding UD analysis, because such a distinction is flattened when converting into UD.

[13] The *dep* relation thus becomes a hypernym of *comp, mod* and *subj*, as well as *cc* and *det*.

[14] Although *comp:obj* and *comp:obl* are clearly sub-functions of *comp*, this is not stricto sensu the case of *comp:rais*. For example, we consider that (Fr.) *dormir* 'to sleep' and *que tu dormes* 'that you sleep' have the same function *comp:obj* in the context *Je veux _* 'I want _', while *que tu dormes* has a different function *comp:obl* in the context *Je m'étonne _* 'I'm surprised _', where it commutes with a PP *de ça* 'of that'. A native SUD annotation could thus distinguish *comp:obj:rais* from *comp:obl:rais* by means of triple labels.

UD dependency	SUD dependency	UPOS of the governor	UPOS of the dependent	Other relations starting on the dependent
obl	dep	ADJ| VERB		
ad		NOUN| PROPN| PRON	ADP	comp ->VERB
ad		NOUN| PROPN| PRON	VERB	
amod			ADJ	
nmod		NOUN| PROPN| PRON	ADP	comp ->NOUN| PROPN| PRON
nummod			NUM	
advd	mod	ADJ| VERB	ADP	comp ->VERB
advd		ADJ| VERB	ADJ| VERB	
advmod			ADV	
obl:mod			ADP	comp ->NOUN| PROPN| PRON
obj	comp:obj		NOUN| PROPN| PRON	
ccomp	comp:obj		VERB	
ccomp	comp:obj		SCONJ	comp ->VERB
ccomp	comp:obl		SCONJ	comp ->VERB
iobj	comp:obl		PRON	
iobj	comp:obl		ADP	comp ->NOUN| PROPN| PRON
obl:arg	comp:obl		ADV	
csubj	subj		VERB	
nsubj	subj		NOUN| PROPN| PRON	
xcomp	comp:rais			

Table 2: UD-SUD transformation correspondences

4 Convertibility between UD and SUD

The conversion UD → SUD is done in three main steps: 1) transforming the bouquet structure into a chaining analysis (for relations *conj, fixed* and *flat*); 2) reversing relations *aux, cop, mark* and *case*; 3) mapping UD relations to SUD relations following Table 2. The reverse conversion (SUD → UD) also proceeds in three steps in the same vein.

The second step is the most problematic because a lexical head can have several function words depending on it (up to 7 in UD_Japanese!). In such a case, we must decide which one depends on which one.

To do this, we rely on a universal hierarchy of relations that the auxiliaries have with the main verb, in particular *mark* relations are higher than *aux* relations and time and aspect auxiliaries are higher than voice auxiliaries (Van Valin 1984, Cinque 1999). When this information is unavailable we rely on the word order: The closest function word is the SUD governor of the lexical head, the next one is the SUD governor of the first one, and so on.

The conversions (UD → SUD and SUD → UD) we proposed are encoded in a rule-based system. The rules are organized by means of a separation of a universal core rule set and a language specific rule set, which for the time being has only been implemented for French.

We use the Grew software (http://grew.fr) based on a computational Graph Rewriting Model. Each conversion is encoded as a graph rewriting system (GRS): a set of rules and a strategy describing how the rule applications must be ordered. Below, we give an example of an UD → SUD rule for the inversion of *mark*:

```
rule left_mark {
    pattern { e:H-[mark]->X1; X1 << H }
    without { H-[aux|aux:pass|aux:caus|cop|
      mark|case]->X2; X1 << X2 }
    commands {
        del_edge e;
        add_edge X1-[comp]-> H;
        shift_out H =[aux|aux:pass|aux:caus|
          cop|mark|case|conj|cc|root]=> X1; } }
```

The rule contains three parts: the *pattern* part says that the rule applies on a dependency *e* labeled *mark*, with a dependent X1 preceding its head H; the *without* part ensures that there is no other element *aux, cop, case* or *mark* depending on H between X1 and H; the *commands* part describes the required modifications on the structure: delete the matched edge *e*, add a new edge *comp* in the reverse order, and the *shift_out* command gives the list of relations that must be moved from node H to node X1. It is worth noting that *aux, case, cop*, and *mark* that remain to be inverted must be raised onto the auxiliary.

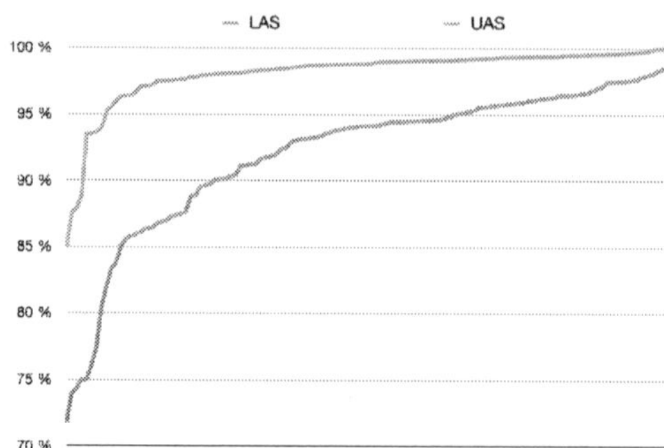

Figure 3: LAS and UAS of UD→SUD→UD transformations across the UD 2.2 treebanks, displayed on the X-axis by ascending LAS (resp. UAS) order.

We have evaluated the results of the double conversion (from UD to SUD first and then from SUD back to UD) against the original UD annotation with the 122 corpora of version 2.2. The experiment were conducted on the test part of each corpus. The median value of the LAS scores is 94.1%. Three corpora have a LAS score below 75%: UD_Korean-Kaist (71.8%), UD_Japanese-BCCWJ (74.0%) and UD_Japanese-GSD (74.4%). The 3 highest values are for UD_Hungarian-Szeged (98.6%), UD_Italian-ParTUT (98.4%), and UD_Italian-PoSTWITA (98.3%). The median value of the UAS scores is 98.8%. The 3 lowest scores are for UD_Yoruba-YTB (85.0%), UD_Japanese-GSD (87.5%) and UD_Japanese-PUD (87.9%). Two corpora have a 100% UAS score: UD_Warlpiri-UFAL and UD_Telugu-MTG.

Figure 4 shows the distribution of LAS (blue curve) and UAS (green curve) on the 122 treebanks. The two curves present the ordered set of values of LAS/UAS (not corresponding to the same corpus ordering). Although the scores are very high, the procedure does not allow to evaluate the two conversion systems separately: A dependency may remain unaffected by both conversions when it should have been, and this error will not be detected.

One central source of the discrepancy between a corpus and its double conversion is the inconsistency between a relation name and the POS of its dependent. For instance, the conversion UD→SUD always produces *dep* for an *amod*, but the SUD→UD is not able to recover *amod* if the dependent is not an ADJ. In the corpus with the lowest LAS score (UD_Korean-Kaist), we observed many unusual associations of relation and POS. In the whole corpus UD_Korean-PUD, 22.4% of the *advmod* relations have a dependent that is not an ADV, and 43.5%

of the *aux* relations have a dependent which is not an AUX. In the corpus UD_Korean-PUD, all the 323 *aux* relations have a dependent which is not an AUX. Until now, we have only designed a set of generic rules that may be refined for each language and it is difficult to draw conclusions about the full set of corpora.

A part of these inconsistencies may also be linked to MWEs: An MWE as a whole often has a POS which is different from the POS of its first token. In UD 2.2, 4 corpora contain the feature MWEPOS to annotate the POS of the MWEs (the conversion in the evaluation curves above does not uses this feature). If this information is taken into account in the conversions, the LAS scores significantly increase in 3 of the 4 cases (UD_French-Sequoia: +1.05%, UD_Catalan-AnCora: +0.80%, UD_Spanish-AnCora: +0.75% and UD_Portuguese-Bosque: +0.08%).

We believe that a further exploration of these inconsistencies could provide a crucial step for the improvement of the treebanks as well as the conversion rules. As a next experiment, we plan to introduce a new feature UDPOS to add the expected POS where the current UD POS is unexpected. Then, each UDPOS have to be interpreted as: 1) an annotation error, 2) a place where a MWEPOS is missing, or 3) a special usage of the relation that should be taken into account in the language specific conversion rules.

5. Conclusion

Based on UD, we propose a new annotation scheme, SUD, which follows standard distributional criteria for headedness and relation labeling and is thus closer to traditional constituency-based surface syntax as well as to dependency-based surface syntax. This means in particular that this new scheme can be employed more easily by users and annotators that are trained in more traditional forms of syntax. As an experiment, we are now developing a new treebank directly in SUD and this treebank will subsequently be converted into UD, the automatic transformation providing a quality and coherence control of the SUD annotation.

Such a format is useful for every computation that concerns the form of the sentence such as word order (Chen et al. submitted) and the relation to prosody, etc. Conversely, UD might be a better entry point to the semantic content of the sentence.

The lower dependency length gives psycholinguistic support to SUD treebanks. Possibly related is the fact that various experiments on parser performance also consistently give an advantage to function-word-headed structures (Schwartz et al. 2012, Silveira and Manning 2015, Kirilin and Versley 2015, Rehbein et al. 2017)[15] which provides another *raison d'être* for parallel SUD treebanks.

The whole UD 2.2 database, with its 122 treebanks, has been converted into SUD and is already accessible at https://gitlab.inria.fr/grew/SUD. We would like to see this alternative to be distributed on the UD website as soon as possible and hope that the new scheme will benefit from discussions with the whole community and evolve in parallel to the UD scheme. Then SUD would become an alternative annotation option for UD treebank developers.

As a last point, it appears that the conversion between UD and SUD sheds light on some potential problems in UD treebanks. We have to better understand why the double conversion UD→SUD→UD gives bad results on some treebanks and to what extent this is due to problems in our conversion grammar, or rather caused by an unexpected usage of the UD scheme that could be fixed, either by correcting the treebank or by adapting the annotation reference guide to include and standardize the new analyses of a given construction. It might be useful to adapt the SUD conversion for each language, which could eventually allow for isomorphic transformations.[16] Making the UD treebanks SUD compliant would lead to a more homogeneous annotation and could lead the way in the ongoing discussion towards the upcoming UD 3.0 annotation scheme.

References

Leonard Bloomfield. 1933. *Language*.

Xinying Chen, Kim Gerdes, Sylvain Kahane. Submitted. Typometrics: From Implicational to Quantitative Universals in Word Order Typology.

Guglielmo Cinque, 1999. Adverbs and functional heads: A cross-linguistic perspective. Oxford University Press.

Marie-Catherine de Marneffe, Bill MacCartney, Christopher D. Manning. 2006. Generating typed dependency parses from phrase structure parses. *Proceedings of LREC.*

Richard Futrell, Kyle Mahowald, Edward Gibson. 2015. Large-scale evidence of dependency length minimization in 37 languages. *Proceedings of the National Academy of Sciences, 112*(33), 10336-10341.

Kim Gerdes, Sylvain Kahane. 2011. Defining dependencies (and constituents). *Proceedings of the First International Conference on Dependency Linguistics (Depling 2011).*

Kim Gerdes, Sylvain Kahane. 2016. Dependency annotation choices: Assessing theoretical and practical issues of universal dependencies. *Proceedings of the 10th Linguistic Annotation Workshop held in conjunction with ACL 2016 (LAW-X 2016).*

Thomas Groß. 2011. Catenae in morphology. *Proceedings of the First International Conference on Dependency Linguistics (Depling 2011).*

Guillaume Bonfante, Bruno Guillaume, Guy Perrier. 2018. *Application of Graph Rewriting to Natural Language Processing.* John Wiley & Sons.

Jan Hajič, Eva Hajičová., Marie Mikulová, Jiří Mírovský. 2017. Prague Dependency Treebank. *Handbook of Linguistic Annotation.* Springer, Dordrecht. 555-594.

Ray Jackendoff. 1977. *X-bar syntax: A Study of Phrase Structure*, Linguistic Inquiry Monograph 2. Cambridge, MA: MIT Press.

Angelika Kirilin, Yannick Versley. 2015. What is hard in Universal Dependency Parsing. *Proceedings of the 6th Workshop on Statistical Parsing of Morphologically Rich Languages (SPMRL 2015).*

Haitao Liu. 2008. Dependency distance as a metric of language comprehension difficulty. *Journal of Cognitive Science, 9(2),* 159-191.

Mitchell P. Marcus, Mary Ann Marcinkiewicz, Beatrice Santorini. 1993. Building a large annotated corpus of English: The Penn Treebank. *Computational linguistics 19.2:* 313-330.

Igor Mel'čuk. 1988. *Dependency Syntax: Theory and Practice*, SUNY Press.

Ines Rehbein, Julius Steen, Bich-Ngoc Do. 2017. Universal Dependencies are hard to parse—or are they? *Proceedings of the Fourth International Conference on Dependency Linguistics (Depling 2017).*

Ivan A. Sag. 2003. Coordination and underspecification. *Proceedings of the 9th International Conference on HPSG.*

Agata Savary, et al. 2015. PARSEME–PARSing and Multiword Expressions within a European multilingual network. *7th Language & Technology Conference: Human Language Technologies as a Challenge for Computer Science and Linguistics (LTC 2015).*

Sebastian Schuster, Christopher D. Manning. 2016. Enhanced English Universal Dependencies: An

---

[15] Although the advances in neural parsers trained on sufficient data probably will ultimately wipe out any differences (because the parser can independently learn the UD-SUD transformation rules).

[16] This aspect distinguishes SUD from Enhanced UD. The latter is clearly a new level of annotation with additional information. On the contrary, SUD is an alternative encoding of UD information.

Improved Representation for Natural Language Understanding Tasks." *Proceedings of LREC*.

Roy Schwartz, Omri Abend, Ari Rappoport. 2012. Learnability-based syntactic annotation design. In *Proceedings of COLING 24*, 2405–2422.

Natalia Silveira, Christopher Manning. 2015. Does Universal Dependencies need a parsing representation? An investigation of English. *Proceedings of the Third International Conference on Dependency Linguistics (Depling 2015)*.

Robert D. Van Valin Jr. 1984. A typology of syntactic relations in clause linkage. In *Annual meeting of the Berkeley Linguistics Society* (Vol. 10, pp. 542-558).

Coordinate Structures in Universal Dependencies
for Head-final Languages

Hiroshi Kanayama
IBM Research
Tokyo, Japan
hkana@jp.ibm.com

Na-Rae Han
University of Pittsburgh
Pittsburgh, PA
naraehan@pitt.edu

Masayuki Asahara
NINJAL, Japan
Tokyo, Japan
masayu-a@ninjal.ac.jp

Jena D. Hwang
IHMC
Ocala, FL
jhwang@ihmc.us

Yusuke Miyao
University of Tokyo
Tokyo, Japan
yusuke@is.s.u-tokyo.ac.jp

Jinho Choi
Emory University
Atlanta, GA
jinho.choi@emory.edu

Yuji Matsumoto
Nara Institute of Science and Technology
Nara, Japan
matsu@naist.jp

Abstract

This paper discusses the representation of coordinate structures in the Universal Dependencies framework for two head-final languages, Japanese and Korean. UD applies a strict principle that makes the head of coordination the left-most conjunct. However, the guideline may produce syntactic trees which are difficult to accept in head-final languages. This paper describes the status in the current Japanese and Korean corpora and proposes alternative designs suitable for these languages.

1 Introduction

The Universal Dependencies (UD) (Nivre et al., 2016, 2017) is a worldwide project to provide multilingual syntactic resources of dependency structures with a uniformed tag set for all languages. The dependency structure in UD was originally designed based on the Universal Stanford Dependencies (De Marneffe et al., 2014), in which the left-most conjunct was selected as the head node in coordinate structures. After some modifications, the current UD (version 2) uses the definition as shown in Figure 1.

The UD principles include a simple mandate: the left word is always the head in parallel and sequential structures, including coordination, apposition and multi-word expressions. The rationale behind this uniformity is that these structures do not involve true dependency, and having a single direction for conj relations on the assumption that coordinate structures are completely paratac-

tic, both within and across languages, is advantageous. However, as discussed in several proposal for extended representation of coordination structures (Gerdes and Kahane, 2015; Schuster and Manning, 2016), they cannot be straightforwardly represented as dependencies. Especially in head-final languages such as Japanese and Korean, the left-headed structure poses some fundamental issues due to hypotactic attributes in terms of syntax in coordinate structures.

This paper points out the issues in the treatment of coordinate structures with evidence of linguistic plausibility and the trainability of parsers, reports on the current status of the corpora in those languages, and proposes alternative representations.

Section 2 describes the linguistic features of head-final languages, and Section 3 points out the problems in the left-headed coordinate structures in head-final languages. Section 4 summarizes the current status of UD Japanese (Tanaka et al., 2016; Asahara et al., 2018) and UD Korean (Chun et al., 2018) corpora released as version 2.2. Section 5 shows the experimental results on multiple corpora in Japanese and Korean to attest the difficulty in training with left-headed coordination. Section 6 proposes a revision to the UD guidelines more suited to head-final languages.

2 Head-final languages

Both Japanese and Korean are strictly head-final agglutinative languages in which most dependencies between content words have the head in the

75

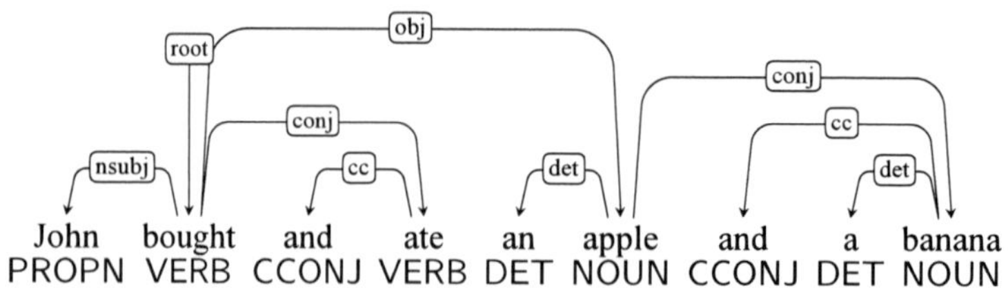

Figure 1: English coordinate structures ("bought and ate" and "an apple and a banana") in UD v2.

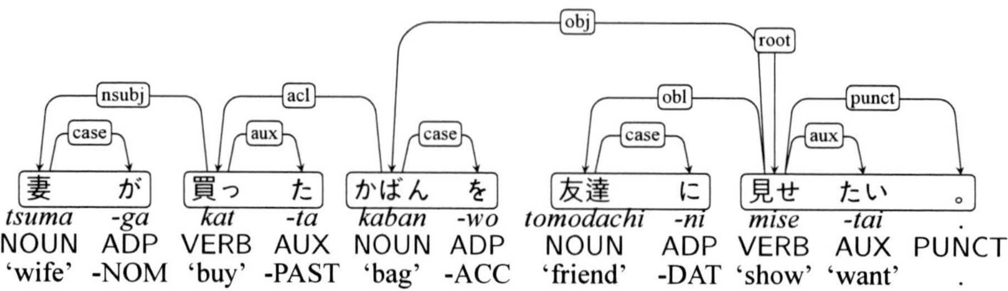

Figure 2: A head-final dependency structure of a Japanese sentence "妻が買ったかばんを友達に見せたい" ('(I) want to show the bag which (my) wife bought to (my) friend').

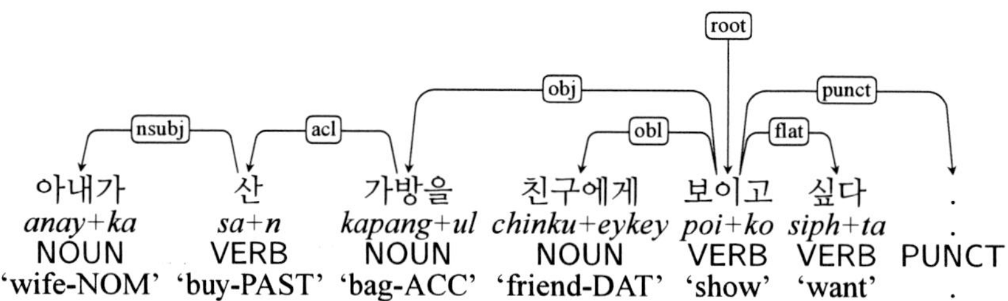

Figure 3: A head-final dependency structure of a Korean sentence "아내가 산 가방을 친구에게 보이고 싶다.", which is parallel to that in Figure 2.

right. Figures 2 and 3 depict the dependency structures in Universal Dependencies for Japanese and Korean sentences, respectively. Both have right-headed dependencies except for functional words and punctuations.

Japanese has a well-known phrasal unit, called *bunsetsu*—each unit is marked with a rounded rectangle in Figure 2. A *bunsetsu* consists of a content word (or multiple words in the case of a compound) and zero or more functional words such as postpositional case markers (ADP), particles (PART) and auxiliary verbs (AUX).

Korean has a similar unit called *eojeol*. It typically consists of a content word optionally followed by highly productive verbal or nominal suffixation, and, unlike Japanese *bunsetsu*, it is marked by white space in orthography. Figure 3

shows a Korean counterpart to Figure 2, where the syntax and the main dependency relations mirror those of the Japanese example. The main departure here is that the Korean UD's treatment of postposition suffixes and verbal endings are dependent morphemes in the *eojeol*-based Korean orthography, and thus, are neither tokenized nor assigned separate dependency relations.

UD corpora from both languages are converted from dependency or constituency corpora based on *bunsetsu* or *eojeol* units. In Japanese, functional words in each *bunsetsu* (ADP, AUX and PUNCT in Figure 2) must depend on the head word in the *bunsetsu* (NOUN and VERB). In the Korean example of Figure 3, the last verb "싶다" ('want') behaves as a function word though it is tagged as VERB, thus it is attached to the main verb with flat label. As for the dependencies between content words, the right-hand unit is always the head. The exceptions are limited to special cases such as annotations using parentheses, but when the UD's left-headedness principle is adopted, multi-word expressions and coordination are added to exceptional cases.

In addition to these two languages, Tamil is categorized as a rigid head-final language (Polinsky, 2012). According to the typological classification using statistics of UD corpora (Chen and Gerdes, 2017), Japanese and Korean fall into a similar class in terms of distance of dependencies. The same goes for Urdu and Hindi, but they have more flexibility in word order including predicates.

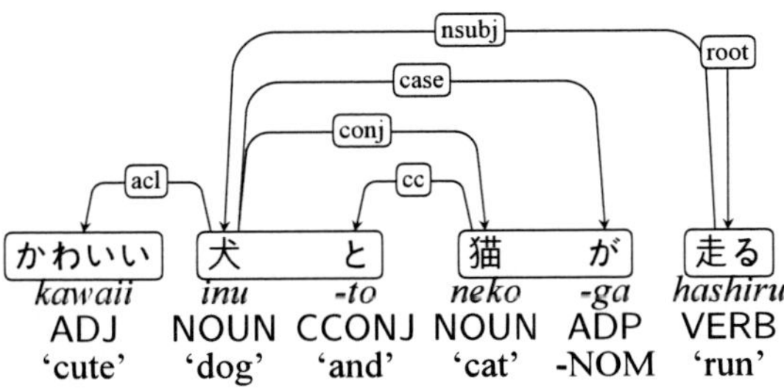

Figure 4: Left-headed representation of a nominal coordination in Japanese "犬と猫" ('dog and cat'), in a sentence "かわいい犬と猫が走る" ('A cute dog and cat run').

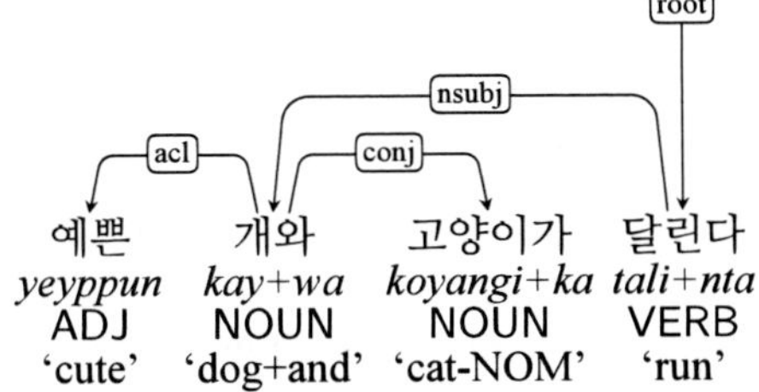

Figure 5: Left-headed representation of a nominal coordination in Korean "개와 고양이" ('dog and cat'), in a sentence "예쁜 개와 고양이가 달린다" ('A cute dog and cat run').

3 Issues with left-headed coordination

This section points out several issues regarding Japanese and Korean coordinate structures in Universal Dependencies when the left-headed rules are strictly applied.

3.1 Nominal coordination

If a Japanese noun phrase "犬と猫" ('dog and cat') is regarded as a coordination and represented in a left-headed manner under UD, the structure is as Figure 4 in a sentence "犬と猫が走る" ('A cute dog and cat run'). When the particle "と" (*to*) is regarded as a conjunction CCONJ to connect two conjuncts, instead of a case marker attached to the preceding noun "犬" ('dog'), it is made a dependent of the right conjunct, breaking the *bunsetsu* unit in the dependency structure.

Also the nominative case marker "が" (*ga*) following "猫" ('cat') should specify the nominative case of the noun phrase ('dog and cat'), then the case marker is a child of "犬" ('dog') as the left conjunct, which produces a long distance dependency for a case marker which is usually attached to the preceding word.

The Korean counterpart in Figure 5 mirrors the Japanese example, except that again due to the different tokenization scheme the conjunctive particle "와" (*wa*) is kept suffixized in the left nominal conjunct *eojeol*, thus the conjunction relation cc is not overtly marked.

A common problem with adjectival modification in UD shown in Figures 4 and 5 is that there is no way to distinguish between modification of the full coordination vs. of the first conjunct (Przepiórkowski and Patejuk, 2018) . For example, there is no way to specify the scope of the adjective 'cute': the two readings (1) only a dog is cute and (2) both animals are cute.

3.2 Verbal coordination

Further critical issues are attested in the verbal coordinate structures. Figure 6 shows the left-headed verbal coordination "食べて走る" ('eat and run') in a noun phrase "食べて走る人" ('a person who eats and runs'), where verb "食べ" ('eat') is the child of "人" ('person'). Despite this dependency relationship, morphological markings tells us a different story: "食べ+て" is an adverbial form that modifies another verb, *i.e.*, "走る" ('run'), and the verb "走る" ('run') is an adnominal form that modifies another noun, *i.e.*, "人" ('person'). Therefore, the dependency between 'eat' and 'person' does not properly reflect the syntactic relationship of the modification of a verb by an adnominal verb, without seeing the whole coordinate structure 'eat and run'. The same set of issues are observed with the corresponding Korean example in Figure 7.

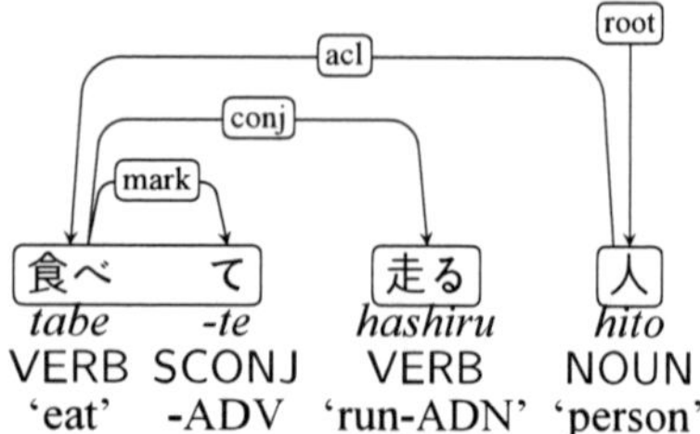

Figure 6: Left-headed representation of a verbal co-ordination in a Japanese phrase "食べて走る人" ('A person who eats and runs').

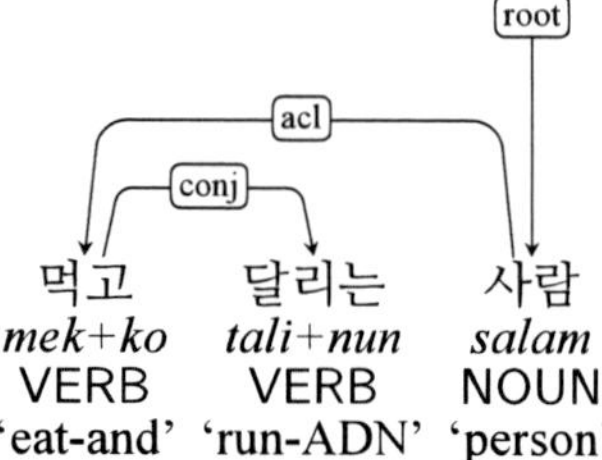

Figure 7: Left-headed representation of a verbal coordination in a Korean phrase "먹고 달리는 사람" ('A person who eats and runs').

3.3 Ellipsis

It is widely acknowledged that the phenomenon of ellipsis in non-constituent coordination is difficult to represent in UD, which does not allow introduction of covert gap words. Such structures can be even trickier to capture in head-final languages.

Figure 8 shows Japanese examples of non-constituent coordination. (a) is the coordination of "父は山に行き" ('he goes to a mountain') and "私は川に行った" ('I went to a river'). The root node is the rightmost word in the left conjunct chunk. The second example (b) ('My father went to the mountain, and I, to the river.') shows the ellipsis of the first verb "行き" ('go'), which is the root node in (a). The dependency relations of the omitted node that include the root are reduced and attached to the daughter node "父" ('father'). The label orphan should be assigned between "私" ('I') and "山" ('mountain'), and then, the first word, "父" ('father'), becomes the root of the sentence. These peculiar tree constructions are caused by the left-headed principle of coordinate structures for a strictly head-final language, where the left conjunct tends to be omitted in this type of ellipsis. Korean likewise exhibits an exact parallel with its predicate ellipsis construction; examples are not

shown in the interest of conserving space.

3.4 Coordination in Japanese and Korean: grammar vs. meaning

Conjunction is typically schematized as 'X and Y', where 'X' and 'Y' are interchangeable: *commutativity* is a defining characteristic of coordination which forms a basis for its headlessness. The Japanese and Korean examples presented so far, however, depart from this in a fundamental way: coordination in the two languages is asymmetric on the levels of syntax and morphology. Their 'and'-counterpart is a dependent morpheme attached to the left conjunct,[1] and it is the right conjunct that bears all inflections and syntactic markings. In ellipsis, it's the left conjunct that is reduced, while the right conjunct, along with requisite inflectional markings, is left standing.

This, then, points strongly towards the right conjunct being the head. Hoeksema (1992) cites four criteria of the 'head', which are: semantic, distributional, morphosyntactic, and technical (*i.e.*, phrasal projection); his morphosyntactic criterion states that the head is the locus of inflection, which applies to the right conjunct in the two languages.

On the other hand, there is one source of commutativity for Japanese and Korean coordination, which is *meaning*: namely, the fact that the lexical portions of left and right conjuncts can be swapped with no impact on truth conditions. In nominal coordination (4, 5) this semantic commutativity is robust; in verbal coordination (6, 7, 8), it is more restricted as temporal-sequential or causal interpretation often slips in (*e.g.*, 6, 7 could be understood as 'eats *and then* runs'), but where it is available it tends to be just as robust (*e.g.*, 8). This would mean that the semantic commutativity is the primary basis for identifying and acknowledging coordination as a phenomenon in these languages, as this property does not extend to grammar.

Back to the grammatical aspect, a natural corollary is that Japanese and Korean coordinate structures are very close to those of nominal modification and subordination. In Korean, "존-의 고양이-가" (*John-uy koyangi-ka*, 'John's cat-NOM') with the genitive marker "-의" (-*uy*) therefore appears to share the same configuration as 'cat-and dog-NOM'; "먹-고서 달리-는 사람" (*mek-kose tali-nun salam*, 'person who eats *and then* runs')

---

[1]Exceptions exist: Korean and Japanese conjunction and disjunction markers "그리고", "及び", "및", "또는", "ない し" are whole words.

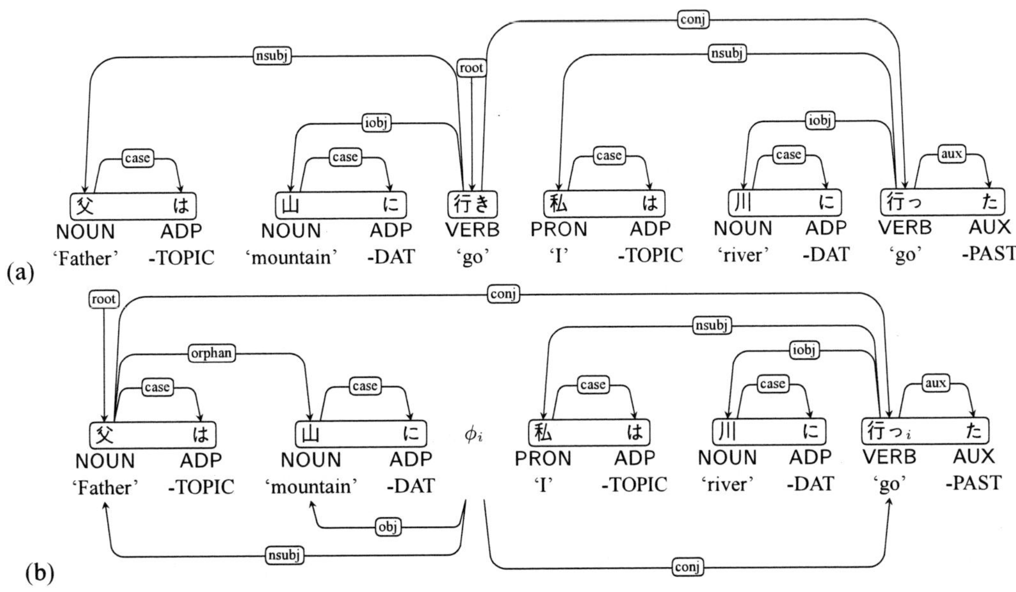

Figure 8: Predicate ellipsis in the non-constituent conjunct coordination.

with the sequential verbal ending "-고서" (*-kose*) likewise is indistinguishable on the surface from the coordination counterpart which uses "-고" (*-ko*, 'and') instead. In both cases, the righthand-side elements are unquestionably the head, syntactically and semantically, and they are treated as such in Japanese and Korean UD. Then, the only criteria for distinguishing the coordinate structures from their headed cousins are (1) choice of the suffix, and (2) semantic commutativity. One unfortunate consequence of the current UD principles is that these seemingly parallel pairs of structures in Korean and Japanese must receive vastly different syntactic treatments – one right-headed and the other left-headed – based on these two, non-syntactic, attributes. This creates a point of incongruence in terms of language-internal grammar; additionally, it becomes an engineering-side liability, as we will see shortly in Section 5.

4 Current status

Despite the complexities outlined in the previous section, the UD Japanese and UD Korean teams had to work within the bounds of the principles laid out by the Universal Dependencies version 2. Therefore, in the official version 2.2 release used for the CoNLL 2018 shared task (Zeman et al., 2018), UD Japanese and UD Korean adopted two separate strategies in order to ensure compliance,

as we will see below.

4.1 UD Japanese

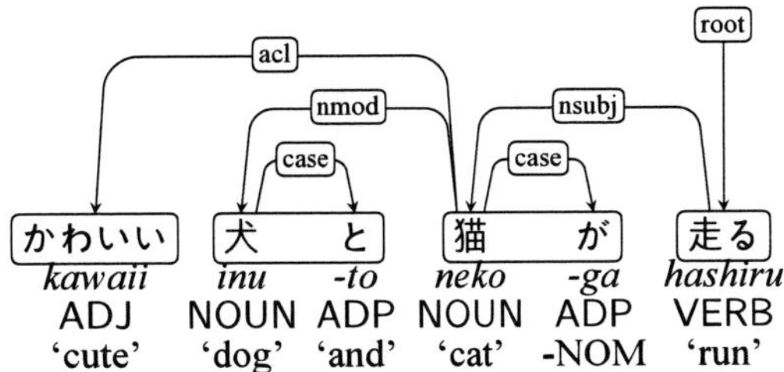

Figure 9: The representation in UD Japanese v2.2 for a sentence "かわいい犬と猫が走る" ('A cute dog and cat run').

To sidestep the issues described in Section 3, UD_Japanese-GSD and -BCCWJ opted against using coordinate structures altogether, that is, no conj label appears in the two corpora. Instead, nominal coordination is represented as a type of nominal modification (nmod) as shown in Figure 9, with "と" (*to*) between 'dog' and 'cat' categorized as ADP along with other case markers. This treatment simplifies the structure: the head of 'cute' is now 'cat', which clearly signals that the adjective modifies both 'dog' and 'cat'. Moreover, 'cat', which is associated with the nominative case marker "が" (*ga*), is seen directly connected with

79

the verb 'run' with the (nsubj) label.

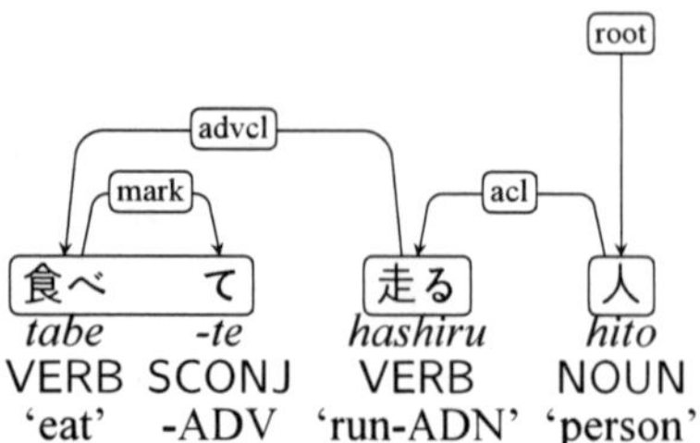

Figure 10: The representation in UD Japanese v2.2 for a phrase "食べて走る人" ('A person who eats and runs').

Additionally, the relationship between verbs are not handled as coordination, as shown in Figure 10. A verb connected with "て" (*te*) is regarded as subordination rather than coordination, because the phrase can be read as 'a person who runs <u>after</u> eating'. It is consistent with the strategy of PoS tagging in UD Japanese to assign SCONJ for conjunctive particles.

Besides the coordination, UD Japanese does not use flat label for sequential nouns, including proper nouns, to avoid the left-headed structures. Instead, compound is used as shown in Figure 11.

UD Japanese_GSD uses fixed for a limited numbers of multi-word functional words, while UD Japanese_BCCWJ does not use it at all. Table 1 shows the distribution of some labels.

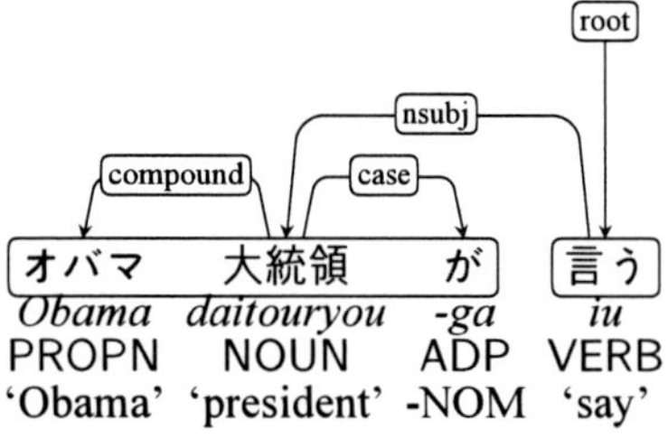

Figure 11: The use of compound in UD Japanese v2.2 for "オバマ大統領が言う" ('President Obama says').

Corpus	root	conj	flat	fixed
GSD	8,232	0	0	338
BCCWJ	57,256	0	0	0

Table 1: Distribution of labels in UD Japanese corpora. root shows the number of sentences.

4.2 UD Korean

Unlike the Japanese UD, the Korean UD effort has made a conscious decision to use right-headedness for conjunction following the coordination guidelines proposed by Choi and Palmer (2011). Thus, the coordinate structures in all three of the Korean UD corpora (Chun et al., 2018) were developed with the rightmost conjunct as the head of the phrase, with each conjunct pointing to its right sibling as its head.

For the latest available UD_Korean-GSD, however, the dependencies were converted to left-headed structures post-development in an effort to fully comply with the UD guidelines despite the problems left-headed structures pose for the language as described in Section 3. The other two Korean UD corpora, namely the Kaist and the Korean Penn Treebank, reflect right-headed coordinate structures (Chun et al., 2018). In addition to coordination, UD Korean extends the right-headed dependency structures to noun-noun structures. Unlike the Japanese that has opted to represent sequential nouns as cases of compound (Figure 11), Korean uses right-headed flat and fixed dependencies (Figure 12(a)), assigning the rightmost nominal with the morphological case marking as the phrasal head. Just as with the coordinate structure, these flat dependencies were converted into left-headed structures for the UD_Korean-GSD (Figure 12(b)). Table 2 shows the distributions of conj, flat and fixed labels.

Corpus	root	conj	flat	fixed
GSD	6,339	3,864	12,247	13
Kaist	27,363	20,774	803	3,186
Penn	5,010	9,960	528	18

Table 2: Distribution of dependency labels in UD Korean corpora.

The differing strategies employed in the Japanese and Korean UD produce very different dependencies over structures that should otherwise receive similar analyses. Effectively, despite the syntactic similarities apparent in the two languages, the differences in the UD structures pose a challenge to the cross-lingual transfer learning (Kanayama et al., 2014).

5 Parsing Experiments

How well will parsers learn the syntactic structures of left-headed coordination in head-final lan-

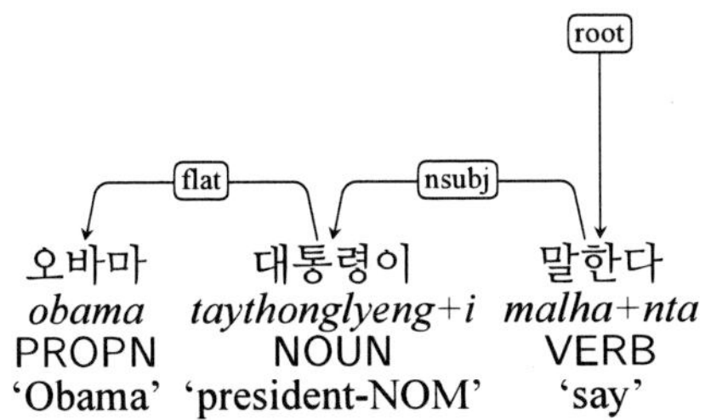

(a) Korean right-headed flat structure.

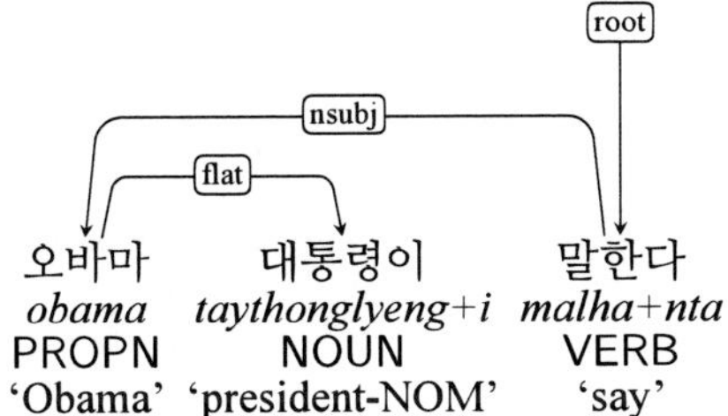

(b) (a) converted to left-headed structure as reflected in the UD_Korean-GSD.

Figure 12: The use of flat in Korean UD v2.2.

guages? To answer this question, we trained and tested UDPipe (Straka et al., 2016) on multiple versions of UD Japanese and Korean corpora.

5.1 Japanese

As described in Section 4.1, the current UD Japanese-GSD corpus does not use conj tags. The corpus was converted into another version with coordinations without changing the dependency structures (right-headed coordination), that is, some of nmod and advcl labels are converted into conj label when the original manual annotation used conj regarding them as nominal or verbal coordinations. Also CCONJ tag and cc label are assigned to the coordinative case markers. The corpus was further converted into left-headed coordination, by changing the dependency structures following the UD guidelines.

For each corpora, two models were trained using train and dev portions; with (1) default UDPipe settings without changing any parameters, and (2) Japanese specific parameters for each phase[2] and

precomputed word embeddings.

Given the model trained with each corpus and the raw input text of the test portion of corresponding corpus, UDPipe processed tokenization, PoS tagging and parsing. Table 3 shows the F1 values of tokenization (word), PoS tagging (UPOS) and UAS and LAS, for three models and two configurations. Tokenization is not straightforward because there is no whitespace between words, and it lowers scores of downstream processes; PoS tagging and parsing. Japanese specific configuration consistently showed better parsing scores by around 2 points.

Compared to the current UD Japanese ('no coordination'), 'right-head coordination' showed similar UAS values because the dependency relations were almost the same. In both configurations, LAS values dropped by 1.4 points because coordination (conj) cannot be deterministically distinguished from other dependencies (nmod or advcl). 'left-head coordination' further confused the model. UAS scores decreased by more than 3 points due to the difficulty to distinguish coordinate structures which completely change the dependency orientation, and the inconsistent syntactic relationship between the left conjunct and the head word. Also, it is known that shorter length of dependencies are preferred (Futrell et al., 2015) and the right-headed coordination strictly reduces the dependency distance in head-final languages. These results support the advantages of the right-headed strategy in Japanese coordinate structures.

5.2 Korean

All three UD corpora in Section 4.2, GSD, Kaist, and Penn Treebanks, are used to conduct similar experiments in Korean. First, raw text from those corpora are combined and fed into the original implementation of Word2Vec (Mikolov et al., 2013)

---

[2]   `--tokenizer=dimension=64;epochs=100;initialization_range=0.1;batch_size=50;learning_rate=0.005;dropout=0.3;early_stopping=1`
`--tagger=models=2;templates_1=tagger;guesser_suffix_rules_1=12;guesser_enrich_dictionary_1=4;guesser_prefixes_max_1=0;use_lemma_1=0;use_xpostag_1=1;use_feats_1=1;provide_lemma_1=`
`0;provide_xpostag_1=1;provide_feats_1=1;prune_features_1=0;templates_2=lemmatizer;guesser_suffix_rules_2=6;guesser_enrich_dictionary_2=6;guesser_prefixes_max_2=4;use_lemma_2=1;use_xpostag_2=1;use_feats_2=1;provide_lemma_2=1;provide_xpostag_2=0;provide_feats_2=0;prune_features_2=0`
`--parser=iterations=30;embedding_upostag=20;embedding_feats=20;embedding_xpostag=0;embedding_form=50;embedding_form_file=ud-2.0-embeddings/ja.skip.forms.50.vectors;embedding_lemma=0;embedding_deprel=20;learning_rate=0.02;learning_rate_final=0.001;l2=0.3;hidden_layer=200;batch_size=10;transition_system=projective;transition_oracle=static;structured_interval=8`

	default parameter				Japanese configuration			
	word	UPOS	UAS	LAS	word	UPOS	UAS	LAS
no coordination [UD v2.2]	91.0	88.4	75.5	74.0	91.8	89.1	77.0	75.4
Left-head coordination	91.0	88.2	71.7	69.9	91.6	88.6	73.6	71.8
Right-head coordination	91.0	88.2	**75.4**	**72.6**	91.6	88.6	**76.7**	**74.0**

Table 3: Parsing performance on Japanese UD corpora. F1 values of tokenization, the Universal POS tagging Score (UPOS), the Unlabeled Attachment Score (UAS), and the Labeled Attachment Score (LAS) are shown here.

	UPOS			UAS			LAS		
	GSD	Kaist	Penn	GSD	Kaist	Penn	GSD	Kaist	Penn
Left-head coordination	89.37	90.12	92.17	69.49	77.54	73.54	61.98	70.37	65.94
Right-head coordination	89.39	90.10	92.41	**77.22**	**83.00**	**78.34**	**65.03**	**75.02**	**69.18**

Table 4: Parsing performance on the three Korean UD corpora, GSD, Kaist, and Penn. The gold-tokenization is used, and F1 values of UPOS tagging, UAS and LAS are reported.

to train word embeddings, where skip-gram with negative sample is used for language modeling and the vector size of 50 and the minimum count of 3 are used for configuration (the default values are used for all the other parameters).

The GSD and Kaist Treebanks are experimented with the configuration recommended by the UDPipe team, which was optimized on the CoNLL'17 shared task dataset.[3] The Penn Treebank is experimented with mostly the same configuration except that the transition-based parsing algorithm using the SWAP transition with the static lazy oracle is applied because this corpus allows multiple roots as well as non-projective dependencies, which is not assumed for the recommended configuration.

Following the annotation guidelines, the conj, flat, and fixed relations in the version 2.2 of the GSD and Kaist Treebanks are all left-headed.

However, the authors of these Korean UD corpora also provide the right-headed version of those corpora from their open-source project. This project provides both left- and right-headed versions of the Penn Treebank as well, which makes it easy for us to make head-to-head comparisons.[4]

Table 4 shows parsing performance of UDPipe on the Korean UD corpora. Significant improvements are found in all three corpora for both the unlabeled and labeled attachment scores when the right-headed version is used. Moreover, our qualitative analysis indicates that the improvements are not just from those three relations, conj, flat, and fixed, but other relations associated with them because the right-headed version makes them more coherent with the other relations.

6 Proposal

The strict left-headed constraint for the coordinate structures in the current Universal Dependencies has tied the hands of the two individual language UD projects, driving them to adopt suboptimal solutions: dropping the conjunction category entirely in the case of Japanese, and maintaining two forks of the same data sets in the case of Korean (Section 4). The former approach incurs the loss of a real and essential cross-linguistic parallelism involving conj which undermines the UD framework's premise of universality; the latter risks splintering of the UD as a linguistically diverse yet unified project.

---

[3]`--tokenizer='dimension=24;epochs=`
```
100;initialization_range=0.1;batch_size=
50;learning_rate=0.01;dropout=0.2;early_
stopping=1'--tagger='models=2;templates_
1=tagger;guesser_suffix_rules_1=8;guesser_
enrich_dictionary_1=6;guesser_prefixes_
max_1=0;use_lemma_1=1;use_xpostag_1=1;use_
feats_1=1;provide_lemma_1=0;provide_xpostag_
1=1;provide_feats_1=1;prune_features_1=
0;templates_2=lemmatizer;guesser_suffix_rules_
2=6;guesser_enrich_dictionary_2=5;guesser_
prefixes_max_2=4;use_lemma_2=1;use_xpostag_
2=0;use_feats_2=0;provide_lemma_2=1;provide_
xpostag_2=0;provide_feats_2=0;prune_features_
2=1'--parser='iterations=30;embedding_upostag=
20;embedding_feats=20;embedding_xpostag=
0;embedding_form=50;embedding_form_file=ko-
all.vec;embedding_lemma=0;embedding_deprel=
20;learning_rate=0.01;learning_rate_final=
0.001;12=0.5;hidden_layer=200;batch_size=
10;transition_system=projective;transition_
oracle=dynamic;structured_interval=10'
```

[4]The official release of the UD Penn Korean Treebank can be obtained only through the Linguistic Data Consortium (LDC) such that the corpus in this open-source project does not include the form field.

Even if one was inclined to regard these drawbacks as merely abstract, hopefully we have sufficiently demonstrated that the adherence to the left-headed principle leads to numerous language-internal inconsistencies (Section 3) and, moreover, has an engineering-side consequence, as parser trainability is negatively impacted (Section 5).

Given these considerations, we propose that the UD guidelines be modified so as to allow flexibility in head orientation for coordinate structures. This move will leave our two UD teams free to apply right-headedness in coordinate structures and hence represent them in a way that is linguistically sound and with engineering-side advantages, all without making a compromise.

Additionally, general UD issues like the scope problem triggered by adjectival modification of coordinate structures (Section 3.1) can be resolved through right-headed attachment (*i.e.*, making the right conjunct ('cat') the head of the coordination). While admittedly right-headed attachment is not a complete solution for UD's general issue of adjectival modification of coordination, for the right-headed languages, at least, would allow the syntax to supply appropriate syntactic structures for the ambiguities present in the text[5].

Furthermore, it is our belief that the change will ultimately prove beneficial to all head-final languages. Rather than viewing this modification as a concession, we invite the UD leadership to consider the fact that coordination manifests differently across languages, and sometimes in a manner that strongly indicates headedness, as it does in Japanese and Korean; extending the head parameter to coordination will therefore strengthen the UD's position of universality. This flexibility may arise another issue in drawing a line between left- or right-headed, but any languages can keep the current strategy without any drawbacks, and apparently, it is beneficial for the rigid head-final languages.

7 Conclusion

In this paper, we presented issues that Japanese and Korean face in the representation of coordinate structures within the current design of Universal Dependencies, followed by a proposal for the UD principles to allow right-headedness in coordination. We hope this proposal will lead to more flexibility in the annotation scheme for the two languages, which will be essential in creating corpora that are useful not only for academic research but also for real-world use cases.

References

Masayuki Asahara, Hiroshi Kanayama, Takaaki Tanaka, Yusuke Miyao, Sumire Uematsu, Shinsuke Mori, Yuji Matsumoto, Mai Omura, and Yugo Murawaki. 2018. Universal Dependencies Version 2 for Japanese. In *Proceedings of the Eleventh International Conference on Language Resources and Evaluation (LREC 2018)*, Miyazaki, Japan.

Xinying Chen and Kim Gerdes. 2017. Classifying languages by dependency structure. typologies of delexicalized Universal Dependency treebanks. In *Proceedings of the Fourth International Conference on Dependency Linguistics (Depling 2017), September 18-20, 2017, Università di Pisa, Italy*, 139, pages 54–63. Linköping University Electronic Press.

Jinho D. Choi and Martha Palmer. 2011. Statistical Dependency Parsing in Korean: From Corpus Generation To Automatic Parsing. In *Proceedings of the IWPT Workshop on Statistical Parsing of Morphologically Rich Languages*, SPMRL'11, pages 1–11, Dublin, Ireland.

Jayeol Chun, Na-Rae Han, Jena D. Hwang, and Jinho D. Choi. 2018. Building Universal Dependency Treebanks in Korean. In *Proceedings of the Eleventh International Conference on Language Resources and Evaluation (LREC 2018)*, Miyazaki, Japan.

Marie-Catherine De Marneffe, Timothy Dozat, Natalia Silveira, Katri Haverinen, Filip Ginter, Joakim Nivre, and Christopher D Manning. 2014. Universal Stanford dependencies: A cross-linguistic typology. In *Proceedings of the 9th International Conference on Language Resources and Evaluation (LREC 2014)*, volume 14, pages 4585–4592.

Richard Futrell, Kyle Mahowald, and Edward Gibson. 2015. Large-scale evidence of dependency length minimization in 37 languages. In *Proceedings of the National Academy of Sciences of the United States of America*.

Kim Gerdes and Sylvain Kahane. 2015. Non-constituent coordination and other coordinative constructions as dependency graphs. In *Proceedings of the Third International Conference on Dependency Linguistics (Depling 2015)*, pages 101–110.

Jack Hoeksema. 1992. The head parameter in morphology and syntax. In Dicky G. Gilbers and S. Looyenga, editors, *Language and Cognition 2*, pages 119–132. University of Groningen.

---

[5]Note that in "犬とかわいい猫" ('dog and cute cat'), where 'cute' modifies 'cat' (the head of coordination), ambiguity is resolved through word order (*i.e.*, cannot be read as both of them are cute).

Hiroshi Kanayama, Youngja Park, Yuta Tsuboi, and Dongmook Yi. 2014. Learning from a neighbor: Adapting a Japanese parser for Korean through feature transfer learning. In *Proceedings of the EMNLP'2014 Workshop on Language Technology for Closely Related Languages and Language Variants*, pages 2–12.

Tomas Mikolov, Ilya Sutskever, Kai Chen, Greg S Corrado, and Jeff Dean. 2013. Distributed Representations of Words and Phrases and their Compositionality. In *Proceedings of Advances in Neural Information Processing Systems 26*, NIPS'13, pages 3111–3119.

Joakim Nivre, Željko Agić, Lars Ahrenberg, et al. 2017. Universal Dependencies 2.0. LINDAT/CLARIN digital library at the Institute of Formal and Applied Linguistics, Charles University, Prague.

Joakim Nivre, Marie-Catherine de Marneffe, Filip Ginter, Yoav Goldberg, Jan Hajič, Christopher Manning, Ryan McDonald, Slav Petrov, Sampo Pyysalo, Natalia Silveira, Reut Tsarfaty, and Daniel Zeman. 2016. Universal Dependencies v1: A multilingual treebank collection. In *Proceedings of the 10th International Conference on Language Resources and Evaluation (LREC 2016)*, Portorož, Slovenia.

Maria Polinsky. 2012. Headness, again. *UCLA Working Papers in Linguistics, Theories of Everything*, 17:348–359.

Adam Przepiórkowski and Agnieszka Patejuk. 2018. Arguments and adjuncts in universal dependencies. In *Proceedings of the 27th International Conference on Computational Linguistics*, pages 3837–3852.

Sebastian Schuster and Christopher D Manning. 2016. Enhanced english universal dependencies: An improved representation for natural language understanding tasks. In *Proceedings of the Tenth International Conference on Language Resources and Evaluation (LREC 2016)*, pages 23–28. Portorož, Slovenia.

Milan Straka, Jan Hajič, and Jana Straková. 2016. UDPipe: trainable pipeline for processing CoNLL-U files performing tokenization, morphological analysis, POS tagging and parsing. In *Proceedings of the 10th International Conference on Language Resources and Evaluation (LREC 2016)*, Portorož, Slovenia. European Language Resources Association.

Takaaki Tanaka, Yusuke Miyao, Masayuki Asahara, Sumire Uematsu, Hiroshi Kanayama, Shinsuke Mori, and Yuji Matsumoto. 2016. Universal Dependencies for Japanese. In *Proceedings of the Tenth International Conference on Language Resources and Evaluation (LREC 2016)*.

Daniel Zeman, Filip Ginter, Jan Hajič, Joakim Nivre, Martin Popel, and Milan Straka. 2018. CoNLL 2018 Shared Task: Multilingual Parsing from Raw Text to Universal Dependencies. In *Proceedings of the CoNLL 2018 Shared Task: Multilingual Parsing from Raw Text to Universal Dependencies*, Brussels, Belgium. Association for Computational Linguistics.

Investigating NP-Chunking with Universal Dependencies for English

Ophélie Lacroix
Siteimprove
Sankt Annæ Plads 28
DK-1250 Copenhagen, Denmark
ola@siteimprove.com

Abstract

Chunking is a pre-processing task generally dedicated to improving constituency parsing. In this paper, we want to show that universal dependency (UD) parsing can also leverage the information provided by the task of chunking even though annotated chunks are not provided with universal dependency trees. In particular, we introduce the possibility of deducing noun-phrase (NP) chunks from universal dependencies, focusing on English as a first example. We then demonstrate how the task of NP-chunking can benefit PoS-tagging in a multi-task learning setting – comparing two different strategies – and how it can be used as a feature for dependency parsing in order to learn enriched models.

1 Introduction

Syntactic chunking consists of identifying groups of (consecutive) words in a sentence that constitute phrases (e.g. noun-phrases, verb-phrases). It can be seen as a shallow parsing task between PoS-tagging and syntactic parsing. Chunking is known as being a relevant preprocessing step for syntactic parsing.

Chunking got a lot of attention when syntactic parsing was predominantly driven by constituency parsing and was highlighted, in particular, through the CoNLL-2000 Shared Task (Tjong Kim Sang and Buchholz, 2000). Nowadays, studies (Søgaard and Goldberg, 2016; Hashimoto et al., 2017) still compare chunking –as well as constituency parsing– performance on these same data from the Penn Treebank. While dependency parsing is spreading to different languages and domains (Kong et al., 2014; Nivre et al., 2017), chunking is restricted to old journalistic data. Nevertheless, chunking can benefit dependency parsing as well as constituency parsing, but gold annotated chunks are not available for universal dependencies.

We want to automatically deduce chunks from universal dependencies (UD) (Nivre et al., 2017) and investigate its benefit for other tasks such as Part-of-Speech (PoS) tagging and dependency parsing. We focus on English, which has properties that make it a good candidate for chunking (low percentage of non-projective dependencies). As a first target, we also decide to restrict the task to the most common chunks: noun-phrases (NP).

We choose to see NP-chunking as a sequence labeling task where tags signal the beginning (B-NP), the inside (I-NP) or the outside (O) of chunks. We thus propose to use multi-task learning for training chunking along with PoS-tagging and feature-tagging to show that the tasks can benefit from each other. We experiment with two different multi-task learning strategies (training parameters in parallel or sequentially). We also intend to make parsing benefit from NP-chunking as a pre-processing task. Accordingly, we propose to add NP-chunk tags as features for dependency parsing.

Contributions. We show how to (i) deduce NP-chunks from universal dependencies for English in order to (ii) demonstrate the benefit of performing chunking along with PoS-tagging through multi-task learning and (iii) evaluate the impact of using NP-chunks as features for dependency parsing.

2 NP-Chunks

While chunks are inherently deduced from constituent trees, we want to deduce chunks from dependency trees in order to not rely on specific constituent annotations which would not be available for other domains or languages. In this case, it means that only partial information is provided by the dependencies to automatically extract the chunks. We thus choose to only deduce noun-phrase (NP) chunks (Ramshaw and Marcus, 1995) from the dependency trees.

Proceedings of the Second Workshop on Universal Dependencies (UDW 2018), pages 85–90
Brussels, Belgium, November 1, 2018. ©2018 Association for Computational Linguistics

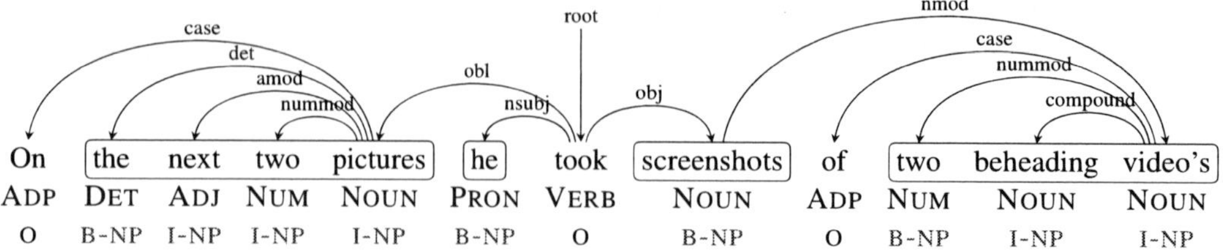

Figure 1: NP-chunks deduced from a UD tree of the English Web Treebank (EWT).

Automatic Deduction. We deduce minimal NP-chunks, which means that embedded prepositional (PP) chunks are not included in our NP-chunks, e.g. in Figure 1 *"screenshots of two beheading video's"* is split in two distinct NPs instead of one long NP with an embedded PP (*"of two beheading video's"*).

We first identify the core tokens of NPs: the nouns (NOUN), proper nouns (PROPN) and some pronouns[1] (PRON). After identifying these core tokens, we form full NPs by joining these core tokens with their direct and indirect children which are not part of PPs. In practice, they are those for which the incoming dependency is labeled with one of the following relations (modulo some individual conditions):

- compound, compound:prt, flat, flat:name, goeswith, fixed, nummod;

- det if the child is located before its head;

- conj if the child and its head are adjectives. We want *"excellent and strong performers"* to be one NP and *"these challenges and possible solutions"* to be split in two NPs;

- amod if the child is not an adverb. We don't want to attach preceding adverbs such as *"not"* to a NP;

- appos if the child is directly before or after its head;

- advmod if the child is not a PART or a VERB and its head an adjective;

- nmod:poss if the child is not a NOUN or a PROPN. We want to group *"your world"* but not *"John's last day* (where *"John"* and *"last day"* would be two distinct NPs;

---

[1] All pronouns but the interrogative and relative pronouns.

- following and preceding obl:npmod and obl:tmod;

- obl if its head has a amod incoming dependency.

In addition, when grouping a core token with one of its det, compound, nummod or nmod:poss children, we automatically attach tokens which are in between. If split chunks remain, we attach the non-attached tokens which are in between two part of a chunk. It allows us to attach the adverbs which modify adjectives such as *"very"* in *"my very best friend"* or some specific punctuation such as the slash in *"The owner/baker"*.

Manual Annotation. To assert the correctness of the automatically deduced chunks, we manually annotate noun-phrases on a small portion of the test set of the EWT UD treebank data. For 50 sentences (from which 233 NP chunks were manually annotated), the accuracy of the automatic deduction reaches 98.7%. Errors in deduction are mostly due to punctual inconsistencies in the UD annotations.

3 Models

3.1 Sequence Labeling

We implement a deep recurrent neural network with an architecture based on bidirectional Long Short-Term Memory (bi-LSTM) (Graves and Schmidhuber, 2005) that can exploit contextual information for processing sequences.

The base network is composed of an embedding layer that feeds two hidden bi-LSTM layers (forward and backward). The outputs of the bi-LSTMs are then concatenated to feed the next layer. Multiple bi-LSTM layers can be stacked. In the end, these outputs are fed to a Softmax output layer. The embedding layer is a concatenation of a word embedding layer and a character embedding layer. It takes as input a sequence of n tokens. The output of the network is a sequence of n tags.

We use this architecture for PoS-tagging, feature-tagging (i.e. morpho-syntactic tagging) and NP-chunking. In order to make the tasks benefit from each other, we adapt the network to multi-task learning. We propose to compare two strategies for multi-task learning : *shared* or *stacked*.

Shared multi-task learning. In this architecture, different tasks are trained at the same level in a similar way as in Søgaard and Goldberg (2016). They share parameters through all the network and feed different outputs.

Stacked multi-task learning. In this architecture, different tasks are trained at different levels as proposed by Hashimoto et al. (2017). A bi-LSTM layer is dedicated to a task. The output of a layer for a given task feeds the next layer dedicated to the next task.

3.2 Dependency Parsing

Our dependency parser is a reimplementation of the arc-hybrid non-projective transition-based parser of de Lhoneux et al. (2017b).

In this version of the arc-hybrid system, the SWAP transition is added to the original transition set (Kuhlmann et al., 2011) made up of the standard transitions RIGHT, LEFT and SHIFT. The SWAP transition allows to build non-projective dependency trees. The standard transitions are trained using a dynamic oracle (Goldberg and Nivre, 2013), which alleviates error propagation, and a static oracle for training the SWAP transition.

The parser uses a bi-LSTM network to learn vector representations of the tokens. These vectors are combined through a feature function and used for learning and evaluating the transitions using a multi-layer perceptron with one hidden layer. In de Lhoneux et al. (2017a), PoS tags are removed from the feature function and instead, the bi-LSTM is fed with only word and character embeddings. In our version of the parser, we reintroduce the PoS tags as features and also make use of the predicted NP-chunks. The PoS and/or NP-chunk tags are turned into embeddings and concatenated with the word and character embeddings to represent the tokens.

4 Experiments

As a baseline for PoS-tagging, feature-tagging and NP-chunking, we first train our sequence tagger for each task separately. We then train the tagger in a multi-task setting –with PoS-tagging as a main task– alternating the auxiliary tasks and the strategies (shared or stacked multi-task learning).

As a baseline for dependency parsing, we train the parser using only word and character embeddings as input to the bi-LSTM. We then add the PoS and NP-chunk embeddings, separately and simultaneously, for training enriched models. As an upper bound, we also propose to run the experiments with "gold" NP-chunks, i.e. we feed the parser (for training and testing) with NP-chunks that were automatically deduced from the dependencies.

Data. We evaluate all tasks on the three English treebanks included in the version 2.1 of the Universal Dependencies project (Nivre et al., 2017) : **EWT** (254k tokens), **LinES** (82k tokens) and **ParTUT** (49k tokens). In average, 3.8, 3.3 and 6.2 NP-chunks per sentence are deduced respectively for each treebank. [2] Note that the LinES treebank does not contain features (morpho-syntactic tags), so we exclude feature-tagging from the evaluation for this treebank.

Hyper-parameters. We use the development data to tune our hyper-parameters and to determine the number of epochs (via early-stopping) for each experiment.

For sequence tagging, we use the RMSProp optimizer with a learning rate at 0.0005. Hidden layers of dimension 300 is used for ParTUT and 100 for EWT and LinES. We use a dropout of 0.2 on the hidden layers. For dependency parsing, the hidden layer of the bi-LSTM has a dimension set at 125 and uses a dropout of 0.33.

The dimension of the word and character embeddings are respectively 200 and 50. For dependency parsing, embedding dimensions for PoS and NP-chunk tags are set respectively to 6 and 3.

Evaluation. We average the scores on 5 runs for each experiment. We evaluate accuracy on PoS-tagging and feature-tagging and F_1 [3] on chunking.

---

[2]EWT is the biggest treebank but the test contains small sentences (12.1 average length) while ParTUT is the smallest treebank but contains long sentences (22.3 average length).

[3]$F_1 = 2*precision*recall/(precision+recall)$ where precision is the percentage of predicted chunks that are cor-

	EWT			LinES		ParTUT		
	PoS acc(%)	**Feats** acc(%)	**Chunks** F_1	**PoS** acc(%)	**Chunks** F_1	**PoS** acc(%)	**Feats** acc(%)	**Chunks** F_1
Baseline	93.16	**94.06**	89.32	**93.00**	82.74	92.61	91.03	88.01
Shared - P+F	93.29	93.97	-	-	-	93.04	91.49	-
Shared - P+C	93.11	-	89.98[†]	92.97	**85.63**[†]	93.19[†]	-	89.20[†]
Shared - P+F+C	**93.30**	94.01	**89.99**[†]	-	-	**93.20**[†]	**91.74**[†]	89.26[†]
Stacked - P+F	93.18	93.92	-	-	-	92.67	91.00	-
Stacked - P+C	93.16	-	89.09	92.82	83.14	92.96	-	88.28
Stacked - P+F+C	93.00	93.75	89.08	-	-	93.13	91.25	**89.74**[†]

Table 1: Results of PoS-tagging (**P**), feature-tagging (**F**) and NP-chunking (**C**) trained as **one task** (baseline) or via multi-task learning (**Shared** vs **Stacked** strategies). Bold scores are the highest of each column. Statistical significance (T-test>0.05) is marked with [†].

	EWT			LinES			ParTUT		
	LA	UAS	LAS	LA	UAS	LAS	LA	UAS	LAS
Baseline	**87.83**	**86.26**	**82.27**	82.54	82.06	75.35	87.28	86.00	81.28
+ P	87.01	85.58	81.20	**83.71**[†]	**83.10**[†]	**76.83**[†]	87.63	86.11	81.51
+ C	87.66	86.19	81.86	82.66	82.53	75.57	87.98	86.53	82.17
+ P+C	87.32	85.98	81.59	83.38[†]	82.87[†]	76.37[†]	**88.05**	**86.88**[†]	**82.24**[†]
+ gold C	89.99	89.07	85.45	84.31	84.05	77.94	89.47	87.92	84.13

Table 2: Results of dependency parsing using PoS (**P**) and/or NP-chunk (**C**) features. The baseline uses only word and character embeddings. Highest scores are in bold. [†] indicates statistical significance.

For dependency parsing, we calculate the label accuracy (LA), the unlabeled attachment score (UAS) and the labeled attachment score (LAS). As for the CoNLL 2017 Shared Task (Hajič and Zeman, 2017), only universal dependency labels are taken into account (ignoring language-specific subtypes), i.e. we consider a predicted label correct if the main type of the gold label is the same, e.g. `flat:name` is correct if the gold label is `flat`. We also exclude punctuations from the evaluation.

5 Results

5.1 Tagging results

See PoS-tagging, feature-tagging and NP-chunking results in Table 1. For all three treebanks, multi-task learning is beneficial for at least one task. Only the LinES treebank does not benefit from it for PoS-tagging (i.e. equivalent performance), however it greatly improves NP-chunking (+2.9). For the smallest treebank (ParTUT), multi-task learning is beneficial for all tasks (at best, +0.6 for PoS-tagging, +0.7 for feature-tagging and +1.73 for NP-chunking). For the EWT treebank, equivalent scores are achieved for feature-tagging but PoS-tagging and NP-chunking are enhanced through multi-task learning (respectively +0.14 and 0.67).

Globally, the shared multi-task learning strategy achieves the best results. The stacked strategy outperforms the baseline for the small treebank but gets lower scores on the big treebank.

It is also worth noting that multi-task learning makes the models more stable. We observe a significant decrease of the standard deviation for most of the experiments.[4]

5.2 Dependency Parsing Results

See dependency parsing results in Table 2. Adding PoS and NP-chunk tags as features significantly improve dependency parsing performance for the smallest treebank, ParTUT (+0.96 LAS). Using

___
rect and recall is the percentage of gold chunks that are correctly predicted.

___
[4]10 out of 12 standard deviations are lower when comparing the baseline to the shared multi-task learning (including chunking as an auxiliary task).

NP-chunks alone is also beneficial on the LinES data (+0.22 LAS over the baseline) but using only PoS-tags is actually more relevant than including both features. For the biggest treebank, EWT, the baseline outperforms all other enriched models. However, the upper-bound shows that the NP-chunk tags as features are relevant for improving dependency parsing, suggesting that the quality of the predicted NP-chunks –as well as the PoS-tags– is not sufficient for improving parsing.

It is worth noting that training converges faster when using features (17.6 epochs on average VS 25.8 for the baseline) which might also indicate a training issue since models that stop after few epochs (11/12) achieve lower performance.

6 Conclusion

We showed that it is possible to extract NP-chunks from universal dependencies that can be useful for improving other tasks such as PoS-tagging and dependency parsing. While the improvement for PoS-tagging is systematic on all English UD treebanks, the results are mixed for dependency parsing suggesting that NP-chunks as features might be useful for training on small datasets.

Further experiments will be performed in future work in order to extend the results to other languages and to investigate the possibility of extracting embedded chunks.

Acknowledgment

The author would like to thank the anonymous reviewers for their comments and suggestions, and add as well a special thanks to her colleagues from the Data Science team at Siteimprove.

References

Yoav Goldberg and Joakim Nivre. 2013. Training Deterministic Parsers with Non-Deterministic Oracles. *Transactions of the Association of Computational Linguistics*, 1:403–414.

Alex Graves and Jürgen Schmidhuber. 2005. Framewise Phoneme Classification with Bidirectional LSTM and Other Neural Network Architectures. *Neural Networks*, pages 5–6.

Jan Hajič and Dan Zeman, editors. 2017. *Proceedings of the CoNLL 2017 Shared Task: Multilingual Parsing from Raw Text to Universal Dependencies*. Association for Computational Linguistics.

Kazuma Hashimoto, Caiming Xiong, Yoshimasa Tsuruoka, and Richard Socher. 2017. A Joint Many-Task Model: Growing a Neural Network for Multiple NLP Tasks. In *Proceedings of the 2017 Conference on Empirical Methods in Natural Language Processing (EMNLP 2017)*.

Lingpeng Kong, Nathan Schneider, Swabha Swayamdipta, Archna Bhatia, Chris Dyer, and Noah A Smith. 2014. A Dependency Parser for Tweets. In *Proceedings of the 2014 Conference on Empirical Methods in Natural Language Processing (EMNLP 2014)*.

Marco Kuhlmann, Carlos Gómez-Rodríguez, and Giorgio Satta. 2011. Dynamic Programming Algorithms for Transition-Based Dependency Parsers. In *Proceedings of the 49th Annual Meeting of the Association for Computational Linguistics (ACL 2011)*.

Miryam de Lhoneux, Yan Shao, Ali Basirat, Eliyahu Kiperwasser, Sara Stymne, Yoav Goldberg, and Joakim Nivre. 2017a. From Raw Text to Universal Dependencies-Look, No Tags!

Miryam de Lhoneux, Sara Stymne, and Joakim Nivre. 2017b. Arc-Hybrid Non-Projective Dependency Parsing with a Static-Dynamic Oracle. In *Proceedings of the 15th International Conference on Parsing Technologies (IWPT 2017)*.

Joakim Nivre, Željko Agić, Lars Ahrenberg, Lene Antonsen, Maria Jesus Aranzabe, Masayuki Asahara, Luma Ateyah, Mohammed Attia, Aitziber Atutxa, Liesbeth Augustinus, Elena Badmaeva, Miguel Ballesteros, Esha Banerjee, Sebastian Bank, Verginica Barbu Mititelu, John Bauer, Kepa Bengoetxea, Riyaz Ahmad Bhat, Eckhard Bick, Victoria Bobicev, Carl Börstell, Cristina Bosco, Gosse Bouma, Sam Bowman, Aljoscha Burchardt, Marie Candito, Gauthier Caron, Gülşen Cebiroğlu Eryiğit, Giuseppe G. A. Celano, Savas Cetin, Fabricio Chalub, Jinho Choi, Silvie Cinková, Çağrı Çöltekin, Miriam Connor, Elizabeth Davidson, Marie-Catherine de Marneffe, Valeria de Paiva, Arantza Diaz de Ilarraza, Peter Dirix, Kaja Dobrovoljc, Timothy Dozat, Kira Droganova, Puneet Dwivedi, Marhaba Eli, Ali Elkahky, Tomaž Erjavec, Richárd Farkas, Hector Fernandez Alcalde, Jennifer Foster, Cláudia Freitas, Katarína Gajdošová, Daniel Galbraith, Marcos Garcia, Moa Gärdenfors, Kim Gerdes, Filip Ginter, Iakes Goenaga, Koldo Gojenola, Memduh Gökırmak, Yoav Goldberg, Xavier Gómez Guinovart, Berta Gonzáles Saavedra, Matias Grioni, Normunds Grūzītis, Bruno Guillaume, Nizar Habash, Jan Hajič, Jan Hajič jr., Linh Hà Mỹ, Kim Harris, Dag Haug, Barbora Hladká, Jaroslava Hlaváčová, Florinel Hociung, Petter Hohle, Radu Ion, Elena Irimia, Tomáš Jelínek, Anders Johannsen, Fredrik Jørgensen, Hüner Kaşıkara, Hiroshi Kanayama, Jenna Kanerva, Tolga Kayadelen, Václava Kettnerová, Jesse Kirchner, Natalia Kotsyba, Simon Krek, Veronika Laippala, Lorenzo Lambertino, Tatiana Lando, John Lee, Phương

Lê Hồng, Alessandro Lenci, Saran Lertpradit, Herman Leung, Cheuk Ying Li, Josie Li, Keying Li, Nikola Ljubešić, Olga Loginova, Olga Lyashevskaya, Teresa Lynn, Vivien Macketanz, Aibek Makazhanov, Michael Mandl, Christopher Manning, Cătălina Mărănduc, David Mareček, Katrin Marheinecke, Héctor Martínez Alonso, André Martins, Jan Mašek, Yuji Matsumoto, Ryan McDonald, Gustavo Mendonça, Niko Miekka, Anna Missilä, Cătălin Mititelu, Yusuke Miyao, Simonetta Montemagni, Amir More, Laura Moreno Romero, Shinsuke Mori, Bohdan Moskalevskyi, Kadri Muischnek, Kaili Müürisep, Pinkey Nainwani, Anna Nedoluzhko, Gunta Nešpore-Bērzkalne, Lương Nguyễn Thị, Huyền Nguyễn Thị Minh, Vitaly Nikolaev, Hanna Nurmi, Stina Ojala, Petya Osenova, Robert Östling, Lilja Øvrelid, Elena Pascual, Marco Passarotti, Cenel-Augusto Perez, Guy Perrier, Slav Petrov, Jussi Piitulainen, Emily Pitler, Barbara Plank, Martin Popel, Lauma Pretkalniņa, Prokopis Prokopidis, Tiina Puolakainen, Sampo Pyysalo, Alexandre Rademaker, Loganathan Ramasamy, Taraka Rama, Vinit Ravishankar, Livy Real, Siva Reddy, Georg Rehm, Larissa Rinaldi, Laura Rituma, Mykhailo Romanenko, Rudolf Rosa, Davide Rovati, Benoît Sagot, Shadi Saleh, Tanja Samardžić, Manuela Sanguinetti, Baiba Saulīte, Sebastian Schuster, Djamé Seddah, Wolfgang Seeker, Mojgan Seraji, Mo Shen, Atsuko Shimada, Dmitry Sichinava, Natalia Silveira, Maria Simi, Radu Simionescu, Katalin Simkó, Mária Šimková, Kiril Simov, Aaron Smith, Antonio Stella, Milan Straka, Jana Strnadová, Alane Suhr, Umut Sulubacak, Zsolt Szántó, Dima Taji, Takaaki Tanaka, Trond Trosterud, Anna Trukhina, Reut Tsarfaty, Francis Tyers, Sumire Uematsu, Zdeňka Urešová, Larraitz Uria, Hans Uszkoreit, Sowmya Vajjala, Daniel van Niekerk, Gertjan van Noord, Viktor Varga, Eric Villemonte de la Clergerie, Veronika Vincze, Lars Wallin, Jonathan North Washington, Mats Wirén, Tak-sum Wong, Zhuoran Yu, Zdeněk Žabokrtský, Amir Zeldes, Daniel Zeman, and Hanzhi Zhu. 2017. Universal dependencies 2.1. LINDAT/CLARIN digital library at the Institute of Formal and Applied Linguistics (ÚFAL), Faculty of Mathematics and Physics, Charles University.

Lance Ramshaw and Mitch Marcus. 1995. Text Chunking using Transformation-Based Learning. In *Third Workshop on Very Large Corpora*.

Anders Søgaard and Yoav Goldberg. 2016. Deep multi-task learning with low level tasks supervised at lower layers. In *Proceedings of the 54th Annual Meeting of the Association for Computational Linguistics (ACL 2016)*.

Erik F. Tjong Kim Sang and Sabine Buchholz. 2000. Introduction to the CoNLL-2000 shared task: Chunking. In *Proceedings of the 2nd Workshop on Learning language in logic and the 4th conference on Computational Natural Language Learning*.

Marrying Universal Dependencies and Universal Morphology

Arya D. McCarthy[1], **Miikka Silfverberg**[2], **Ryan Cotterell**[1],
Mans Hulden[2], and **David Yarowsky**[1]

[1]Johns Hopkins University
[2]University of Colorado Boulder
{arya,rcotter2,yarowsky}@jhu.edu
{miikka.silfverberg,mans.hulden}@colorado.edu

Abstract

The Universal Dependencies (UD) and Universal Morphology (UniMorph) projects each present schemata for annotating the morphosyntactic details of language. Each project also provides corpora of annotated text in many languages—UD at the token level and UniMorph at the type level. As each corpus is built by different annotators, language-specific decisions hinder the goal of universal schemata. With compatibility of tags, each project's annotations could be used to validate the other's. Additionally, the availability of both type- and token-level resources would be a boon to tasks such as parsing and homograph disambiguation. To ease this interoperability, we present a deterministic mapping from Universal Dependencies v2 features into the UniMorph schema. We validate our approach by lookup in the UniMorph corpora and find a macro-average of 64.13% recall. We also note incompatibilities due to paucity of data on either side. Finally, we present a critical evaluation of the foundations, strengths, and weaknesses of the two annotation projects.

1 Introduction

The two largest standardized, cross-lingual datasets for morphological annotation are provided by the Universal Dependencies (UD; Nivre et al., 2017) and Universal Morphology (UniMorph; Sylak-Glassman et al., 2015; Kirov et al., 2018) projects. Each project's data are annotated according to its own cross-lingual schema, prescribing how features like gender or case should be marked. The schemata capture largely similar information, so one may want to leverage both UD's token-level treebanks and UniMorph's type-level lookup tables and unify the two resources. This would permit a leveraging of both the token-level UD treebanks and the type-level UniMorph tables of paradigms. Unfortunately, neither resource perfectly realizes

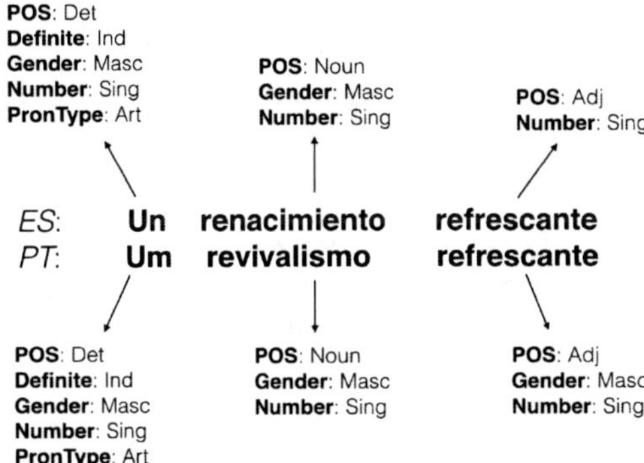

Figure 1: Example of annotation disagreement in UD between two languages on translations of one phrase, reproduced from Malaviya et al. (2018). The final word in each, *"refrescante"*, is not inflected for gender: It has the same surface form whether masculine or feminine. Only in Portuguese, it is annotated as masculine to reflect grammatical concord with the noun it modifies.

its schema. On a dataset-by-dataset basis, they incorporate annotator errors, omissions, and human decisions when the schemata are underspecified; one such example is in Figure 1.

A dataset-by-dataset problem demands a dataset-by-dataset solution; our task is not to translate a *schema*, but to translate a *resource*. Starting from the idealized schema, we create a rule-based tool for converting UD-schema annotations to UniMorph annotations, incorporating language-specific post-edits that both correct infelicities and also increase harmony between the datasets themselves (rather than the schemata). We apply this conversion to the 31 languages with both UD and UniMorph data, and we report our method's recall, showing an improvement over the strategy which just maps corresponding schematic features to each other. Further, we show similar downstream performance for each annotation scheme in the task of morphological tagging.

Proceedings of the Second Workshop on Universal Dependencies (UDW 2018), pages 91–101
Brussels, Belgium, November 1, 2018. ©2018 Association for Computational Linguistics

This tool enables a synergistic use of UniMorph and Universal Dependencies, as well as teasing out the annotation discrepancies within and across projects. When one dataset disobeys its schema or disagrees with a related language, the flaws may not be noticed except by such a methodological dive into the resources. When the maintainers of the resources ameliorate these flaws, the resources move closer to the goal of a universal, cross-lingual inventory of features for morphological annotation.

The contributions of this work are:

- We detail a deterministic mapping from UD morphological annotations to UniMorph. Language-specific edits of the tags in 31 languages increase harmony between converted UD and existing UniMorph data (§5).

- We provide an implementation of this mapping and post-editing, which replaces the UD features in a CoNLL-U file with UniMorph features.[1]

- We demonstrate that downstream performance tagging accuracy on UD treebanks is similar, whichever annotation schema is used (§7).

- We provide a partial inventory of missing attributes or annotation inconsistencies in both UD and UniMorph, a guidepost for strengthening and harmonizing each resource.

2 Background: Morphological Inflection

Morphological **inflection** is the act of altering the base form of a word (the **lemma**, represented in `fixed-width type`) to encode morphosyntactic features. As an example from English, `prove` takes on the **form** "proved" to indicate that the action occurred in the past. (We will represent all surface forms in quotation marks.) The process occurs in the majority of the world's widely-spoken languages, typically through meaningful affixes. The breadth of forms created by inflection creates a challenge of data sparsity for natural language processing: The likelihood of observing a particular word form diminishes.

A classic result in psycholinguistics (Berko, 1958) shows that inflectional morphology is a fully productive process. Indeed, it cannot be that humans simply have the equivalent of a lookup table,

Simple label	Form	PTB tag
Present, 3rd singular	"proves"	VBZ
Present, other	"prove"	VBP
Past	"proved"	VBD
Past participle	"proven"	VBN
Present participle	"proving"	VBG

Table 1: Inflected forms of the English verb `prove`, along with their Penn Treebank tags

where they store the inflected forms for retrieval as the syntactic context requires. Instead, there needs to be a mental process that can generate properly inflected words on demand. Berko (1958) showed this insightfully through the "wug"-test, an experiment where she forced participants to correctly inflect out-of-vocabulary lemmata, such as the novel noun `wug`.

Certain features of a word do not vary depending on its context: In German or Spanish where nouns are gendered, the word for `onion` will always be grammatically feminine. Thus, to prepare for later discussion, we divide the morphological features of a word into two categories: the modifiable **inflectional features** and the fixed **lexical features**.

A **part of speech (POS)** is a coarse syntactic category (like "verb") that begets a word's particular menu of lexical and inflectional features. In English, verbs express no gender, and adjectives do not reflect person or number. The part of speech dictates a set of inflectional **slots** to be filled by the surface forms. Completing these slots for a given lemma and part of speech gives a **paradigm**: a mapping from slots to surface forms. Regular English verbs have five slots in their paradigm (Long, 1957), which we illustrate for the verb `prove`, using simple labels for the forms in Table 1.

A morphosyntactic **schema** prescribes how language can be annotated—giving stricter categories than our simple labels for `prove`—and can vary in the level of detail provided. Part of speech tags are an example of a very coarse schema, ignoring details of person, gender, and number. A slightly finer-grained schema for English is the Penn Treebank tagset (Marcus et al., 1993), which includes signals for English morphology. For instance, its VBZ tag pertains to the specially inflected 3rd-person singular, present-tense verb form (e.g. "proves" in Table 1).

If the tag in a schema is detailed enough that it exactly specifies a slot in a paradigm, it is

---

[1]Available at `https://www.github.com/unimorph/ud-compatibility`.

called a **morphosyntactic description (MSD)**.[2] These descriptions require varying amounts of detail: While the English verbal paradigm is small enough to fit on a page, the verbal paradigm of the Northeast Caucasian language Archi can have over $1{,}500{,}000$ slots (Kibrik, 1998).

3 Two Schemata, Two Philosophies

Unlike the Penn Treebank tags, the UD and UniMorph schemata are cross-lingual and include a fuller lexicon of attribute-value pairs, such as PERSON: 1. Each was built according to a different set of principles. UD's schema is constructed bottom-up, adapting to include new features when they're identified in languages. UniMorph, conversely, is top-down: A cross-lingual survey of the literature of morphological phenomena guided its design. UniMorph aims to be linguistically complete, containing all known morphosyntactic attributes. Both schemata share one long-term goal: a total inventory for annotating the possible morphosyntactic features of a word.

3.1 Universal Dependencies

The Universal Dependencies morphological schema comprises part of speech and 23 additional attributes (also called features in UD) annotating meaning or syntax, as well as language-specific attributes. In order to ensure consistent annotation, attributes are included into the general UD schema if they occur in several corpora. Language-specific attributes are used when only one corpus annotates for a specific feature.

The UD schema seeks to balance language-specific and cross-lingual concerns. It annotates for both inflectional features such as case and lexical features such as gender. Additionally, the UD schema annotates for features which can be interpreted as derivational in some languages. For example, the Czech UD guidance uses a COLL value for the NUMBER feature to denote mass nouns (for example, "*lidstvo*" "humankind" from the root "*lid*" "people").[3]

UD represents a confederation of datasets (see, e.g., Dirix et al., 2017) annotated with dependency relationships (which are not the focus of this work) and morphosyntactic descriptions. Each dataset

is an annotated treebank, making it a resource of **token-level** annotations. The schema is guided by these treebanks, with feature names chosen for relevance to native speakers. (In §3.2, we will contrast this with UniMorph's treatment of morphosyntactic categories.) The UD datasets have been used in the CoNLL shared tasks (Zeman et al., 2017, 2018 to appear).

3.2 UniMorph

In the Universal Morphological Feature Schema (UniMorph schema, Sylak-Glassman, 2016), there are at least 212 values, spread across 23 attributes. It identifies some attributes that UD excludes like information structure and deixis, as well as providing more values for certain attributes, like 23 different noun classes endemic to Bantu languages. As it is a schema for marking morphology, its part of speech attribute does not have POS values for punctuation, symbols, or miscellany (PUNCT, SYM, and X in Universal Dependencies).

Like the UD schema, the decomposition of a word into its lemma and MSD is directly comparable across languages. Its features are informed by a distinction between **universal categories**, which are widespread and psychologically "real" to speakers; and **comparative concepts**, only used by linguistic typologists to compare languages (Haspelmath, 2010). Additionally, it strives for identity of meaning across languages, not simply similarity of terminology. As a prime example, it does not regularly label a dative case for nouns, for reasons explained in depth by Haspelmath (2010).[4]

The UniMorph resources for a language contain complete paradigms extracted from Wiktionary (Kirov et al., 2016, 2018). Word **types** are annotated to form a database, mapping a lemma–tag pair to a surface form. The schema is explained in detail in Sylak-Glassman (2016). It has been used in the SIGMORPHON shared task (Cotterell et al., 2016) and the CoNLL–SIGMORPHON shared tasks (Cotterell et al., 2017, 2018). Several components of the UniMorph schema have been adopted by UD.[5]

---

[2]Other sources will call this a morphological tag or bundle. We avoid the former because of the analogy to POS tagging; a morphological tag is not atomic.

[3]Note that NUMBER: COLL does not actually figure in the Czech corpus.

[4]"The Russian Dative, the Korean Dative, and the Turkish Dative are similar enough to be called by the same name, but there are numerous differences between them and they cannot be simply equated with each other. Clearly, their nature is not captured satisfactorily by saying that they are instantiations of a crosslinguistic category 'dative'." (Haspelmath, 2010)

[5]`http://universaldependencies.org/v2/`
`features.html#comparison-with-unimorph`

Schema	Annotation				
UD	VERB	MOOD=IND|NUMBER=SING|PERSON=3|TENSE=IMP|VERBFORM=FIN			
UniMorph	V;IND;PST;1;SG;IPFV				
	V;IND;PST;3;SG;IPFV				

Table 2: Attested annotations for the Spanish verb form *"mandaba"* "I/he/she/it commanded". Note that UD separates the part of speech from the remainder of the morphosyntactic description. In each schema, order of the values is irrelevant.

3.3 Similarities in the annotation

While the two schemata annotate different features, their annotations often look largely similar. Consider the attested annotation of the Spanish word *"mandaba"* "(I/he/she/it) commanded". Table 2 shows that these annotations share many attributes.

Some conversions are straightforward: VERB to V, MOOD=IND to IND, NUMBER=SING to SG, and PERSON=3 to 3.[6] One might also suggest mapping TENSE=IMP to IPFV, though this crosses semantic categories: IPFV represents the imperfective *aspect*, whereas TENSE=IMP comes from **imperfect**, the English name often given to Spanish's *pasado continuo* form. The imperfect is a verb form which combines both past tense and imperfective aspect. UniMorph chooses to split this into the atoms PST and IPFV, while UD unifies them according to the familiar name of the tense.

4 UD treebanks and UniMorph tables

Prima facie, the alignment task may seem trivial. But we've yet to explore the humans in the loop. This conversion is a hard problem because we're operating on idealized schemata. We're actually annotating human decisions—and human mistakes. If both schemata were perfectly applied, their overlapping attributes could be mapped to each other simply, in a cross-lingual and totally general way. Unfortunately, the resources are imperfect realizations of their schemata. The cross-lingual, cross-resource, and within-resource problems that we'll note mean that we need a tailor-made solution for each language.

Showcasing their schemata, the Universal Dependencies and UniMorph projects each present large, annotated datasets. UD's v2.1 release (Nivre et al., 2017) has 102 treebanks in 60 languages. The large resource, constructed by independent parties, evinces problems in the goal of a universal inventory of annotations. Annotators may choose to omit certain values (like the coerced gender of *refrescante* in Figure 1), and they may disagree on how a linguistic concept is encoded. (See, e.g., Haspelmath's (2010) description of the dative case.) Additionally, many of the treebanks "were created by fully- or semi-automatic conversion from treebanks with less comprehensive annotation schemata than UD" (Malaviya et al., 2018). For instance, the Spanish word *"vas"* "you go" is incorrectly labeled **GENDER: FEM\|NUMBER: PL** because it ends in a character sequence which is common among feminine plural nouns. (Nevertheless, the part of speech field for *"vas"* is correct.)

UniMorph's development is more centralized and pipelined.[7] Inflectional paradigms are scraped from Wiktionary, annotators map positions in the scraped data to MSDs, and the mapping is automatically applied to all of the scraped paradigms. Because annotators handle languages they are familiar with (or related ones), realization of the schema is also done on a language-by-language basis. Further, the scraping process does not capture lexical aspects that are not inflected, like noun gender in many languages. The schema permits inclusion of these details; their absence is an artifact of the data collection process. Finally, UniMorph records only exist for nouns, verbs, and adjectives, though the schema is broader than these categories.

For these reasons, we treat the corpora as imperfect realizations of the schemata. Moreover, we contend that ambiguity in the schemata leave the door open to allow for such imperfections. With no strict guidance, it's natural that annotators would take different paths. Nevertheless, modulo annota-

---

[6] The curious reader may wonder why there are two rows of UniMorph annotation for *"mandaba"*, each with a different recorded person. The word displays **syncretism**, meaning that a single form realizes multiple MSDs. UniMorph chooses to mark these separately for the sake of its decomposable representation. As this ambiguity is systematic and pervasive in the language, one can imagine a unified paradigm slot V;IND;PST;{1/3};SG;IPFV (Baerman et al., 2005).

[7] This centralization explains why UniMorph tables exist for only 49 languages, or 50 when counting the Norwegian Nynorsk and Bokmål writing forms separately.

| tegarg | **latme**-ye | bad-i | be | ba:q-e | man | **zad**. |
| Hail | damage-EZ | bad-INDEF PAR | to | garden-EZ | 1.S | beat-PST. |

"The hail caused bad damage to my garden." *or* "The hail damaged my garden badly."

Figure 2: Transliterated Persian with a gloss and translation from Karimi-Doostan (2011), annotated in a Persian-specific schema. The light verb construction *"latme zadan"* ("to damage") has been spread across the sentence. Multiword constructions like this are a challenge for word-level tagging schemata.

tor disagreement, we assume that within a particular corpus, one word form will always be consistently annotated.

Three categories of annotation difficulty are missing values, language-specific attributes, and multiword expressions.

Missing values In both schemata, irrelevant attributes are omitted for words to which they do not pertain. For instance, an English verb is not labeled **GENDER**=NULL; the **GENDER** attribute is simply excluded from the annotation, making the human-readable representations compact. Unfortunately, in both resources, even relevant attributes are intentionally omitted. A verb's positiveness, activeness, or finiteness can be taken as implicit, and it will be omitted arbitrarily on a language-by-language basis. For instance, in our example in Table 2 only UD tags Spanish finite verbs: **VERB-FORM**=**FIN**. Not only UniMorph makes such elisions: we note that *neither* resource marks verb forms as active—an action entirely permitted by the schemata. This is one source of discrepancy, both between the projects and across languages within a project, but it is straightforward to harmonize.

Language-specific attributes UD records a set of features that are kept language-specific, including **POSITION** in Romanian, **DIALECT** in Russian, and **NUMVALUE** in Czech and Arabic.[8] UniMorph has (potentially infinite) language-specific features **LGSPEC1**, **LGSPEC2**, ..., which are sparsely used but opaque when encountered. For instance, **LGSPEC1** in Spanish distinguishes between the two (semantically identical) forms of the imperfect subjunctive: the "-se" and "-ra" forms (e.g. *"estuviese"* and *"estuviera"* from *"estar"* "to be"). UD does not annotate the forms differently. If a language has multiple language-specific attributes, their order is not prescribed by the UniMorph schema, and separate notes that explain the use of such tags must accompany datasets.

Multiword expressions A final imperfection is how to represent multiword constructions. Both UD and UniMorph are word-level annotations, espousing what has alternately been called the **lexical integrity principle** (Chomsky, 1970; Bresnan and Mchombo, 1995) or **word-based morphology** (Aronoff, 1976, 2007; Spencer, 1991). Unfortunately, not all morphological manifestations occur at the level of individual words. The Farsi (Persian) **light verb construction** illustrates the deficiency (see Karimi-Doostan, 2011). Farsi expresses many actions by pairing a light verb (one with little meaning) with a noun that gives a concrete meaning. The example in Figure 2 uses the light verb construction *"latme zadan"* ("to damage"). The parts of the verb construction are separated in the sentence, seeming to require a morphosyntactic parse. When attempting to annotate these constructs, neither schema provides guidance. In languages where these occur, language-specific decisions are made. It should be noted that multiword expressions are a general challenge to natural language processing, not specifically morphology (Sag et al., 2002).

5   A Deterministic Conversion

In our work, the goal is not simply to translate one schema into the other, but to translate one *resource* (the imperfect manifestation of the schema) to match the other. The differences between the schemata and discrepancies in annotation mean that the transformation of annotations from one schema to the other is not straightforward.

Two naive options for the conversion are a lookup table of MSDs and a lookup table of the individual attribute-value pairs which comprise the MSDs. The former is untenable: the table of all UD feature combinations (including null features, excluding language-specific attributes) would have

---

[8]The complete list is at `http://universaldependencies.org/v2/features.html#inventory-of-features-that-will-stay-language-specific`

2.445×10^{17} entries. Of course, most combinations won't exist, but this gives a sense of the table's scale. Also, it doesn't leverage the factorial nature of the annotations: constructing the table would require a massive duplication of effort. On the other hand, attribute-value lookup lacks the flexibility to show how a pair of values interacts. Neither approach would handle language- and annotator-specific tendencies in the corpora.

Our approach to converting UD MSDs to UniMorph MSDs begins with the attribute-value lookup, then amends it on a language-specific basis. Alterations informed by the MSD and the word form, like insertion, substitution, and deletion, increase the number of agreeing annotations. They are critical for work that examines the MSD monolithically instead of feature-by-feature (e.g. Belinkov et al., 2017; Cotterell and Heigold, 2017): Without exact matches, converting the individual tags becomes hollow.

Beginning our process, we relied on documentation of the two schemata to create our initial, language-agnostic mapping of individual values. This mapping has 140 pairs in it. Because the mapping was derived purely from the schemata, it is a useful approximation of how well the schemata match up. We note, however, that the mapping does not handle idiosyncrasies like the many uses of "dative" or features which are represented in UniMorph by argument templates: possession and ergative–absolutive argument marking. The initial step of our conversion is using this mapping to populate a proposed UniMorph MSD.

As shown in §7, the initial proposal is often frustratingly deficient. Thus we introduce the post-edits. To concoct these, we looked into UniMorph corpora for these languages, compared these to the conversion outputs, and then sought to bring the conversion outputs closer to the annotations in the actual UniMorph corpora. When a form and its lemma existed in both corpora, we could directly inspect how the annotations differed. Our process of iteratively refining the conversion implies a table which exactly maps any combination of UD MSD and its related values (lemma, form, etc.) to a UniMorph MSD, though we do not store the table explicitly.

Some conversion rules we've created must be applied before or after others. These sequential dependencies provide conciseness. Our post-editing procedure operates on the initial MSD hypothesis as follows:

1. First, we collect all arguments relating to a possessor or an ergative–absolutive language's argument agreement, because UniMorph represents both categories as a single templatic value.

2. We discard any values that UniMorph doesn't annotate for a particular part of speech, like gender and number in French verb participles, or German noun genders.

3. We make MSD additions when they are unambiguously implied by the resources, like PFV to accompany PST in Spanish "pasado simple", but PST to accompany IPFV in Spanish "pasado continuo".

4. We also incorporate fixes using information outside of the MSD like the LGSPEC1 tag for Spanish's "-ra" forms, as described in §4, and other language-specific corrections, like mapping the various dative cases to the cross-lingually comparable case annotations used in UniMorph.

What we left out We did, however, reject certain changes that would increase harmony between the resources. Usually, this decision was made when the UniMorph syntax or tagset was not obeyed, such as in the case of made-up tags for Basque arguments (instead of the template mentioned above) or the use of idiopathic colons (:) instead of semicolons (;) as separators in Farsi. Other instances were linguistically motivated. UD acknowledges Italian imperatives, but UniMorph does not have any in its table. We could largely alter these to have subjunctive labels, but to ill effect. A third reason to be conservative in our rules was cases of under-specification: If a participle is not marked as past or present in UD, but both exist in UniMorph, we could unilaterally assign all to the majority category and increase recall. This would pollute the data with fallacious features, so we leave these cases under-specified. In other words, we do not add new values that cannot be unequivocally inferred from the existing data.

Output The Universal Dependencies data are presented in the CoNLL-U format.[9] Each sentence

---

[9] `http://universaldependencies.org/format.html`

is represented in tabular form to organize annotations like lemmas, parts of speech, and dependencies of each word token. The MSDs are held in a column called `FEATS`. Our MSD conversion tool produces a CoNLL-U file whose `FEATS` column now contains a UniMorph-style MSD. For more straightforward interface with UniMorph, the feature bundle includes the part of speech tag. As the `POS` column of the CONLL-U file is preserved, this can easily be stripped from the `FEATS` column, depending on use case.

Why not a learned mapping? One can imagine learning the UniMorph MSD corresponding to a UD dataset's MSD by a set-to-set translation model like IBM Model 1 (Brown et al., 1993). Unfortunately, statistical (and especially neural) machine translation generalizes in unreliable ways. Our goal is a straightforward, easily manipulable and extensible conversion that prioritizes correctness over coverage.

6   Experiments

We evaluate our tool on two tasks:

Intrinsic assessment: Once we convert UD MSDs to UniMorph MSDs, how many of the converted ones are attested in UniMorph's paradigm tables.

Extrinsic assessment: Whether performance on a downstream task is comparable when using pre- and post-conversion MSDs.

To be clear, our scope is limited to the schema conversion. Future work will explore NLP tasks that exploit both the created token-level UniMorph data and the existing type-level UniMorph data.

Data We draw our input data from the UD v2.1 treebanks (Nivre et al., 2017). When multiple treebanks exist for a language, we select the one with a basic name, e.g. "Spanish" instead of "Spanish-AnCora". We leave the construction of additional converters to future work, and we invite the community to participate in designing the mappings for all UD treebanks. UniMorph modifies its language packs individually instead of offering versioned releases. Our UniMorph lookup tables are the latest versions at the time of writing.[10] There are 31 languages which possess both a UD and a UniMorph corpus.

---

[10]As of 19 June 2018, the latest modification to a UniMorph language resource was to Finnish on 3 August 2017.

6.1   Intrinsic evaluation

We transform all UD data to the UniMorph. We compare the simple lookup-based transformation to the one with linguistically informed post-edits on all languages with both UD and UniMorph data. We then evaluate the recall of MSDs without partial credit.

Calculating recall Because the UniMorph tables only possess annotations for verbs, nouns, adjectives, or some combination, we can only examine performance for these parts of speech. We consider two words to be a match if their form and lemma are present in both resources. Syncretism allows a single surface form to realize multiple MSDs (Spanish *"mandaba"* can be first- or third-person), so we define success as the computed MSD matching *any* of the word's UniMorph MSDs. This gives rise to an equation for recall: of the word–lemma pairs found in both resources, how many of their UniMorph-converted MSDs are present in the UniMorph tables?

Why no held-out test set? Our problem here is not a learning problem, so the question is ill-posed. There is no *training* set, and the two resources for a given language make up a test set. The quality of our model—the conversion tool—comes from how well we encode prior knowledge about the relationship between the UD and UniMorph corpora.

6.2   Extrinsic evaluation

If the UniMorph-converted treebanks perform differently on downstream tasks, then they convey different information. This signals a failure of the conversion process. As a downstream task, we choose morphological tagging, a critical step to leveraging morphological information on new text.

We evaluate taggers trained on the transformed UD data, choosing eight languages randomly from the intersection of UD and UniMorph resources. We report the macro-averaged F1 score of attribute-value pairs on a held-out test set, with official train/validation/test splits provided in the UD treebanks. As a reference point, we also report tagging accuracy on those languages' untransformed data.

We use the state-of-the-art morphological tagger of Malaviya et al. (2018). It is a factored conditional random field with potentials for each attribute, attribute pair, and attribute transition. The potentials are computed by neural networks, predicting the values of each attribute jointly but not monolithically. Inference with the potentials is performed approximately by loopy belief propagation. We use the authors' hyperparameters.

We note a minor implementation detail for the sake of reproducibility. The tagger exploits explicit guidance about the attribute each value pertains to. The UniMorph schema's values are globally unique, but their attributes are not explicit. For example, the UniMorph MASC denotes a masculine gender. We amend the code of Malaviya et al. to incorporate attribute identifiers for each UniMorph value.

7 Results

We present the intrinsic task's recall scores in Table 3. Bear in mind that due to annotation errors in the original corpora (like the "*vas*" example from §4), the optimal score is not always 100%. Some shortcomings of recall come from irremediable annotation discrepancies. Largely, we are hamstrung by differences in choice of attributes to annotate. When one resource marks gender and the other marks case, we can't infer the gender of the word purely from its surface form. The resources themselves would need updating to encode the relevant morphosyntactic information. Some languages had a very low number of overlapping forms,[11] and no tag matches or near-matches between them: Arabic, Hindi, Lithuanian, Persian, and Russian. A full list of observed, irremediable discrepancies is presented alongside the codebase.

There are three other transformations for which we note no improvement here. Because of the problem in Basque argument encoding in the UniMorph dataset—which only contains verbs—we note no improvement in recall on Basque. Irish also does not improve: UD marks gender on nouns, while UniMorph marks case. Adjectives in UD are also underspecified. The verbs, though, are already correct with the simple mapping. Finally, with Dutch, the UD annotations are impoverished compared to the UniMorph annotations, and missing attributes cannot be inferred without external knowledge.

For the extrinsic task, the performance is reasonably similar whether UniMorph or UD; see Table 4. A large fluctuation would suggest that the two annotations encode distinct information. On the contrary, the similarities suggest that the UniMorph-mapped MSDs have similar content. We recognize

---

[11] Fewer than 250 overlapping form–lemma pairs. The other languages had overlaps in the thousands.

Language	CSV	Post-editing
Ar	0.00	-
Bg	34.61	87.88
Ca	23.23	99.78
Cs	0.48	81.71
Da	1.55	4.70
De	17.20	60.81
En	42.17	90.10
Es	17.20	97.86
Eu	0.00	0.00
Fa	0.00	-
Fi	59.19	92.81
Fr	18.61	99.20
Ga	0.41	0.41
He	4.08	46.61
Hi	0.00	-
Hu	15.46	24.94
It	22.32	94.89
La	11.73	64.25
Lt	0.00	-
Lv	0.17	90.58
Nb	2.11	38.88
Nl	12.12	12.12
Nn	2.40	40.21
Pl	7.70	88.17
Pt	20.11	99.34
Ro	0.00	25.16
Ru	0.00	-
Sl	37.57	90.27
Sv	13.20	83.44
Tr	0.00	65.14
Uk	4.06	96.45
Ur	0.00	55.72

Table 3: Token-level recall when converting Universal Dependencies tags to UniMorph tags. CSV refers to the lookup-based system. Post-editing refers to the proposed method.

Language	UD F1	UniMorph F1
Da	90.58	92.59
Es	78.31	96.44
Fi	93.78	94.98
Lv	84.20	86.94
Pt	95.57	95.77
Ru	89.89	89.95
Bg	95.54	95.79
Sv	92.39	93.83

Table 4: Tagging F1 using UD sentences annotated with either original UD MSDs or UniMorph-converted MSDs

that in every case, tagging F1 increased—albeit by amounts as small as 0.16 points. This is in part due to the information that is lost in the conversion. UniMorph's schema does not indicate the type of pronoun (demonstrative, interrogative, etc.), and when lexical information is not recorded in Uni-Morph, we delete it from the MSD during transformation. On the other hand, UniMorph's atomic tags have more parts to guess, but they are often related. (E.g. IPFV always entails PST in Spanish.) Altogether, these forces seem to have little impact on tagging performance.

8   Related Work

The goal of a tagset-to-tagset mapping of morphological annotations is shared by the Interset project (Zeman, 2008). Interset decodes features in the source corpus to a *tag interlingua*, then encodes that into target corpus features. (The idea of an interlingua is drawn from machine translation, where a prevailing early mindset was to convert to a universal representation, then encode that representation's semantics in the target language. Our approach, by contrast, is a direct flight from the source to the target.) Because UniMorph corpora are noisy, the encoding from the interlingua would have to be rewritten for each target. Further, decoding the UD MSD into the interlingua cannot leverage external information like the lemma and form.

The creators of HamleDT sought to harmonize dependency annotations among treebanks, similar to our goal of harmonizing across resources (Zeman et al., 2014). The treebanks they sought to harmonize used multiple diverse annotation schemes, which the authors unified under a single scheme.

Petrov et al. (2012) present mappings into a coarse, "universal" part of speech for 22 languages. Working with POS tags rather than morphological tags (which have far more dimensions), their space of options to harmonize is much smaller than ours.

Our extrinsic evaluation is most in line with the paradigm of Wisniewski and Lacroix (2017) (and similar work therein), who compare syntactic parser performance on UD treebanks annotated with two styles of dependency representation. Our problem differs, though, in that the dependency representations express different relationships, while our two schemata vastly overlap. As our conversion is lossy, we do not appraise the learnability of representations as they did.

In addition to using the number of extra rules as a proxy for harmony between resources, one could perform cross-lingual projection of morphological tags (Drábek and Yarowsky, 2005; Kirov et al., 2017). Our approach succeeds even without parallel corpora.

9   Conclusion and Future Work

We created a tool for annotating Universal Dependencies CoNLL-U files with UniMorph annotations. Our tool is ready to use off-the-shelf today, requires no training, and is deterministic. While under-specification necessitates a lossy and imperfect conversion, ours is interpretable. Patterns of mistakes can be identified and ameliorated.

The tool allows a bridge between resources annotated in the Universal Dependencies and Universal Morphology (UniMorph) schemata. As the Universal Dependencies project provides a set of treebanks with token-level annotation, while the UniMorph project releases type-level annotated tables, the newfound compatibility opens up new experiments. A prime example of exploiting token- and type-level data is Täckström et al. (2013). That work presents a part-of-speech (POS) dictionary built from Wiktionary, where the POS tagger is also constrained to options available in their type-level POS dictionary, improving performance. Our transformation means that datasets are prepared for similar experiments with morphological tagging. It would also be reasonable to incorporate this tool as a subroutine to UDPipe (Straka and Straková, 2017) and Udapi (Popel et al., 2017). We leave open the task of converting in the opposite direction, turning UniMorph MSDs into Universal Dependencies MSDs.

Because our conversion rules are interpretable, we identify shortcomings in both resources, using each as validation for the other. We were able to find specific instances of incorrectly applied Uni-Morph annotation, as well as specific instances of cross-lingual inconsistency in both resources. These findings will harden both resources and better align them with their goal of universal, cross-lingual annotation.

Acknowledgments

We thank Hajime Senuma and John Sylak-Glassman for early comments in devising the starting language-independent mapping from Universal Dependencies to UniMorph.

References

Mark Aronoff. 1976. Word formation in generative grammar. *Linguistic Inquiry Monographs Cambridge, Mass.*, 1:1–134.

Mark Aronoff. 2007. In the beginning was the word. *Language*, 83(4):803–830.

Matthew Baerman, Dunstan Brown, Greville G Corbett, et al. 2005. *The syntax-morphology interface: A study of syncretism*, volume 109. Cambridge University Press.

Yonatan Belinkov, Nadir Durrani, Fahim Dalvi, Hassan Sajjad, and James Glass. 2017. What do neural machine translation models learn about morphology? In *Proceedings of the 55th Annual Meeting of the Association for Computational Linguistics (Volume 1: Long Papers)*, volume 1, pages 861–872.

Jean Berko. 1958. The child's learning of English morphology. *Word*, 14(2-3):150–177.

Joan Bresnan and Sam A. Mchombo. 1995. The lexical integrity principle: Evidence from Bantu. *Natural Language & Linguistic Theory*, 13(2):181–254.

Peter F Brown, Vincent J Della Pietra, Stephen A Della Pietra, and Robert L Mercer. 1993. The mathematics of statistical machine translation: Parameter estimation. *Computational linguistics*, 19(2):263–311.

Noam Chomsky. 1970. Remarks on nominalization. In R. Jacobs and P. Rosenbaum, editors, *Reading in English Transformational Grammar*, pages 184–221. Ginn and Co., Waltham.

Ryan Cotterell and Georg Heigold. 2017. Cross-lingual character-level neural morphological tagging. In *Proceedings of the 2017 Conference on Empirical Methods in Natural Language Processing*, pages 748–759. Association for Computational Linguistics.

Ryan Cotterell, Christo Kirov, John Sylak-Glassman, Géraldine Walther, Ekaterina Vylomova, Arya D. McCarthy, Katharina Kann, Sebastian Mielke, Garrett Nicolai, Miikka Silfverberg, David Yarowsky, Jason Eisner, and Mans Hulden. 2018. The CoNLL–SIGMORPHON 2018 shared task: Universal morphological reinflection. In *Proceedings of the CoNLL–SIGMORPHON 2018 Shared Task: Universal Morphological Reinflection*, Brussels, Belgium. Association for Computational Linguistics.

Ryan Cotterell, Christo Kirov, John Sylak-Glassman, Géraldine Walther, Ekaterina Vylomova, Patrick Xia, Manaal Faruqui, Sandra Kübler, David Yarowsky, Jason Eisner, et al. 2017. CoNLL-SIGMORPHON 2017 shared task: Universal morphological reinflection in 52 languages. *Proceedings of the CoNLL–SIGMORPHON 2017 Shared Task: Universal Morphological Reinflection*, pages 1–30.

Ryan Cotterell, Christo Kirov, John Sylak-Glassman, David Yarowsky, Jason Eisner, and Mans Hulden. 2016. The SIGMORPHON 2016 shared task—morphological reinflection. In *Proceedings of the 14th SIGMORPHON Workshop on Computational Research in Phonetics, Phonology, and Morphology*, pages 10–22.

Peter Dirix, Liesbeth Augustinus, Daniel van Niekerk, and Frank Van Eynde. 2017. Universal dependencies for Afrikaans. In *Proceedings of the NoDaLiDa 2017 Workshop on Universal Dependencies, 22 May, Gothenburg Sweden*, 135, pages 38–47. Linköping University Electronic Press.

Elliott Franco Drábek and David Yarowsky. 2005. Induction of fine-grained part-of-speech taggers via classifier combination and crosslingual projection. In *Proceedings of the ACL Workshop on Building and Using Parallel Texts*, pages 49–56. Association for Computational Linguistics.

Martin Haspelmath. 2010. Comparative concepts and descriptive categories in crosslinguistic studies. *Language*, 86(3):663–687.

Gholamhossein Karimi-Doostan. 2011. Separability of light verb constructions in Persian. *Studia Linguistica*, 65(1):70–95.

Aleksandr E. Kibrik. 1998. *Archi (Caucasian–Daghestanian)*. Wiley Online Library.

Christo Kirov, Ryan Cotterell, John Sylak-Glassman, Géraldine Walther, Ekaterina Vylomova, Patrick Xia, Manaal Faruqui, Arya D. McCarthy, Sandra Kübler, David Yarowsky, Jason Eisner, and Mans Hulden. 2018. UniMorph 2.0: Universal Morphology. In *Proceedings of the Eleventh International Conference on Language Resources and Evaluation (LREC 2018)*, Miyazaki, Japan. European Language Resources Association (ELRA).

Christo Kirov, John Sylak-Glassman, Rebecca Knowles, Ryan Cotterell, and Matt Post. 2017. A rich morphological tagger for English: Exploring the cross-linguistic tradeoff between morphology and syntax. In *Proceedings of the 15th Conference of the European Chapter of the Association for Computational Linguistics: Volume 2, Short Papers*, volume 2, pages 112–117.

Christo Kirov, John Sylak-Glassman, Roger Que, and David Yarowsky. 2016. Very-large scale parsing and normalization of Wiktionary morphological paradigms. In *LREC*.

Ralph B. Long. 1957. Paradigms for English verbs. *Publications of the Modern Language Association of America*, pages 359–372.

Chaitanya Malaviya, Matthew R. Gormley, and Graham Neubig. 2018. Neural factor graph models for cross-lingual morphological tagging. In *Proceedings of the 56th Annual Meeting of the Association for Computational Linguistics (Volume 1: Long Papers)*, pages 2652–2662. Association for Computational Linguistics.

Mitchell P. Marcus, Mary Ann Marcinkiewicz, and Beatrice Santorini. 1993. Building a large annotated corpus of English: The Penn Treebank. *Computational linguistics*, 19(2):313–330.

Joakim Nivre, Željko Agić, Lars Ahrenberg, Lene Antonsen, Maria Jesus Aranzabe, Masayuki Asahara, Luma Ateyah, Mohammed Attia, Aitziber Atutxa, Liesbeth Augustinus, et al. 2017. Universal dependencies 2.1. LINDAT/CLARIN digital library at the Institute of Formal and Applied Linguistics (ÚFAL), Faculty of Mathematics and Physics, Charles University.

Slav Petrov, Dipanjan Das, and Ryan McDonald. 2012. A universal part-of-speech tagset. In *Proceedings of the Eight International Conference on Language Resources and Evaluation (LREC'12)*, Istanbul, Turkey. European Language Resources Association (ELRA).

Martin Popel, Zdeněk Žabokrtský, and Martin Vojtek. 2017. Udapi: Universal API for universal dependencies. In *Proceedings of the NoDaLiDa 2017 Workshop on Universal Dependencies (UDW 2017)*, pages 96–101.

Ivan A. Sag, Timothy Baldwin, Francis Bond, Ann Copestake, and Dan Flickinger. 2002. Multiword expressions: A pain in the neck for NLP. In *International Conference on Intelligent Text Processing and Computational Linguistics*, pages 1–15. Springer.

Andrew Spencer. 1991. *Morphological theory: An introduction to word structure in generative grammar*, volume 2. Basil Blackwell Oxford.

Milan Straka and Jana Straková. 2017. Tokenizing, POS tagging, lemmatizing and parsing UD 2.0 with UDPipe. In *Proceedings of the CoNLL 2017 Shared Task: Multilingual Parsing from Raw Text to Universal Dependencies*, pages 88–99, Vancouver, Canada. Association for Computational Linguistics.

John Sylak-Glassman. 2016. The composition and use of the universal morphological feature schema (UniMorph schema). Technical report, Department of Computer Science, Johns Hopkins University.

John Sylak-Glassman, Christo Kirov, David Yarowsky, and Roger Que. 2015. A language-independent feature schema for inflectional morphology. In *Proceedings of the 53rd Annual Meeting of the Association for Computational Linguistics and the 7th International Joint Conference on Natural Language Processing (Volume 2: Short Papers)*, pages 674–680, Beijing, China. Association for Computational Linguistics.

Oscar Täckström, Dipanjan Das, Slav Petrov, Ryan McDonald, and Joakim Nivre. 2013. Token and type constraints for cross-lingual part-of-speech tagging. *Transactions of the Association for Computational Linguistics*, 1:1–12.

Guillaume Wisniewski and Ophélie Lacroix. 2017. A systematic comparison of syntactic representations of dependency parsing. In *Proceedings of the NoDaLiDa 2017 Workshop on Universal Dependencies (UDW 2017)*, pages 146–152.

Daniel Zeman. 2008. Reusable tagset conversion using tagset drivers. In *LREC*, volume 2008, pages 28–30.

Daniel Zeman, Ondřej Dušek, David Mareček, Martin Popel, Loganathan Ramasamy, Jan Štěpánek, Zdeněk Žabokrtský, and Jan Hajič. 2014. Hamledt: Harmonized multi-language dependency treebank. *Language Resources and Evaluation*, 48(4):601–637.

Daniel Zeman, Martin Popel, Milan Straka, Jan Hajic, Joakim Nivre, Filip Ginter, Juhani Luotolahti, Sampo Pyysalo, Slav Petrov, Martin Potthast, et al. 2017. CoNLL 2017 shared task: multilingual parsing from raw text to universal dependencies. *Proceedings of the CoNLL 2017 Shared Task: Multilingual Parsing from Raw Text to Universal Dependencies*, pages 1–19.

Enhancing Universal Dependency Treebanks: A Case Study

Joakim Nivre[*] Paola Marongiu[†] Filip Ginter[‡] Jenna Kanerva[‡]
Simonetta Montemagni[◦] Sebastian Schuster[⋆] Maria Simi[•]

[*]Uppsala University, Department of Linguistics and Philology
[†]University of Pavia, Department of Linguistics
[‡]University of Turku, Department of Future Technologies
[◦]Institute for Computational Linguistics «A. Zampolli» – CNR, Italy
[⋆]Stanford University, Department of Linguistics
[•]University of Pisa, Department of Computer Science

Abstract

We evaluate two cross-lingual techniques for adding enhanced dependencies to existing treebanks in Universal Dependencies. We apply a rule-based system developed for English and a data-driven system trained on Finnish to Swedish and Italian. We find that both systems are accurate enough to bootstrap enhanced dependencies in existing UD treebanks. In the case of Italian, results are even on par with those of a prototype language-specific system.

1 Introduction

Universal Dependencies (UD) is a framework for cross-linguistically consistent treebank annotation (Nivre et al., 2016). Its syntactic annotation layer exists in two versions: a *basic* representation, where words are connected by syntactic relations into a dependency tree, and an *enhanced* representation, which is a richer graph structure that adds external subject relations, shared dependents in coordination, and predicate-argument relations in elliptical constructions, among other things.

Despite the usefulness of enhanced representations (see e.g., Reddy et al. 2017; Schuster et al. 2017), most UD treebanks still contain only basic dependencies[1] and therefore cannot be used to train or evaluate systems that output enhanced UD graphs. In this paper, we explore cross-lingual methods for predicting enhanced dependencies given a basic dependencies treebank. If these predictions are accurate enough, they can be used as a first approximation of enhanced representations for the nearly 100 UD treebanks that lack them,

and as input to manual validation. Further, enhanced UD graphs are in many respects very similar to semantic dependency representations that encode predicate-argument structures (e.g., Böhmová et al. 2003; Miyao and Tsujii 2004; Oepen and Lønning 2006). While the latter exist only for a small number of languages and are typically either produced by complex hand-written grammars or by manual annotation, basic UD treebanks currently exist for more than 60 languages. Hence, automatic methods capable of predicting enhanced dependencies from UD treebanks, have the potential to drastically increase the availability of semantic dependency treebanks.

In this paper, we evaluate a rule-based system developed for English and a data-driven system trained on de-lexicalized Finnish data, for predicting enhanced dependencies on a sample of 1,000 sentences in two new languages, namely Swedish and Italian. For Italian, we also compare to a rule-based system developed specifically for that language using language-specific information. The results show that both cross-lingual methods give high precision, often on par with the language-specific system, and that recall can be improved by exploiting their complementary strengths.

2 Basic and Enhanced Dependencies

Basic dependencies are strict surface syntax trees that connect content words with argument and modifier relations, and attach function words to the content word they modify (Figure 1). Enhanced dependencies restructure trees and add relations that have been shown useful for semantic downstream applications. Although the enhanced representation is in most cases a monotonic exten-

---

[1]Out of 102 treebanks in UD release v2.1, only 5 contain enhanced dependencies.

Proceedings of the Second Workshop on Universal Dependencies (UDW 2018), pages 102–107
Brussels, Belgium, November 1, 2018. ©2018 Association for Computational Linguistics

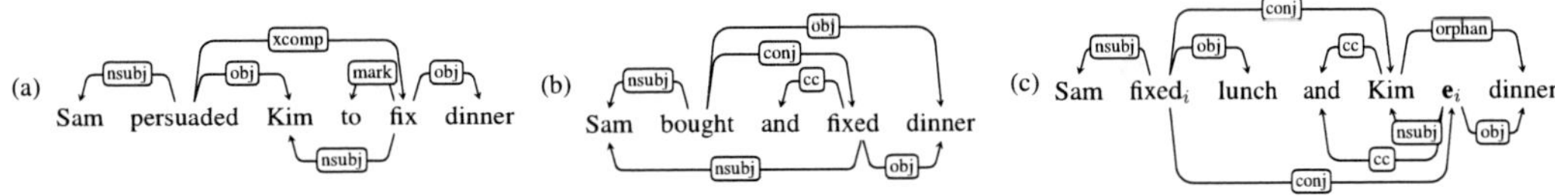

Figure 1: UD basic (top) and enhanced (bottom) dependencies: (a) control, (b) coordination, (c) gapping. For clarity, we show only those enhanced dependencies that are not shared with the basic layer.

sion of the basic one, this does not hold in general (as shown by the treatment of ellipsis below). The current UD guidelines define five enhancements:

1. Added subject relations in control and raising
2. Null nodes for elided predicates (gapping)
3. Shared heads and dependents in coordination
4. Co-reference in relative clause constructions
5. Modifier relations typed by case markers

The last two enhancements can in most cases be predicted deterministically from the basic representation and are mainly a practical convenience. We therefore limit our attention to the first three types, illustrated in Figure 1 (a–c).

Added subject relations Basic dependencies do not specify whether the implicit subject of *fix* in (a) is controlled by *Sam* (subject) or *Kim* (object), but enhanced dependencies do. Similar relations are added also in raising constructions.

Shared heads and dependents in coordination In coordinated structures, incoming and outgoing relations are connected only to the first conjunct in basic dependencies. Enhanced dependencies add explicit links from all conjuncts to shared dependents, like the subject *Sam* and the object *dinner* in (b), as well as from the shared head (not shown).

Null nodes for elided predicates Basic dependencies cannot represent predicate-argument relations in gapping constructions like (c), because of the missing verb, and therefore connect arguments and modifiers using a special *orphan* relation. By adding a null node with lexical information copied from the verb in the first clause, enhanced dependencies can assign the real argument relations to the subject *Kim* and the object *dinner*.

3 Adding Enhanced Dependencies

We describe three systems for predicting enhanced dependencies from basic dependencies. The first two systems have been adapted for cross-lingual use, while the third one uses language-specific information and will be used only for comparison in

the evaluation in the next section. Other language-specific systems have been developed, such as the one by Candito et al. (2017) for French, but this is the first attempt to predict enhanced dependencies in a language-independent way.

3.1 The Rule-Based English System

The system is an adaptation of the work by Schuster and Manning (2016), developed for English. It relies on Semgrex (Chambers et al., 2007) patterns to find dependency structures that should be enhanced and applies heuristics-based processing steps corresponding to the five types of enhancement described in Section 2. We briefly discuss the three steps that are relevant to our study.

Added subject relations For any node attached to a higher predicate with an `xcomp` relation, the system adds a subject relation to the object of the higher predicate if an object is present (object control) or to the subject of the higher predicate if no object is present (subject control or raising). This heuristic gives the right result in Figure 1 (a).

Shared heads and dependents in coordination For conjoined clauses and verb phrases, the system adds explicit dependencies to shared core arguments (i.e., (i) `obj`, n/`csubj`, x/`ccomp`). Thus, in Figure 1(b), the system adds the `nsubj` and `obj` relations from *fixed* to *Sam* and *dinner*, respectively. For other types of coordination, it only adds dependencies from the shared head.

Null nodes Following Schuster et al. (2018), the system aligns arguments and modifiers in the gapped clause to the full clause. This alignment determines main clause predicates for which an empty node should be inserted. Finally, the gapped clause arguments and modifiers are re-attached to the empty node, obtaining a structure such as the one in Figure 1 (c). This method uses word embeddings for the alignment of arguments; here we use the embeddings from the 2017 CoNLL Shared Task (Zeman et al., 2017).

	Subjects					Coordination					Null	
	Swe		Ita			Swe		Ita			Swe	Ita
	RBE	DDF	RBE	DDF	LSI	RBE	DDF	RBE	DDF	LSI	RBE	RBE
Count	127	36	115	43	88	559	981	421	653	660	112	162
Precision	0.87	0.83	0.80	0.95	0.91	0.94	0.91	0.89	0.82	0.85	0.85	0.76
Recall (pooled)	0.98	0.27	0.79	0.35	0.69	0.55	0.97	0.64	0.91	0.78		
Basic errors	12	1	14	0	2	25	28	12	32	19	15	0
Enhanced errors	4	5	9	2	6	9	69	34	86	65	2	35

Table 1: Evaluation of predicted enhanced dependencies for Italian and Swedish (RBE = rule-based English system, DDF = data-driven Finnish system, LSI = language-specific Italian system).

3.2 The Data-Driven Finnish System

This data-driven approach is adapted from the supervised method of Nyblom et al. (2013) originally developed for Finnish. First, patterns identify candidate relations, which are subsequently classified with a linear SVM, trained on gold standard annotation. The original method does not predict null nodes, and therefore we only discuss added subject relations and coordination below.

Added subject relations   A binary classifier is used to decide whether an `nsubj` relation should be added from an `xcomp` dependent to the subject of its governor, accounting for subject control or raising (in the positive case). Object control is not handled by the original system, and we chose not to extend it for this initial case study.

Shared heads and dependents in coordination Candidate relations are created for all possible shared heads (incoming relation to the first conjunct) and dependents (outgoing relations from the first conjunct), striving for high recall. A classifier then predicts the relation type, or negative.

Feature representation   To enable transfer from models trained on Finnish to other languages, we remove lexical and morphological features except universal POS tags and morphological categories that we expect to generalize well: `Number`, `Mood`, `Tense`, `VerbForm`, `Voice`. Language-specific dependency type features are generalized to universal types (e.g., from `nmod:tmod` to `nmod`).

3.3 The Language-Specific Italian System

The language-specific Italian system builds on the rule-based enhancer developed for the Italian Stanford Dependencies Treebank (Bosco et al., 2013, 2014). It has been adapted to predict enhanced dependencies according to the UD guidelines but does not yet handle null nodes. It provides an interesting point of comparison for the cross-lingual systems but cannot really be evaluated on the same conditions since it has been developed using data from the Italian treebank.

Added subject relations   For any infinitive verb attached to a higher predicate with an `xcomp` relation, the system adds a subject relation to a core or (dative) oblique dependent of the governing verb. In contrast to the other systems, this system uses external language-specific resources that specify the control/raising properties of Italian verbs.

Shared heads and dependents in coordination For coordination, the system works similarly to the English rule-based system but includes additional heuristics for different types of coordination (clausal, verbal, nominal, etc.) to prevent the addition of multiple dependents of the same type (e.g., multiple subjects) if this leads to incorrect graphs.

4 Evaluation

Systems were evaluated on the Italian and Swedish UD treebanks. Since these lack enhanced dependencies annotation, the output is manually evaluated by native speakers with extensive experience with the UD guidelines. This allows us to report precision, while recall can only be measured relative to the union of correct predictions. The data-driven system was trained on the training set of the UD Finnish-TDT treebank.

We evaluate added subjects and coordination in a sample of 1,000 sentences from the training set of each treebank; the evaluation of null nodes for elided predicates, which occur more rarely, is based on the entire training sets. The results are shown in Table 1, with errors categorized as *basic errors* caused by errors in the basic dependencies, and *enhanced errors* attributed to the systems.

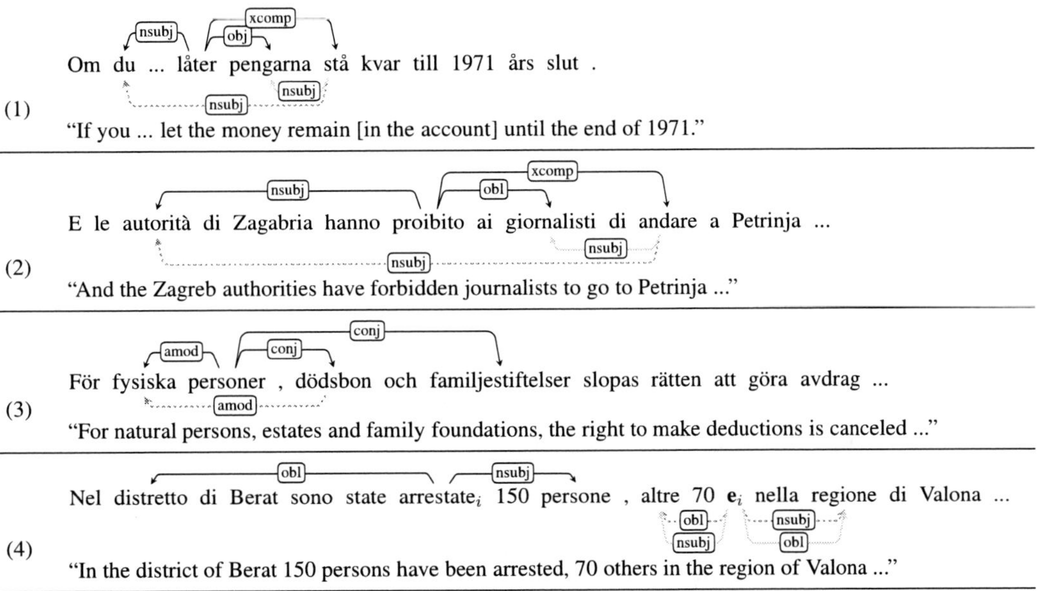

Figure 2: Error examples: added subjects (1–2), coordination (3), null nodes (4). Basic dependencies above, enhanced dependencies below; dotted red = incorrect; solid green = correct.

Added subject relations For Swedish, the rule-based English system (RBE) performs better than the data-driven Finnish system (DDF), especially on recall. The advantage in precision comes from object control, as illustrated in (1) in Figure 2 where DDF predicts subject control despite the presence of a direct object. The lower recall for DDF comes from only considering added subjects of infinitives (as opposed to all `xcomp` predicates). For Italian, the precision results are reversed, which is in part due to non-core arguments occurring more frequently as controllers in Italian. In this case, RBE will always predict a core argument (subject or object) as controller while DDF can abstain from predicting a dependency. The language-specific Italian system (LSI) correctly predicts most of the non-core controllers, thanks to lexical information, leading to higher precision than RBE. This is exemplified in (2) in Figure 2, where RBE predicts subject control while LSI finds the oblique controller and DDF makes no prediction at all. The lower recall for LSI is again caused by its restriction to infinitives.[2]

Shared heads and dependents in coordination The results for coordination are indicative of the different adopted strategies. RBE achieves high precision (0.94 for Swedish, 0.89 for Italian) by limiting shared dependent predictions to core arguments. DDF instead opts for high recall (0.97 for Swedish, 0.91 for Italian) by considering all dependents of the first conjunct as potential shared dependents. As a result, both systems outperform the language-specific system on one metric, but lose out on the other. The most common type of error, especially for the high-recall systems, is to treat a left-dependent of the first conjunct as shared by all conjuncts. This is exemplified by (3) in Figure 2, where DDF incorrectly predicts that the adjectival modifier in *fysiska personer* (natural persons) also applies to *dödsbon* (estates).

Null nodes for elided predicates The method developed to resolve gapping in English seems to generalize very well to Swedish, where almost all the observed errors are in fact due to errors in the basic annotation (mostly incorrect uses of the `orphan` relation). The results are somewhat lower for Italian, which allows word order variations that cannot be captured by the algorithm of Schuster et al. (2018). A case in point is (4) in Figure 2, where the order of the remnants in the gapped clause (`nsubj-obl`) is inverted compared to the complete clause (`obl-nsubj`).

---

[2]It is worth noting that the recall of both DDF and LSI could easily be improved by lifting the restriction to infinitives, since the non-infinitive cases are rarely ambiguous.

5 Conclusion

Our main conclusion is that both the rule-based English and the data-driven Finnish systems are accurate enough to be useful for enhancing treebanks in other languages. Precision is often above 0.9 (and never below 0.8) and recall is complementary, with the English system giving better coverage on added subjects and the Finnish one on coordination. The error analysis furthermore shows how both systems can be further improved. The results are especially encouraging given that one of the "source languages", Finnish, is typologically quite different from the others, which indicates that UD does generalize across languages.

For future research, it would be interesting to investigate how much language-specific training data would be needed for the data-driven system to exceed the cross-lingual results reported here. In addition, the same techniques can of course be used not only for treebank enhancement but also to post-process basic dependencies in parsing, which would potentially be useful for many downstream applications. An interesting question there is how much results would deteriorate because of parsing errors in the basic dependencies.

Acknowledgments

We are grateful to two reviewers for constructive comments on the first version of the paper. This work was supported in part by a gift from Google, Inc.

References

Alena Böhmová, Jan Hajič, Eva Hajičová, and Barbora Hladká. 2003. The Prague dependency treebank. In *Treebanks*, Springer, pages 103–127.

Cristina Bosco, Felice DellâĂŹOrletta, Simonetta Montemagni, Manuela Sanguinetti, and Maria Simi. 2014. The evalita 2014 dependency parsing task. In *Proceedings of the First Italian Conference on Computational Linguistics CLiC-it 2014 and of the Fourth International Workshop EVALITA 2014*. Pisa University Press, volume II, pages 1–8.

Cristina Bosco, Simonetta Montemagni, and Maria Simi. 2013. Converting italian treebanks: Towards an italian stanford dependency treebank. In *Proceedings of the 7th ACL Linguistic Annotation Workshop and Interoperability with Discourse*. pages 61–69.

Marie Candito, Bruno Guillaume, Guy Perrie, and Djamé Seddah. 2017. Enhanced UD dependencies with neutralized diathesis alternation. In *Proceedings of the Fourth International Conference on Dependency Linguistics (Depling 2017)*. pages 42–53.

Nathanael Chambers, Daniel Cer, Trond Grenager, David Hall, Chloe Kiddon, Bill MacCartney, Marie-Catherine de Marneffe, Daniel Ramage, Eric Yeh, and Christopher D. Manning. 2007. Learning alignments and leveraging natural logic. In *Proceedings of the Workshop on Textual Entailment and Paraphrasing*. pages 165–170.

Yusuke Miyao and Jun'ichi Tsujii. 2004. Deep linguistic analysis for the accurate identification of predicate-argument relations. In *Proceedings of the 20th International Conference on Computational Linguistics (COLING 2004)*. pages 1392–1397.

Joakim Nivre, Marie-Catherine de Marneffe, Filip Ginter, Yoav Goldberg, Jan Hajič, Christopher D. Manning, Ryan McDonald, Slav Petrov, Sampo Pyysalo, Natalia Silveira, Reut Tsarfaty, and Dan Zeman. 2016. Universal Dependencies v1: A multilingual treebank collection. In *Proceedings of the 10th International Conference on Language Resources and Evaluation (LREC)*.

Jenna Nyblom, Samuel Kohonen, Katri Haverinen, Tapio Salakoski, and Filip Ginter. 2013. Predicting conjunct propagation and other extended stanford dependencies. In *Proceedings of the Second International Conference on Dependency Linguistics (DepLing 2013)*. pages 252–261.

Stephan Oepen and Jan Tore Lønning. 2006. Discriminant-based MRS banking. In *Proceedings of the Fifth International Conference on Language Resources and Evaluation (LREC 2006)*.

Siva Reddy, Oscar Täckström, Slav Petrov, Mark Steedman, and Mirella Lapata. 2017. Universal semantic parsing. In *Proceedings of the 2017 Conference on Empirical Methods in Natural Language Processing (EMNLP 2017)*. pages 89–101.

Sebastian Schuster and Christopher D. Manning. 2016. Enhanced english universal dependencies: An improved representation for natural language understanding tasks. In *Proceedings of the 10th International Conference on Language Resources and Evaluation (LREC)*.

Sebastian Schuster, Joakim Nivre, and Christopher D. Manning. 2018. Sentences with gapping: Parsing and reconstructing elided predicates. In *Proceedings of the 16th Annual Conference of the North American Chapter of the Association for Computational Linguistics: Human Language Technologies (NAACL 2018)*.

Sebastian Schuster, Éric Villemonte de la Clergerie, Marie Candito, Benoît Sagot, Christopher D. Manning, and Djamé Seddah. 2017. Paris and Stanford at EPE 2017: Downstream evaluation of graph-based dependency representations. In *Proceedings of the 2017 Shared Task on Extrinsic Parser Evaluation (EPE 2017).*

Daniel Zeman, Martin Popel, Milan Straka, Jan Hajic, Joakim Nivre, Filip Ginter, Juhani Luotolahti, Sampo Pyysalo, Slav Petrov, Martin Potthast, Francis Tyers, Elena Badmaeva, Memduh Gokirmak, Anna Nedoluzhko, Silvie Cinkova, Jan Hajic jr., Jaroslava Hlavacova, Václava Kettnerová, Zdenka Uresova, Jenna Kanerva, Stina Ojala, Anna Missilä, Christopher D. Manning, Sebastian Schuster, Siva Reddy, Dima Taji, Nizar Habash, Herman Leung, Marie-Catherine de Marneffe, Manuela Sanguinetti, Maria Simi, Hiroshi Kanayama, Valeria dePaiva, Kira Droganova, Héctor Martínez Alonso, ÇağrÄś Çöltekin, Umut Sulubacak, Hans Uszkoreit, Vivien Macketanz, Aljoscha Burchardt, Kim Harris, Katrin Marheinecke, Georg Rehm, Tolga Kayadelen, Mohammed Attia, Ali Elkahky, Zhuoran Yu, Emily Pitler, Saran Lertpradit, Michael Mandl, Jesse Kirchner, Hector Fernandez Alcalde, Jana Strnadová, Esha Banerjee, Ruli Manurung, Antonio Stella, Atsuko Shimada, Sookyoung Kwak, Gustavo Mendonca, Tatiana Lando, Rattima Nitisaroj, and Josie Li. 2017. Conll 2017 shared task: Multilingual parsing from raw text to universal dependencies. In *Proceedings of the CoNLL 2017 Shared Task: Multilingual Parsing from Raw Text to Universal Dependencies.* pages 1–19.

Enhancing Universal Dependencies for Korean

Youngbin Noh[1]   Jiyoon Han[2]   Taehwan Oh[3]   Hansaem Kim[2][†]

[1]Department of Cognitive Science, Yonsei University, Seoul, South Korea
[2] Institution of Language and Information Studies, Yonsei University, Seoul, South Korea
[3] Department of Korean Language and Literature, Yonsei University, Seoul, South Korea
{vincenoh, clinamen35, ghksl0604, khss}@yonsei.ac.kr

Abstract

In this paper, for the purpose of enhancing Universal Dependencies for the Korean language, we propose a modified method for mapping Korean Part-of-Speech(POS) tagset in relation to Universal Part-of-Speech (UPOS) tagset in order to enhance the Universal Dependencies for the Korean Language. Previous studies suggest that UPOS reflects several issues that influence dependency annotation by using the POS of Korean predicates, particularly the distinctiveness in using verb, adjective, and copula.

1   Introduction

The Universal Dependencies (UD) approach aims to find morphological and syntactic characteristics that can be applied to several languages for cross-lingual language processing. This approach converts the language resources of each language has into one unified format (CoNLL U-Format) in order to simplify general language processing.

The number of language resources varies among all languages. Designed with a focus on the characteristics of resource-rich languages, the CoNLL U-Format does not completely reflect the distinctiveness of Korean annotation. The CoNLL U-Format sets up minimum processing unit based on eojeol (white space), However, in Korean, the basic unit for language processing is not only eojeol but the also morphemes with eojeol. Therefore, an analysis of the Korean language with white space as the minimum unit may lead to the omission of some important information, or yield inaccurate results.

In Korean, the unit divided by white space is called eojeol, this is composed of a noun or verb stem combined with a postposition (josa) or ending (eomi) that function as inflectional and derivational particles. Significantly, based on the type of ending with which the stem of the predicate is combined to form an eojeol, the eojeol takes on different functions. Therefore, this paper suggests that Universal Part-of-speech (UPOS) be analyzed by taking this characteristic into consideration.

The CoNLL U-Format assigns a UPOS to each eojeol, and marks it with a language-specific part-of-speech tag (XPOS) beside it. This paper suggests a methodology that is able to clarify the UPOS and Dependency annotation by using XPOS after processing the Korean language.

For the purpose of enhancing Korean UD, the focus should be on the processing of predicates. In the Korean, most predicates consist of the combination of a stem and an ending, which is similar to Japanese predicate construction but differs from that of English and European languages. However, unlike Japanese text which can be segmented into stem and ending separately to give UPOS, as there is no white space in the language itself, Korean text includes a white space unit which has a construction that is different from English, and thus, we should consider this specific property.

This paper suggests a scheme for the mapping of part-of-speech that forms Korean predicates on UPOS, as well as suggests a method of annotating the dependency relations in case of verb sequences. In section 2, we examine the attempts to convert and build Korean language resources into UD. Furthermore, based on an analysis of the contents of previous Part-of-Speech (POS) annotations and dependency annotations, we search for the necessary areas of improvement for Korean annotation. In section 3, we suggest a UPOS for several issues that can have influences the dependency annotation by using XPOS of Korean predicates. In section 4, we will suggest a Korean

---

† corresponding author

Proceedings of the Second Workshop on Universal Dependencies (UDW 2018), pages 108–116
Brussels, Belgium, November 1, 2018. ©2018 Association for Computational Linguistics

dependency annotation modified through the suggested UPOS.

2 Previous works

Since the late 1990s, there have been attempts to build a syntactic parsing corpus of the Korean language based on the dependency structure. Korean National Corpus in the 21st Century Sejong Project (KNC), which has been established and is the most well-known syntactic parsing corpus, is based on the binary phrase structure and can easily to be converted to have a dependency structure. In fact, the dependency structure analysis corpus has been used widely in Korean language processing, and with a recent attempt to unify its form with UD. The efforts to apply current tag system of UD to the Korean language began with the Google Universal Dependency Treebank (UDT) Project (McDonald et al., 2013), which attempted to combine the Stanford Tag System and the Google System.

This paper discusses a total of three corpora: the Google Korean Universal Dependency Treebank (GKT), the Parallel Universal Korean Dependency Treebank (PUD), and the KAIST Korean Universal Dependency Treebank (KTB). All of the three corpora were tagged in CoNLL U-Format. The Google Korean Universal Dependency Treebank was first converted from the Universal Dependency Treebank v2.0 (legacy), and then enhanced by Chun et al. (2018). The KAIST Korean Universal Dependency Treebank was generated by Chun et al. (2018) from the constituency-based trees in the KAIST Tree-Tagging Corpus. The Parallel Universal Dependencies (PUD) treebanks are created from Raw Text to Universal Dependencies for the CoNLL 2017 shared task on Multilingual Parsing.

As stated in the Introduction, it is necessary to focus on predicate processing for enhanced Korean UD. Therefore, in section 2, this paper, examines GKT, PUD, and KTB centered on predicates; In 2.1, we will compare and analyze POS annotation methods of eojeols containing predicates in three corpora; and in 2.2, we will examine the Dependency annotation methods of these three corpora for eojeols containing predicates.

2.1 Part-of-speech annotation

For the POS annotation of eojeols containing predicates, all GKT, PUD, and KTB currently published on the UD Website follow the types of predicates contained in the eojeols without considering the function of the eojeols. It designates itself as VERB if the predicate in the eojeol is a verb and designates itself as ADJ if the predicate in the eojeol is an adjective, similar to the process of lemmatization.

(1) GKT Example - UPOS annotation as VERB for verb (VV) contained eojeol

text = 조화가 잘 되어 아담한 감을 준다.

조화+가	잘	되+어	아담하+ㄴ	감+을	주+ㄴ다	.
jo-hwa-ga	jal	doe-eo	a-dam-han	gam-eul	jun-da	
"Harmony + tpc"	"well"	"become"	"neat"	"Impression + obj"	make	

UPOS	NOUN	ADV	**VERB**	ADJ	NOUN	**VERB** PUNCT
XPOS			VV+EC			VV+EF

For copula, GKT and KTB adopt a similar methods of POS annotation while PUD takes different one. GKT and KTB label all eojeols that contain copula as VERB; however, PUD segments the copula from eojeols and assigns an AUX.

(2) GKT Example - UPOS annotation as VERB for copula (VCP) contained eojeol

text = 바로 이곳입니다.

	바로	이곳+이+ㅂ니다	.
	ba-lo	i-gos-ib-ni-da	
	"exactly"	"here"	
UPOS	ADV	**VERB**	PUNCT
XPOS		NP+VCP+EF	

text = 설립 이사장인 청암 박태준

	설립	이사장+이+ㄴ	청암	박태준
	seol-lib	i-sa-jang-in	cheong-am	park-tae-jun
	"Establishing"	"chairman"	"Cheongahm"	"Park Tae jun"
UPOS	NOUN	**VERB**	NOUN	NOUN
XPOS		NNG+VCP+ETM		

(3) PUD Example - UPOS annotation as AUX for copula(VCP) contained eojeol

text = 비협조적인 사람이며

	비협조적	이+ㄴ	사람	이+며
	bi-hyeob-jo-jeog	in	sa-lam	i-myeo
	"Uncooperative"	"is"	"person"	"is"
UPOS	NOUN	**AUX**	NOUN	**AUX**
XPOS		VCP+ETM		VCP+EC

In addition, GKT and PUD tag both the main predicate as well as the auxiliary predicate as VERB. On the other hand, KTB gives an AUX tag to auxiliary predicates to differentiate between main predicates and auxiliary predicates.

(4) GKT Example - UPOS annotation as VERB for eojeol containing auxiliary verb(VX)

text = 사용이 두드러지고 있다.

	사용+이	두드러지+고	있+다	
	sa-yong-i	du-deu-leo-ji-go	iss-da	
	"Use+tpc"	"prominent"	"is"	
UPOS	NOUN	**VERB**	**VERB**	PUNCT
XPOS		**VV+EC**	**VX+EF**	

(5) KTB Example - UPOS annotation as AUX for eojeol containing auxiliary verb(VX)

text = 현판이 달려 있었습니다.

	현판+이	달리+어	있+었+습니다	
	hyeon-pan-i	dal-lyeo	iss-eoss-seub-ni-da	
	"Signboard+tpc"	"hang"	"being"	
UPOS	NOUN	**VERB**	**AUX**	PUNCT
XPOS		**VV+EC**	**VX+EF**	

2.2 Dependency annotation

Of the 37 universal syntactic relations labels that represent Universal Dependency Relations, GKT, PUD, and KTB show the biggest difference in the aux (Auxiliary) and labels related to MEW (multi-word-expression), compound (Compound), fixed (Fixed Multiword Expression), and flat (Flat Multiword Expression). GKT demonstrates quite a low frequency of aux, which is because auxiliary predicates are not classified separately in the POS annotation process but are processed with VERB. Since an auxiliary predicate is not used alone but appears next to the main predicate, AUX which is a POS tag, and aux, which is a label and syntactic tag, should be proportional to each other. As such, it is natural for aux to show high frequency, as is the case with KTB. Instead, a flat label appears in GKT with high frequency whereas it appears with low frequency in other corpus as the relationship between the auxiliary predicate and the main predicate is processed as flat.

In this way, the Korean language has a predicate formed with continual eojeols in several cases; therefore it becomes critical to establish dependency relations between eojeols that form a predicate in the Korean language.

(6) GKT Example – tags VX as flat

text = 이야기를 하려 하지 않았다.

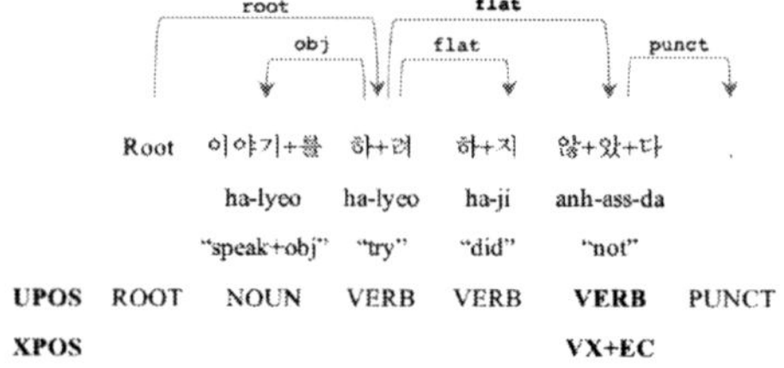

(7) KTB Example – tags VX as(with) aux

text = 말을 하지 않았다.

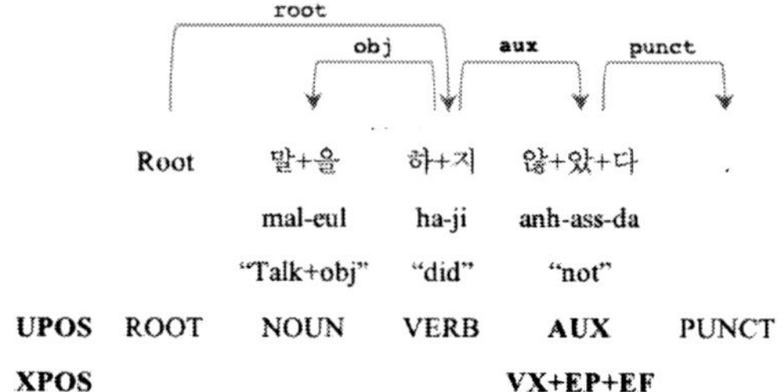

3 Part-of-speech annotation

The target of this paper is limited only to the POS that can be used as a predicate in a sentence. In the Korean language, the POS applicable to the predicates are verb, adjective, copula, and auxiliary. The predicates of the Korean language can be composed of either a single eojeol or multiple ones. In the former case, one eojeol composed of a stem and ending with a verb or adjective functions as a predicate; alternatively, noun and copula combined with ending form an eojeol. In the latter case, stems of the main verb and auxiliary verbs are combined with an ending forming two or more eojeols in sequence, or many types of main verb stems are combined with an ending forming two or more eojeols in a sequence.

In this manner, the Korean language is very diverse in terms of predicate configurations; as the morphological and syntactic functions of predicate-related POS contained in these configurations are different, the POS annotation method in the prior process of parsing becomes an important issue that influences clear dependency annotation thereafter.

3.1 Verb

A Korean verb stem cannot be used alone in a sentence; it must be combined with an ending to form an eojeol. The types of ending are broadly categorized into final endings, connective endings, and conversion endings, and the function of an eojeol in a sentence is dependent on the ending with which the stem is combined. When combined with a final or connective ending, it has the function of a predicate, whereas it has the function of a modifier or substantive on being combined with a conversion ending.

As described in section 2, in GKT, KTB, and PUD, eojeols that contain Korean verbs are mostly tagged as VERB regardless of the type of ending that is combined with the verb stem. This simple labeling method does not consider the actual function of an eojeol in which the verb is contained. When this approach is used, the POS annotation is very likely to become redundant, which does not improve the accuracy of the dependency annotation.

This paper suggests that POS annotation should be performed according to the function of each eojeol within a sentence. In an eojeol where the verb stem functions as a predicate by being combined with a final or connective ending, the POS tag of VERB can be given. On the other hand, in an eojeol where the verb stem functions as modifying the following noun by being combined with an adnominal ending, the POS tag of ADJ can be given. When a verb stem is combined with a nominal ending, the function of the eojeol can be changed according to the type of combined inflectional particle.

Therefore, the POS tag of the eojeol follows the type of the combined inflectional particle. For helpful information in deciding the POS annotation of each eojeol, we can refer to the KNC POS tagset, which analyzes eojeol in morpheme units. Specifically, if the morpheme unit annotation of an eojeol is "VV (verb) + EF (final ending)" or "VV + EC (connective ending)", the UPOS of VERB is allotted; if the morpheme unit annotation is "VV + ETM (adnominal ending)", the tag ADJ is allotted.

However, among other connective endings combined with verb stem, "-게 (-ge)" provides an adverbial function to the eojeol, and it can often be tagged as ADV rather than VERB. It is the same in the case of the adjective and copula below. An eojeol made with a verb stem combined with a nominal ending and inflectional particle can be tagged with NOUN if it is "VV + ETN (nominal ending) + {JKS (subjective case particle), JKC (compliment case particle), JKO (objective case particle), JC (conjunctive particle)}," with ADJ if "VV + ETN + JKG (adjective case particle)", and with ADV if "VV + ETN + JKB (adverbial case particle)". The POS assignment method described above is applied only when the eojeol is not a part of a paragraph that presupposes a subject-predicate relation.

By following this method, more accurate UPOS annotation can be obtained by using morphological annotation information of the existing KNC. The UPOS established in this way would also be helpful in determining the dependencies relations.

(8) Verb contained eojeol UPOS annotation obtained from XPOS

# text = 자전거 타고 대전역 가는 길				
자전거	타+고	대전역	가+는	길
ja-jeon-geo	ta-go	dae-jeon-yeog	ga-neun	gil
"Bicycle"	"ride"	"Daejeon Station"	"go"	"way"
UPOS NOUN	**VERB**	NOUN	**ADJ**	NOUN
XPOS	**VV+EC**		**VV+ETM**	

3.2 Adjective

Unlike English adjectives, Korean adjectives are sometimes classified as stative verbs, because a Korean adjective can function as predicate without a support verb. Therefore, it is hard to apply ADJ of UPOS to intact Korean adjectives. An English adjective does not change its form depending on whether it takes the role of predicate or modifier, and it can even form an eojeol on its own. Hence, it does not result in problem if it is tagged as ADJ. However, a Korean adjective stem, just like a verb, can complete an eojeol and be used in a sentence only when it is combined with an ending, and its function within the sentence can be changed based on the type of ending it is combined with.

In GKT, PUD, and KTB, eojeols that contain Korean adjectives are mostly tagged as ADJ regardless of the type of ending that is combined with the adjective stem in the sentence, or the function of the eojeol, in which the adjective is contained. Sometimes, an eojeol that functions as a predicate rather than a modifier is tagged as ADJ; and if this eojeol containing an adjective which functions as a predicate by being combined with a final ending or connective ending, is tagged as POS of ADJ, the sentence becomes a non-sentence, as it does not have a predicate.

Focusing on this characteristic of Korean adjectives, this paper suggests performing POS annotation for an eojeol that contains an adjective based on the function of the eojeol within the sentence. The approach is to annotate an eojeol in which an adjective stem functions as a predicate within a sentence when combined with a final or connective ending as VERB, and to annotate an eojeol in which an adjective stem functions as a modifier within sentence by being combined with adnominal ending as ADJ.

As stated above, Korean adjectives are analogous with stative verbs; hence, if one is combined with a final or connective ending, it functions as a predicate within a sentence. Therefore, a UPOS annotation as VERB is not irrational in the least, and it is suitable to give an ADJ tag to an eojeol that modifies a following eojeol by being combined with an adnominal ending. In addition, if an adjective stem is combined with a nominal ending, in the manner described in section 3.1, its function is changes according to the type of postposition with which it is combined; therefore, the POS of the eojeol can be determined according to the type of postposition.

(9) Adjective contained eojeol UPOS annotation obtained from XPOS

# text =	제일 가까운 스타벅스가 어디 있지			
제일	가깝+ㄴ	스타벅스+가	어디	있+지
je-il	ga-kka-un	Starbucks+ga	eo-di	iss-ji
"Most"	"close"	"Starbucks +tpc"	"where"	"be"
UPOS NOUN	**ADJ**	NOUN	NOUN	**VERB**
XPOS	**VA+ETM**			**VA+EF**

An eojeol containing an adjective can also be annotated by referring to the KNC POS tagset that performs analysis in morpheme units. This information will be helpful in clarifying the dependency relations of a sentence by being used in dependency annotation.

3.3 Copula

The Korean copula "-이-(-*i*-)" is a unique POS that gives a predicate function to a noun. It appears with a noun and is similar to the English verb "be," as it has the function of a predicate. But unlike the verb "be" which functions as a predicate alone by forming an eojeol without a noun, it can form an eojeol only by forming a "noun+copula+ending"

structure. In addition, Korean copula, just like verb stem or adjective stem, can function as a predicate by combining it with a final or connective ending, or as a modifier or substantive by combining with a conversion ending.

In GKT and KTB, eojeols that contain copula are mostly tagged as VERB regardless of the type of ending that is combined with copula, similar to the eojeols that contain a Korean verb; in PUD, a copula is segmented from the eojeol and tagged as AUX. The former does not consider the actual function of the eojeol containing the copula, and the latter takes a method out of UD's POS annotation guideline, which considers the eojeol as a basic unit.

This paper suggests differentiating the POS annotation of eojeols that contain copula according to the function of the eojeol in a sentence, just like the Korean verb or adjective stated above. To be specific, if an ending that completes an eojeol located next to a "noun+copula" structure is a final or connective ending when the eojeol functions as a predicate within the sentence, it is tagged as VERB; if the adnominal ending functions as a modifier, it is tagged as ADJ; and if combined with a nominal ending, POS annotation is done according to the type of inflectional particle. Here, we can also refer to the KNC POS tagset that annotates Korean language in morpheme units. Unlike Korean verbs or adjectives, the KNC POS tagset analysis on the eojeol containing copula that forms an eojeol by combining it with a noun would be like "NN* (noun) + VCP (copula) + E* (ending)."

(10) Copula contained eojeol UPOS annotation ontained from XPOS

# text =	설립 이사장인 청암 박태준		
설립	이사장+이+ㄴ	청암	박태준
seol-lib	i-sa-jang-in	cheong-am	park-tae-jun
"Establishing"	"chairman"	"Cheongahm"	"Park Tae jun"
UPOS NOUN	**ADJ**	NOUN	NOUN
XPOS	**NNG+VCP+ETM**		

3.4 Auxiliary

The Korean auxiliary verb is different from the English auxiliary verb in several respects. Firstly, most English auxiliary verbs take forms that are different from main verbs; however in several cases, Korean auxiliary verbs are homonyms that take the same forms as the main verbs. Additionally, unlike English, which has completely different figures of "main verb‖auxiliary verb" combinations and "main verb‖main verb" combinations, in the Korean language the "main verb‖auxiliary verb" combinations and "main verb‖main verb" combinations, these combinations have the same syntactic structure in the Korean Language. Finally, in principle the Korean auxiliary verb is written with a space separating it from the main verb in order to form a separate eojeol, but sometimes it forms one eojeol with main verb in order to take the function of one predicate.

(11) 'Main verb‖main verb' combination

 # text = 김치를 맛있게 먹고 나오다

김치를	맛있+게	먹+고	나오+다
gim-chi-leul	mas-iss-ge	meog-go	na-o-da
"Kimchi+obj"	"delicious"	"eat"	"out"
XPOS		**VV+EC**	**VV+EF**

(12) 'Main verb‖auxiliary verb' combination

 # text = 사용이 두드러지고 있다.

사용+이	두드러지+고	있+다
sa-yong-i	du-deu-leo-ji-go	iss-da
"Use+tpc"	"prominent"	"is"
XPOS	**VV+EC**	**VX+EF**

In GKT and PUD, eojeols that contain the main verb and auxiliary verb are not divided; however, both of them are tagged as VERB. In this case, "main verb‖main verb" combinations and "main verb‖auxiliary verb" combinations are not distinguished, and in the case of the "main verb‖auxiliary verb" combinations, it is hard to understand which one of two eojeols takes the role of the main predicate and which one takes the auxiliary function. In addition, "main verb‖main verb" combinations and "main verb‖auxiliary verb" combinations form different dependency relations. If POS annotation is unable to give this information properly, the whole sentence has to be analyzed again in the dependency annotation process.

This paper suggests applying different tags to the "main verb‖main verb" combinations as wel as the "main verb‖auxiliary verb" combinations by strictly classifying both of them. Sometimes the form of a Korean auxiliary verb is difficult to be distinguished from the main verb, but it is a closed set and small in number. In the KNC POS tagset that analyzes the Korean language in morpheme units, the main verb stem is tagged as VV or VA while the auxiliary verb is tagged as VX; Using this information, we can clearly and simply classify main verbs and auxiliary verbs in UD POS annotation. Therefore, the main verb can be tagged by VERB and the auxiliary verb by AUX, and when a main verb and an auxiliary verb form an eojeol, it can be tagged as VERB without segmenting the eojeol.

(13) 'Main verb‖main verb' combination UPOS annotation obtained from XPOS

 # text = 김치를 맛있게 먹고 나오다

김치를	맛있+게	먹+고	나오+다
gim-chi-leul	mas-iss-ge	meog-go	na-o-da
"Kimchi+obj"	"delicious"	"eat"	"out"
UPOS		**VERB**	**VERB**
XPOS		**VV+EC**	**VV+EF**

(14) 'Main verb‖auxiliary verb' combination UPOS annotation obtained from XPOS

 # text = 사용이 두드러지고 있다.

사용+이	두드러지+고	있+다
sa-yong-i	du-deu-leo-ji-go	iss-da
"Use+tpc"	"prominent"	"is"
UPOS	**VERB**	**AUX**
XPOS	**VV+EC**	**VX+EF**

3.5 Application result

When applying our proposal to GSD, the results are the same as in Table 1.

XPOS	UPOS	correct	total	revise	%
VV+EC	VERB	3,443	3,602	159	4%
VV+EF	VERB	414	560	146	26%
VV+ETM	ADJ	8	2,385	2,377	100%
VV+-게	ADV	14	161	147	91%
VV+ETN+JKB	ADV	23	26	3	12%
XPOS	UPOS	correct	total	revise	%
VA+EC	VERB	609	1152	543	47%
VA+EF	VERB	7	278	271	97%
VA+ETM	ADJ	497	839	342	41%
VA+-게	ADV	233	250	17	7%
VA+ETN+JKB	ADV	2	5	3	60%
XPOS	UPOS	correct	total	revise	%
NN+VCP+EC	VERB	355	403	48	12%
NN+VCP+EF	VERB	575	575	0	0%
NN+VCP+ETM	ADJ	4	268	264	99%
NN+VCP+ETN+JKB	ADV	1	1	0	0%
XPOS	UPOS	correct	total	revise	%
VX+*	AUX	55	1,730	1,675	97%

Table 1 : application result on GSD

Because the UPOS is based on information of XPOS inside CoNLL U-Format, it can be automatically converted. The eojeol contaning VV showed the highest conversion rates to ADJ and ADV. And for eojeols contaning VA, the conversion rates to VERB and ADV was highest. In the case of eojeols contaning VCP, the conversion rates to VERB and ADJ was highest. Most eojeols starting with VX were converted to AUX.

4   Dependency annotation

4.1   Head final

Unlike English, Korean language is a head-final language in which complement comes first followed by a head of verb phrase. This head is marked as `root` in the tag system of Universal Dependency Relations. This `root` is the core of dependency annotation as other sentence components are subordinated to this label. There are two kinds of Korean sentences; simple sentences and compound-complex. Compound-complex sentences can be divided into compound sentences that contain two consecutive simple sentences, and complex sentences that contain clauses with various kinds of sentence functions. It is easy to set up the root for a simple sentence, as there is only one predicate in the sentence.

However, it is difficult to determine the head of the sentence in compound-complex sentences. In the case of complex sentences, the last predicate is likely to be the head, but in the case of compound sentences, it is hard to assign a head as the ranks of two predicates within the sentence are equal. Accordingly, we would like to apply the head-final principle to compound sentences based on the cases of simple sentence and complex sentences.

In the Japanese language, there is a tendency of setting up the right-most predicate stem in a sentence as the root while examining GSD, PUD, Modern, BCCWJ, and KTC corpora revealed by UD. In Korean, based on this criterion, it is necessary to set up the right-most eojeol containing a predicate as the root. This can be used to minimize confusion in the Korean language, which has a complex sentence structure.

Korean predicates play various role by being combined with endings; therefore, it is essential to first check whether the eojeol actually plays the role of predicate, upon setting up a predicate located in places other than the sentence final as

the root. The error rate can increase if this process is omitted. The error rate can increase if this process is omitted. Therefore, following the principle of head final will reduce analysis errors and increase the efficiency of the processing.

(15) Simple sentence

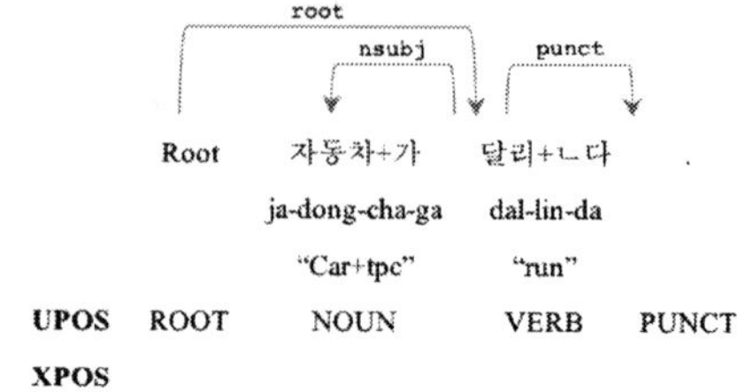

(16) Compound sentence

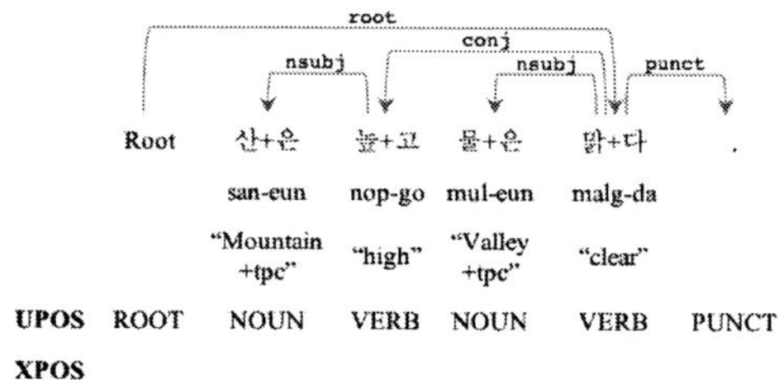

(17) Complex sentence

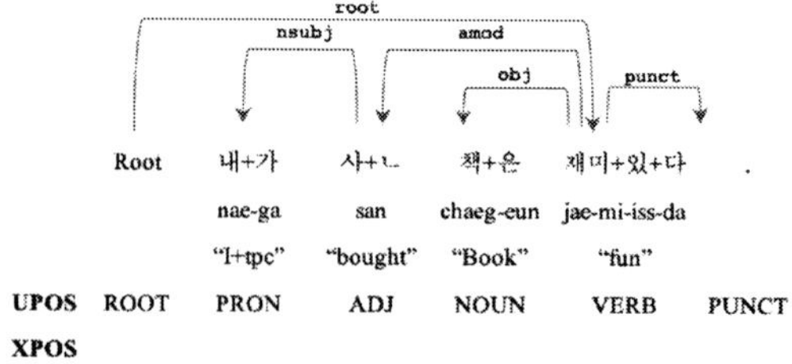

4.2   Verb sequence separated by white space

If two or more consecutive eojeols take on the same role of predicate within a sentence, the relationship between these eojeols should be revealed. Predicate eojeols are combined in the following cases: combination of main predicate with auxiliary predicate; and combination of two main predicate and main predicate.

In the first case, `root` is assigned to the main predicate and `aux` is assigned to the auxiliary predicate. In the existing dependency syntactic parsing or structure analysis, if the head final is provided, head position is allotted to the auxiliary predicate; however, following the UD system, `aux` position is given to the auxiliary predicate and the head position is not. This shows that the auxiliary predicate does not describe actual contents of a sentence, but takes on an auxiliary function. Through this processing, we can resolve the controversy over whether to accept the Korean language should be accepted as a head final language.

In the case of a combination of two main predicates, the relationship is determined by the ending of the preceding main predicate. The following main predicate is labeled as `root`. However, if the preceding main predicate is combined with a connective ending, it can be assigned as `flat`; if the preceding main predicate is combined with an adverbial ending, it can be designated as `advcl` or `advmod`, depending on the combination relationship of the preceding Eojeol. Based on the KNC tagset, the connective ending is tagged by EC, and if the morpheme is "-게," it can be considered as an adverbial ending. In the case of an adnominal ending, there is an extra label of ETM in the KNC tagset.

(18) Aux

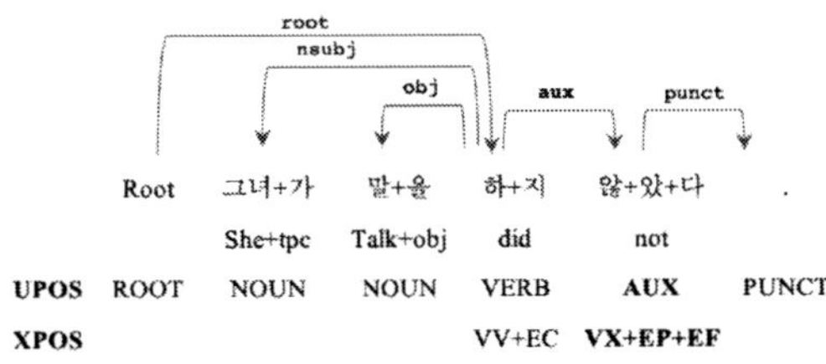

(19) flat

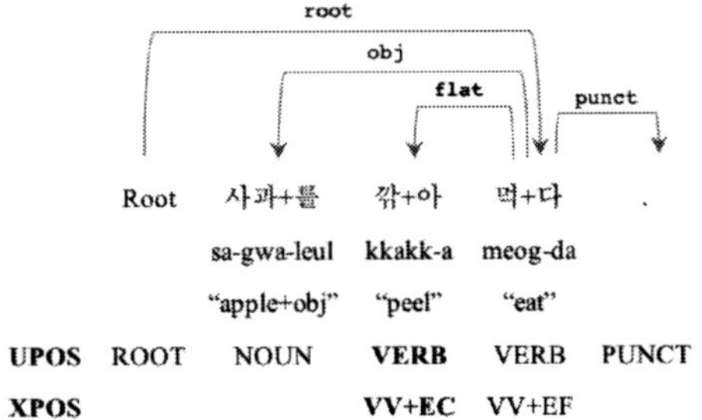

(20) advcl

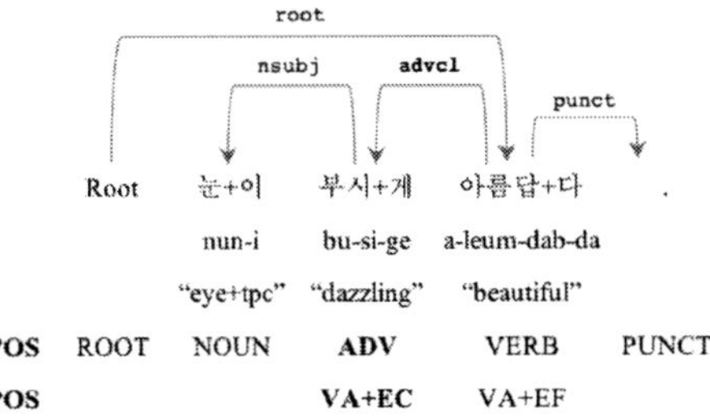

(21) advmod

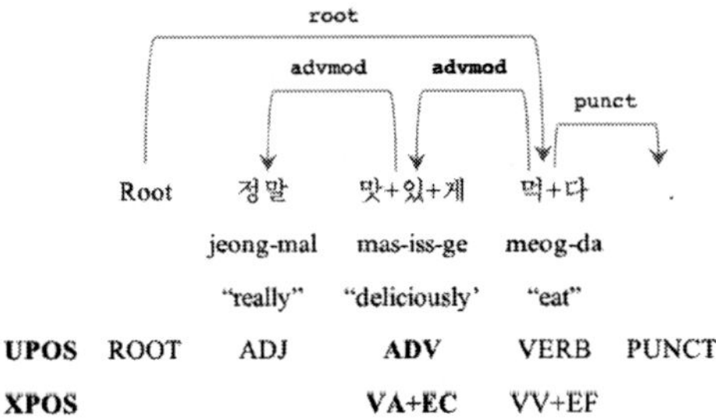

5 Conclusion and Future works

This paper aimed to suggest a plan for improving UD Tagging by focusing on the predicate. A Korean eojeol consists of nouns and verbs combined with propositions and endings that function as inflectional and derivational particles. The function of the stem of predicate depends on which ending is combined with the eojeol. Therefore, we proposed modified UPOS tagging and dependency annotation to reflect the syntactic characteristics of the Korean language using language-specific XPOS.

This paper developed the discussion by focusing only on predicates-related contents. eojeols with other functions that were not considered in this paper will be examined in future studies.

Acknowledgments

This work was supported by the National Research Foundation of Korea (NRF), funded by the Korean Government (MSIT) (NRF-2017 M3C4A7068186).

This work was supported by the National Research Foundation of Korea (NRF), funded by the Korean Government (MSIT) (NRF-2009-361-A00027).

References

De Marneffe, M. C., & Manning, C. D. 2008. Stanford typed dependencies manual (pp. 338-345). Technical report, Stanford University.

Hansaem Kim, Korean National Corpus in the 21st Century Sejong Project(2006), Proceedings of the 13th National Institute of Japanese Literature (NIJL) International Symposium(pp 49–54)

Jayeol Chun1 , Na-Rae Han2 , Jena D. Hwang3 , Jinho D. Choi1, 2018. Building Universal Dependency Treebanks in Korean, In LREC.

Nivre, J., De Marneffe, M. C., Ginter, F., Goldberg, Y., Hajic, J., Manning, C. D., ... & Tsarfaty, R. 2016. Universal Dependencies v1: A Multilingual Treebank Collection. In LREC.

McDonald, R., Nivre, J., Quirmbach-Brundage, Y., Goldberg, Y., Das, D., Ganchev, K., ... & Bedini, C. 2013. Universal dependency annotation for multilingual parsing. In Proceedings of the 51st Annual Meeting of the Association for Computational Linguistics (Volume 2: Short Papers) (Vol. 2, pp. 92-97).

Park, J., Hong, J. P., & Cha, J. W. 2016. Korean Language Resources for Everyone. In Proceedings of the 30th Pacific Asia Conference on Language, Information and Computation: Oral Papers pp. 49-58.

Sag, Ivan A., Thomas Wasow, and Emily M. Bender. 2003. Syntactic Theory: A Formal Introduction, second edition. CSLI Publications.

Tanaka, T., Miyao, Y., Asahara, M., Uematsu, S., Kanayama, H., Mori, S., & Matsumoto, Y. 2016. Universal Dependencies for Japanese. In LREC.

金山博, 宮尾祐介, 田中貴秋, 森信介, 浅原正幸, & 植松すみれ. 2015. 日本語 Universal Dependencies の試案. 言語処理学会第 21 回年次大会, 505-508.

UD-Japanese BCCWJ: Universal Dependencies Annotation for the Balanced Corpus of Contemporary Written Japanese

Mai Omura and **Masayuki Asahara**
National Institute for Japanese Language and Linguistics
{mai-om, masayu-a}@ninjal.ac.jp

Abstract

In this paper, we describe a corpus UD Japanese-BCCWJ that was created by converting the Balanced Corpus of Contemporary Written Japanese (BCCWJ), a Japanese language corpus, to adhere to the UD annotation schema. The BCCWJ already assigns dependency information at the level of the bunsetsu (a Japanese syntactic unit comparable to the phrase). We developed a program to convert the BCCWJto UD based on this dependency structure, and this corpus is the result of completely automatic conversion using the program. UD Japanese-BCCWJ is the largest-scale UD Japanese corpus and the second-largest of all UD corpora, including 1,980 documents, 57,109 sentences, and 1,273k words across six distinct domains.

1 Introduction

The field of Natural Language Processing has seen growing interest in multilingual and cross-linguistic research. One such cross-linguistic research initiative is the Universal Dependencies (UD) (McDonald et al., 2013) Project, which defines standards and schemas for parts of speech and dependency structures and distributes multilingual corpora. As part of our efforts to import the UD annotation schema into the Japanese language, we defined a part-of-speech (PoS) system and set of dependency structure labels for Japanese, which are documented on GitHub [1], and we are currently preparing reference corpora. This paper describes our Japanese UD corpus **UD Japanese-BCCWJ**, which is based on the Balanced Corpus of Contemporary Written Japanese (BCCWJ) (Maekawa et al., 2014), and which we have prepared as part of our efforts to design a Japanese version of UD.

Previous applications of UD to Japanese corpora can be found in Table 1, which is based on (Asahara et al., 2018). Tanaka et al. (2016) have published a Japanese UD treebank, UD Japanese-KTC, which was converted from the Japanese Phrase Structure Treebank (Tanaka and Nagata, 2013). Other corpora include an unlabelled UD Japanese treebank derived from Wikipedia, UD Japanese-GSD, and a Japanese-PUD corpus, UD Japanese-PUD (Zeman et al., 2017), derived from parallel corpora, but all of these have had to be partially manually corrected. According to Table 1, UD Japanese-BCCWJ is the largest UD Japanese corpus. Furthermore, it is the second largest of all UD corpora and includes many documents across various domains as shown in Table 3.

Existing Japanese-language corpora tagged with dependency structures include the Kyoto University Text Corpus (Kurohashi and Nagao, 2003) and the Japanese Dependency Corpus (Mori et al., 2014). These corpora frequently use **bunsetsu** as the syntactic dependency annotation units for Japanese. Also, the BCCWJ, based on UD Japanese-BCCWJ, is annotated using a bunsetsu-level dependency structure (Asahara and Matsumoto, 2016), which we must thus convert from a bunsetsu-level dependency structure to a Universal Dependencies schema. Figure 1 shows an example of BCCWJ with the UD annotation schema.

In this paper, we describe the conversion of the BCCWJ to the UD annotation schema. To accomplish the conversion, the following information must be combined: word-morphological information, bunsetsu-level dependency structure, coordination structure annotation, and predicate argument structure information. We also attempt to convert the BCCWJ to a UD schema, which allows us to respond to changes in the tree structures based on ongoing discussions in the UD commu-

---

[1] https://github.com/UniversalDependencies/

Proceedings of the Second Workshop on Universal Dependencies (UDW 2018), pages 117–125
Brussels, Belgium, November 1, 2018. ©2018 Association for Computational Linguistics

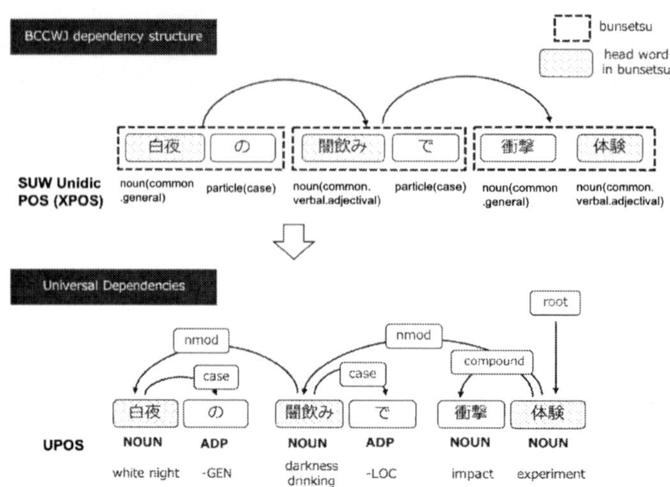

(There is an) impact experiment on the darkness drinking party on white night.

Figure 1: Summary of conversion of BCCWJ to UD. (The sample is from `PB_00001`). The left example is the BCCWJ schema, bunsetsu-level dependency structure, and the right is the Universal Dependencies schema.

Table 1: Comparison of existing UD Japanese resources.

Treebank	Tokens	Version	Copyright	Media
UD Japanese-BCCWJ	**1273k**	v2.2	masked surface	Newspaper, Books, Magazines, Blogs, etc.
UD Japanese-KTC	189k	v1.2	masked surface	Newspaper
UD Japanese-GSD	186k	v2.1	CC-BY-NC-SA	Wikipedia
UD Japanese-PUD	26k	v2.1	CC-BY-SA	Wikipedia Parallel Corpus
UD Japanese-Modern	14k	v2.2	CC-BY-NC-SA	Magazines in 19th century

Table 2: Genres in BCCWJ core data. Please refer to Table 3 about the number of sentences/tokens.

Abbr.	description
OC	Bulletin board (Yahoo! Answers)
OW	Government white papers
OY	Blog (*Yahoo! Blogs*)
PB	Books
PM	Magazines
PN	Newspaper

nity. The next section is a brief description of our current conversion.[2]

2 Balanced Corpus of Contemporary Written Japanese (BCCWJ)

The *Balanced Corpus of Contemporary Written Japanese* (BCCWJ) (Maekawa et al., 2014) is a 104.3-million-word corpus that covers a range of genres including general books and magazines, newspapers, white papers, blogs, Internet bulletin board postings, textbooks, and legal statutes. It is currently the largest balanced corpus of Japanese. The copyright negotiation process has also been completed for BCCWJ DVD purchasers. [3]

All BCCWJ data are automatically tokenized and PoS-tagged by NLP analysers in a three-layered tokenization of Short Unit Word (SUW), Long Unit Word (LUW), and bunsetsu as in Figure 2.[4] There are subcorpora to be checked manually to improve their quality after analysis, as well as a subcorpus of the 1% of the BCCWJ data called 'core data' consisting of 1,980 samples and 57,256 sentences with morphological information (word boundaries and PoS information). Table 2 describes each genre in the BCCWJ core data. The distribution, including the BCCWJ core data, is shown in Figure 3. The UD Japanese-BCCWJ is based on the BCCWJ core data.

The BCCWJ provides bunsetsu-level dependency information as BCCWJ-DepPara (Asahara and Matsumoto, 2016) including bunsetsu dependency structures, coordination structures, and information on

---

[2]UD Japanese-BCCWJ was released in Universal Dependencies on 2018 March; however, we noticed and addressed some problems after release, and so the development version is as described in this paper.

[3]`http://pj.ninjal.ac.jp/corpus_center/bccwj/en/`
[4]The details of these layers are described in Section 3.1.

Table 3: Genre distribution including BCCWJ core data. A description of each genes is given in the Table 2.

Genre / Type		OC	OW	OY	PB	PM	PN	total
Documents	train	421	45	214	58	63	286	1,087
	dev	259	9	129	13	12	27	449
	test	258	8	128	12	11	27	444
	total	938	62	471	83	86	340	1,980
Sentences	train	2,838	4,456	3,278	7,196	9,546	13,487	40,801
	dev	1,650	780	1,920	1,131	1,510	1,436	8,427
	test	1,619	589	1,722	1,351	1,486	1,114	7,881
	total	6,107	5,825	6,920	9,678	12,542	16,037	57,109
Tokens(SUWs)	train	50,415	168,909	51,310	174,394	177,947	300,786	923,761
	dev	29,961	31,471	32,164	27,315	30,328	29,528	180,767
	test	29,624	26,421	28,485	29,612	28,183	26,434	168,759
	total	110,000	226,801	111,959	231,321	236,458	356,748	1,273,287

predicate-argument structures through BCCWJ-DepPara-PAS (Ueda et al., 2015). This information is exploited in the conversion of BCCWJ to the UD schemas.

3 Conversion of BCCWJ to UD

As shown in Figure 1, there are some differences between the BCCWJ and UD schemas. One concerns PoS: BCCWJ's and UD's PoS Unidic (Den et al., 2007) and Universal PoS (Petrov et al., 2012), respectively (e.g. `noun(common.general)` and NOUN in Figure 1). Second, the structure is different between bunsetsu-level and word-level dependency, for example in the directions and units of dependency (compare BCCWJ with the UD schema in Figure 1). Finally, the bunsetsu-level dependency structures in Japanese have less detailed syntactic dependency roles than the relations in Universal Dependencies like `nmod` and `case`. We need to convert UD Japanese-BCCWJ while taking into consideration the differences between the UD and BCCWJ schemata. In addition, we need to choose or detect apposite word units for the basic word unit based on UD guidelines from SUWs, LUWs, and others because these layers are not always appropriate as given by BCCWJ. Therefore, we convert BCCWJ to UD Japanese-BCCWJ using the following steps:

1. Detect the word unit.
2. Convert Unidic PoS to UD PoS.
3. Convert bunsetsu-level dependency to UD word-level dependency.
4. Attach a UD relation label to each dependency.

We will describe each step in the following sections.

3.1 Word Unit

Japanese, unlike English as well as many other languages, text is not explicitly divided into words using spaces. UD guidelines specify that the basic units of annotation are *syntactic words* [5]. The first task is therefore to decide what counts as a token and what counts as a syntactic word.

All the samples in the BCCWJ are morphologically analysed based on linguistic units called 'Short Unit Words' (SUWs) and 'Long Unit Words' (LUWs), as in Figure 2. SUWs are defined on the basis of their morphological properties in the Japanese language. They are minimal atomic units that can be combined in ways specific to particular classes of Japanese words. LUWs are defined on the basis of their syntactic properties. The bunsetsu are word grouping units defined in terms of the dependency structure (the so-called *bunsetsu-kakariuke*). The bunsetsu-level dependency structure annotations in BCCWJ-DepPara (Asahara and Matsumoto, 2016) rely on LUWs. As shown in Figure 2, the SUWs, LUWs, and bunsetsu exist in a hierarchical relationship: SUW $<=$ LUW $<=$ bunsetsu; SUWs render 魚/フライ/を as three words, LUWs as 魚フライ/を or two words, and bunsetsu as 魚フライを or one word. SUWs and LUWs also entail different PoS systems, as will be described in Section 3.2.

UD Japanese-BCCWJ adopts the SUW word unit, which corresponds to the BCCWJ's basic PoS system, as its fundamental linguistic unit. However, as described in the following sections, usage information associated with LUWs is also required to conform to UD standards and to achieve consistency with annotations for other languages. We will discuss the differences between

---

[5] http://universaldependencies.org/u/overview/tokenization.html

119

| | 魚フライを食べたかもしれないペルシャ猫 | | | | | | | | | | |
	"It is the Persian cat that may have eaten fried fish."										
SUW	魚	フライ	を	食べ	た	か	も	しれ	ない	ペルシャ	猫
	NOUN	NOUN	ADP	VERB	AUX	PART	ADP	VERB	AUX	PROPN	NOUN
	fish	fry	—ACC	eat	—PAST			know	—NEG	Persia	cat
LUW	魚フライ		を	食べ	た	かもしれない				ペルシャ猫	
	NOUN		ADP	VERB	AUX	AUX				NOUN	
	fried fish		—ACC	eat	—PAST	may				Persia	cat
bunsetsu	魚フライを			食べたかもしれない						ペルシャ猫	

Figure 2: An example of a Japanese word unit: 'It is the Persian cat that may have eaten fried fish' in Japanese.

SUWs and LUWs in Section 5.1.

3.2 Conversion to Universal PoS tags

UD has adopted Universal PoS tags, version 2.0 (Petrov et al., 2012), as a system for aggregating the parts of speech of all languages; in this system 17 distinct parts of speech are defined. For the Japanese-language version of UD, we defined the UD parts of speech by constructing a table of correspondences using UniDic (Den et al., 2007) and the Universal PoS tags. For SUWs, BCCWJ adopts a PoS system based on a word's possible lexical categories. For example, the PoS tag `noun(common.adverbial)` (名詞-普通名詞-副詞可能) means that the word can be a common noun (普通名詞) or an adverb (副詞). In contrast, LUWs are used to specify PoS tags based on *usage principles*, which resolve usage ambiguities based on context. The `noun(common.adverbial)` tag in the SUW PoS system resolves to a common noun or an adverb depending on context. We selected the SUW PoS system because SUWs are the base annotation of word units of the BCCWJ; broadly speaking, there is no significant difference between the SUW and LUW PoS systems for our purposes.

However, for certain words we need to use a LUW PoS system based on usage principles in order to conform to the UD standards and to achieve consistency with other languages. For example, in the case of a nominal verb (`noun(common.verbal_suru)`, which can add -する) or nominal adjective (`noun(common.adjectival)`, which can add -な), the SUW PoS system, based on lexical principles, is not appropriate because if a word is a verb or adjective depending on the context, the SUW PoS system cannot detect this. Instead, here we use LUW PoS tags based on usage principles that resolve ambiguities based on context. The LUW PoS tags based on usage principles have the advantage of being easier to map onto other lan-

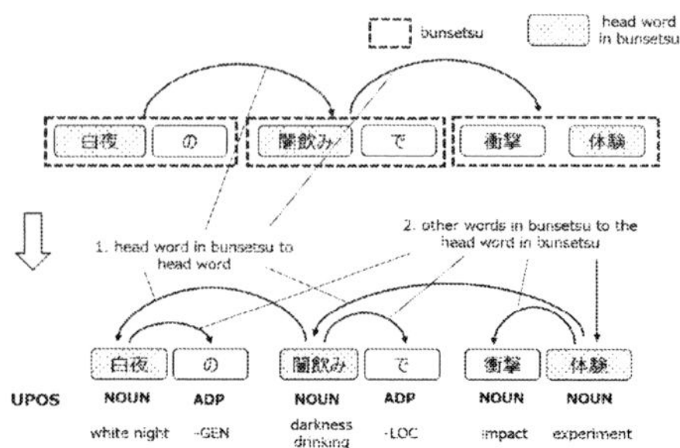

Figure 3: Illustration of the conversion of bunsetsu-level dependency to UD word-level dependency.

guages, and the reduced ambiguity associated with word endings makes it easier to specify the conditions for a VERB or ADJ tag.

Table 4 shows the mapping between Universal PoS tags and UniDic based on these principles. Note that the mapping is for Unidic SUW PoS; using Unidic LUW PoS would be simpler, as described in the following Section 5.1. The fact is, however, that there are several problems involved in using LUW PoS, as will be described presently.

3.3 Conversion of dependency structure

For syntactic information for Japanese, we use BCCWJ-DepPara (Asahara and Matsumoto, 2016), which includes bunsetsu dependency and coordination information for the BCCWJ. In order to convert bunsetsu-level into word-level dependencies, we identify the head word in the bunsetsu and then attach all other elements in the bunsetsu to the head word, as in Figure 3. Note that the UD dependency arrow is from the head to the dependent word, whereas the BCCWJ dependency arrow is from the dependent to the head word; this is merely a notational issue and the substantive description is the same. Moreover, the head-word

---

[6]Japanese uses various suffixes to make an adjective phrase using a noun, -的; to express an honorific meaning, such as -さん; and so on. However, we use the NOUN for the time being for various reasons.

Table 4: Some of example of labeling rule UPOS, which of the number is about forty.

SUW POS	Basic form	LUW POS	UD rel
`adjective_i(bound)`		`auxiliary`	AUX
`adjective_i(bound)`		`adjective_i(general)`	ADJ
`adnominal`	`^[こそあど此其彼] の` (ko/so/a/do/ko/ka-no)		DET
`adnominal`	`^[こそあど此其彼]` (ko/so/a/do/ko/ka)		PRON
`verb(bound)`	為る (suru)		AUX
`verb`			VERB
`noun(proper.*.*)`			PROPN
`noun(common.adverbial)`		`adverb`	ADV
`noun(common.adverbial)`			NOUN
`prefix`		`adverb`	NOUN
`suffix`			NOUN[6]

in the bunsetsuis selected as the rightmost content word after separating content and function words; for example, the head-word is 体験 'experiments' in 衝撃体験 ' impact experiments ' in Figure 3. [7]

While BCCWJ-DepPara includes dependency information, it does not include syntactic dependency roles corresponding to the Universal Dependencies relations (de Marneffe et al., 2014) (such as the labels `nsubj`, `obj`, and `iobj`). We therefore determined and assigned the UD relation labels based on the case-marking (`particle(case|binding|adverbial)`) or predicate-argument structure information in BCCWJ-PAS (Ueda et al., 2015). This predicate-argument structure information is semantic-level information, so *basically* we use the case-marking, and the predicate-argument information is just for reference. Since Japanese, unlike languages such as English, can omit core arguments and case-marking and the case-marking *always* corresponds with grammatical arguments in UD relations, predicate-argument structure is necessarily expressed by the case marker. For example, the case marker は *ha* usually indicates a nominal subject `nsubj`, but also frequently appears as a topic marker. [8]

Table 5 shows the rules for assigning UD relations. These conversions combine various rules like bunsetsu information, case information, and coordination relations between the head word and the dependent word.

Our current rules, which are unable to identify clauses, thus cannot effectively handle clause-related labels such as `csubj`, `advcl`, and `acl`; this is because clauses in Japanese are vaguer than in English, as described in Section 5.2. In the future, we will solve this problem by establishing

Table 5: Some of example of rules for assigning UD relations, which of the number is about sixty. It is more detailed in the actual implementation.

Rule	Label
root of sentence and head word in bunsetsu.	`root`
have UD POS NUM	`nummod`
have UD POS ADV	`advmod`
include case 'ga' (nominative case) in bunsetsu	`nsubj`
include case 'o' (accusative case) in bunsetsu	`obj`
have UD POS VERB and the dependency have UD POS VERB if the relation is above bunsetsu.	`aux`
have UD POS VERB and the dependency have UD POS VERB if the relation is not above bunsetsu	`compound`

Table 6: MISC field on UD Japanese-BCCWJ. It is a development version, so may be changed.

label	description
`BunsetuBILabel`	BI-tags on bunsetsu (B=top of bunsetsu, I=others.)
`BunsetuPositionType`	Type of bunsetsu
`LUWBILabel`	BI-tags on LUW. (B=top word of LUW, I=others.)
`LUWPOS`	LUW Unidic POS tag.

criteria for identifying clauses.

BCCWJ-DepPara also contains coordinate structure information, but our current conversion rules do not yet have defined rules related to coordinate structures such as `cc` and `conj`. The issue will be presented in (Kanayama et al., 2018).

3.4 Format

Through this process we can convert the BCCWJ to a UD schema. UD Japanese-BCCWJ is formatted by CoNLL-U. UD Japanese-BCCWJ provides the word form, lemma of the word form, universal part-of-speech tag, language-specific part-of-speech tag (Unidic POS), and Universal Depen-

---

[7]As described in (Kanayama et al., 2018), this property affects coordinate structures.

[8]Please refer to Section 3.4 in (Asahara et al., 2018) for a discussion of case markers in Japanese.

dencies relation. Note that the provided POS is the **SUW** POS serves as the language-specific PoS tag in UD Japanese-BCCWJ.

UD allows us to insert any annotation using the `MISC` field, so we can give syntactic information using this field for LUW word units and bunsetsu. This information may be useful for Japanese parsing. Table 6 summarizes the MISC fields in UD Japanese-BCCWJ.

4 Parsing by genre

UD Japanese-BCCWJ is attractive in that it includes documents in various genres. We present the parsing results that indicate differences by genre. In this paper we do not show part-of-speech tagging results, because there are some Japanese POS tagging tools (for example, Kudo et al. (2004)'s implementation, MeCab), which make it easier to convert Unidic to UD POS, as mentioned.

We use UDPipe (Straka and Straková, 2017) as a tool to train the parsing model and evaluate the parsing accuracy. UDPipe is a trainable pipeline for tokenization, tagging, lemmatization, and dependency parsing from CoNLL-U format files. The parsing uses Parsito (Straka et al., 2015), which is a transition-based parser using a neural-network classifier. We use default parameters in UDPipe. [9] We use the labelled attachment score (LAS) and unlabelled attachment score (UAS) as evaluation metrics.

The results are shown in Table 7 and Table 8. The columns in the Tables represent the parsing model by genre, the rows the genre tests, and 'all' is the full core data, so a given cell represents the result of evaluating the genre parsing model by the genre test set.

Whereas the genres of OW, PB, PM, and PN contain more than 200K tokens, the genres of OC and OY contain only around 100K, tokens as shown in Table 3.

It is in principle one of the advantages of UD Japanese-BCCWJ that it can utilize a relatively large scale sub-corpus. In fact, however, the UAS results show that if a genre has more than 200K tokens, the result from using only the in-domain data is better than that with the data for all 1.2 million tokens, including the out-domain data.

---

[9]The version using UDPipe is 1.2.1-devel, and executes with no options.

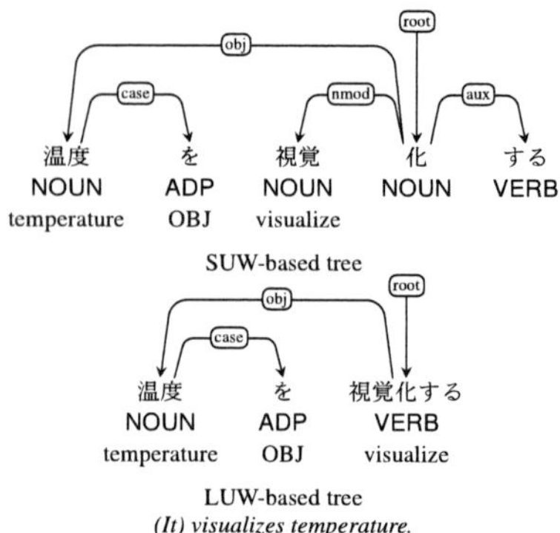

Figure 4: PoS variation between SUW and LUW

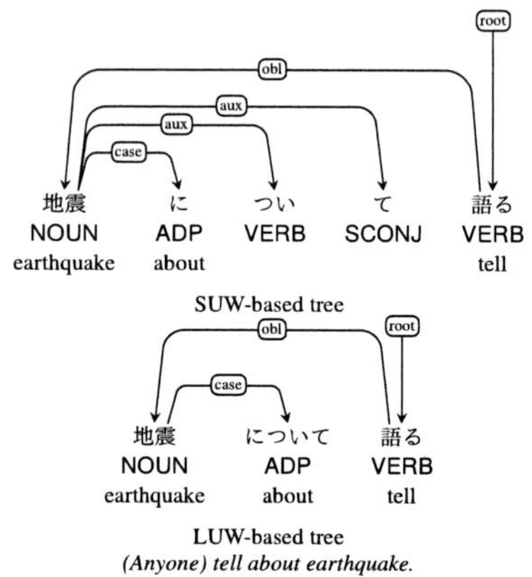

Figure 5: Multi-Word Expression

5 Discussion

In this section, we will take up a problem related to UD Japanese that centres on UD Japanese-BCCWJ. The overall discussion of UD Japanese is summarized by (Asahara et al., 2018).

We must also still discuss the issue of coordinate structures in Japanese. The issue will be presented in (Kanayama et al., 2018).

5.1 Word units

The choice of word unit is one of the important issues in UD Japanese. BCCWJ includes three sorts of word unit standards, as noted: SUWs, LUWs, and bunsetsu. We used SUWs for UD Japanese-BCCWJ.

However, the UD project stipulates that word delimitation in the UD standard should be for 'syntactic words'. LUWs in BCCWJ are thus a more preferable word delimitation standard than SUWs.

Figure 4 shows the difference between SUW PoS and LUW PoS. The top of Figure 4 shows the

Table 7: Results of unlabeled attachment score (UAS).

train \ test	OC	OW	OY	PB	PM	PN	all.
OC	89.70	81.99	88.46	87.93	88.45	87.21	**90.49**
OW	80.21	**88.62**	78.08	83.66	84.74	84.95	88.55
OY	86.35	79.54	86.15	84.62	85.67	84.66	**88.21**
PB	89.23	86.23	88.34	**91.56**	90.91	90.63	91.48
PM	87.28	85.57	86.64	89.65	**89.74**	89.32	89.67
PN	86.40	87.66	85.88	88.65	89.31	**91.20**	90.83
all.	86.64	84.84	85.71	87.74	88.18	88.00	**89.89**

Table 8: Results of LAS (Labeled attachment score). LAS consider the UD relation label unlike UAS.

train \ test	OC	OW	OY	PB	PM	PN	all.
OC	87.35	78.19	85.76	85.06	85.67	84.32	**88.17**
OW	78.36	**87.16**	76.16	82.06	83.03	83.23	87.00
OY	83.31	75.87	83.24	81.43	82.62	81.43	**85.33**
PB	86.60	83.47	85.73	89.21	88.58	88.07	**89.30**
PM	84.32	82.59	83.81	86.63	**87.16**	86.79	87.14
PN	83.65	85.03	83.34	85.93	87.06	**89.28**	88.90
all.	84.04	81.94	83.12	85.10	85.72	85.51	**87.65**

SUW-based PoS. The verb する 'do' and the verbal noun make a compound verb, as in the bottom of Figure 4 in the LUW-based segmentation.

Figure 5 presents a functional multi-word expression について, which includes three words in SUW units and one word in LUW units. We can mask the morphological construction of the syntactic word within a LUW.

However, currently we nevertheless continue to use SUWs as the UD Japanese word delimitation standard. This is because (1) LUWs are difficult to produce with word segmenters, and (2) some functional multi-word expressions in Japanese do not conform to the LUW standards.

5.2 Clause

The UD dependency labels are designed to be split between the word/phrase and the clause. The difference between clauses and words/phrases is vague in Japanese, because cases, including the subject, do not necessarily overtly appear in sentences.

Figure 6 shows an adjective clause and an adjective phrase in Japanese. At the top of Figure 6 is an overt adjective clause with a nominal subject. In contrast, however, in the example at the bottom of Figure 6 it cannot be determined whether the adjective is attributive or predicative, since the nominal subject of adjective predicate can be omitted in Japanese (in this case, しっぽ 'tail' may be omitted). Thus, we define `acl` for all adjectives which attach to noun phrases as the current state.

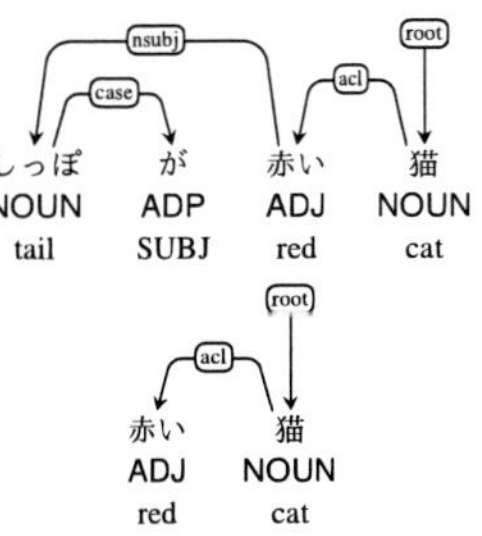

Figure 6: Clause or Phrase.

6 Other UD Japanese resources

In this section, we describe other UD Japanese resources at the time of writing. Table 2 shows a summary of these. As noted, there are five UD Japanese corpora as of March 2018, which in scale constitute the second largest of all UD corpora with the addition of the UD Japanese-BCCWJ.

UD Japanese-KTC (Tanaka et al., 2016) is based on the NTT Japanese Phrase Structure Treebank (Tanaka and Nagata, 2013), which contains the same original text as the Kyoto Text Corpus (KTC) (Kurohashi and Nagao, 2003). KTC is a bunsetsu-level dependency structure like BCCWJ, but with its own word delimitation schema and POS tag set. We are now modifying the UD Japanese KTC from the version 1.0 schema to version 2.0.

UD Japanese-GSD consists of sentences from Japanese Wikipedia that have been automatically split into words by IBM's word segmenter. The dependencies are automatically resolved using the bunsetsu-level dependency parser (Kanayama et al., 2000) with the attachment rules for functional words defined in UD Japanese.

UD Japanese-PUD (Zeman et al., 2017) was created in the same manner as UD Japanese-GSD, with the goal of maintaining consistency with UD Japanese-GSD. It is a parallel corpus with multiple other languages.

UD Japanese-Modern (Omura et al., 2017) is a small UD annotation corpus based on the *Corpus of Historical Japanese: Meiji-Taisho Series I Magazines* (CHJ) (Ogiso et al., 2017). The CHJ is large-scale corpus with morphological information of Old Japanese and has morphological information compatible with the BCCWJ. We annotated bunsetsu-level syntactic dependency and coordinated structures using the BCCWJ-DepPara annotation schema and predicate-argument relations, and utilized the conversion script used for UD Japanese-BCCWJ because the two corpora share the same annotation schema. There are two characteristic syntactic structures in Old Japanese. One is inversion, found in Sino-Japanese literary styles. The other is predicative adnominals.

As mentioned, each UD Japanese corpus has been developed in a different manner since the resources are derived from annotation with other standards. For example, UD Japanese-KTC is converted from a phrase structure treebank, while UD Japanese-Modern is based on compatible annotation with UD Japanese-BCCWJ. However, the syntactic structures of Old Japanese are very different from contemporary Japanese, as described above.

Presently we are trying to standardize UD Japanese resources under the UD Japanese-BCCWJ schema by annotating BCCWJ-DepPara with standard syntactic dependency notation for other resources. Then, we will use the conversion rules of this article for the other UD Japanese resources.

7 Summary and Outlook

In this paper, we described a corpus created by converting the Balanced Corpus of Contemporary Written Japanese (BCCWJ), a Japanese language corpus, into the UD annotation schema. There are differences between BCCWJ and UD schemas, and so we have tried to develop and implement

rules to convert BCCWJ to UD.

The UD Japanese-BCCWJ was released in March 2018. Note that though the corpus does not include the surface form due to the original text copyright, the BCCWJ DVD Edition purchaser can add the surface form using the scripts in the UD package. However, this is a matter of debate, as described in this paper, so we are going to continue to update it based on ongoing discussion, for instance regarding the apposite word unit for Japanese.

At the time of writing, we have completed the process of UD conversion based on SUWs. We also need to implement a corpus based on LUWs, and will publicly release our Japanese UD data based on both SUW and LUW analyses.

Acknowledgements

This work was supported by JSPS KAKENHI Grants Number 17H00917, and 18H05521 and a project of the Centre for Corpus Development, NINJAL.

References

Masayuki Asahara, Hiroshi Kanayama, Takaaki Tanaka, Yusuke Miyao, Sumire Uematsu, Shinsuke Mori, Yuji Matsumoto, Mai Omura, and Yugo Murawaki. 2018. Universal Dependencies Version 2 for Japanese. In *Proceedings of the Eleventh International Conference on Language Resources and Evaluation (LREC 2018)*, pages 1824–1831, Miyazaki, Japan.

Masayuki Asahara and Yuji Matsumoto. 2016. BCCWJ-DepPara: A Syntactic Annotation Treebank on the 'Balanced Corpus of Contemporary Written Japanese'. In *Proceedings of the 12th Workshop on Asian Langauge Resources (ALR12)*, pages 49–58, Osaka, Japan.

Yasuharu Den, Toshinobu Ogiso, Hideki Ogura, Atsushi Yamada, Nobuaki Minematsu, Kiyotaka Uchimoto, and Hanae Koiso. 2007. *The development of an electronic dictionary for morphological analysis and its application to Japanese corpus linguistics (in Japanese)*.

Hiroshi Kanayama, Na-Rae Han, Masayuki Asahara, Jena D. Hwang, Yusuke Miyao, Jinho Choi, and Yuji Matsumoto. 2018. Coordinate structures in universal dependencies for head-final languages. In *Proceedings of Universal Dependencies Workshop 2018 (UDW 2018)*, Brussels, Belgium. (to appear).

Hiroshi Kanayama, Kentaro Torisawa, Yutaka Mitsuishi, and Jun'ichi Tsujii. 2000. A hybrid Japanese parser with hand-crafted grammar and statistics. In

Proceedings of the 18th International Conference on Computational Linguistics (COLING '00), pages 411–417, Saarbrücken, Germany.

Taku Kudo, Kaoru Yamamoto, and Yuji Matsumoto. 2004. Applying conditional random fields to Japanese morphological analysis. In *Proceedings of the 2004 Conference on Empirical Methods in Natural Language Processing (EMNLP 2014)*, Barcelona, Spain.

Sadao Kurohashi and Makoto Nagao. 2003. *Building a Japanese Parsed Corpus – while Improving the Parsing System*, Treebanks: Building and Using Parsed Corpora, chapter 14. Springer, Dordrecht.

Kikuo Maekawa, Makoto Yamazaki, Toshinobu Ogiso, Takehiko Maruyama, Hideki Ogura, Wakako Kashino, Hanae Koiso, Masaya Yamaguchi, Makiro Tanaka, and Yasuharu Den. 2014. Balanced Corpus of Contemporary Written Japanese. *Language Resources and Evaluation*, 48(2):345–371.

Marie-Catherine de Marneffe, Timothy Dozat, Natalia Silveira, Katri Haverinen, Filip Ginter, Joakim Nivre, and Christopher D Manning. 2014. Universal stanford dependencies: A cross-linguistic typology. In *Proceedings of 9th International Conference on Language Resources and Evaluation (LREC 2014)*, pages 4585–4592, Reykjavik, Iceland.

R. McDonald, J. Nivre, Y. Quirmbach-Brundage, Y. Goldberg, D. Das, K.Ganchev, K. Hall, S. Petrov, H. Zhang, O. Täckström, C. Bedini, N. B. Castelló, and J. Lee. 2013. Universal Dependency annotation for multilingual parsing. In *Proceedings of the 51st Annual Meeting of the Association for Computational Linguistics (ACL 2013)*, pages 92–97, Sofia, Bulgaria.

Shinsuke Mori, Hideki Ogura, and Tetsuro Sasada. 2014. A Japanese word dependency corpus. In *Proceedings of 9th International Conference on Language Resources and Evaluation (LREC 2014)*, pages 753–758, Reykjavik, Iceland.

Toshinobu Ogiso, Asuko Kondo, Yoko Mabuchi, and Noriko Hattori. 2017. Construction of the "Corpus of Historical Japanese: Meiji-Taisho Series I - Magazines". In *Proceedings of the 2017 Conference of Digital Humanities (DH2017)*, Montrèal, Canada.

Mai Omura, Yuta Takahashi, and Masayuki Asahara. 2017. Universal Dependency for Modern Japanese. In *Proceedings of the 7th Conference of Japanese Association for Digital Humanities (JADH2017)*, pages 34–36.

Slav Petrov, Dipanjan Das, and Ryan McDonald. 2012. A universal part-of-speech tagset. In *Proceedings of the Eight International Conference on Language Resources and Evaluation (LREC 2012)*, pages 2089–2096.

Milan Straka, Jan Hajič, Jana Straková, and Jan Hajič jr. 2015. Parsing universal dependency treebanks using neural networks and search-based oracle. In *Proceedings of Fourteenth International Workshop on Treebanks and Linguistic Theories (TLT 2015)*.

Milan Straka and Jana Straková. 2017. Tokenizing, pos tagging, lemmatizing and parsing ud 2.0 with udpipe. In *Proceedings of the CoNLL 2017 Shared Task: Multilingual Parsing from Raw Text to Universal Dependencies*, pages 88–99, Vancouver, Canada.

Takaaki Tanaka, Yusuke Miyao, Masayuki Asahara, Sumire Uematsu, Hiroshi Kanayama, Shinsuke Mori, and Yuji Matsumoto. 2016. Universal Dependencies for Japanese. In *Proceedings of the Tenth International Conference on Language Resources and Evaluation (LREC 2016)*, pages 1651–1658.

Takaaki Tanaka and Masaaki Nagata. 2013. Constructing a practical constituent parser from a Japanese treebank with function labels. In *Proceedings of 4th Workshop on Statistical Parsing of Morphologically-Rich Languages (SPMRL'2013)*, pages 108–118, Seattle, Washington, USA.

Yoshiko Ueda, Ryu Iida, Masayuki Asahara, Yuji Matsumoto, and Takenobu Tokunaga. 2015. Predicate-argument structure and coreference relation annotation on 'Balanced Corpus of Contemporary Written Japanese' (in Japanese). In *Proceedings of the 8th Workshop on Japanese Language Corpus*, pages 205–214, Tokyo, Japanese.

Daniel Zeman, Martin Popel, Milan Straka, Jan Hajič, Joakim Nivre, Filip Ginter, Juhani Luotolahti, Sampo Pyysalo, Slav Petrov, Martin Potthast, Francis Tyers, Elena Badmaeva, Memduh Gökırmak, Anna Nedoluzhko, Silvie Cinková, Jan Hajič jr., Jaroslava Hlaváčová, Václava Kettnerová, Zdeňka Urešová, Jenna Kanerva, Stina Ojala, Anna Missilä, Christopher Manning, Sebastian Schuster, Siva Reddy, Dima Taji, Nizar Habash, Herman Leung, Marie-Catherine de Marneffe, Manuela Sanguinetti, Maria Simi, Hiroshi Kanayama, Valeria de Paiva, Kira Droganova, Hěctor Martínez Alonso, Hans Uszkoreit, Vivien Macketanz, Aljoscha Burchardt, Kim Harris, Katrin Marheinecke, Georg Rehm, Tolga Kayadelen, Mohammed Attia, Ali Elkahky, Zhuoran Yu, Emily Pitler, Saran Lertpradit, Michael Mandl, Jesse Kirchner, Hector Fernandez Alcalde, Jana Strnadova, Esha Banerjee, Ruli Manurung, Antonio Stella, Atsuko Shimada, Sookyoung Kwak, Gustavo Mendonça, Tatiana Lando, Rattima Nitisaroj, and Josie Li. 2017. CoNLL 2017 Shared Task: Multilingual Parsing from Raw Text to Universal Dependencies. In *Proceedings of the CoNLL 2017 Shared Task: Multilingual Parsing from Raw Text to Universal Dependencies*, pages 1–19.

The First Komi-Zyrian Universal Dependencies Treebanks

Niko Partanen[1], Rogier Blokland[2], KyungTae Lim[3], Thierry Poibeau[3], Michael Rießler[4]

`niko.partanen@kotus.fi, rogier.blokland@moderna.uu.se,`
`kyungtae.lim@ens.fr, thierry.poibeau@ens.fr,`
`michael.riessler@uni-bielefeld.de`

[1]Institute for the Languages of Finland
[2]University of Uppsala
[3]LATTICE (CNRS & ENS / PSL & Université Sorbonne nouvelle / USPC)
[4]University of Bielefeld

Abstract

Two Komi-Zyrian treebanks were included in the Universal Dependencies 2.2 release. This article contextualizes the treebanks, discusses the process through which they were created, and outlines the future plans and timeline for the next improvements. Special attention is paid to the possibilities of using UD in the documentation and description of endangered languages.

1 Introduction

Komi-Zyrian is a Uralic language spoken in the north-eastern corner of the European part of Russia. Smaller Komi settlements can also be found elsewhere in northern Russia, from the Kola Peninsula to Western Siberia. The language has approximately 160,000 speakers and, although not moribund, is still threatened by the local majority language, Russian. There is a long history of research on Komi, but contemporary descriptions and computational resources could be greatly improved. Over the last few years some larger documentation projects have been carried out on Komi. These projects have focused on the most endangered spoken varieties, while at the same time, new written resources for Standard Komi have became available.

This paper discusses the creation of two Komi treebanks, one containing written and another spoken data. Both the treebanks and the scripts used to create them are included in this paper as supplementary materials, and the treebanks are part of the Universal Dependencies 2.2 release (Nivre et al., 2018). The treebanks are called **Lattice** and **IKDP**, due to the fact that most of the work on them has been carried out at the LATTICE-CNRS

laboratory in Paris, and the work has been done collaboratively with the IKDP-2[1] project, which is a continuation of earlier work that produced a language documentation corpus of Komi called IKDP (Blokland et al., 2009-2018). A comprehensive descriptive grammar of Komi with a focus on syntax is currently being written by members of the team. The present treebanks are intended to support the grammatical description.

The authors' recent research at LATTICE laboratory has focused on dependency parsing of low-resource languages, using Komi and North Saami as examples (Lim et al., 2018). The Lattice treebank was initially created for use in testing dependency parsers, and the IKDP treebank was created at a later date with the aim of also including spoken language data.

2 Language Documentation

Language documentation refers to a linguistic practice aiming at the provision of long-lasting and accountable records of speech events, usually carried out in the context of endangered languages and with the goal of understanding spoken communication beyond mere structural grammar. Himmelmann (1998) was the first to define "Documentary Linguistics" as separate from "Descriptive Linguistics", although with considerable overlap between the two. He also pays special attention to the interface between research outputs and primary data, ideally including audio and video recordings (Himmelmann, 2006). This has generally been the approach in the present work too, so that the spoken language UD corpus is directly connected to the documentary multimedia corpus

---

[1]`https://langdoc.github.io/IKDP-2`

Proceedings of the Second Workshop on Universal Dependencies (UDW 2018), pages 126–132
Brussels, Belgium, November 1, 2018. ©2018 Association for Computational Linguistics

through matching sentence IDs. This allows the treebank sentences to be connected to rich non-linguistic metadata. Additionally, the coded time-alignment in the original utterances provides information about turn-taking and overlapping at the millisecond level. The documentary corpus refers to the materials collected and processed within the language documentation activities, which are usually fieldwork-based and aim to represent various genres and speech practices, all of which are often under a threat of disappearance.

In language documentation, traditional annotation methods have mainly consisted of so-called interlinear glossing.[2] This is normally done manually or semi-manually, i.e. with little or no use of natural language processing tools (cf. Gerstenberger et al., 2016). With the available Komi data in our project, however, we wanted to apply an annotation method that would connect our work more closely to established corpus linguistics and NLP. Universal Dependencies appeared to be a very attractive annotation scheme as it aims at cross-linguistic comparability and already contains several Uralic languages. Komi-Zyrian is currently the sixth Uralic language to be included in the project.

Work with Komi complements well the developments associated with the emergence of new Uralic treebanks in 2017, with new repositories created for North Saami[3] and Erzya (Rueter and Tyers, 2018). Another noteworthy trend is that there are several treebanks currently being created for endangered languages in situations similar to that of Komi. As far as we have been able to ascertain, these are, at least: Dargwa spoken in the Caucasus (Kozhukhar, 2017), Pnar[4] spoken in South-East Asia and Shipibo-Konibo[5] spoken in Peru. The description of the last treebank mentioned does not indicate the use of language documentation materials, but as the language is very small, the context is comparable. To our knowledge, the IKDP treebank discussed here is the first treebank included in the UD release that is directly

based on language documentation material. It is too early to say whether there will be more similar treebanks in the future and within what timeframe, but having more materials like these included in UD would fit into the original ideas of the multifunctional language documentation enterprise very well.

3 Methodology

The initial analysis of Komi plain text was created using Giellatekno's[6] open infrastructure (Moshagen et al., 2014), which is currently at a rather mature level for Komi. The syntactic analysis component demands the most further work, which in turn can be guided by the work on treebanks. Similar rule-based architectures have already been used for other treebanks as well. The Northern Saami and Erzya corpora, for example, seem to have been created using a similar approach. Some work has been conducted with integrating these NLP tools into workflows commonly used in language documentation (Gerstenberger et al., 2017a,b, 2016). Since these languages often lack larger annotated resources, the use of infrastructures other than rule-based ones has not been common or possible, but these workflows have been implemented in a modular fashion that would make enable the integration of other tools when they become available or reach needed accuracy.

It has been demonstrated that it is possible to convert annotations from Giellatekno's annotation scheme into the UD scheme (Sheyanova and Tyers, 2017), and this has also worked well in our case, although the exact procedure will continue to be refined while the token count of the corpus grows, which will ultimately also reveal rarer and not-yet-analysed morphosyntactic features. After starting with manually editing CoNLL-U files, the UD Annotatrix tool (Tyers et al., 2018) was adopted in January 2018, which marked the midpoint in the project's timeline. This greatly improved the annotation speed and consistency.

The treebank creation thus consisted of the following steps:

1. Sending Komi sentences to the Giellatekno morphosyntactic analyser (consisting of an FST component for morphological categories and a syntactic component using Constraint Grammar)

---

[2]Cf., e.g., the Leipzig Glossing Rules `https://www.eva.mpg.de/lingua/resources/glossing-rules.php`

[3]`https://github.com/UniversalDependencies/UD_North_Sami-Giella`

[4]`https://github.com/UniversalDependencies/UD_Pnar-PTB`

[5]`https://github.com/UniversalDependencies/UD_Shipibo_Konibo-PUCP`

[6]`http://giellatekno.uit.no`

2. Resolving the remaining ambiguity manually

3. Adding the missing syntactic relations manually to the UD Annotatrix

4. Automatically converting the analyzer's XPOS-tags into UPOS-tags and converting morphological feature tags into their UD counterparts

5. Manual correction and verification

The current workflow involves a rather large amount of manual work. We are interested in testing various approaches to morphological and syntactic analysis so that different (rule-based, statistic-based and hybrid) parsers can eventually replace the manual work. Some tests have already been carried out with the dependency parser used by the Lattice team in the CoNLL-U Shared Task 2017 (Lim and Poibeau, 2017) and a follow-up project (Partanen et al., 2018).

The treebank processing pipeline has been tied to several scripts and existing tools. The primary analysisis done within the Giellatekno toolkit (building on FST Morphology and Constraint Grammar), where tokenization, morphological analysis and rule-based disambiguation are tied to the script 'kpvdep'. The script returns a vislcg3 file that contains all ambiguities left after the analysis. Once the ambiguities are resolved manually, the vislcg3 file can be imported into the UD Annotatrix tool. As a final step, the Giellatekno POS-tags and morphological features are converted to follow the UD standard with a Python script, originally written by Francis Tyers[7]. A modified version of the script with the conversion pattern file is stored in **not-to-release** folder in the dev-branch of the Lattice treebank, which is the location where all development scripts of both treebanks will be maintained.

4 Data Sources and Design Principles

Most of the work on the Komi language is currently being done by collaborators of FU-Lab[8] in Syktyvkar, the capital of the Komi Republic in Russia. The work of FU-Lab, led by Marina Fedina, has been particularly exceptional, as it has resulted in a significant number of Komi-language

books being digitalized, made available online[9] and converted into a linguistic corpus.[10] The corpus is currently 40 million words large, and the long-term goal is to digitalize all books and other printed texts ever published in Komi-Zyrian. The number of publications is approximately 4,500 books, plus tens of thousands of newspaper and journal issues. A significant portion of the latter are available in the Public Domain as part of the Fenno-Ugrica project of the National Library of Finland[11]. We have exclusively chosen to use openly available data for the Lattice treebank in order to ensure as broad and simple reuse as possible. The forthcoming releases will include more genres of text, such as newspaper texts and longer sections of Wikipedia articles.

All sentences in the Lattice treebank are presented in the contemporary orthography, even when they were originally published using various earlier Komi writing systems. The proportion of texts originally written in the Molodcov alphabet will rise dramatically in the next releases, as this is probably the most commonly used orthography in the upcoming texts. Storing several orthographic variants may be necessary. Conversion between systems has been carried out using FU-Lab's Molodcov converter[12]. The data originates from scanned books through text recognition, currently with loss of page coordinates. This connects to the question of how to retrieve arbitrary information from different sources that can be connected to the sentence IDs: metadata, page positions, page images, time codes and audio segments.

We considered it very important to also include spoken language in the treebank, ideally eventually covering all dialects. During the last years, one of the largest research projects investigating spoken Komi has been the IKDP project, led by Rogier Blokland in 20142016, which resulted in a large transcribed spoken language corpus (Blokland et al., 2009-2018). The IKDP treebank contains dialectal texts taken from this corpus, and since written Komi does not follow the exact same principles employed in the transcriptions, it seems problematic to mix these materials together. The orthographic conventions

---

[7]https://github.com/ftyers/ud-scripts/blob/master/conllu-feats.py

[8]http://fu-lab.ru

[9]http://komikyv.org

[10]http://komicorpora.ru

[11]https://fennougrica.kansalliskirjasto.fi

[12]http://fu-lab.ru/convertermolodcov

of the spoken treebank are basically similar to those used in the recent Komi dialect dictionary (Beznosikova et al., 2012), with only relatively subtle differences.What it comes to spoken features, corrections are kept and marked with the relation reparandum, but features such as pauses are not separately marked. The user can access the original archived audio, which enables a more detailed analysis of spoken phenomena if desired. In their typographic simplicity, the transcribed texts are reminiscent of some of the dialect texts published previously in various printed text collections (without the original audio recordings). The context of the spoken data here is therefore not only a faithful representation of the spoken signal, which could include also more exact phonetic transcriptions, but also the larger landscape of spoken language resources which we would like to integrate into our NLP ecosystem.

Furthermore, because local Komi speech and research communities are often conscious of orthographic norms, we wanted to draw a clear boundary between written and spoken representations. Additionally, the spoken language treebank contains a large number of Russian phrases due to code-switching, which makes it to some degree a multilingual treebank. In the IKDP treebank, Russian items are currently marked with a language tag in the misc-field, but verification that Russian annotations are consistent with monolingual Russian treebanks is a topic that requires further attention.

The sentences represent running texts and narratives, and, to a great extent, they link together into continuous larger text units. There are deviations from this in situations where individual examples have been selected in order to include instances of each dependency relation in the treebank. This was done particularly in the early stages of the treebanks when it was important to gain more understanding of how different syntactic relations are tagged consistently in UD. In the upcoming releases, occurrences of each morphosyntactic phenomena present in Komi may also be hand-picked from corpora to ensure that they occur in the treebanks, the need for which is discussed next.

5 Some Questions Arising From Komi-Zyrian

As the majority of languages in UD are larger Indo-European languages, the project does not yet include many examples of languages with very complex case systems. For example, Komi has two values of nominal case that were not yet included in the earlier documentation, namely the **approximative** and the **egressive**. One issue arising when comparing current treebanks is the cross-comparability of the case labels applied. Komi has two cases that express a path of some sort, traditionally called prolative and transitive in Komi and Uralic linguistics. These would match closely with a case label already in the UD documentation, perlative, found in Warlpiri, but the fact that there are two very similar cases already makes the labeling problematic. Differences in case labeling are related to further linguistic analyses that are possible with the corpora, as well as to parsing accuracy in multilingual scenarios. In the present treebanks, the traditional labels for Komi cases are used.

Another theoretical question arising from Komi concerns the way different cases can be combined, resulting in "double case marking". For example, it is entirely possible to use several spatial case markers linearly combined in one and the same inflected noun form, and, although this is somewhat rare, examples can be easily found even for more marginal combinations. For example, the case suffixes for elative and terminative can combine to mark subtle changes in focus: vengrija-iç-edʒ Hungary-ELA-TER 'all the way from Hungary' (see e.g. (Bartens, 2003, 53). This raises the question of how to best annotate this in UD. Of course each combination could be labeled as a new case, which is also sometimes seen in the literature on Komi nominal case (Kuznetsov, 2012, p. 374), but this would greatly increase the number of case values that need to be documented, and most of them would be very marginal and specific to individual languages. Another solution would be to allow several case affixes to be added to one word form. However, this would only help when several cases are clearly combined and would not be useful when new spatial cases have emerged from postpositions, a phenomenon typical of Komi and Udmurt dialects.

Currently, a large portion of the cases in UD documentation are used only in Hungarian. Including more languages with large case systems, such as Uralic or Northeast Caucasian languages like Lezgian, would only increase the number of names for case values used mainly in individual languages. Eventually this also boils down to the question of how comparable the cases in different languages actually are. Haspelmath has argued convincingly that case labels are valid only for particular languages (Haspelmath, 2009, 510), and the issue probably cannot be explicitly solved within UD either, but for the sake of usability of treebanks and their suitability for multilingual NLP applications, some harmonization would seem desirable. One alternative could be to create a higher layer of mapping that connects language-specific labels to broader shared categories. In this way, both Komi cases expressing a path could be connected to a concept of *movement along a path*, but the language-specific nuances would not be lost.

6   Conclusion and Further Work

The written and spoken treebanks have 1389 and 988 tokens, respectively. Due to their small size, they have not been split into test and development sets. Based on this experience, it already seems clear that providing annotations in this framework has several advantages compared to traditional methods used in language documentation projects. The main benefit is the comparability between different languages, and also straightforward licensing and distribution within UD framework.

It can be argued that tagging according the UD principles is necessarily a compromise, and that it may not express all particularities of individual languages. One possible way to solve this problem is to include further annotations in the misc-column. Another possible approach would be to provide different parts of the documentary corpus with varying degrees of annotations. In any case, based on our experience, we would strongly encourage endangered language documentation projects to take a small segment of their materials and add to it an additional layer of annotations in the Universal Dependencies framework. Language documentation data is usually stored in archives that require access requests. This is not very compatible with openly available treebanks. Still, it should be possible to collect small subsets of materials with the clear intention and permission for these recordings to be openly licensed, or to use texts old enough that they are copyright free.

New material is currently being brought into the Lattice treebank. The main genres obtained from Fenno-Ugrica collection are newspaper texts, nonfiction works and schoolbooks. Samples of these, along with some larger Wikipedia texts, will be included in the next UD release 2.3. The next phase of the IKDP treebank will include individual texts from the Komi recordings made by Eric Vászolyi in the 1950s and 1960s (Vászolyi-Vasse, 2003), which the present authors have acquired permission to re-publish electronically. These texts originate from a time and place of intensive language contact between Komi-Zyrian and Tundra Nenets, what makes them a particularly interesting target for further study.

One possibly useful addition to the treebank could be English glosses in the misc-field, since many linguists are used to working with data from endangered languages in a format like this. The English gloss could contain a contextual translation of the lemma, for example, which would make the sentences in the treebank much more accessible to different linguistic audiences.

In terms of size, the target is to reach 5,000 tokens in both treebanks during 2018, and to increase this to 20,000 in the first half of 2019. Our long-term goal is to create a resource that would contribute to research on Komi and provide better resources for Natural Language Processing of this language, which has yet to receive sufficient attention in computational linguistic research.

7   Acknowledgements

We want to thank the reviewers for their useful comments. This work has been developed in the framework of the LAKME project funded by a grant from Paris Sciences et Lettres (IDEX PSL reference ANR-10-IDEX-0001-02). Thierry Poibeau is partially supported by a RGNF-CNRS (grant between the LATTICE-CNRS Laboratory and the Russian State University for the Humanities in Moscow). Kyungtae Lim is partially supported by the ERA-NET Atlantis project. Niko Partanen's work has been carried out at the LATTICE laboratory, and besides Partanen, both Rogier Blokland and Michael Rießler collaborate within the project Language Documentation meets Language Technology: the Next Step in the Description of Komi, funded by the Kone Foundation. Thanks to Jack Rueter for numerous discussions on Komi and Erzya, and to Alexandra Kellner for proofreading the paper.

References

Raija Bartens. 2003. Kahden kaasuspäätteen jonoista suomalais-ugrilaisissa kielissä. In Bakró-Nagy Marianne and Károly Rédei, editors, *Ünnepi kötet Honti László tiszteletére*, pages 46–54. MTA, Budapest.

L.M. Beznosikova, E.A. Ajbabina, N.K. Zaboeva, and R.I. Kosnyreva. 2012. *Komi sërnisikas kyvčukör. Slovar dialektov komi âzyka: v 2-h tomah.* Institut âzyka, literatury i istorii Komi naunogo centra Uralskogo otdeleniâ Rossijskoj akademii nauk, Syktyvkar.

Rogier Blokland, Marina Fedina, Niko Partanen, and Michael Rießler. 2009-2018. IKDP. In *The Language Archive (TLA): Donated Corpora*. Max Planck Institute for Psycholinguistics, Nijmegen.

Ciprian Gerstenberger, Niko Partanen, and Michael Rießler. 2017a. Instant annotations in ELAN corpora of spoken and written Komi, an endangered language of the Barents Sea region. In *Proceedings of the 2nd Workshop on the Use of Computational Methods in the Study of Endangered Languages*, pages 57–66. ACL.

Ciprian Gerstenberger, Niko Partanen, Michael Rießler, and Joshua Wilbur. 2016. Utilizing language technology in the documentation of endangered Uralic languages. *Northern European Journal of Language Technology*, 4:29–47.

Ciprian Gerstenberger, Niko Partanen, Michael Rießler, and Joshua Wilbur. 2017b. Instant annotations: Applying NLP methods to the annotation of spoken language documentation corpora. In *Proceedings of the 3rd International Workshop on Computational Linguistics for Uralic languages*, pages 25–36. ACL.

Martin Haspelmath. 2009. Terminology of case. In Andrew Spencer and Andrej L. Malchukov, editors, *The Oxford handbook of case*, pages 505–517. OUP, Oxford.

Nikolaus Himmelmann. 2006. Language documentation: What is it and what is it good for? In Jost Gippert, Ulrike Mosel, and Nikolaus Himmelmann, editors, *Essentials of Language Documentation*, pages 1–30. Mouton de Gruyter, Berlin.

Nikolaus P. Himmelmann. 1998. Documentary and descriptive linguistics. *Linguistics*, 36:161–195.

Alexandra Kozhukhar. 2017. Universal dependencies for Dargwa Mehweb. In *Proceedings of the Fourth International Conference on Dependency Linguistics*, pages 92–99. ACL.

Nikolay Kuznetsov. 2012. Matrix of cognitive domains for Komi local cases. *Journal of Estonian and Finno-Ugric Linguistics*, 3(1):373–394.

KyungTae Lim, Niko Partanen, and Thierry Poibeau. 2018. Multilingual Dependency Parsing for Low-Resource Languages: Case Studies on North Saami and Komi-Zyrian. In *Proceedings of the Eleventh International Conference on Language Resources and Evaluation*. ELRA.

KyungTae Lim and Thierry Poibeau. 2017. A system for multilingual dependency parsing based on bidirectional LSTM feature representations. In *Proceedings of the CoNLL 2017 Shared Task: Multilingual Parsing from Raw Text to Universal Dependencies*, pages 63–70. ACL.

Sjur Moshagen, Jack Rueter, Tommi Pirinen, Trond Trosterud, and Francis M Tyers. 2014. Open-source infrastructures for collaborative work on underresourced languages. In *Proceedings of the Ninth International Conference on Language Resources and Evaluation*, pages 71–77. ELRA.

Joakim Nivre, Mitchell Abrams, Željko Agić, Lars Ahrenberg, Lene Antonsen, Maria Jesus Aranzabe, Gashaw Arutie, Masayuki Asahara, Luma Ateyah, Mohammed Attia, Aitziber Atutxa, Liesbeth Augustinus, Elena Badmaeva, Miguel Ballesteros, Esha Banerjee, Sebastian Bank, Verginica Barbu Mititelu, John Bauer, Sandra Bellato, Kepa Bengoetxea, Riyaz Ahmad Bhat, Erica Biagetti, Eckhard Bick, Rogier Blokland, Victoria Bobicev, Carl Börstell, Cristina Bosco, Gosse Bouma, Sam Bowman, Adriane Boyd, Aljoscha Burchardt, Marie Candito, Bernard Caron, Gauthier Caron, Gülşen Cebiroğlu Eryiğit, Giuseppe G. A. Celano, Savas Cetin, Fabricio Chalub, Jinho Choi, Yongseok Cho, Jayeol Chun, Silvie Cinková, Aurélie Collomb, Çağrı Çöltekin, Miriam Connor, Marine Courtin, Elizabeth Davidson, Marie-Catherine de Marneffe, Valeria de Paiva, Arantza Diaz de Ilarraza, Carly Dickerson, Peter Dirix, Kaja Dobrovoljc, Timothy Dozat, Kira Droganova, Puneet Dwivedi, Marhaba Eli, Ali Elkahky, Binyam Ephrem, Tomaž Erjavec, Aline Etienne, Richárd Farkas, Hector Fernandez Alcalde, Jennifer Foster, Cláudia Freitas, Katarína Gajdošová, Daniel Galbraith, Marcos Garcia, Moa Gärdenfors, Kim Gerdes, Filip Ginter, Iakes Goenaga, Koldo Gojenola, Memduh Gökırmak, Yoav Goldberg, Xavier Gómez Guinovart, Berta Gonzáles Saavedra, Matias Grioni, Normunds Grūzītis, Bruno Guillaume, Céline Guillot-Barbance, Nizar Habash, Jan Hajič, Jan Hajič jr., Linh Hà Mỹ, Na-Rae Han, Kim Harris, Dag Haug, Barbora Hladká, Jaroslava Hlaváčová, Florinel Hociung, Petter Hohle, Jena Hwang, Radu Ion, Elena Irimia, Tomáš Jelínek, Anders Johannsen, Fredrik Jørgensen, Hüner Kaşıkara, Sylvain Kahane, Hiroshi Kanayama, Jenna Kanerva, Tolga Kayadelen, Václava Kettnerová, Jesse Kirchner, Natalia Kotsyba, Simon Krek, Sookyoung Kwak, Veronika Laippala, Lorenzo Lambertino, Tatiana Lando, Septina Dian Larasati, Alexei Lavrentiev, John Lee, Phng Lê Hồng, Alessandro Lenci, Saran Lertpradit, Herman Leung, Cheuk Ying Li, Josie Li, Keying Li, KyungTae Lim, Nikola Ljubešić,

131

Olga Loginova, Olga Lyashevskaya, Teresa Lynn, Vivien Macketanz, Aibek Makazhanov, Michael Mandl, Christopher Manning, Ruli Manurung, Cătălina Mărănduc, David Mareček, Katrin Marheinecke, Héctor Martínez Alonso, André Martins, Jan Mašek, Yuji Matsumoto, Ryan McDonald, Gustavo Mendonça, Niko Miekka, Anna Missilä, Cătălin Mititelu, Yusuke Miyao, Simonetta Montemagni, Amir More, Laura Moreno Romero, Shinsuke Mori, Bjartur Mortensen, Bohdan Moskalevskyi, Kadri Muischnek, Yugo Murawaki, Kaili Müürisep, Pinkey Nainwani, Juan Ignacio Navarro Horñiacek, Anna Nedoluzhko, Gunta Nešpore-Bērzkalne, Lng Nguyễn Thị, Huyền Nguyễn Thị Minh, Vitaly Nikolaev, Rattima Nitisaroj, Hanna Nurmi, Stina Ojala, Adédayọ Olúòkun, Mai Omura, Petya Osenova, Robert Östling, Lilja Øvrelid, Niko Partanen, Elena Pascual, Marco Passarotti, Agnieszka Patejuk, Siyao Peng, Cenel-Augusto Perez, Guy Perrier, Slav Petrov, Jussi Piitulainen, Emily Pitler, Barbara Plank, Thierry Poibeau, Martin Popel, Lauma Pretkalniņa, Sophie Prévost, Prokopis Prokopidis, Adam Przepiórkowski, Tiina Puolakainen, Sampo Pyysalo, Andriela Rääbis, Alexandre Rademaker, Loganathan Ramasamy, Taraka Rama, Carlos Ramisch, Vinit Ravishankar, Livy Real, Siva Reddy, Georg Rehm, Michael Rießler, Larissa Rinaldi, Laura Rituma, Luisa Rocha, Mykhailo Romanenko, Rudolf Rosa, Davide Rovati, Valentin Roca, Olga Rudina, Shoval Sadde, Shadi Saleh, Tanja Samardžić, Stephanie Samson, Manuela Sanguinetti, Baiba Saulīte, Yanin Sawanakunanon, Nathan Schneider, Sebastian Schuster, Djamé Seddah, Wolfgang Seeker, Mojgan Seraji, Mo Shen, Atsuko Shimada, Muh Shohibussirri, Dmitry Sichinava, Natalia Silveira, Maria Simi, Radu Simionescu, Katalin Simkó, Mária Šimková, Kiril Simov, Aaron Smith, Isabela Soares-Bastos, Antonio Stella, Milan Straka, Jana Strnadová, Alane Suhr, Umut Sulubacak, Zsolt Szántó, Dima Taji, Yuta Takahashi, Takaaki Tanaka, Isabelle Tellier, Trond Trosterud, Anna Trukhina, Reut Tsarfaty, Francis Tyers, Sumire Uematsu, Zdeňka Urešová, Larraitz Uria, Hans Uszkoreit, Sowmya Vajjala, Daniel van Niekerk, Gertjan van Noord, Viktor Varga, Veronika Vincze, Lars Wallin, Jonathan North Washington, Seyi Williams, Mats Wirén, Tsegay Woldemariam, Tak-sum Wong, Chunxiao Yan, Marat M. Yavrumyan, Zhuoran Yu, Zdeněk Žabokrtský, Amir Zeldes, Daniel Zeman, Manying Zhang, and Hanzhi Zhu. 2018. Universal dependencies 2.2. LINDAT/CLARIN digital library at the Institute of Formal and Applied Linguistics (ÚFAL), Faculty of Mathematics and Physics, Charles University.

Niko Partanen, KyungTae Lim, Michael Rießler, and Thierry Poibeau. 2018. Dependency parsing of code-switching data with cross-lingual feature representations. In *Proceedings of the 4th International Workshop on Computational Linguistics for Uralic languages*, pages 1–17. ACL.

Jack Rueter and Francis Tyers. 2018. Towards an open-source universal-dependency treebank for Erzya. In *Proceedings of the 4th International Workshop on Computational Linguistics for Uralic languages*, pages 106–118. ACL.

Mariya Sheyanova and Francis M. Tyers. 2017. Annotation schemes in North Sámi dependency parsing. In *Proceedings of the Third Workshop on Computational Linguistics for Uralic Languages*, pages 66–75. ACL.

Francis M Tyers, Mariya Sheyanova, and Jonathan North Washington. 2018. UD Annotatrix: An annotation tool for universal dependencies. In *Proceedings of the 16th International Workshop on Treebanks and Linguistic Theories*, pages 10–17. ACL.

Eric Vászolyi-Vasse. 2003. *Syrjaenica: Narratives, folklore and folk poetry from eight dialects of the Komi language. Vol. 1, Upper Izhma, Lower Ob, Kanin Peninsula, Upper Jusva, Middle Inva, Udora.* Savariae, Szombathely.

The Hebrew Universal Dependency Treebank:
Past, Present and Future

Shoval Sadde
Open University of Israel
shovalsa@openu.ac.il

Amit Seker
Open University of Israel
amitse@openu.ac.il

Reut Tsarfaty
Open University of Israel
reutts@openu.ac.il

Abstract

The Hebrew treebank (HTB), consisting of 6221 morpho-syntactically annotated newspaper sentences, has been the only resource for training and validating statistical parsers and taggers for Hebrew, for almost two decades now. During these decades, the HTB has gone through a trajectory of automatic and semi-automatic conversions, until arriving at its UDv2 form. In this work we manually validate the UDv2 version of the HTB, and, according to our findings, we apply scheme changes that bring the UD HTB to the same theoretical grounds as the rest of UD. Our experimental parsing results with UDv2New confirm that improving the coherence and internal consistency of the UD HTB indeed leads to improved parsing performance. At the same time, our analysis demonstrates that there is more to be done at the point of intersection of UD with other linguistic processing layers, in particular, at the points where UD interfaces external morphological and lexical resources.

1 Introduction

The Hebrew Treebank (HTB), initially introduced by Sima'an et al. (2001), is the first, and so far only, gold standard for morphologically and syntactically annotated sentences in Modern Hebrew. It was created with the main goal in mind to enable the development of statistical models for morphological and syntactic parsing for Hebrew, but also to facilitate linguistic investigations into the structure and distribution of linguistic Semitic phenomena. The pilot version of Sima'an et al. (2001) has been minimal — it consisted of 500 sentences, morphologically and syntactically annotated by hand. This modest start, however, defined linguistic conventions and annotation principles that would continue to affect many treebank versions derived from the HTB for many years, including the *universal dependencies* (UD) HTB version.

During these two decades, the HTB has expanded from 500 to 6221 sentences and changed several forms. The different versions of the treebank reflect different theories and formal representation types, that in turn reflect different, and sometimes contradictory, linguistic annotation principles. The reasons for these differences were sometimes practical, e.g., a new version was derived to answer an emerging technological need, and sometimes socio-academic, e.g., because different teams adopted different linguistic theories as their underlying annotation principles.

The HTB thus enabled the development of many statistical morphological and syntactic processing models (Adler, 2007; Bar-haim et al., 2008; Shacham and Wintner, 2007; Tsarfaty, 2006; Goldberg and Tsarfaty, 2008; Goldberg and Elhadad, 2009; Tsarfaty, 2010; Goldberg and Elhadad, 2010, 2011; More and Tsarfaty, 2016; More et al., In Press), but these models were trained on vastly different versions of the treebank, obeying different theories and annotation schemes, which then rendered the reported results mostly non-comparable.

Hebrew dependency parsing presents an acute version of this syndrome. Studies such as Goldberg and Elhadad (2011), Tsarfaty et al. (2012), More et al. (In Press), as well as the SPMRL shared tasks (Seddah et al., 2013, 2014), all present attachment scores on Hebrew dependency parsing. But for reporting these scores they use HTB versions that reflect distinct schemes, sometime reporting different metrics, which makes the numerical comparison between the respective results meaningless (Tsarfaty et al., 2011). This is why the UD initiative comes as a blessing, not only for the cross-linguistic parsing community but also for the Hebrew NLP community — by presenting a unique opportunity to standardize the resources and metrics used for Hebrew parsing.

133

Proceedings of the Second Workshop on Universal Dependencies (UDW 2018), pages 133–143
Brussels, Belgium, November 1, 2018. ©2018 Association for Computational Linguistics

Ideally, the current UDv2 version would make for such a standard Hebrew resource. Unfortunately though, many of the conversion processes since Sima'an et al. (2001) to the present UDv2 have been automatic or semi-automatic, with no point of systematic qualitative validation. This resulted in odd, and sometime plain wrong, dependency structures, with respect to the UD scheme.

In this work we take the opportunity to validate the UDv2 HTB, by manually going through the published trees, identifying systematic errors or annotation inconsistencies, and locating cases where the annotated structures contradict the UD guidelines (or spirit). We identified and corrected three main points of failure in the UD HTB: (i) the classification of argument types, deriving from the classification in the original HTB (ii) a mix-up of morphological and syntactic properties, where morphological features serve as syntactic sub-relations and vice versa, and (iii) a mix up of language-specific versus universal phenomena, where label sub-typing is exploited to indicate a supposedly language-specific phenomenon, which in fact has a designated universal label elsewhere.

Based on these corrections, we present a revised version of the HTB that we call UDv2New. We use UDv2 and UDv2New to train a morphosyntactic parser (More et al., In Press) and provide baseline results on Hebrew UD parsing, in both ideal and realistic scenarios. Comparing our Hebrew parsing results on UDv2 and UDv2New, we verify that the improvement of linguistic coherence and annotation consistency has also led to improved parsing performance. Lessons learned from our empirical analysis concern the systematic organization of natural language grammar in UD, and in particular (i) the need to standardize the interface of UD treebanks to external morphological and lexical resources, and (ii) the need to organize the form-function mapping in a language-specific vs. family-specific vs. strictly-universal relations taxonomy, within and across treebanks.

The remainder of this paper is organized as follows. In Section 2 we describe the trajectory of the HTB from its inception to UDv2. In Section 3 we present our validation process and the scheme changes we applied. In Section 4 we present raw-to-dependencies Hebrew parsing results and in Section 5 we share our future plans and lessons learned. Finally, in Section 6 we conclude.

2 Previous Work and the Trajectory of the Modern Hebrew Treebank

Following the first treebanking efforts, in English (Marcus et al., 1993), Chinese (Xue et al., 2005), and Arabic (Maamouri and Bies, 2004), and with the surge of interest in developing statistical, broad-coverage, parsing models, Sima'an et al. (2001) introduced a pilot treebanking study and a Hebrew treebank (HTB), which included 500 sentences from the Hebrew newspaper *ha'aretz*, morphologically segmented and morpho-syntactically annotated with part-of-speech tags, morphological features, and labeled phrase-structure trees. Following the annotation practices at the time, much of the tagging and labeling scheme was adopted almost as is from the UPenn Treebank (Marcus et al., 1993). However, due to its rich morphology and Semitic phenomena, several annotation decisions in the HTB diverged from these practices.

Firstly, the basic units that appear as leaves of the trees are not space-delimited tokens, but segmented units that we call morphemes.[1] Various prefixes that mark independent function words, including[2] *B* (in), *L* (to), *M* (from), *F* (that), *KF* (when) and *H* (definite article) are segmented away from their host. In addition, pronominal suffixes that appear on top of function words are also segmented away. So, the tokens *FLW* (of him), *LK* (to you), and *AITM* (with them), are segmented into *FL* (of) + *HWA* (he) , *L* (to) + *ATH* (you) , *EM* (with) + *HM* (them) respectively.[3]

The POS tags labeling scheme in the HTB includes quite a few changes from PTB, including the addition of special tags lexicalizing important functional elements in Hebrew: AT (for the accusative marker), H (the definite article), POSS (the possesive marker), and HAM (the yes/no question marker). In addition, the HTB introduces the NNT, JJT, CDT labels, marking the construct-state variants of NN, JJ, CD in the PTB, and a specific tag MOD that tags modifier words which is neither an adjective nor an adverb. On top of that, all open class POS tags as well as auxiliaries have been marked for their inflectional features (gender, number, person, time), yielding in total hundreds of possible fine-grained POS categories.

---

[1]In the UD terminology these are called syntactic words.

[2]We use the transliteration of Sima'an et al. (2001), and describe the transliteration in our supplementary material.

[3]Note that while combining *prefixes* is fairly straightforward, *suffixes* are fused to hosts in idiosyncratic and non-systematic morpho-phonological processes.

The syntactic labels in the phrase structure trees of the HTB were adopted from the Penn Treebank (PTB) almost as is, with the addition of a PREDP label for marking verbless predicates. The syntactic trees themselves looked superficially like the PTB but they differ in several aspects. Due to word-order freedom at the clause level, S-level categories present a flat structure, where the positions of the arguments do not entail anything about their grammatical function. The HTB provided 3 types of manually verified function tags to indicate such functions: SUBJect, OBJect, and COMplement, the latter marking obligatory arguments of the verb. Finally the HTB defined three types of null elements: *T* marking phonologically empty anaphors, *PRO* for pro-drop subjects, and *NONE* for elliptical elements.

The work of Guthmann et al. (2008) extended the HTB to 6501 sentences, in a manually-validated automatic process.[4] During this process they further added a systematic marking of *mother-daughter* dependencies. That is — due to feature-spreading in Hebrew, morphological features of phrases may be contributed by different daughters, and not necessarily via a single *head*. So they marked each daughter with the role it plays in determining its mothers' features (gender, number, tense, etc.). Using these feature-based dependencies, they performed feature-percolation from daughter to mother, so that phrasal nodes are also marked with their morphological signatures.[5]

Still, the phrase-structure trees yielded by HTB-trained parsers were not useful for downstream applications in Hebrew. This is because Hebrew is a relatively-free word order language, where the position of a constituent does not entail its grammatical function or semantic role. This in particular precludes the use of well known 'head tables' for selecting a single head and deriving labeled and unlabeled dependencies. To overcome this, Tsarfaty (2010) devised a set of rules based on the *daughter-dependencies, function tags* and *empty elements*, to automatically derive the *relational-realizational* (RR) version of the HTB. In the RR HTB, each node is marked with its relational network (an unordered set of grammatical functions) mapped to the ordered syntactic constituents. The RR HTB retained the morphological conventions and core non-core distinction of the original HTB.

In a parallel effort, and with the surge of interest in dependency parsing (Buchholz and Marsi, 2006; Nivre et al., 2007),[6] Goldberg (2011) automatically converted the HTB into its first, unlabeled, dependency version. The automatic conversion procedure assumed that heads are functional rather than lexical. As a result, the coordination marker would head coordination structures, the accusative marker would head direct object phrases, and so on. On top of that, in order to remain compatible with the wide-coverage lexicon of Itai and Wintner (2008), this version of the HTB adopted the POS tags scheme of Adler (2007), rather than the POS tags of Sima'an et al. (2001)

Based on this version, Goldberg and Elhadad (2009) presented the first Hebrew dependency parsing results, only *unlabeled attachment scores* (UAS) at this point. Here too, as with the phrase-structure trees, it was impossible to devise an external procedure that would infer dependency labels for the unlabeled arcs — and there were no labeled dependencies to train such a labeler on.

At that point, where the need for Hebrew labeled dependencies had become pressing, Tsarfaty (2013) presented the Unified-Stanford Dependencies (Unified-SD) version of the HTB, extending the *Stanford dependencies* (SD) scheme to cover both morphological and syntactic phenomena. Similar to SD, U-SD assumed a labeling hierarchy, with several changes: the hierarchy now included branches for *head-types (hd), dependency types (dep)*, and *functional types (func)*. In particular, dependencies in the *func* branch mark syntactic functions that are in fact interchangeable with morphology, when considering these functions from a typological perspective.

Tsarfaty used the U-SD labels to edit three versions of the HTB: (i) to mark the original phrase-structure trees in the HTB with the labels as dash-features, (ii) to relabel the relational networks in RR trees with U-SD labels, and (iii) to derive a *labeled* dependencies version of the HTB. As with the unlabeled dependencies of Goldberg, the U-SD HTB assumed functional heads across the board, and the POS tags layer was again changed to comply with the wide-coverage lexicon (HEBLEX) of Itai and Wintner (2008). The labeled dependencies treebank of U-SD then provided the Hebrew section of the SPMRL shared tasks (Seddah et al., 2013, 2014).

---

[4] Excluding repeated sentences, we have 6221 trees.

[5] This marking did not specify a single *head* since a mother node could have multiple *daughter-dependencies*.

[6] Notably, Hebrew did not take part in these shared tasks.

3 The Hebrew UD Treebank

3.1 Overview

The RR version of the Unified-SD HTB provided
the basis for automatically converting the Hebrew
trees into UDv1 trees. The UD HTB assumes the
same segmentation principles as the first edition
of the HTB, segmenting off prefixes and suffixes,
with the addition of splitting off genitive pronominal clitics from nouns.

Goldberg and Tsarfaty (2014) devised an automatic process that chooses a *lexical head* in each
relational network of each constituent in the RR
treebank. They also mapped the fine-grained POS
categories to the coarse-grained UPOS categories
in UD, and remaining POS distinctions in HebLex
(HebBinyan, construct-states, etc.) are stored in
FEATS. The label set of U-SD was automatically
mapped to UD, and relations from U-SD outside
of UD were kept as relation:subtype.

The conversion of UDv1 to UDv2 was also done
automatically, by augmenting the script of Goldberg and Tsarfaty (2014). Points of failure of the
UDv1 version of the HTB to comply with UDv2
were identified by aiming to locate skewed distributions of tags or labels, and they were corrected
in the conversion script on a case by case basis.
This process has stopped when the treebank com-
plied with the UDv2 validation script. The converted HTB is documented on the UD webpage.[7]

3.2 Validation

The present version of UDv2 thus results from a
sequence of automatic and semi-automatic conversions on the trees of Guthmann et al. (2008). In
order to validate the current UDv2 trees, we re-
viewed the list of UD POS tags, relation labels
and features, and for each of these items we identified the dependency structures in the HTB *dev set*
that contain them. At this point, for each item, a
linguist characterized the role such item actually
fulfills in the Hebrew grammatical structures, (as
opposed to the role it was designed to fulfill in the
UD scheme).

During this process the linguist documented errors and inconsistencies that were found, either between the realistic use of a function in the UDv2
HTB and the UDv2 guidelines, or simply attesting
insufficient or incorrect coverage of the linguistic
structure that this particular label, tag or feature is
supposed to describe.

This validation process[8] was conducted on the
entire HTB UDv2 *dev set*[9] and it was followed by
a sequence of discussions in which our research
team, consisting of two linguists, two NLP spe-
cialists, and a senior NLP researcher, discussed
possible solutions for each error. The discussions were focused on explicitly assessing the
merits of each solution alternative according to the
six criteria of the Mannings Law. That is: linguistically adequate, typologically adequate, suitable for rapid, consistent annotation, suitable for
parsing with high accuracy, easily comprehended
by non-linguists, and provides good support for
downstream NLP tasks.[10] After narrowing down
the list of adequate solutions, the final decision
about which revisions to make leaned on their importance and feasibility. For example, a very important, yet easily executable revision was to simply replace all instances of prepositional *iobj* with
obl. Just as important, but far more complex,
was to switch between a head and a dependent in
the case of structures containing *auxiliaries* (e.g.,
modals, as we illustrate shortly).

All revisions were made with the python Pan-
das package, and they were applied to all, *dev*,
train and *test*, sets. Revisions were made with
respect to linguistic patterns that refer to existing
labels, tags or features, with no consideration of
any particular (lexicalized) Hebrew words. Furthermore, we refrained from manual changes of
specific errors, considering that their source might
be a vaster problem, to be dealt with in the future.
As an example for simple edits, consider adding a
label compound:affix. For this, all rows containing the feature 'Prefix=Yes' had to be retrieved,
and the label was changed to *compound:affix*. As
a more complex case, consider the case involving
modality mentioned above. Here, all rows with
the *xcomp* label were retrieved. For each row,
if the head had a morphological feature 'Verb-
Type=Mod', the head's label was relabeled 'aux',

---

[8]It is important to note that our analysis proceeded label-
by-label, and tag-by-tag, which is a faster process than going
through the treebank trees one-by-one. But it also bears the
risk of missing out rare peculiarities and singleton errors.

[9]In this work we primarily aimed to correct the main issues that appeared across the board, rather than tackling idiosyncratic or incidental errors. So, observing the *dev set* was
enough, as it well reflects the main linguistic phenomena in
the language.

[10] en.wikipedia.org/wiki/Manning%27s_Law

[7]http://universaldependencies.org/
treebanks/he_htb/index.html.

ID	FORM	UPOSTAG	FEATS	HEAD	DEPREL
6	IS	AUX	VerbType=Mod	0	root
7	LPNWT	VERB	VerbForm=Inf	6	xcomp
6	IS	AUX	VerbType=Mod	7	aux
7	LPNWT	VERB	VerbForm=Inf	0	root

Table 1: Turning Auxiliary Heads into Modal Dependents. The top pair represents the UDv2 structure, the lower pair represents the UDv2New revision.

the row itself was relabeled with the original label of the head, and the numbers were changed respectively in the 'HEAD' column (see Table 1).

3.3 Revision

Adhering to UDv2 guidelines provided an opportunity to make a consistent decision about topics under debate, and to generally revise inconsistencies in the system. Our revisions typically fall under one of the following three categories: predicate/argument types distinctions (3.3.1), morphological vs. syntactic distinctions (3.3.2), and Hebrew-specific vs. universal distinctions (3.3.3).

3.3.1 Predicate Argument Types Distinctions

Open Clausal Complements. In the UDv2 HTB, predicative complements were labeled advmod when adjectival. Following the UDv2 guidelines, we label them xcomp, as they are subordinated predicates, after all, even if not verbal.

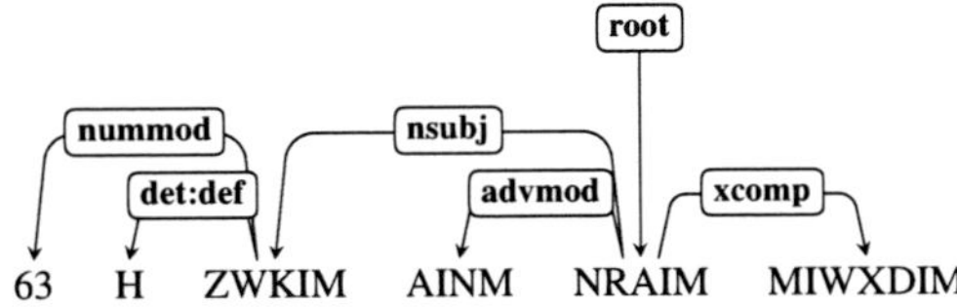

Figure 1: UDv2New treatment of predicative complements as xcomp rather than advmod. The adjective *MIWXDIM* 'special' is a complement of *NRAIM* 'look'

"63 H-ZWKIM AINM NRAIM
63 DET-winner.PL.M be.NEG.PL.M look.PL.M
MIWXDIM."
special.PL.M

'The 63 winners do not look special'

Argument iobj vs. obl. Some UD definitions stand in clear contrast with the canonical syntactic analysis of Hebrew. Perhaps the most salient case is of core arguments. The canonical view of Hebrew core arguments (Coffin and Bolozky (2005) p. 290) is of a direct object, marked by an accusative case when definite, and an indirect object, marked by an oblique case marker when a pronoun, and preceded by a preposition when common or proper noun. UDv2 dedicates an iobj (indirect object) relation to secondary core arguments which are not preceded by prepositions, and arguments which are do follow a preposition are labeled obl, whether core or non-core. We revised the labels accordingly.

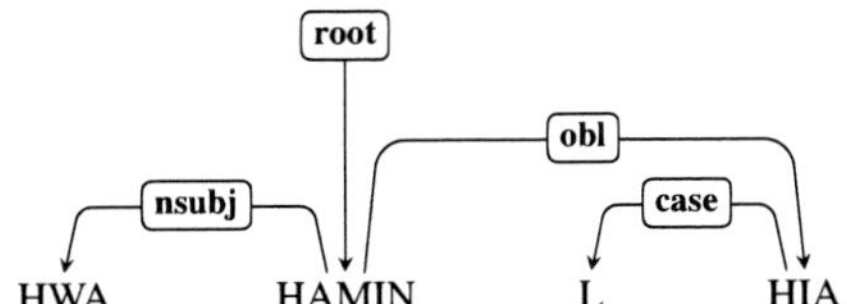

Figure 2: The noun *HIA*, following the preposition *L*, although being a core argument of the verb *HAMIN*, is labeled obl in UDv2New, as opposed to iobj in previous versions.

"HWA HAMIN L-HIA."
he.3SG.M believe.Tsg.PST DAT-she.3SG.F

'He believed her'

Predicate types: the case of auxiliaries As part of the shift towards a lexically-driven analysis, structural changes were made to sentences containing auxiliary elements and copulas. There are three main sets of these: (i) Auxiliary elements marking modality, (ii) Auxiliary verbs which mostly mark habituality, but occasionally participate in negation or tense inflection when the predicate has no past/future form, and (iii) Positive or negative copulars.

Modals do not constitute any uniform syntactic class in Hebrew, and there is an ongoing debate as to the POS of each modal expression (cf. Netzer et al. (2007)). In line with Netzer et al's conclusion, these are tagged as AUX in the UD HTB. In UDv2, the modal served as the head of the clause, while the following predicate was labeled xcomp, as it is consistently realized in Hebrew in infinitive form. As of UDv2New, those modals which are tagged as AUX are also labeled aux, and the subsequent predicate receives the label which was attributed to the modal. See Table 1.

In the opposite direction, auxiliary verbs, such as the ones in sets ii and iii were tagged as VERB. As the UDv2 scheme dedicates an AUX tag to function words in auxiliary functions even when they are verbs, we changed them to AUX as well in UDv2New. Finally, consistency across sets ii and iii was achieved by unifying the labeling of copular verbs as cop regardless of their inflection, whereas previous versions labeled past and future inflections of copular verbs as aux.

3.3.2 Morphology vs. Syntax

Eliminating acl:inf to acl. The automatic conversion to UD has kept fine-grained labels as sub-relations, resulting with the language-specific label acl:inf. Since the UD guidelines permit infinitive structures in acl, it is unnecessary to mark infinity as a sub-relation. Moreover, all cases of acl:inf bear the feature 'VerbForm=Inf'. So eliminating the morphological feature inf from the sub-relation acl:inf does not lead to any information loss.

> "NSIWN-W H-AXRWN FL MILR
> attempt.SG.M-POSS DET-last POSS Miller
> LHFIG KSPIM"
> get.INF money.PL

'Miller's last attempt to get money'

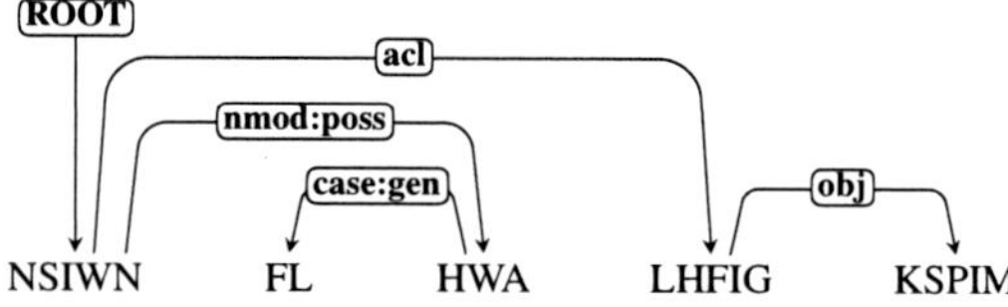

Figure 3: The label acl:inf was reduced into simply acl for the infinitive verb *LHFIG* (to get)

Adding compound:affix This new relation is dedicated to non-standalone words, which function semantically like affixes, but syntactically surface as separate words, at times separated by a hyphen and in others by white-space. A subset of these words are loan words (mainly from English, like 'non', 'multi' etc.) where originally they surface syntactically as affixes. In UDv2 these items were marked by the feature Prefix=Yes. However, since they mark a certain type of Hebrew compounds, we used sub-typing to indicate it.[11] In "KLL-EWLMIT" for example, *KLL* 'uni-' is semantically a prefix to *EWLMIT* 'worldly', but in Hebrew the two are separate words.

3.3.3 HTB-to-UD: language-specific representation with relation:subtype

As UD aspires to present a set of tags which are relevant to as many languages as possible, naturally many language-specific phenomena are left unanswered. To allow representation of these, the UD scheme allows for sub-relations in the form of relation:subtype, as exemplified above. However, although originally aiming toward coverage of language-specific phenomena, this structure can be frequently seen as a subtype of relation which is present in many languages (e.g. nsubj:pass, which is in use for subjects of passive sentences - not unique to any one language or even a family of languages). In our revision to adhere to UDv2 guidelines, we tried as much as possible to narrow the use of relation:subtype to Hebrew-specific phenomena, eliminating any hierarchical structure of dependency relations. As a result, the following subtypes were reduced to their parent relation: (i) det:quant, originally marking an arbitrary subset of existential quantifiers, was reduced to simply det , and (ii) advmod:phrase, originally marking multi-word adverbials, were re-structured as advmod+fixed, in line with the UD guidelines for multi-word-expressions.

From conj:discourse to parataxis An interesting case is with labels not used at all in the older versions of the UD HTB, while language-specific labels stand to mark their function. The UD label parataxis, for instance, describes a relation between two (or more) sentences which are syntactically independent (i.e. do not stand in subordination or conjunction relation to one another), but are thematically connected, and consequently punctuated as the same sentence. Previously, this relation was labeled in the HTB as conj:discourse, simply classifying conjunctions that are not explicitly marked as of type discourse. In our revised version, we comply with UD guidelines and label this relation 'parataxis'.

From PART to ADP The accusative and possessive case markers in Hebrew, AT and FL respectively, are realised as separate tokens, as opposed to some other case markers, which prefix the following nouns. Furthermore, a possessive case marker may also morphologically suffix the noun, whether instead of or in addition to the above-mentioned particle. In older versions of HTB, while preposition (whether standalone or not) were tagged IN, the accusative case marker was tagged AT and the possessive case marker was tagged POSS. As a result, automatic conversions led to converting IN to ADP across the board,

---

[11]All analyses are visualized in the supp. materials.

while AT and FL were converted into PART. As there is no real difference between AT and FL and prepositions according to the UDv2 scheme, and as they are in no way particles, we converted them into ADP.

3.4 Unsolved Issues

Some inconsistencies in the treebank were spotted but not yet fixed as their automatic full retrieval and change is more complicated [12]. For example, *it*-extraposition construction is represented in UDv2 by a combination of nsubj and ccomp or advcl, but should be a combination of expl+csubj, as defined in the guidelines (see example 9 in the supplements).

In another case, lack of congruence was found between our treatment of participles and Adler et al. (2008). The feature of VerbForm=Part marks both deverbal nouns and present tense clauses, as in the following sentence.

"EFRWT ANFIM   MGIEIM
ten.PL.F person.PL.M arrive.PTCP
M-TAILND   L-ISRAL"
from-Thailand to-Israel

'Tens of people come from Thailand to Israel.'

Hebrew makes various uses of the dative case, some of them fulfill purely discursive functionality (Borer and Grodzinsky, 1986). The current representation of the dative case marker in UDv2New does not give way to all possible meanings, including experiencer dative (Berman, 1982) as opposed to ethical dative, the regular dative where the dative argument is subcategorized by the verb. The current UDv2 guidelines do not distinguish between the different types of dative, so an educated decision must be made locally as for how to tell them apart.

- IS **LW** HMIWMNWT HNXWCH BFBIL LHIWT MWFL
  '**He** has what it takes to be a governer.'

- HRAF HIHWDI MMCIA **LNW** PTNTIM.
  'The Jewish mind invents (**us**) patents'

- HW QRA **LH** FQRNIT
  'He called **her** a liar.'

---

[12] For reasons of brevity we do not discuss all of them in this work.

4   HTB Experiments and Parsing Results

Goal: We wish to examine the empirical impact of our effort to correct the treebank and retain linguistic (as well as cross-treebank) coherence in its annotation scheme. Indeed, ease of parsing should not be the indication for selecting one scheme over another, but the hypothesis is that, within *one and the same set of guidelines*, a version that presents better coherence and consistency will also be more suitable for statistical training and will yield better results.

Settings: To gauge the effect of our revision we conducted two sets of experiments: one with the HTB UDv2 version used in the recent shared task, and another our revised UDv2New. We use the syntactic evaluation script provided by the CoNLL shared task 2018. We train on the portion defined as train set and report results on the dev set. For training and parsing we used *yap*,[13] a transition-based morphosyntactic parser written in go, which includes a morphological analyzer, a morphological disambiguator, and syntactic parser. In previous work *yap* was shown to obtain state of the art results on Hebrew parsing using the SPMRL version of the treebank (More et al., In Press). Here we report its performance on the UD HTB.

Scenarios: Because of its rich morphology and orthographic convention to attach or fuse adpositions and pronominals onto open-class categories, there is severe ambiguity in the morphological analysis of the Hebrew input tokens. This is further magnified by the lack of diacritics in Hebrew written texts. Hence, it is unknown upfront how many morphemes (in the HTB terminology) or syntactic words (in the UD terminology) are in the space-delimited tokens. We examine two kinds of scenarios:

- *ideal:* assuming gold morphological analysis and disambiguation given by an oracle.

- *realistic:* assuming automatically predicted morphological analysis and disambiguation.

We use *yap* for predicting morphological analysis (MA) and morphological disambiguation (More, 2016), and we contrast the use of a data-driven lexicon *baselinelex* with an external broad-coverage lexicon *HebLex*. To gauge the effect of the lexical

---

[13] https://github.com/habeanf/yap

coverage of the morphological resource, we contrast each variant with an *infused* scenario, where the correct analysis is injected into the lattice. Note that the input in the infused cases is still high as there are many MA alternatives. However, the correct morphological disambiguation is guaranteed to be one of the morphological MA provided to the system as input.

Results: Table 2 shows the parsing results in an ideal scenario, assuming gold morphology. Here we see that there is a consistent improvement for all metrics. This supports our conjecture that a more consistent and coherent annotation of the treebank will benefit parsing, and it corroborates a wider conjecture, that, when it comes to supervised learning, the quality of the annotated data is as important as the learning algorithm (and maybe more important).

Table 3 shows the parsing results in realistic scenarios, where we assume automatically predicted morphological analysis and disambiguation. As expected, the results substantially drop relative to the ideal scenario. Also expected is the result that assuming an external broad-coverage lexicon substantially improves the results relative to a data-driven lexicon learned from the treebank. The result that seems less expected here is that, as opposed to the ideal scenario, we see no improvement in the results of UDv2New relative to UDv2. For some of the metrics the results slightly drop.

This drop could be either due to parser errors, or due to the lack of lexical coverage of the lexicon with respect to our revised UDv2New scheme. To test this, we execute an *infused* scenario where the morphological analysis lattices are guaranteed to also include the correct analysis. Here we see a substantial improvement for both types of lexica, on all the different metrics, for the UDv2New version. This result suggests that the drop has indeed been due to the insufficient lexical coverage of the resources, or due to mismatches between the lexicon and the new scheme. As far as the statistical components for morphological and syntactic analysis and disambiguation go, the revised version helps the parser obtain better disambiguation, in line of our results in the gold experiments.

5   Discussion and Lessons Learned

The original HTB (Sima'an et al., 2001; Guthmann et al., 2008) has seen many revisions all of which executed automatically, or semi-

UDv2 Shared-Task Version	LAS	MLAS	BLEX
he_htb-ud-dev-*yap*-gold	79.51	72.76	47.76
UDv2New Revised Version	LAS	MLAS	BLEX
he_htb-ud-dev-*yap*-gold	81.24	75.58	50.16

Table 2: Parsing Results of the HTB *dev* set for UDv2 vs UDv2New, in an *ideal* parsing scenario assuming GOLD morphology.

UDv2 Shared-Task Version	LAS	MLAS	BLEX
he_htb-dev-*yap*_baselinelex	51.99	37.62	29.50
he_htb-dev-*yap*_heblex	60.71	39.53	33.82
he_htb-dev-*yap*_baselinelex-infused	58.45	43.70	32.94
he_htb-dev-*yap*_heblex-infused	71.19	61.08	41.71
UDv2New Revised Version	LAS	MLAS	BLEX
he_htb-dev-*yap*-baselinelex	52.42	38.08	30.32
he_htb-dev-*yap*_heblex	60.34	37.95	34.71
he_htb-dev-*yap*-baselinelex-infused	58.54	44.06	33.30
he_htb-dev-*yap*_heblex-infused	73.66	64.73	44.32

Table 3: Parsing Results of the HTB *dev* set for UDv2 vs UDv2New, in a *realistic* parsing scenario assuming PREDICTED morphology. We compare a data-driven *baseline* lexicon with an external lexicon, *heblex*, and we contrast *uninfused* or *infused* setting for both

automatically.   Our endeavor here has been to manually verify the current version of the UD HTB resulting analyses, and to correct lingering errors. Apart from being linguistically justified, this process has proven to be also empirically valuable, as indeed this revision has led to a improvement in parsing results.

Much work is still needed in order to bring the level of performance to be adequate for downstream applications, in particular in realistic scenarios. We conjecture that in order to obtain decent performance, the work on the treebank should be complemented by adapting language-specific lexica to the set of guidelines for word segmentation and for representing morphology, as defined by UD. Even when external lexica assumes the same labeling scheme as UD, gaps between the theories underlying the development of these resources could lead to lack of coverage that substantially harms parsing performance.

Additional lessons learned from our manual verification process have to do with the organization of morphological features and syntactic subtypes within the HTB and in the UD treebanks collection in general. In the HTB UDv2, there appeared to be a mix between the linguistic notions expressed using these two mechanisms. For example, subtypes were sometimes used to indicate morphological features (see the case for acl:inf) while the features column is exploited to express syntactic properties. We argue that clearer guidelines are needed in the general UD scheme, instructing directly what kind of linguistic information should go where, by which formal means.

Furthermore, it seems to us that the language-specific mechanisms are exploited for expressing phenomena that could potentially be cross-linguistic, or at least shared by a language family. An example to this is the feature *HebBinyan* in the UD HTB, which stores the value of the morphological template of the verb. The phenomenon of *Binyan* (a root-template construction) is clearly not Hebrew specific — in fact all Semitic languages have *Binyanim* (morphological constructions) in their grammar, so we see no good reason for not unifying this feature across the Semitic sub-family. Same goes with marking construct state nouns, a phenomenon that extends beyond Semitic languages, and is currently marked differently in each language (Hebrew, Arabic, Persian, etc.).

We propose that the next major revision of the UD treebank scheme could ideally focus on *the universal organization of the grammar*, and will center around these themes:

- *subtypes:* A universal inventory and management of the sub-label system which will define what linguistic phenomena can count as subtype of a label, and will maintain cross-linguistic consistency in its use for shared phenomena.

- *features:* A universal inventory and management of features which will define what can count as a feature, and will foster cross-linguistic reuse.

- *lexical resources:* For languages that have external lexica, especially in the case of morphologically rich and resource scarce languages, an effort is needed to verify that the labeling scheme theoretical guidelines underlying lexica are harmonized with the UD guidelines. Such lexica can be made available via the CoNLL-UL format (More et al., 2018) to benefit the entire UD community.

- *semantic applications:* in addition to aligning lexical resources, it is important to advance the usability of UD in down-stream application scenarios, by making available the additional layer of *enhanced* dependencies.

6   Conclusion

In this paper we describe the long and multi-phased process of coming-into-existence of the Hebrew version of the HTB. Most of the process has consisted of automatic conversions between different schemes. In this work we manually verified the recent UD HTB version and corrected lingering errors. The revised version is more linguistically and cross-linguistically consistent and obtains better parsing results in scenarios that are not dependent on the coverage of external lexica. Our future plans include a comprehensive revision of the lexical and morphological resources associated with the UD scheme, to improve the empirical parsing results in realistic scenarios, and the addition of enhanced dependencies, which would be more adequate for downstream semantic tasks.

Acknowledgments

We thank the ONLP team at the Open University of Israel for fruitful discussions throughout the process. We further thank two anonymous reviewers for their detailed and insightful comments. This research is supported by the European Research Council, ERC-StG-2015 scheme, Grant number 677352, and by the Israel Science Foundation (ISF), Grant number 1739/26, for which we are grateful.

References

Meni Adler. 2007. *Hebrew Morphological Disambiguation: An Unsupervised Stochastic Word-based Approach.* Ph.D. thesis, Ben-Gurion University of the Negev, Beer-Sheva, Israel.

Meni Adler, Yael Dahan Netzer, Yoav Goldberg, David Gabay, and Michael Elhadad. 2008. Tagging a hebrew corpus: the case of participles. In *LREC*. Citeseer.

Roy Bar-haim, Khalil Sima'an, and Yoad Winter. 2008. Part-of-speech tagging of Modern Hebrew text. *Natural Language Engineering*, 14(2):223–251.

Ruth A Berman. 1982. Dative marking of the affectee role: Data from modern hebrew.

Hagit Borer and Yosef Grodzinsky. 1986. Syntactic cliticization and lexical cliticization: The case of hebrew dative clitics in the syntax of pronominal clitics. *Syntax and semantics*, 19:175–217.

Sabine Buchholz and Erwin Marsi. 2006. CoNLL-X shared task on multilingual dependency parsing. In *Proceedings of CoNLL-X*, pages 149–164.

Edna Amir Coffin and Shmuel Bolozky. 2005. *A reference grammar of Modern Hebrew.* Cambridge University Press.

Yoav Goldberg. 2011. *Automatic syntactic processing of Modern Hebrew.* Ben Gurion University of the Negev.

Yoav Goldberg and Michael Elhadad. 2009. Hebrew dependency parsing: Initial results. In *Proceedings of the 11th International Conference on Parsing Technologies*, IWPT '09, pages 129–133, Stroudsburg, PA, USA. Association for Computational Linguistics.

Yoav Goldberg and Michael Elhadad. 2010. Easy first dependency parsing of modern hebrew. In *Proceedings of the NAACL HLT 2010 First Workshop on Statistical Parsing of Morphologically-Rich Languages*, SPMRL '10, pages 103–107, Stroudsburg, PA, USA. Association for Computational Linguistics.

Yoav Goldberg and Michael Elhadad. 2011. Joint Hebrew segmentation and parsing using a PCFGLA lattice parser. In *Proceedings of ACL.*

Yoav Goldberg and Reut Tsarfaty. 2008. A single framework for joint morphological segmentation and syntactic parsing. In *Proceedings of ACL.*

Yoav Goldberg and Reut Tsarfaty. 2014. Htb to ud conversion.

Noemie Guthmann, Yuval Krymolowski, Adi Milea, and Yoad Winter. 2008. Automatic annotation of morpho-syntactic dependencies in a modern hebrew treebank. *LOT Occasional Series*, 12:77–90.

Alon Itai and Shuly Wintner. 2008. Language resources for hebrew. *Language Resources and Evaluation*, 42(1):75–98.

Mohamed Maamouri and Ann Bies. 2004. Developing an arabic treebank: Methods, guidelines, procedures, and tools. In *Proceedings of the Workshop on Computational Approaches to Arabic Script-based Languages*, Semitic '04, pages 2–9, Stroudsburg, PA, USA. Association for Computational Linguistics.

Mitchell P. Marcus, Mary Ann Marcinkiewicz, and Beatrice Santorini. 1993. Building a large annotated corpus of english: The penn treebank. *Comput. Linguist.*, 19(2):313–330.

Amir More. 2016. *Joint Morpho-Syntactic Processing of Morphologically Rich Languages in a Transition-Based Framework.* Ph.D. thesis, The Interdisciplinary Center, Herzliya.

Amir More, Özlem Çetinoğlu, Çağri Çöltekin, Nizar Habash, Benoît Sagot, Djamé Seddah, Dima Taji, and Reut Tsarfaty. 2018. Conll-ul: Universal morphological lattices for universal dependency parsing. In *11th Language Resources and Evaluation Conference.*

Amir More, Amit Seker, Victoria Basmova, and Reut Tsarfaty. In Press. Joint transition-based models for morpho-syntactic parsing: Parsing strategies for mrls and a case study from modern hebrew. In *Transactions of ACL.*

Amir More and Reut Tsarfaty. 2016. Data-driven morphological analysis and disambiguation for morphologically rich languages and universal dependencies. In *Proceedings of COLING*, pages 337–348. The COLING 2016 Organizing Committee.

Yael Dahan Netzer, Meni Adler, David Gabay, and Michael Elhadad. 2007. Can you tag the modal? you should. In *Proceedings of the 2007 Workshop on Computational Approaches to Semitic Languages: Common Issues and Resources, SEMITIC@ACL 2007, Prague, Czech Republic, June 28, 2007*, pages 57–64.

Joakim Nivre, Johan Hall, Sandra Kübler, Ryan McDonald, Jens Nilsson, Sebastian Riedel, and Deniz Yuret. 2007. The CoNLL 2007 shared task on dependency parsing. In *Proceedings of the CoNLL Shared Task Session of EMNLP-CoNLL 2007*, pages 915–932.

Djamé Seddah, Sandra Kübler, and Reut Tsarfaty. 2014. Introducing the spmrl 2014 shared task on parsing morphologically-rich languages. In *Proceedings of the First Joint Workshop on Statistical Parsing of Morphologically Rich Languages and Syntactic Analysis of Non-Canonical Languages*, pages 103–109, Dublin, Ireland. Dublin City University.

Djamé Seddah, Reut Tsarfaty, Sandra Kübler, Marie Candito, Jinho D. Choi, Richárd Farkas, Jennifer Foster, Iakes Goenaga, Koldo Gojenola Galletebeitia, Yoav Goldberg, Spence Green, Nizar Habash, Marco Kuhlmann, Wolfgang Maier, Joakim Nivre, Adam Przepiórkowski, Ryan Roth, Wolfgang Seeker, Yannick Versley, Veronika Vincze, Marcin Woliński, Alina Wróblewska, and Eric Villemonte de la Clergerie. 2013. Overview of the SPMRL 2013 shared task: A cross-framework evaluation of parsing morphologically rich languages. In *Proceedings of the Fourth Workshop on Statistical Parsing of Morphologically-Rich Languages*, pages 146–182, Seattle, Washington, USA. Association for Computational Linguistics.

Danny Shacham and Shuly Wintner. 2007. Morphological disambiguation of Hebrew: A case study in classifier combination. In *Proceedings of the 2007 Joint Conference on Empirical Methods in Natural Language Processing and Computational Natural Language Learning (EMNLP-CoNLL)*, pages 439–447, Prague, Czech Republic. Association for Computational Linguistics.

Khalil Sima'an, Alon Itai, Yoad Winter, Alon Altman, and N. Nativ. 2001. Building a tree-bank of Modern Hebrew text. *Traitement Automatique des Langues*, 42(2).

Reut Tsarfaty. 2006. Integrated morphological and syntactic disambiguation for modern Hebrew. In *Proceedings ACL-CoLing Student Research Workshop*, pages 49–54, Stroudsburg, PA, USA. ACL.

Reut Tsarfaty. 2010. *Relational-realizational parsing*. Ph.D. thesis.

Reut Tsarfaty. 2013. A unified morphosyntactic scheme for stanford dependencies. In *Proceedings of ACL*.

Reut Tsarfaty, Joakim Nivre, and Evelina Andersson. 2012. Joint evaluation of morphological segmentation and syntactic parsing. In *Proceedings of ACL*, ACL '12, pages 6–10, Stroudsburg, PA, USA.

Reut Tsarfaty, Joakim Nivre, and Evelina Ndersson. 2011. Evaluating dependency parsing: robust and heuristics-free cross-nnotation evaluation. In *Proceedings of the Conference on Empirical Methods in Natural Language Processing*, pages 385–396. Association for Computational Linguistics.

Naiwen Xue, Fei Xia, Fu-dong Chiou, and Marta Palmer. 2005. The penn chinese treebank: Phrase structure annotation of a large corpus. *Nat. Lang. Eng.*, 11(2):207–238.

Multi-source synthetic treebank creation for improved cross-lingual dependency parsing

Francis M. Tyers
Department of Linguistics
Indiana University
Bloomington, IN
ftyers@prompsit.com

Mariya Sheyanova
School of Linguistics
Higher School of Economics
Moscow
marija.shejanova@gmail.com

Alexandra Martynova
School of Linguistics
Higher School of Economics
Moscow
alex250396@gmail.com

Pavel Stepachev
School of Linguistics
Higher School of Economics
Moscow
pavel.stepachev@yandex.ru

Konstantin Vinogradovsky
School of Linguistics
Higher School of Economics
Moscow
kvinog54@gmail.com

Abstract

This paper describes a method of creating synthetic treebanks for cross-lingual dependency parsing using a combination of machine translation (including pivot translation), annotation projection and the spanning tree algorithm. Sentences are first automatically translated from a lesser-resourced language to a number of related highly-resourced languages, parsed and then the annotations are projected back to the lesser-resourced language, leading to multiple trees for each sentence from the lesser-resourced language. The final treebank is created by merging the possible trees into a graph and running the spanning tree algorithm to vote for the best tree for each sentence. We present experiments aimed at parsing Faroese using a combination of Danish, Swedish and Norwegian. In a similar experimental setup to the CoNLL 2018 shared task on dependency parsing we report state-of-the-art results on dependency parsing for Faroese using an off-the-shelf parser.

1 Introduction

In this paper, we describe and compare a number of approaches to cross-lingual parsing for Faroese, a Nordic language spoken by approximately 66,000 people on the Faroe Islands in the North Atlantic. Faroese is a moderately under-resourced language. It has a standardised orthography and fairly long written tradition, but lacks large syntactically-annotated corpora. There are however related well-resourced languages, such as Norwegian (both Bokmål and Nynorsk), Dan-ish and Swedish for which large syntactically-annotated corpora exist.

Compared with the other Nordic languages, Faroese has a full nominal case system of four cases: Nominative, Genitive, Accusative and Dative, where the other languages have only a Genitive case. It has three grammatical genders, like Norwegian Nynorsk, but unlike Norwegian Bokmål, Danish and Swedish, which have a two-gender agreement system. Like the other Nordic languages, it is a verb-second (V2) language and the word order is generally similar. Faroese is however not mutually intelligible with any of the mainland Nordic languages.

Using these treebanks we perform experiments using two well-known methods, delexicalised parsing (Zeman and Resnik, 2008; McDonald et al., 2011) and synthetic treebanking using annotation projection (Tiedemann and Agić, 2016), and in addition propose a new method based on voting over possible projected trees using the maximum spanning tree algorithm. This can be thought of as creating a synthetic treebank where the tree for each sentence is the result of voting over the set of trees generated by parsing different translations.

The remainder of the paper is laid out as follows: Section 2 describes prior work on both Faroese and on cross-lingual dependency parsing; Section 3 describes the resources we used for the experiments, including a description of how the gold-standard for Faroese was made; Section 4 describes the methodology, including both the baseline models and our proposed method. Sections 5 and 6 de-

Proceedings of the Second Workshop on Universal Dependencies (UDW 2018), pages 144–150
Brussels, Belgium, November 1, 2018. ©2018 Association for Computational Linguistics

scribe the experiments we performed and the results and discussion respectively and finally: Section 7 describes future avenues for research and Section 8 concludes.

2 Prior work

Our work is closely related to two main trends in cross-lingual dependency parsing. The first is multi-source delexicalised dependency parsing as described by McDonald et al. (2011).

The second is the work on synthetic treebanking by Tiedemann and Agić (2016); Tiedemann (2017). In these works, sentences in the target language (e.g. Faroese) is first translated by a machine translation system to a well-resourced language (e.g. Norwegian). The machine-translated Norwegian sentences are then parsed by a parser trained on a treebank of Norwegian, and word aligned to the Faroese originals. The output tree from the Norwegian parser is then *projected* back to the Faroese sentences via the word alignments.

In terms of voting for parse trees, the CoNLL shared task on dependency parsing in 2007 (Nivre et al., 2007) reported that using a similar architecture to the one we describe here, they were able to get significantly better results by combining the trees produced by the top three systems, and found that even after adding all the systems, including the worst-performing system, the performance did not drop below that of the top-performing system.

Our work is very similar to Agić et al. (2016), in that we use spanning tree to find the best parse in a graph that has been induced from aligned parallel corpora. However, their focus is on cross-linguality rather than on producing the best system for a related language, and as such the performance they report is lower.

It is also worth noting the work by Schlichtkrull and Søgaard (2017), who present a system that can learn from dependency graphs over tokens as opposed to over the well-formed dependency trees that are typically assumed for other systems.

In terms of dependency parsing specifically for Faroese, we can include the work by Antonsen et al. (2010), who apply a slightly-modified rule-based parser written for North Sámi to parsing Faroese. They achieved good results, F-score of over 0.98, on a small test set of 100 sentences. Unfortunately their work is not directly comparable as it relies on a very different annotation scheme to that which we use in our work, in addition they did not evaluate end-to-end results (the evaluation was done over gold standard POS and morphology).

3 Resources

In the experiments we used raw Faroese text extracted from Wikipedia, a manually created gold-standard corpus of trees, treebanks for the source languages (Danish, Swedish and Norwegian) and machine translation systems between the languages. The following subsections describe these resources.

3.1 Raw data

The Faroese raw data that we used in our experiments comes from Wikipedia dump which was preliminary cleaned of all the markup using the `WikiExtractor` script.[1] Then, both manually and via regular expressions, we deleted non-Faroese texts, poetic texts, reference lists, short sentences with little or no dependencies. All sentences containing only non-alphanumeric symbols were also deleted.

For sentence segmentation we used regular expressions splitting on sentence-final punctuation, but taking care to ignore month names, ordinal numbers and abbreviations. After cleaning the corpus we ended up with a total of 28,862 sentences. This data was used in the creation of the gold standard (§3.2) and in creating the parallel data used for the synthetic treebanking experiments (§4.2).

3.2 Gold standard

In order to evaluate the methods we needed to create a gold-standard treebank of Faroese. This was done manually by annotating sentences from the Faroese Wikipedia.[2] The gold standard contains 10,002 tokens in 1,208 sentences. The annotation procedure was as follows: We extracted sentences from the Faroese Wikipedia and analysed them using the Faroese morphological analyser and constraint grammar described by Trosterud (2009). This gave us a corpus where for each token in each sentence we had a lemma, a part of speech and a set of morphological features. These were checked manually and on top of these analyses, a dependency tree was added according to the guidelines in version 2.0 of Universal Dependencies (Nivre et al., 2016). Each tree was added manually by the

---

[1] `https://github.com/attardi/wikiextractor`
[2] The treebank is available online at `https://github.com/UniversalDependencies/UD_Faroese-OFT`.

Treebank	Sentences	Tokens
UD_Swedish-Talbanken	4,304	66,673
UD_Danish	4,384	80,378
UD_Norwegian-Nynorsk	14,175	245,330
UD_Norwegian-Bokmaal	15,696	243,887

Table 1: Number of sentences and tokens in UD treebanks for training the delexicalised models

first author in discussion with a native speaker of Faroese and members of the Universal Dependencies community.[3] The part-of-speech tags and features were converted automatically to ones compatible with Universal Dependencies using a lookup table and the longest-match set overlap procedure described in Gökırmak and Tyers (2017).

3.3 Other treebanks

For training the delexicalised models we used the following treebanks: `UD_Swedish-Talbanken`, `UD_Danish-DDT` (Johannsen et al., 2015), `UD_Norwegian-Bokmaal` (Øvrelid and Hohle, 2016) and `UD_Norwegian-Nynorsk`. Some statistics about these treebanks are presented in Table 1.

3.4 Machine translation

Faroese is not supported by the mainstream online machine translation engines and there are very few parallel sentence pairs available. For example, the widely-cited OPUS collection (Tiedemann, 2016) contains fewer than 7,000 sentences pairs for Faroese–Danish, Faroese–English, Faroese–Norwegian and Faroese–Swedish. This makes creating a corpus-based machine translation model unlikely to succeed. There is however a prototype rule-based machine translation system from Faroese to Norwegian Bokmål available through the Apertium project (Forcada et al., 2011).[4] This system has a vocabulary coverage of approximately 90% on the Faroese Wikipedia and supports translation of compound words. In addition to this system, systems for Norwegian Bokmål to Norwegian Nynorsk (Unhammer and Trosterud, 2009) and Norwegian Bokmål to Swedish and Danish also exist. As a result of this, we decided to use pivotting via Norwegian Bokmål to produce the translations (see §4.2).

---

[3]Some of the discussions can be found in the issues page of the `UD_Faroese-OFT` repository: `https://github.com/UniversalDependencies/UD_Faroese-OFT/issues`

[4]`https://github.com/apertium/apertium-fao-nor`

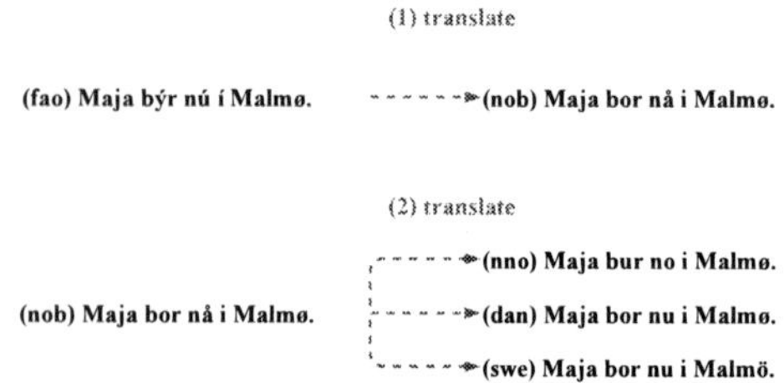

Figure 1: Example of pivot translation from Faroese to Swedish, Danish and Norwegian Nynorsk via Norwegian Bokmål. The sentence *Maja býr nú í Malmø* translates in English as 'Maja now lives in Malmø'. The translation to the other Nordic languages is word-by-word and monotonic.

4 Methodology

In this section we describe the two baseline methods and our multi-source approach.

4.1 Delexicalised parsing

For the delexicalised parsing baseline, we trained delexicalised models on the Swedish, Danish, Norwegian Bokmål and Norwegian Nynorsk Universal Dependencies treebanks. Delexicalised models are models trained only on the sequence of POS-tags and morphological features, omitting both lemmas and surface forms. The idea behind this is to make the model maximally language independent.

4.2 Annotation projection

For each of the source languages (Swedish, Danish, Norwegian Bokmål, and Norwegian Nynorsk), we first translated the Faroese Wikipedia (§3.1) to that language using the Apertium machine translation system. In the case of Swedish, Danish and Norwegian Nynorsk, the translation is pivoted via Norwegian Bokmål. This is demonstrated in Figure 1.

The original Faroese text and the translation is then aligned using `fastalign` (Dyer et al., 2013), a word-aligned based on IBM Model 2. Both translations and alignments are largely word-for-word and monotonic.

We then parse the translation using a lexicalised model trained on the training portion of the relevant treebank using UDPipe (Straka and Straková, 2017). This results in a collection of: original Faroese sentences, translations of those sentences, a word-by-word alignment between the Faroese sentences and the translated sentences, and a tree for each of the translated sentences.

The next step is to take the trees over the translated sentences and *project* them back to the original Faroese sentences, as is shown in Figure 2.

The final trees are then used for training a *lexicalised* model using UDPipe for parsing Faroese.

Language	Sentences	Tokens
Swedish	28,701	758,999
Danish	28,632	768,662
Norwegian Bokmål	28,016	765,203
Norwegian Nynorsk	28,611	753,597

Table 2: Number of valid sentences in synthetic UD treebanks for single-language models

4.3 Multi-source projection

With multi-source projection we add some additional steps. Instead of training a model on sentences which have had annotation projected from a single source language, we take into account the annotation for the sentence from all of the languages.

We first build a dependency graph for each Faroese sentence using the arcs found in all of the parsed translations of that sentence. The arcs are weighted, like in the voting scheme from the CoNLL-07 shared task (Nivre et al., 2007), such that each language is counted as a single vote for that arc. The dependency relations are voted for independently after the best tree has been found.

To find the best tree in the weighted graph, we use the maximum-spanning tree (MST) algorithm of Chu (1965); Edmonds (1967). This algorithm is widely used in dependency parsing, cf. McDonald et al. (2005). The algorithm is composed of the following steps:

1. For each vertex, pick the the incoming edge with the highest weight.

2. Check the graph for cycles. If there are no cycles and the graph is a tree, then return this graph as the resulting MST.

3. If there are cycles, then, for each cycle, isolate the cycle from the tree, find the incoming (to any vertex of the cycle), edge with the highest weight, then remove all the edges within the cycle which conflict with it.

4. Then repeat the steps 2-3 until there are no cycles.

Figure 3 shows the graph produced from the running example and the result of running the spanning tree algorithm.

5 Experiments

In order to evaluate the performance of multi-source synthetic treebank model, we conduct several experiments in which we compare the performance of our models to the baseline methods: delexicalised parsing (see §4.1) and synthetic treebanking (see §4.2).

For each model, we trained tagger and parser UDPipe models with the default settings (20 epochs for tagger and 10 epochs for parser).

6 Results

Here we present a comparison between the performance of baseline models described in Section 4 and that of the model trained on the multi-source synthetic treebank described in Section 4.3 measured against the gold standard.

Table 3 shows the F-measure for POS tagging and labelled-attachment score (LAS) and unlabelled-attachment score (UAS) for dependency relations. The best results for each approach are shown in bold.

7 Future work

One promising avenue for future work is to improve the way in which trees are projected into the lesser-resourced language. At the moment this is done in a deterministic fashion using the 1-best alignment from the word aligner. This has two primary drawbacks: (1) It could be however that there exist better alignments, but we miss them by choosing only the best; and (2) we then have to use imperfect heuristics to attempt to make a valid tree when the alignments do not result in one. One idea we have had would be to view the projection problem as one of finding the best tree in a graph of alignments. These alignments could come from several word aligners, or even from using simple attachment rules such as in e.g. Alonso et al. (2017).

Another avenue is to improve how arcs in the projected graph are weighted. At the moment we do only raw voting, but information from other languages in terms of distribution of part-of-speech tags, features and dependency relations could potentially improve the results.

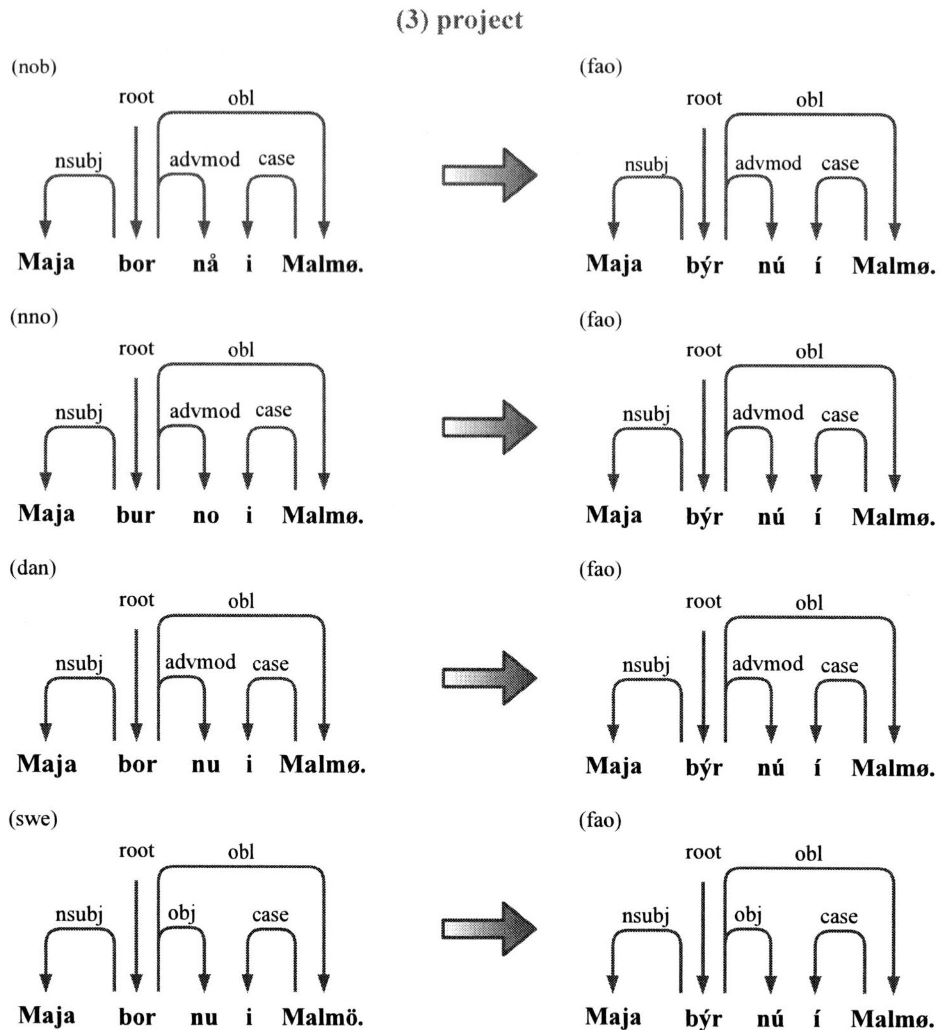

Figure 2: The sentences in the source languages are parsed, and then the trees are projected via the alignments back to the target language. In this case, the trees are identical with the exception of the annotation of *nu* 'now' as an object obj in Swedish.

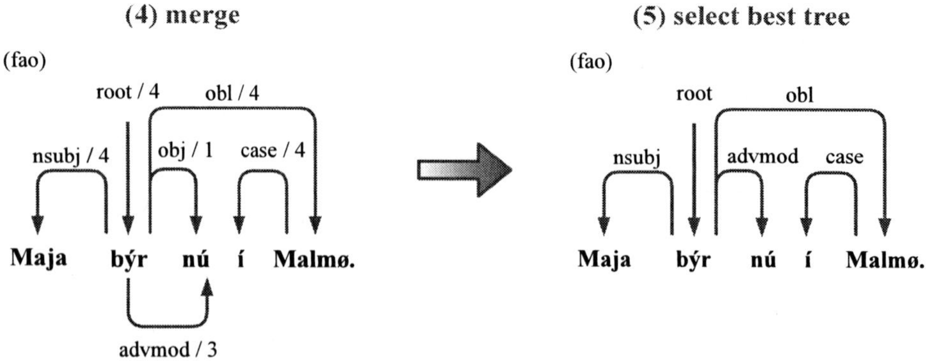

Figure 3: The projected trees from Figure 2 are merged into a weighted dependency graph where the weight of each edge is the number of times that edge is seen in the source trees. After merging the spanning tree algorithm is run to find the tree with the highest weight.

Model	Delexicalised			Projected		
	POS	UAS	LAS	POS	UAS	LAS
Swedish	43.83	23.14	10.32	73.06	65.66	58.53
Danish	46.15	21.27	13.01	74.76	68.74	59.84
Norwegian Bokmål	44.29	24.51	15.62	**74.89**	**72.04**	**63.95**
Norwegian Nynorsk	**51.30**	**27.76**	**18.93**	72.93	70.62	62.27
Multi-source	—	—	—	**74.49**	**72.90**	**64.43**

Table 3: Results for the systems. Delexicalised models are trained directly on the target language treebank and applied directly. In bold are the best results for delexicalised parsing, projected parsing and parsing with multi-source trees. In all cases the multi-source model outperforms all others.

In addition, we would like to try increasing the number of trees used to build the graph in the source language. One possibility is to use different parsers to generate different trees, and another is to use more machine translation systems to produce more translations to align.

We would also like to try the approach with other language groups for which there are several related treebanks in the Universal Dependencies project, for instance Upper Sorbian.

8 Conclusion

We have presented a method of creating synthetic training data for parsing a moderately under-resourced language for dependency parsing by using pivot machine translation into several closely-related better-resourced languages. By training an off-the-shelf parser on this synthetic treebank we are able to substantially improve on the state of the art for dependency parsing of Faroese, a moderately under-resourced language. All of the code is available under a free/open-source licence online.[5]

Acknowledgements

The article was prepared within the framework of the Academic Fund Programme at the National Research University Higher School of Economics (HSE) in 2016 — 2018 (grant №17-05-0043) and by the Russian Academic Excellence Project «5-100». The authors would like to thank Bjartur Mortensen for his help in preparing the gold standard, and the anonymous reviewers for their helpful comments.

References

Agić, □., Johannsen, A., Plank, B., Martínez Alonso, H., Schluter, N., and Søgaard, A. (2016). Multilingual projection for parsing truly low-resource languages. *Transactions of the Association for Computational Linguistics*, 4:301–312.

Alonso, H. M., Željko Agić, Plank, B., and Søgaard, A. (2017). Parsing Universal Dependencies without training. In *Proceedings of the 15th Conference of the European Chapter of the Association for Computational Linguistics*, volume 1, pages 230–240.

Antonsen, L., Trosterud, T., and Wiechetek, L. (2010). Reusing grammatical resources for new languages. In *Proceedings of the Seventh International Conference on Language Resources and Evaluation, LREC10*, pages 2782–2789.

Chu, Y.-J. (1965). On the shortest arborescence of a directed graph. *Science Sinica*, 14:1396–1400.

Dyer, C., Chahuneau, V., and Smith, N. A. (2013). A simple, fast, and effective reparameterization of IBM Model 2. In *Proceedings of NAACL-HLT 2013*, pages 644–648. Association for Computational Linguistics.

Edmonds, J. (1967). Optimum branchings. *Journal of Research of the National Bureau of Standards*, 71:233–240.

Forcada, M. L., Ginestí-Rosell, M., Nordfalk, J., O'Regan, J., Ortiz-Rojas, S., Pérez-Ortiz, J. A., Sánchez-Martínez, F., Ramírez-Sánchez, G., and Tyers, F. M. (2011). Apertium: a free/open-source platform for rule-based machine translation. *Machine Translation*, 25(2):127–144.

Gökırmak, M. and Tyers, F. M. (2017). A dependency treebank for Kurmanji Kurdish. In *Proceedings of the Fourth International Conference on Dependency Linguistics (DepLing, 2017)*, pages 64–73.

Johannsen, A., Martínez Alonso, H., and Plank, B. (2015). Universal dependencies for danish. In *Proceedings of the 14th International Workshop on Treebanks and Linguistic Theories (TLT14)*.

---

[5] `https://github.com/ftyers/cross-lingual-parsing`

McDonald, R., Pereira, F., Ribarov, K., and Hajič, J. (2005). Non-projective dependency parsing using spanning tree algorithms. In *Proceedings of the Conference on Human Language Technology and Empirical Methods in Natural Language Processing*, HLT '05, pages 523–530, Stroudsburg, PA, USA. Association for Computational Linguistics.

McDonald, R., Petrov, S., and Hall, K. (2011). Multi-source transfer of delexicalized dependency parsers. In *Proceedings of the 2011 Conference on Empirical Methods in Natural Language Processing*, pages 62–72.

Nivre, J., de Marneffe, M.-C., Ginter, F., Goldberg, Y., Hajič, J., Manning, C. D., McDonald, R., Petrov, S., Pyysalo, S., Silveira, N., Tsarfaty, R., and Zeman, D. (2016). Universal dependencies v1: A multilingual treebank collection. In *Proceedings of the 10th International Conference on Language Resources and Evaluation, LREC16*.

Nivre, J., Hall, J., Kübler, S., McDonald, R. T., Nilsson, J., Riedel, S., and Yuret, D. (2007). The conll 2007 shared task on dependency parsing. In *EMNLP-CoNLL 2007, Proceedings of the 2007 Joint Conference on Empirical Methods in Natural Language Processing and Computational Natural Language Learning, June 28-30, 2007, Prague, Czech Republic*, pages 915–932.

Schlichtkrull, M. S. and Søgaard, A. (2017). Cross-lingual dependency parsing with late decoding for truly low-resource languages. In *Proceedings of the 15th Conference of the European Chapter of the Association for Computational Linguistics: Volume 1, Long Papers*, pages 222–229. Association for Computational Linguistics.

Straka, M. and Straková, J. (2017). Tokenizing, POS tagging, lemmatizing and parsing UD 2.0 with UD-Pipe. In *Proceedings of the CoNLL 2017 Shared Task: Multilingual Parsing from Raw Text to Universal Dependencies*, pages 88–99, Vancouver, Canada. Association for Computational Linguistics.

Tiedemann, J. (2016). Opus - Parallel corpora for everyone. *Baltic Journal of Modern Computing*, 4(2).

Tiedemann, J. (2017). Cross-lingual dependency parsing for closely related languages – Helsinki's submission to VarDial 2017. In *Proceedings of the Fourth Workshop on NLP for Similar Languages, Varieties and Dialects*, pages 131–136. Association for Computational Linguistics.

Tiedemann, J. and Agić, Z. (2016). Synthetic treebanking for cross-lingual dependency parsing. *Journal of Artificial Intelligence Research*, 55:209–248.

Trosterud, T. (2009). A constraint grammar for Faroese. In *Proceedings of the NODALIDA 2009 workshop Constraint Grammar and robust parsing*.

Unhammer, K. and Trosterud, T. (2009). Reuse of free resources in machine translation between Nynorsk and Bokmål. In *Proceedings of the First International Workshop on Free/Open-Source Rule-Based Machine Translation*, pages 35–42.

Zeman, D. and Resnik, P. (2008). Cross-language parser adaptation between related languages. In *Proceedings of the IJCNLP-08 Workshop on NLP for Less Privileged Languages*, pages 35–42.

Øvrelid, L. and Hohle, P. (2016). Universal Dependencies for Norwegian. In *Proceedings of the 10th International Conference on Language Resources and Evaluation, LREC16*.

Toward Universal Dependencies for Shipibo-Konibo

Alonso Vasquez[1,3]**, Renzo Ego Aguirre**[1]**, Candy Angulo**[1]**, John Miller**[1]**,
Claudia Villanueva**[1]**, Željko Agić**[2]**, Roberto Zariquiey**[1] **and Arturo Oncevay**[1]
[1] Dpto. de Humanidades and Dpto. de Ingeniería, Pontificia Universidad Católica del Perú
[2] Department of Computer Science, IT University of Copenhagen
[3] Department of Linguistics, University of California, Santa Barbara
arturo.oncevay@pucp.edu.pe

Abstract

We present an initial version of the Universal Dependencies (UD) treebank for Shipibo-Konibo, the first South American, Amazonian, Panoan and Peruvian language with a resource built under UD. We describe the linguistic aspects of how the tagset was defined and the treebank was annotated; in addition we present our specific treatment of linguistic units called *clitics*. Although the treebank is still under development, it allowed us to perform a typological comparison against Spanish, the predominant language in Peru, and dependency syntax parsing experiments in both monolingual and cross-lingual approaches.

1 Introduction and Background

Shipibo-Konibo is a language of the Panoan family spoken by around 35,000 native speakers in the Amazon region of Peru. It is a language with agglutinative processes, with a majority presence of suffixes and some clitics (neither a word nor an affix). Additionally, it presents word orders different from the dominant Spanish language.

To the best of our knowledge, there are no other Universal Dependencies (UD) treebanks for an indigenous language of South America, as surveyed by Mager et al. (2018). The closest resource is a treebank developed for a Quechuan variant; however, it was not designed under the UD guidelines (Rios et al., 2008). Another related case is the application of UD for the annotation of the native North American language Arapaho (Algonquian) (Wagner et al., 2016). Thus, Shipibo-Konibo would be the first South American indigenous language with this kind of computational resource[1].

Natural Language Processing (NLP) efforts for Shipibo-Konibo have developed a POS-tagger, a

lemmatizer, a spell-checker, and a machine translation prototype with Spanish as the paired language (Mager et al., 2018). Each functionality has been published alongside its annotated corpus. A UD treebank would enhance the NLP toolkit for the language, as it is the core element for being able to train a dependency parser.

This paper describes the steps and decisions made towards a UD treebank for Shipibo-Konibo. First, §2 presents the annotation process. Then, §3 details the information of the UD treebank itself, such as the POS tags, morphological features and dependency relations, including the specific ones for Shipibo-Konibo. Moreover, it describes relevant decisions regarding clitics and word segmentation, including an analysis of the generated multiword tokens. Finally, we take advantage of the built treebank, and perform a typological comparison against Spanish in §4, as well as dependency parsing tests for monolingual and cross-lingual scenarios in §5.

2 Treebank Annotation

The annotation workflow of the Universal Dependencies (UD) treebank for Shipibo-Konibo is described in §2.1. In particular, specific consideration has been given for word segmentation with respect to clitics, which is detailed in §2.2.

2.1 Annotation Workflow

Annotation followed a sequential flow:

1. To annotate Shipibo-Konibo corpus in ChAnot (Mercado et al., 2018) and BRAT (Stenetorp et al., 2012). The former tool was specifically used for the morpheme segmentation of raw text into prefixes, root morphemes and suffixes in appropriate morphological detail. The provided interface with BRAT allows the graphical

---

[1] The treebank will be available for the next UD release

Proceedings of the Second Workshop on Universal Dependencies (UDW 2018), pages 151–161
Brussels, Belgium, November 1, 2018. ©2018 Association for Computational Linguistics

annotation of syntactic information over the segmentation. We used part of speech and relation names determined prior to the decision to conform to UD v2.0.

2. To compile segmented corpus into UD v2.0 format: Gather all annotations from ChAnot and BRAT into single file in UD v2.0 format. Compress detail segmentation of prefixes and suffixes to only segment on clitic boundaries. Add clitic features, and convert non-standard to UD v2.0 standard universal POS and dependency relation notation.

2.2 Clitics and Segmentation

In terms of its morphological profile, Shipibo-Konibo favors synthetic word formations. That is, in Shipibo-Konibo, words are often composed of a root and one or more bound morphemes. Some of these morphemes may be considered *clitics*, linguistic elements that do not fit either the prototype of word or that of affix. Similar elements are labelled *particles* in the Universal Dependencies tradition, but we prefer *clitics*, following the arguments presented in Zwicky (1977, 1985). In the Panoan literature, these intermediate linguistic units have also been called *clitics* (Fleck, 2013; Valenzuela, 2003; Zariquiey, 2015), so we consider it appropriate to follow this terminology in the development of our Shipibo-Konibo treebank.

As *clitics*, these linguistic units exhibit some features that resemble those attested in words. This intermediate nature clashes with the dichotomic division between morphology and syntax, in which linguistic units belong to one of these domains (see Dixon and Aikhenvald (2002); Haspelmath (2011) for discussion).

Taking all this into consideration, we have made the methodological decision of treating clitics as independent syntactic words. Therefore, the relationships between words and clitics is rendered as syntactic and is annotated by means of the appropriate dependency. All clitics in Shipibo-Konibo are phrasal in nature and treating them as independent words captures this in a more precise way (although annotation may be more time-consuming). In section 2.3 we present some examples.

Furthermore, following the principles for tokenizing a surface word into multiple *inflectional groups* (IGs) proposed by Çöltekin (2016, p. 2), we segment clitics as independent words because they and their host may participate in different syntactic relations. For instance, in the Shipibo-Konibo sentence *ea=ra joke* (I came), *ea* is the pronoun (I) in a dependency of `nsubj` from the verb *joke* (came), whereas *=ra* is an evidential clitic in the dependency of `aux:valid`.

Languages with similar morphological profiles have treebanks in Universal Dependencies, such as Finnish (Pyysalo et al., 2015), Turkish (Sulubacak et al., 2016) or Kazakh (Tyers and Washington, 2015). Nevertheless, those treebanks do not tend to systematically label bound morphemes as independent words, as we aim to do in the development of our treebank because of the reasons mentioned above.

2.3 Language Examples

We present two Shipibo-Konibo sentences in anticipation of further discussion.

The sentence *Jatianra en ja maxko bake panshin kírika menike* (So, I give this little boy a yellow book) in Figure 1 presents a ditransitive verb with direct and indirect objects. The clitic *=ra* has an evidential function, hence it projects the dependency relation `aux:valid` to the main verb *menike* (gave). The clitic *=n* expresses nominal case and projects to the token's core word. In Shipibo-Konibo, adjectives tend to precede nominal heads, with determiners preceding both adjectives and nominal heads as shown in the phrase *ja maxko bake*.

The sentence *Joninronki yoyo aká iki: "Jen, enra moa onanke"* (They say the man said, "Ah, I already knew that") in Figure 2 presents a direct speech construction showing two main verbs, each one with a evidentiality clitic. There are two multiword tokens with three syntactic words each, *joni =n =ronki* and *e =n =ra*.

3 Shipibo-Konibo Treebank

Our current Shipibo-Konibo treebank is the result of the syntactic annotation of 407 sentences extracted from parallel Shipibo-Konibo and Spanish educational materials and storybooks – complemented with elicited sentences produced and translated by the Shipibo-Konibo members of our team. This is a small treebank with work still ongoing (Table 1).

3.1 Typological features of Shipibo-Konibo

Shipibo-Konibo presents a basic AOV/SV constituent order (Figures 1 & 2), but it exhibits other

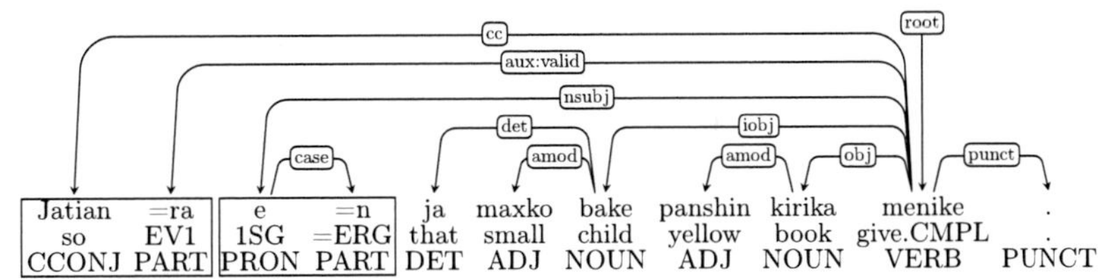

Figure 1: Dependency graph - clitic example (So, I gave that little boy a yellow book.)

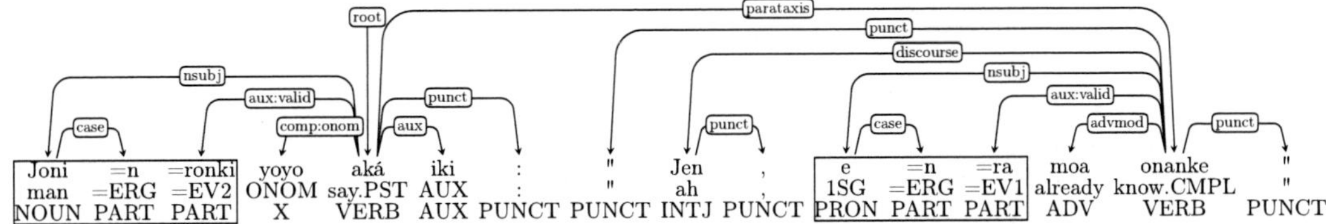

Figure 2: Dependency graph - complex clitic example (They say the man said, "Ah, I already knew that.")

Item	Count
Sentences	407
Orthographic tokens	2706
Syntactic words	3148

Table 1. Corpus Description.

pragmatically conditioned orders. NP-modifiers often precede their head (Figure 1) and verbs do not show either subject or object cross-reference.

As this is first treebank for any South-American indigenous language, there could well be novel grammatical features of Shipibo-Konibo not included in any other treebanks.

3.2 Universal Part of Speech (POS) Tags

Universal Dependencies (UD) introduces a tagset of 17 POS tags, mainly based in the Google universal part-of-speech tags (Petrov et al., 2012). All of them have been employed in the development of the Shipibo-Konibo treebank. The POS tags and frequencies in the treebank are shown in table 2.

The POS tag X is used for labelling onomatopoeia, which is a relevant POS in various Panoan languages, including Shipibo-Konibo (Valenzuela, 2003; Zariquiey, 2015, 2011). UD does not have an onomatopoeia POS tag. Hence, we opted to use X to label it. In other treebanks, onomatopoeias were ascribed to different POS tags. For example, Badmaeva (2016) in her "Universal Dependencies for Buryat" states that "the case of onomatopoeia is also an interjection" (2016, p. 40). However,

onomatopoeias in Shipibo-Konibo are members of a special closed part of speech. They are used in combination with semantically generic verbs or auxiliaries as a productive strategy in order to form new words. Therefore, we considered it appropriate to label them as a different and independent POS.

As discussed in §2.2, Shipibo-Konibo *clitics* are a special type of linguistic unit that ought to be treated as an independent POS. Since Universal Dependencies does not present a clitic POS tag, but it does present a particle POS tag, PART, we opted to treat the Shipibo-Konibo clitics as particles, since *clitics* are often called *particles* (§2.2). These linguistic units are divided into three different categories: nominal clitic (expressing case and only used with nominal phrases), second position clitics (mainly expressing evidentiality and following the first constituent of a sentence), and less-fixed clitics (expressing adverbial value and used with any kind of POS). In this sense, it is important to remark that we are not considering them as adpositions ADP, since they belong to a closed set of items that occur before (preposition) or after (postposition) a complement composed of a noun phrase, noun, pronoun, or clause that functions as a noun phrase. Thus, they form a single structure with the complement to express its grammatical and semantic relation to another unit within a clause.

The high PART frequency noted in table 2 could impact performance in tasks as part-of-speech tagging or even syntax dependency parsing if it would require prior POS tag information. This was discussed and analyzed by Endresen et al. (2016) in a Russian corpus. We believe it will be important to measure whether the impact would be positive or negative in morphosyntactic tasks for Shipibo-Konibo as well, and thus, we would like to extend the discussion to a multilingual approach as further work.

POS	Count	%
Open class words		
NOUN	574	18.2
VERB	575	18.3
ADJ	119	3.8
ADV	103	3.3
PROPN	52	1.7
INTJ	7	0.2
Closed class words		
PART	440	14.0
PRON	177	5.6
AUX	162	5.1
DET	123	3.9
CCONJ	93	3.0
ADP	36	1.1
NUM	22	0.7
X (ONOM)	4	0.1
SCONJ	1	<0.1
Other		
PUNCT	654	20.8
SYM	2	0.1

Table 2: Universal POS.

3.3 Universal Morphological Features

The universal morphological features of UD are based on Zeman (2008)'s "Reusable tagset conversion using tagset drivers" with the concept of an expandable feature structure that could support any tagset. Tagset labels aim to "distinguish additional lexical and grammatical properties of words, not covered by the POS tags" (Nivre et al., 2017). A list of the morphological features and values used in the Shipibo-Konibo treebank annotation are given in Table 3; most are already defined in Universal Dependencies. The few morphological features of Shipibo-Konibo that require labels not currently in Universal Dependencies are underlined in Table 3.

The new morphological features are further defined below.

Aspect=And, Ven Shipibo-Konibo uses a set of

Feature	Values
Animacy	Inam, Anim
Aspect	Perf, Hab, Iter, Imp, <u>And</u>, <u>Ven</u>
Case	Loc, Ela, Abl, Abs, Dat, Dis, Gen, Ill, Abe, Equa, Erg, Com, All, Tem, Ine, Voc, <u>Chez</u>
Evidentiality	Fh, Nfh
Mood	Jus, Frus, Des, Imp, Prev, Ind, <u>Int</u>
Number	Sing, Plur, Dual
Person	1, 2, 3
Polarity	Neg, Pos
Tense	<u>Past1</u>, <u>Past2</u>, <u>Past3</u>, <u>Past4</u>, <u>Past5</u>, <u>Past6</u>, <u>Fut1</u>, <u>Fut2</u>
VerbForm	Part, Inf
Voice	Mid, Rcp, Act, Cau, App
<u>Clitic</u>	<u>Nomcl</u>, <u>Spcl</u>, <u>Lfcl</u>

Table 3: Features in Shipibo-Konibo

deictic morphemes which indicate associated motion, *going* (andative) versus *coming* (venitive). Although there is literature arguing that associated motion should be treated as an independent grammatical category, the interaction between associated motion and aspect is well known (Guillaume, 2009).

Case=Chez Valenzuela defines a chezative case, which can be translated as "to/at the place where X is/lives" (2003, p. 232). Shipibo-Konibo encodes this case with the clitic *-ibá* ∼ *-ibat*.

Mood=Int Questions in Shipibo-Konibo are encoded by bound morphemes which are labeled by the dependency relation `aux:valid` (see §3.4.1).

Tense=Past1, Past2, Past3, Past4, Past5, Past6 Shipibo-Konibo presents six productive past categories. These tense categories are expressed by verbal bound morphemes. These features are presented in Table 4.

Tense=Fut1, Fut2 Shipibo-Konibo also has two different classes of future tense, expressed by bound morphemes. These features are also presented in Table 4.

Clitic=Nomcl, Spcl, Lfcl In §3.2 we introduced clitics with the `PART` POS tag, while also defining the three clitic categories as nominal clitic (`Nomcl`), second position clitic (`Spcl`), and less-fixed clitic (`Lfcl`).

Features currently annotated in the Shipibo-Konibo treebank are shown in Table 5. These

Universal features	Bound morpheme	Meaning
Past1	-wan	earlier the same day
Past2	-ibat ∼ -ibá	yesterday, a few days ago
Past3	-yantan	some months, a few years ago
Past4	-rabe	ca. 9 months to 3 years ago
Past5	-kati(t)	distant past, many years ago
Past6	-ni	remote past
Fut1	-nonx(iki)	indefinite future
Fut2	-yá ∼ -yat	tomorrow

Adapted from Valenzuela (2003, p. 284-285)

Table 4: Tense Features

have been automatically inferred based on POS tag, dependency relation, lexical, and, in the case of `AdpType`, language type information. Our next work update should deliver manually annotated features as well.

Feature	Value	Count
Clitic	Nomcl	263
Clitic	Spcl	176
Clitic	Lfcl	1
PronType	Int	86
AdpType	Post	36

Table 5: Inferred Features.

3.4 Dependency Relations

UD defines a set of 37 dependency relations, mainly based on "Universal Stanford Dependencies: A cross-linguistic typology" by Marneffe et al. (2014). Thirty-one of these 37 relations were employed in our Shipibo-Konibo treebank. One of the main characteristics of UD is that relations link content words rather than abstract nodes, i.e., *lexicalism* (Nivre et al., 2017). Dependency relations and frequencies in the treebank are reported in Table 6. It is worth mentioning that the frequency of `acl` and `ccomp` relation labels is low due to the choice of annotated sentences rather than a specific property of the language.

Shipibo-Konibo specific relations

While UD aims to provide "a universal inventory of categories and guidelines to facilitate consistent annotation of similar constructions across languages" (Nivre et al., 2017), it also allows language-specific subtype relation labels when necessary. For the Shipibo-Konibo treebank, we considered the inclusion of two new subtype relation labels: `aux:valid` and `compound:onom`.

Relation	Count	%
punct	654	20.8
root	407	12.9
nsubj	314	10.0
case	299	9.5
obj	189	6.0
aux:valid	176	5.6
aux	172	5.5
amod	133	4.2
det	130	4.1
advcl	112	3.6
advmod	103	3.3
cc	93	3.0
obl	87	2.8
cop	67	2.1
nmod	67	2.1
compound	46	1.5
conj	39	1.2
iobj	21	0.7
nummod	15	0.5
discourse	6	0.2
appos	6	0.2
flat	4	0.1
vocative	3	0.1
acl	1	<0.1
ccomp	1	<0.1

Table 6: Dependency Relations

3.4.1 Relation subtype - aux:valid

An auxiliary is an element that may express different grammatical categories such as time, aspect, mood, voice and evidentiality. In Shipibo-Konibo, evidentiality and mood are expressed through a subset of clitics. These clitics are ascribed to the relation `aux`, but in order to distinguish them from verbal auxiliaries, they receive the subtype relation label `val`. This subcategory refers to the notion of *validator*, as defined by Cerrón-Palomino (2008, p. 166) for Quechua. For example, the sentence *Enra yapa yoá akai* (I cook fish) uses the first-hand evidentiality clitic =*ra* (Valenzuela, 2003, p. 534) to express that the speaker witnessed the event. See Figures 1 & 2 for more examples.

Note the high frequency of use for `aux:valid` shown in Table 6. At 176 instances, 5.6% of all syntactic words, almost half of Shipibo-Konibo sentences would include an expression of evidentiality (given seldom more than one `aux:valid` is used per sentence). This high frequency expression of evidentiality is an intriguing linguistic phenomenon and worth further study.

3.4.2 Relation subtype - compound:onom

Similar to other languages of the Panoan language family, in Shipibo-Konibo, onomatopoeias are considered as a closed word class (Valenzuela, 2003). In this language there are constructions that include two *semantically generic* verbs: *ati* (do) or *iti* (be) (Valenzuela, 2003, p. 83). These elements may be combined with onomatopoeias in order to create a type of compound verb.

We decided to use the subtype relation label `compound:onom` for those specific types of compound verbs. For example, the verb *yoyo iti* (to speak) corresponds to a compound formed by the verb *iti* (be) and the onomatopoeia *yoyo* (speech noise). In spite of the fact that they are two differentiated entities, both elements constitute a unit at the semantic level, and therefore are compounds in Universal Dependencies. See Figure 2 as another example.

There is a significant use of compounds, 46 instances and 1.5% of syntactic words (Table 6), but only a few are due to onomatopoeia. While deemed important in the language, onomatopoeias have low frequency representation in the current instance of the treebank.

3.5 Segmentation and Multiword Tokens

Our decision to split orthographic tokens on clitic boundaries in §2.2 results in an abundance of multiple syntactic word tokens (Table 7) with 402 multiword tokens (MWTs) of 2706 total tokens. The clitic of second position, `Spcl`, invokes the dependency relation `aux:valid` typically with the clausal head and not with the core word of the MWT. The nominal clitic, `Nomcl`, invokes the dependency relation `case` with the core word of the MWT.

The cases where a token contains multiple clitics, the `Spcl` comes later. This has the effect of preserving projectivity. We continue to follow this issue of multiple clitic MWTs and projectivity.

3.6 Multiword Tokens vs Other Languages

Indeed, Shipibo-konibo has proportionally many more Multiword tokens (MWTs) than Spanish or Turkish, a language considered agglutinative, but less than Hebrew. Table 8 shows the differences where ~15% of Shipibo-Konibo tokens are multiword versus ~3% for Turkish, much less for Spanish, and ~32% for Hebrew.

Property	Value	Count
MWTs	All	402
Num words	2	362
Relation	case	260
Relation	aux:valid	138
Relation	other	4
Head	not MWT core	137
Num words	3	40
Relation	aux:valid	35
Relation	other	5
Head	not MWT core	39

Table 7: Multiword Tokens

The big differences in MWT relative frequency is surprising given the UD documentation's explicit encouragement to use MWTs for annotating clitics (Universal Dependencies contributors, 2018). Our decision to segment tokens by phrasal clitic boundaries likely explains part of this large difference versus even other agglutinative languages.

Item	Quantity			
	Shipibo	Spanish	Turkish	Hebrew
Sentences	407	17680	5635	6216
Tokens	2706	547681	56422	115535
Multiword Tokens				
Count	402	1887	1640	37035
% tokens	14.86	0.34	2.91	32.06

See Spanish (Martínez Alonso and Zeman, 2017), Hebrew (Goldberg et al., 2017), and Turkish (Sulubacak et al., 2016) treebanks.

Table 8: Multiword Tokens Comparison

4 Word Order vs Spanish

We examined word order differences between the dominant Spanish and Shipibo-Konibo. Spanish results are from the training set of the Es-Ancora treebank (Martínez Alonso and Zeman, 2017), while Shipibo-Konibo results are from our treebank. Table 9 reports counts and relative frequencies of a constituent *preceding* its head. Constituents are reported either by their dependency relation with their head or POS in the case of single syntactic word constituents. Relative frequency of following the head is just the complement of that of preceding the head.

Direct and oblique objects usually follow the head (typically a verb) in Spanish and precede the head in Shipibo-konibo. Auxiliary verbs usually precede the head in Spanish and follow the head in Shipibo-Konibo. Spanish uses prepositions and Shipibo-Konibo postpositions, but determiners precede their heads in both languages. Similar differences and similarities follow for the less common constituents as well.

Constituent	Shipibo		Spanish	
≺ Head	Count	%	Count	%
obj	157	83.1	898	24.3
obl	64	73.6	209	15.3
iobj	19	90.5	62	71.3
nmod	59	88.1	8	0.3
acl	*	*	0	0.0
advcl	75	67.0	18	3.1
ccomp	*	*	1	0.4
advmod	91	88.4	298	52.1
amod	106	79.7	261	18.4
nummod	12	80.0	80	77.7
appos	1	16.7	0	0.0
cop	37	55.2	181	99.5
AUX	2	1.2	737	95.3
ADV	91	91.0	333	55.9
DET	123	100.0	5661	99.1
ADJ	77	75.5	279	16.8
ADP	1	2.8	5373	98.8

* Zero or one occurrence in Shipibo-Konibo corpus.

Table 9: Phrase or word order - Shipibo vs Spanish

Full confirmation of Shipibo-Konibo features versus the WALS database (Dryer and Haspelmath, 2013) awaits further progress. But a review of word order from Table 9 versus WALS largely confirms comparable word order features in WALS. An exception is adjective and noun head order. Our corpus shows ~75% adjective preceding head (~80% for adjective preceding *noun* head). So adjective precedes noun head order *dominates* versus the earlier finding by Faust (1973) reported in WALS of *no dominant order*.

5 Parsing for Shipibo-Konibo

Dependency syntax parsing is a complex task that usually requires a lot of annotated data, thus we decided to perform experiments in two different scenarios. The first one treats the treebank as an isolated corpus using monolingual methods, whereas the second one presents a cross-lingual experiment to identify which other languages from the UD v2.0 collection can support the parsing task for Shipibo-Konibo.

5.1 Monolingual Parsing

A straightforward test was performed using a greedy transition-based parser (Parsito) (Straka et al., 2015) from UDPipe (Straka and Straková, 2017) and the Yara Parser (Rasooli and Tetreault, 2015), which is also a transition-based method but uses beam search. The obtained results with 10-fold cross-validation are presented in Table 10, where we perform parses with POS gold annotations and raw text.

Input	Parser	UAS	LAS
Gold POS	Parsito	83.66±4.12	77.81±4.33
	Yara	87.32±2.90	81.25±3.45
Raw text	Parsito	37.68±1.23	30.39±1.34
	Yara	42.15±6.20	29.19±3.90

Table 10: Monolingual parsing accuracy for unlabeled (UAS) and labeled (LAS) attachment with gold POS tags and raw text as inputs

With the gold annotations, UAS and LAS scores from Parsito are greater than the language average of 78.59% and 72.81%, respectively, from Straka and Straková (2017); and the Yara Parser provides slightly better results in most cases. The low difference may be caused by the different search approaches (greedy versus global beam search) in the transition-based parsers. Meanwhile, parsing raw text scored much worse, which was expected for the corpus size. However, most of the cross-validation results has presented high variance; and thus, these results must not be treated as definitive ones, and only as a reference, as there could be overfitting and scarcity issues.

5.2 Cross-Lingual Parsing

We conducted an experiment with single-source cross-lingual delexicalized parser transfer from the UD v2.0 source languages into Shipibo-Konibo as the target language, in the vein of Zeman and Resnik (2008).

In the experiment, we used the `mate-tools` graph-based parser by Bohnet (2010) with default settings. The entire Shipibo-Konibo treebank was our test set. We tagged the treebank for POS using MarMoT (Mueller et al., 2013) via 10-fold cross-validation with a mean accuracy of 93.94±1.38 (s.d.). As we performed delexicalized transfer, all training and test data used only the following CoNLL-U features: ID, POS, HEAD, and DE-

kk	66.42	pl	54.02	hr	48.80	got	43.97
ja_ktc	63.26	lv	53.81	ja	48.46	no	42.26
eu	58.77	cs_cac	53.29	en	48.29	nl	42.22
tr	58.73	ro	53.29	sv	47.86	vi	41.57
ta	57.49	el	53.04	sv_lines	47.78	swl	41.49
fa	57.01	grc	52.69	sa	46.71	pt_bosque	40.98
hi	56.89	cs	51.63	id	46.49	grc_proiel	40.72
hu	56.46	sl	51.50	es_ancora	46.15	fi	39.31
et	55.77	cop	50.60	gl_treegal	46.15	it	39.31
bg	55.56	ru	50.51	pt	45.98	la_proiel	38.11
fi_ftb	55.43	sk	50.04	es	45.42	nl_lassysmall	37.98
de	55.35	gl	49.79	en_esl	45.38	cu	37.38
la_ittb	55.26	ru_syntagrus	49.57	ca	45.17	da	36.10
sl_sst	54.88	la	49.02	zh	45.17	ar	33.96
ug	54.58	en_lines	48.97	uk	44.91	ga	30.50
cs_cltt	54.23	fr	48.85	pt_br	44.31	he	23.22

Table 11: Cross-lingual parsing accuracy (UAS) for single-source delexicalized transfer parsers with Shipibo-Konibo as the target language. The source treebanks and their codes are from UD v2.0.

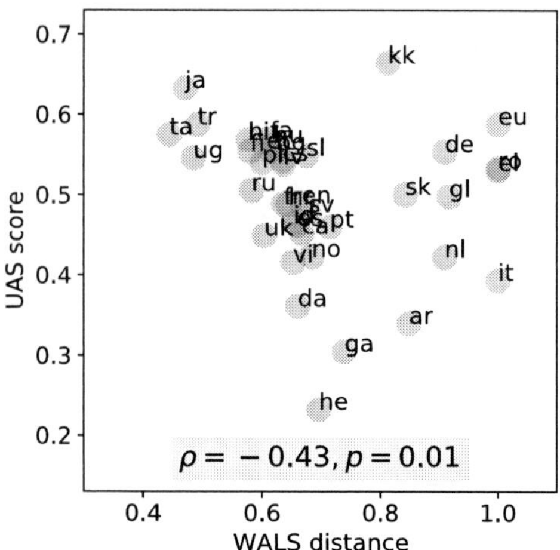

Figure 3: Cross-lingual parsing UAS scores correlated with source language WALS vector Hamming distance to Shipibo-Konibo. The correlation coefficient is Spearman's ρ.

PREL. Yet, to avoid any dependency label inconsistencies since our treebank is small, we evaluated for UAS only. We excluded all multiword tokens from the experiment, while retaining their respective syntactic words. A single delexicalized parser was trained for each UD v2.0 source treebank and applied on the Shipibo-Konibo test data.

Table 11 presents the results of the transfer parsing experiment. We achieve by far the best parsing results via the Kazakh delexicalized parser (66% UAS), closely followed by Japanese (63%), Basque and Turkish (ca 59%), and then Tamil, Persian, and Hindi (57%). Specifically, Kazakh presents morphosyntactic features similar to Shipibo-Konibo, such as SOV word order, high presence of agglutinative suffixes and head-final directionality (Mukhamedova, 2015). Moreover, the results are interesting as the top-performing cluster of sources for Shipibo-Konibo comprises languages that mainly feature as outliers in most cross-lingual parsing research, owing to the strong mainstream bias towards experimenting with resource-rich languages, as argued by Agić et al. (2016).

To further support our findings, we correlate the cross-lingual parsing UAS scores with language similarity of UD v2.0 source languages to Shipibo-Konibo. We express language similarity as pairwise Hamming distance between WALS vectors (Dryer and Haspelmath, 2013) for Shipibo-Konibo and the respective UD v2.0 source languages similar to Agić (2017). We depict this set of results in Figure 3, where we show a moderate negative correlation (Spearman's $\rho = -0.43$) between UAS and WALS distance, that is unlikely to be random at $p < 0.05$. In other words, the source languages that are more similar to Shipibo-Konibo in terms of WALS are more likely to provide Shipibo-Konibo with good delexicalized parsers. That said, some of the best source parsers are outliers in the figure: Kazakh and Basque yield good parsers for Shipibo-Konibo, but their WALS distance to it is large. This is due to the sparsity of WALS features for these languages: for example, 183 of 202 WALS features are null for Kazakh, and 188 for Basque, but only 41 for Japanese. Fixing these WALS feature deficiencies would in turn arguably strengthen the correlations to further support our findings. Besides, this analysis could be complemented by using a subset of WALS features that are generally available, as well as by inferring empty Kazakh features from related languages in the Kypchak group.

6 Conclusion and Future Work

We've presented Shipibo-Konibo from the Amazon region of Peru and our ample progress in building a treebank conforming to Universal Dependencies v2.0. We argued for segmenting syntactic words (versus tokens) along phrasal clitic boundaries and provided parse examples of this.

While our treebank is still a work in progress with 407 sentences, we've learned much already about what distinguishes us from other languages and treebanks. Segmenting on phrasal clitics and POS tagging as PART resulted in a phenomenal 14% of clitics tagged as PART in our treebank, following only PUNCT, NOUN, VERB in popularity.

Several morphological features were added to account for past and future verb tenses, And and Ven aspects, Chez case, and Nomcl, Spcl, and Lfcl clitics. Each of these additions matters in the meaningful annotation of Shipibo-Konibo.

We considered two new dependency relation subtypes: aux:valid and compound:onom. The aux:valid relation occurred 176 times (5.6% of words and almost half of sentences). This high use evidentiality function invites further linguistic study.

By segmenting on phrasal clitics Shipibo-Konibo stands out in its use of multiword tokens (MWTs) including both two and three word MWTs. The Spcl clitic usually projects to the verbal head, but since it succeeds other clitics, projectivity is preserved. Shipibo-Konibo has a huge fives times as many MWTs (∼15% versus ∼3% for Turkish) versus other (agglutinative) languages.

Word order of Shipibo-Konibo versus Spanish reveals dramatic differences, which informs our work on machine translation between them. We largely confirmed WALS word order features for Shipibo-Konibo, except for our finding that adjective precedes noun is *dominant* as opposed to *no dominant order* as reported in WALS.

Results on a monolingual parser show promise with better than the language average performance for gold POS tags. Delexicalized cross-lingual parsing using parsers trained on all UD v2.0 treebanks, showed a maximum 66% unlabeled attachment score (UAS) for Kazakh, a language with similar morphosyntactic features, followed closely by Japanese at 63%. A plot of UAS versus Hamming distance from WALS vectors reveals the expected inverse correlation between WALS distance and UAS (lesser WALS distance related to higher UAS). Japanese showed a low WALS distance and a high UAS, but Kazakh showed both high WALS distance and high UAS (seemingly an outlier).

As future work, we will increase the size of the UD treebank, as well as annotate the morphological features in a semi-supervised way. There has been developed an FSM-based morphological analyzer (Cardenas Acosta and Zeman, 2018) that could support the annotation for that purpose. Moreover, as Shipibo-Konibo is one of many in the Panoan linguistic family, the next step would be the definition of the UD tagsets and guidelines for closely related languages, such as Iskonawa or Amawaka. We hope these efforts could extend language technologies development for minority languages in Peru.

Acknowledgments

We gratefully acknowledge the support of the "Consejo Nacional de Ciencia, Tecnología e Innovación Tecnológica" (CONCYTEC, Peru) under the contract 225-2015-FONDECYT. Furthermore, we appreciate the detailed feedback of the anonymous reviewers.

References

Željko Agić. 2017. Cross-lingual parser selection for low-resource languages. In *Proceedings of the NoDaLiDa 2017 Workshop on Universal Dependencies (UDW 2017)*, pages 1–10, Gothenburg, Sweden. Association for Computational Linguistics.

Željko Agić, Anders Johannsen, Barbara Plank, Héctor Martínez Alonso, Natalie Schluter, and Anders Søgaard. 2016. Multilingual projection for parsing truly low-resource languages. *Transactions of the Association for Computational Linguistics*, 4:301–312.

Elena Badmaeva. 2016. Universal Dependencies for Buryat. Master's thesis, Universidad del País Vasco/ Euskal Herriko Unibersitate.

Bernd Bohnet. 2010. Top accuracy and fast dependency parsing is not a contradiction. In *Proceedings of the 23rd International Conference on Computational Linguistics (Coling 2010)*, pages 89–97, Beijing, China. Coling 2010 Organizing Committee.

Ronald Cardenas Acosta and Daniel Zeman. 2018. Morphological analyzer for shipibo-konibo. LINDAT/CLARIN digital library at the Institute of Formal and Applied Linguistics (ÚFAL), Faculty of Mathematics and Physics, Charles University.

Rodolfo Cerrón-Palomino. 2008. *Quechumara: Estructuras paralelas del quechua y del aimara*. Universidad Mayor de San Simón, Cochabamba, Bolivia.

Çağrı Çöltekin. 2016. (When) do we need inflectional groups? In *The First International Conference on Turkic Computational Linguistic*.

R. M. W. Dixon and Alexandra Y. Aikhenvald, editors. 2002. *Word: a cross-linguistic typology*, volume 20. Cambridge University Press, Cambridge.

Matthew S. Dryer and Martin Haspelmath, editors. 2013. *WALS Online - World Atlas of Language Structures*. Max Planck Institute for Evolutionary Anthropology, Leipzig.

Anna Endresen, Laura A Janda, Robert Reynolds, and Francis M Tyers. 2016. Who needs particles? A challenge to the classification of particles as a part of speech in Russian. *Russian Linguistics*, 40(2):103–132.

Norma Faust. 1973. *Lecciones para el aprendizaje del idioma shipibo-conibo*, volume 1 of *Documento de Trabajo*. Instituto Lingüístico de Verano, Yarinacocha.

David W. Fleck. 2013. *Panoan languages and linguistics*. 99. American Museum of Natural History.

Yoav Goldberg, Reut Tsarfaty, Amir More, and Yuval Pinter. 2017. UD Hebrew HTB. http://universaldependencies.org/treebanks/he_htb/index.html.

Antoine Guillaume. 2009. Les suffixes verbaux de mouvement associé en cavineña. *Faits de Langues : Les Cahiers*, 1:181–204.

Martin Haspelmath. 2011. The indeterminacy of word segmentation and the nature of morphology and syntax. *Folia Linguistica*, 45(1):31 –80.

Manuel Mager, Ximena Gutierrez-Vasques, Gerardo Sierra, and Ivan Meza-Ruiz. 2018. Challenges of language technologies for the indigenous languages of the americas. pages 55–69.

Marie-Catherine de Marneffe, Timothy Dozat, Natalia Silveira, Katri Haverinen, Filip Ginter, Joakim Nivre, and Christopher D. Manning. 2014. Universal Stanford dependencies: A cross-linguistic typology. In *Proceedings of the Ninth International Conference on Language Resources and Evaluation (LREC-2014)*. European Language Resources Association (ELRA).

Héctor Martínez Alonso and Daniel Zeman. 2017. UD Spanish AnCora. http://universaldependencies.org/treebanks/es_ancora/index.html.

Rodolfo Mercado, José Pereira, Marco Antonio Sobrevilla Cabezudo, and Arturo Oncevay. 2018. ChAnot: An intelligent annotation tool for indigenous and highly agglutinative languages in Peru. In *Proceedings of the Eleventh International Conference on Language Resources and Evaluation (LREC 2018)*, Miyazaki, Japan. European Language Resources Association (ELRA).

Thomas Mueller, Helmut Schmid, and Hinrich Schütze. 2013. Efficient higher-order CRFs for morphological tagging. In *Proceedings of the 2013 Conference on Empirical Methods in Natural Language Processing*, pages 322–332, Seattle, Washington, USA. Association for Computational Linguistics.

Raikhangul Mukhamedova. 2015. *Kazakh: A comprehensive grammar*. Routledge.

Joakim Nivre, Željko Agić, Lars Ahrenberg, Maria Jesus Aranzabe, Masayuki Asahara, Aitziber Atutxa, Miguel Ballesteros, John Bauer, Kepa Bengoetxea, Riyaz Ahmad Bhat, Eckhard Bick, Cristina Bosco, Gosse Bouma, Sam Bowman, Marie Candito, Gülşen Cebiroğlu Eryiğit, Giuseppe G. A. Celano, Fabricio Chalub, Jinho Choi, Çağrı Çöltekin, Miriam Connor, Elizabeth Davidson, Marie-Catherine de Marneffe, Valeria de Paiva, Arantza Diaz de Ilarraza, Kaja Dobrovoljc, Timothy Dozat, Kira Droganova, Puneet Dwivedi, Marhaba Eli, Tomaž Erjavec, Richárd Farkas, Jennifer Foster, Cláudia Freitas, Katarína Gajdošová, Daniel Galbraith, Marcos Garcia, Filip Ginter, Iakes Goenaga, Koldo Gojenola, Memduh Gökırmak, Yoav Goldberg, Xavier Gómez Guinovart, Berta Gonzáles Saavedra, Matias Grioni, Normunds Grūzītis, Bruno Guillaume, Nizar Habash, Jan Hajič, Linh Hà Mỹ, Dag Haug, Barbora Hladká, Petter Hohle, Radu Ion, Elena Irimia, Anders Johannsen, Fredrik Jørgensen, Hüner Kaşıkara, Hiroshi Kanayama, Jenna Kanerva, Natalia Kotsyba, Simon Krek, Veronika Laippala, Alessandro Lenci, Nikola Ljubešić, Olga Lyashevskaya, Teresa Lynn, Aibek Makazhanov, Christopher Manning, Cătălina Mărănduc, David Mareček, Héctor Martínez Alonso, André Martins, Jan Mašek, Yuji Matsumoto, Ryan McDonald, Anna Missilä, Verginica Mititelu, Yusuke Miyao, Simonetta Montemagni, Amir More, Shunsuke Mori, Bohdan Moskalevskyi, Kadri Muischnek, Nina Mustafina, Kaili Müürisep, Huyền Nguyễn Thị Minh, Vitaly Nikolaev, Hanna Nurmi, Stina Ojala, Petya Osenova, Lilja Øvrelid, Elena Pascual, Marco Passarotti, Cenel-Augusto Perez, Guy Perrier, Slav Petrov, Jussi Piitulainen, Barbara Plank, Martin Popel, Lauma Pretkalniņa, Prokopis Prokopidis, Tiina Puolakainen, Sampo Pyysalo, Alexandre Rademaker, Loganathan Ramasamy, Livy Real, Laura Rituma, Rudolf Rosa, Shadi Saleh, Manuela Sanguinetti, Baiba Saulīte, Sebastian Schuster, Djamé Seddah, Wolfgang Seeker, Mojgan Seraji, Lena Shakurova, Mo Shen, Dmitry Sichinava, Natalia Silveira, Maria Simi, Radu Simionescu, Katalin Simkó, Mária Šimková, Kiril Simov, Aaron Smith, Alane Suhr, Umut Sulubacak, Zsolt Szántó, Dima Taji, Takaaki Tanaka, Reut Tsarfaty, Francis Tyers, Sumire Uematsu, Larraitz Uria, Gertjan van Noord, Viktor Varga, Veronika Vincze, Jonathan North Washington, Zdeněk Žabokrtský, Amir Zeldes, Daniel Zeman, and Hanzhi Zhu. 2017. Universal dependencies 2.0. http://hdl.handle.net/11234/1-1983. LINDAT/CLARIN digital library at the Institute of Formal and Applied Linguistics (ÚFAL), Faculty of Mathematics and Physics, Charles University.

Slav Petrov, Dipanjan Das, and Ryan McDonald. 2012. A universal part-of-speech tagset. In *Proceedings of the Eight International Conference on Language Resources and Evaluation (LREC'12)*, Istanbul, Turkey. European Language Resources Association (ELRA).

Sampo Pyysalo, Jenna Kanerva, Anna Missilä, Veronika Laippala, and Filip Ginter. 2015. Universal Dependencies for Finnish. In *Proceedings of the 20th Nordic Conference of Computational Linguistics (Nodalida 2015)*, pages 163–172.

Mohammad Sadegh Rasooli and Joel R. Tetreault. 2015. Yara Parser: A fast and accurate dependency parser. *CoRR*, abs/1503.06733.

Annette Rios, Anne Göhring, and Martin Volk. 2008. A Quechua-Spanish parallel treebank. *LOT Occasional Series*, 12:53–64.

Pontus Stenetorp, Sampo Pyysalo, Goran Topić, Tomoko Ohta, Sophia Ananiadou, and Jun'ichi Tsujii. 2012. Brat: a web-based tool for nlp-assisted text annotation. In *Proceedings of the Demonstrations at the 13th Conference of the European Chapter of the Association for Computational Linguistics*, pages 102–107. Association for Computational Linguistics.

Milan Straka, Jan Hajic, Jana Straková, and Jan Hajic jr. 2015. Parsing universal dependency treebanks using neural networks and search-based oracle. In *International Workshop on Treebanks and Linguistic Theories (TLT14)*, pages 208–220.

Milan Straka and Jana Straková. 2017. Tokenizing, pos tagging, lemmatizing and parsing UD 2.0 with UDPipe. In *Proceedings of the CoNLL 2017 Shared Task: Multilingual Parsing from Raw Text to Universal Dependencies*, pages 88–99, Vancouver, Canada. Association for Computational Linguistics.

Umut Sulubacak, Memduh Gokirmak, Francis Tyers, Çağrı Çöltekin, Joakim Nivre, and Gülşen Eryiğit. 2016. Universal Dependencies for Turkish. In *Proceedings of COLING 2016, the 26th International Conference on Computational Linguistics: Technical Papers*, pages 3444–3454. The COLING 2016 Organizing Committee.

Francis M. Tyers and Jonathan N. Washington. 2015. Towards a free/open-source universal-dependency treebank for kazakh. In *3rd International Conference on Turkic Languages Processing, (TurkLang 2015)*, pages 276–289.

Universal Dependencies contributors. 2018. Universal dependencies. http://universaldependencies.org.

Pilar Valenzuela. 2003. *Transitivity in Shipibo-Konibo Grammar*. Ph.D. thesis, University of Oregon.

Irina Wagner, Andrew Cowell, and Jena D Hwang. 2016. Applying universal dependency to the arapaho language. In *Proceedings of the 10th Linguistic Annotation Workshop held in conjunction with ACL 2016 (LAW-X 2016)*, pages 171–179.

Roberto Zariquiey. 2011. Uchumataqu, the lost language of the Urus of Bolivia: A grammatical description of the language as documented between 1894 and 1952 (hannß). *International Journal of American Linguistics*, 77:316–318.

Roberto Zariquiey. 2015. *Bosquejo gramatical de la lengua iskonawa*. Latinoamericana Editores/ CELACP/ Revista Crítica Literaria Latinoamericana, Lima, Boston.

Daniel Zeman. 2008. Reusable tagset conversion using tagset drivers. In *Proceedings of the Sixth International Conference on Language Resources and Evaluation (LREC'08)*, Marrakech, Morocco. European Language Resources Association (ELRA).

Daniel Zeman and Philip Resnik. 2008. Cross-language parser adaptation between related languages. In *Proceedings of the IJCNLP-08 Workshop on NLP for Less Privileged Languages*.

Arnold M Zwicky. 1977. On clitics. Handout of Indiana University Linguistics Club.

Arnold M Zwicky. 1985. Cilitics and particles. *Working Papers in Linguistics*, 61(2):283–305.

Transition-based Parsing with Lighter Feed-Forward Networks

David Vilares
Universidade da Coruña
FASTPARSE Lab, LyS Group
Departamento de Computación
Campus de Elviña s/n, 15071
A Coruña, Spain
`david.vilares@udc.es`

Carlos Gómez-Rodríguez
Universidade da Coruña
FASTPARSE Lab, LyS Group
Departamento de Computación
Campus de Elviña s/n, 15071
A Coruña, Spain
`carlos.gomez@udc.es`

Abstract

We explore whether it is possible to build lighter parsers, that are statistically equivalent to their corresponding standard version, for a wide set of languages showing different structures and morphologies. As testbed, we use the Universal Dependencies and transition-based dependency parsers trained on feed-forward networks. For these, most existing research assumes *de facto standard* embedded features and relies on pre-computation tricks to obtain speed-ups. We explore how these features and their size can be reduced and whether this translates into speed-ups with a negligible impact on accuracy. The experiments show that *grand-daughter* features can be removed for the majority of treebanks without a significant (negative or positive) LAS difference. They also show how the size of the embeddings can be notably reduced.

1 Introduction

Transition-based models have achieved significant improvements in the last decade (Nivre et al., 2007; Chen and Manning, 2014; Rasooli and Tetreault, 2015; Shi et al., 2017). Some of them already achieve a level of agreement similar to that of experts on English newswire texts (Berzak et al., 2016), although this does not generalize to other configurations (e.g. lower-resource languages). These higher levels of accuracy often come at higher computational costs (Andor et al., 2016) and lower bandwidths, which can be a disadvantage for scenarios where speed is more relevant than accuracy (Gómez-Rodríguez et al., 2017). Furthermore, running neural models on small devices for tasks such as part-of-speech tagging or word segmentation has become a matter of study (Botha et al., 2017), showing that small feed-forward networks are suitable for these challenges. However, for parsers that are trained using

neural networks, little exploration has been done beyond the application of pre-computation tricks, initially intended for fast neural machine translation (Devlin et al., 2014), at a cost of affordable but larger memory.

Contribution We explore efficient and light dependency parsers for languages with a variety of structures and morphologies. We rely on neural feed-forward dependency parsers, since their architecture offers a competitive *accuracy vs bandwidth* ratio and they are also the inspiration for more complex parsers, which also rely on embedded features but previously processed by bidirectional LSTMs (Kiperwasser and Goldberg, 2016). In particular, we study if the *de facto standard* embedded features and their sizes can be reduced without having a significant impact on their accuracy. Building these models is of help in downstream applications of natural language processing, such as those running on small devices and also of interest for syntactic parsing itself, as it makes it possible to explore how the same configuration affects different languages. This study is made on the Universal Dependencies v2.1, a testbed that allows us to compare a variety of languages annotated following common guidelines. This also makes it possible to extract a robust and fair comparative analysis.

2 Related Work

2.1 Computational efficiency

The usefulness of dependency parsing is partially thanks to the efficiency of existing transition-based algorithms, although to the date it is an open question which algorithms suit certain languages better. To predict projective structures, a number of algorithms that run in $\mathcal{O}(n)$ with respect to the length of the input string are available. Broadly speaking, these parsers usually keep two

Proceedings of the Second Workshop on Universal Dependencies (UDW 2018), pages 162–172
Brussels, Belgium, November 1, 2018. ©2018 Association for Computational Linguistics

structures: a stack (containing the words that are waiting for some arcs to be created) and a buffer (containing words awaiting to be processed). The ARC-STANDARD parser (Nivre, 2004) follows a strictly bottom-up strategy, where a word can only be assigned a head (and removed from the stack) once every daughter node has already been processed. The ARC-EAGER parser avoids this restriction by including a specific transition for the reduce action. The ARC-HYBRID algorithm (Kuhlmann et al., 2011) mixes characteristics of both algorithms. More recent algorithms, such as ARC-SWIFT, have focused on the ability to manage *non-local* transitions (Qi and Manning, 2017) to reduce the limitations of transition-based parsers with respect to graph-based ones (McDonald et al., 2005; Dozat and Manning, 2017), that consider a more global context. To manage non-projective structures, there are also different options available. The Covington (2001) algorithm runs in $\mathcal{O}(n^2)$ in the worst case, by comparing the word in the top of the buffer with a subset of the words that have been already processed, deciding whether or not to create a link with each of them. More efficient algorithms such as SWAP (Nivre, 2009) manage non-projectivity by learning when to swap pairs of words that are involved in a crossing arc, transforming it into a projective problem, with expected execution in linear time. The 2-PLANAR algorithm (Gómez-Rodríguez and Nivre, 2010) decomposes trees into at most two planar graphs, which can be used to implement a parser that runs in linear time. The NON-LOCAL COVINGTON algorithm (Fernández-González and Gómez-Rodríguez, 2018) combines the advantages of the wide coverage of the Covington (2001) algorithm with the non-local capabilities of the Qi and Manning (2017) transition system, running in quadratic time in the worst case.

2.2 Fast dependency parsing strategies

Despite the advances in transition-based algorithms, dependency parsing still is the bottleneck for many applications. This is due to collateral issues such as the time it takes to extract features and the multiple calls to the classifier that need to be made. In traditional dependency parsing systems, such as MaltParser (Nivre et al., 2007), the oracles are trained relying on machine learning algorithms, such as support vector machines,

and hand-crafted (Huang et al., 2009; Zhang and Nivre, 2011) or automatically optimized sets of features (Ballesteros and Nivre, 2012). The goal usually is to maximize accuracy, which often comes at a cost of bandwidth. In this sense, efforts were made in order to obtain speed-ups. Using linear classifiers might lead to faster parsers, at a cost of accuracy and larger memory usage (Nivre and Hall, 2010). Bohnet (2010) illustrates that mapping the features into weights for a support vector machine is the major issue for the execution time and introduces a hash kernel approach to mitigate it. Volokh (2013) made efforts on optimizing the feature extraction time for the Covington (2001) algorithm, defining the concept of *static features*, which can be reused through different configuration steps. The concept itself does not imply a reduction in terms of efficiency, but it is often employed in conjunction with the reduction of *non-static features*, which causes a drop in accuracy.

In more modern parsers, the oracles are trained using feed-forward networks (Titov and Henderson, 2007; Chen and Manning, 2014; Straka et al., 2015) and sequential models (Kiperwasser and Goldberg, 2016). In this sense, to obtain significant speed improvements it is common to use the pre-computation trick from Devlin et al. (2014), initially intended for machine translation. Broadly speaking, they precompute the output of the hidden layer for each individual feature and each position in the input vector where they might occur, saving computation time during the test phase, with an affordable memory cost. Vacariu (2017) proposes an optimized parser and also includes a brief evaluation about reducing features that have a high cost of extraction, but the analysis is limited to English and three treebanks. However, little analysis has been made on determining if these features are relevant across a wide variety of languages that show different particularities. Our work is also in line with this line of research. In particular, we focus on feed-forward transition-based parsers, which already offer a very competitive accuracy vs bandwidth ratio. The models used in this work do not use any pre-computation trick, but it is worth pointing out that the insights of this paper could be used in conjunction with it, to obtain further bandwidth improvements.

3 Motivation

Transition-based dependency parsers whose oracles are trained using feed-forward neural networks have adopted as the *de facto standard* set of features the one proposed by Chen and Manning (2014) to parse the English and Chinese Penn Treebanks (Marcus et al., 1993; Xue et al., 2005).

We hypothesize this *de facto standard* set of features and the size of the embeddings used to represent them can be reduced for a wide variety of languages, obtaining significant speed-ups at a cost of a marginal impact on their performance. To test this hypothesis, we are performing an evaluation over the Universal Dependencies v2.1 (Nivre et al., 2017) a wide multilingual testbed to approximate relevant features over a wide variety of languages from different families.

4 Methods and Materials

This section describes the parsing algorithms (§4.1), the architecture of the feed-forward network (§4.2) and the treebanks (§4.3).

4.1 Transition-based algorithms

Let $w = [w_1, w_2, ..., w_{|w|}]$ be an input sentence, a *dependency tree* for w is an edge-labeled directed tree $T = (V, A)$ where $V = \{0, 1, 2, ..., |w|\}$ is the set of nodes and $A = V \times D \times V$ is the set of labeled arcs. Each arc $a \in A$, of the form (i, d, j), corresponds to a syntactic *dependency* between the words w_i and w_j; where i is the index of the *head* word, j is the index of the *child* word and d is the *dependency type* representing the kind of syntactic relation between them. Each transition configuration is represented as a 3-tuple $c = (\sigma, \beta, A)$ where:

- σ is a stack that contains the words that are awaiting for remaining arcs to be created. In $\sigma|i$, i represents the first word of the stack.

- β is a buffer structure containing the words that still have not been processed (awaiting to be moved to σ. In $i|\beta$, i denotes the first word of the buffer.

- A is the set of arcs that have been created.

We rely on two transition-based algorithms: the stack-based ARC-STANDARD (Nivre, 2008) algorithm for projective parsing and its corresponding version with the SWAP operation (Nivre, 2009)

to manage non-projective structures. The election of the algorithms is based on their computational complexity as both run in $\mathcal{O}(n)$ empirically. The set of transitions is shown in Table 1. Let $c_i = ([0], \beta, \{\})$ be an initial configuration, the parser will apply transitions until a final configuration $c_f = ([0], [], A)$ is reached.

Transition		Step t	Step *t+1*
STANDARD	LEFT-ARC$_l$	$(\sigma|i|j, \beta, A)$	$(\sigma|j, \beta, A \cup (j, l, i))$
(projective)	RIGHT-ARC$_l$	$(\sigma|i|j, \beta, A)$	$(\sigma|i, \beta, A \cup (i, l, j))$
	SHIFT	$(\sigma, i|\beta, A)$	$(\sigma|i, \beta, A)$
SWAP	SWAP	$(\sigma|i|j, \beta, A)$	$(\sigma|j, i|\beta, A)$
(above +)			

Table 1: Transitions for the projective version of the stack-based ARC-STANDARD algorithm and its non-projective version including the SWAP operation

4.2 Feed-forward neural network

We reproduce the Chen and Manning (2014) architecture and more in particular the Straka et al. (2015) version. These two parsers report the fastest architectures for transition-based dependency parsing (using the pre-computation trick from Devlin et al. (2014)), and obtain results close to the state of the art. Let $\text{MLP}_\theta(\mathbf{v})$ be an abstraction of our multilayered perceptron parametrized by θ, the output for an input $\mathbf{v}$ (in this paper, a concatenation of embeddings, as described in §5) is computed as:

$$\text{MLP}_\theta(\mathbf{v}) = softmax(\mathbf{W_2} \cdot relu(\mathbf{W_1} \cdot \mathbf{v} + \mathbf{b_1}) + \mathbf{b_2}) \tag{1}$$

where $\mathbf{W_i}$ and $\mathbf{b_i}$ are the weights and bias tensors to be learned at the ith layer and *softmax* and *relu* correspond to the activation functions in their standard form.

4.3 Universal Dependencies v2.1

Universal dependencies (UD) v2.1 (Nivre et al., 2017) is a set of 101 dependency treebanks for up to 60 different languages. They are labeled in the CoNLLU format, heavily inspired in the CoNLL format (Buchholz and Marsi, 2006). For each word in a sentence there is available the following information: ID, WORD, LEMMA, UPOSTAG (universal postag, available for all languages), XPOSTAG (language-specific postag, available for some languages), FEATS (additional morphosyntactic information, available for some languages), HEAD, DEPREL and other optional columns with additional information.

In this paper, we are only considering experiments on the *unsuffixed* treebanks (where UD_English is an unsuffixed treebank and UD_English-PUD is a suffixed treebank). The motivation owes to practical issues and legibility of tables and discussions.

5 Experiments

We followed the training configuration proposed by Straka et al. (2015). All models where trained using mini-batches (size=10) and stochastic gradient descent (SGD) with exponential decay ($lr = 0.02$, decay computed as $lr \times e^{-0.2 \times epoch}$). Dropout was set to 50%. With our implementation dropout was observed to work better than regularization with less effort in terms of tuning. We used internal embeddings, initialized according to a Glorot uniform (Glorot and Bengio, 2010), which are learned together with the oracle during the training phase. In the experiments we use no external embeddings, following the same criteria as Straka et al. (2015). The aim was to evaluate all parsers under a homogeneous configuration, and high-quality external embeddings may be difficult to obtain for some languages.

The experiments explore two paths: (1) is it possible to reduce the number of features without a significant loss in terms of accuracy? and (2) is it possible to reduce the size of the embeddings representing those features, also without causing significant loss in terms of accuracy? To evaluate this, we used as baseline the following configuration.

5.1 Baseline configuration

This configuration reproduces that of Straka et al. (2015) which is basically a version of the Chen and Manning (2014) parser whose features were specifically adapted to the UD treebanks:

De facto standard features The initial set of features, which we call the *de facto standard* features, is composed of: FORM, UPOSTAG and FEATS for the first 3 words in β and the first 3 words of σ. The FORM, UPOSTAG, FEATS and DE-PREL[1] for the 2 leftmost and rightmost children of the first 2 words in σ. And the FORM, UPOSTAG, FEATS and DEPREL of the leftmost of the leftmost and rightmost of the rightmost children of the first 2 words in σ. This makes a total of 18 elements

and 66 different features. In the case of UD treebanks, it is worth noting that for some languages the FEATS features are not available. We thought of two strategies in this situation: (1) not to consider any FEATS vector as input or (2) assume that a dummy input vector is given to represent the FEATS of an element of the tree. The former would be more realistic in a real environment, but we believe the latter offers a fairer comparison of speeds and memory costs, as the input vector is homogeneous across all languages. Thus, this is the option we have implemented. The dummy vector is expected to be given no relevance by the neural network during the training phase. We also rely on gold UPOSTAGS and FEATS to measure the impact of the reduced features and their reduced size in an isolated environment.[2]

Size of the embeddings The embedding size for the FORM features is set to 50 and for the UP-OSTAG, FEATS and DEPREL features it is set to 20. Given an input configuration, the final dimension of the input vector is 1860: 540 dimensions from directly accessible nodes in σ and β, 880 dimensions corresponding to daughter nodes and 440 dimensions corresponding to grand-daughter nodes.

Metrics We use LAS (Labeled Attachment Score) to measure the performance. To determine whether the gain or loss with respect to the *de facto standard* features is significant or not, we used Bikel's randomized parsing evaluation comparator ($p < 0.05$), a stratified shuffling significance test. The null hypothesis is that the two outputs are produced by equivalent models and so the scores are equally likely. To refute it, it first measures the difference obtained for a metric by the two models. Then, it shuffles scores of individual sentences between the two models and recomputes the evaluation metrics, measuring if the new difference is smaller than the original one, which is an indicator that the outputs are significantly different. *Thousands of tokens parsed per second* is the metric used to compare the speed between different feature sets. To diminish the impact of running time outliers, this is averaged across five runs.

Hardware All models were run on the test set on a single thread on a Intel(R) Core(TM) i7-7700 CPU @ 3.60GHz.

---

[1] Once it has been assigned

[2] The use of predicted PoS-tags and/or tokenization would make harder to measure which is the actual impact of using different features and size of embeddings.

No precomputation trick All the parsers proposed in this work do not use the precomputation trick from Devlin et al. (2014). There is no major reason for this, beyond measuring the impact of the strategies in a simple scenario. We would like to remark that the speed-ups obtained here by reducing the number of features could also be applied to the parsers implementing this precomputation trick, in the sense that the feature extraction time is lower. No time will be further gained in terms of computation of the hidden activation values. However, in this context, at least in the case of the Chen and Manning (2014) parser, the pre-computation trick is only applied to the 10 000 most common words. The experiments here proposed are also useful to save memory resources, even if the trick is used.

5.2 Reducing the number of features

Table 2 shows the impact of ignoring features that have a larger cost of extraction, i.e., daughter and grand-daughter nodes, for both the ARC-STANDARD and SWAP algorithms. It compares three sets of features in terms of performance and speed: (1) *de facto standard* features, (2) *no grand-daughter* (NO-GD) features (excluding every leftmost of leftmost and rightmost of rightmost feature) and (3) *no daughter* (NO-GD/D) features (excluding every daughter and grand-daughter feature from nodes of σ).

Impact of using the NO-GD feature set The results show that these features can be removed without causing a significant difference in most of the cases. In the case of the ARC-STANDARD algorithm, for 47 out of 52 treebanks there is no significant accuracy loss with respect to the *de facto standard* features. In fact, for 22 treebanks there was a gain with respect to the original set of features, from which 5 of them were statistically significant. With respect to SWAP, we observe similar tendencies. For 38 out of 52 treebanks there is no loss (or the loss is again not statistically significant). There is however a larger number of differences that are statistically significant, both gains (11) and losses (13). On average, the ARC-STANDARD models trained with these features lost 0.1 LAS points with respect to the original models, while the average speed-up was ~23%. The models trained with SWAP gained instead 0.15 points and the bandwidth increased by ~28%.

Impact of the NO-GD/D features As expected, the results show that removing *daughter* features in conjunction with *grand-daughter* causes a big drop in performance for the vast majority of cases (most of them statistically significant). Due to this issue and despite the (also expected) larger speed-ups, we are not considering this set of features for the next section.

5.3 Reducing the embedding size of the selected features

We now explore whether by reducing the size of the embeddings for the FORM, POSTAG, FEATS and DEPREL features the models can produce better bandwidths without suffering a lack of accuracy. We run separate experiments for the ARC-STANDARD and SWAP algorithms, using as the starting point the NO-GD feature set, which had a negligible impact on accuracy, as tested in Table 2. Table 3 summarizes the experiments when reducing the size of each embedding from 10% to 50%, at a step size of 10 percentage points, for the ARC-STANDARD. The results include information indicating whether the difference in performance is statistically significant from that obtained by the *de facto* standard set. In general terms, reducing the size of the embeddings causes a small but constant drop in the performance. However, for the vast majority of languages this drop is not statistically significant. Reducing the size of the embeddings by a factor of 0.2 was the configuration with the minimum number of significant losses (6), and reducing them by a factor of 0.5 the one with the largest (14). On average, the lightest models lost 0.45 LAS points to obtain an speed-up of ~40%. Similar tendencies were observed in the case of the non-projective algorithm, whose results reducing the size of the embeddings by a factor of 0.1 and 0.5 can be found in Table 4.

5.4 Discussion

Different deep learning frameworks to build neural networks might present differences and implementation details that might cause the speed obtained empirically to differ from theoretical expectations.

From a theoretical point of view, both tested approaches (§5.2, 5.3) should have a similar impact, as their use directly affects the size of the input to the neural network. The smaller the input size, the lighter and faster parsers are obtained. As a side note, with respect to the case of reducing the

Treebank	ARC-STANDARD						SWAP					
	STANDARD		NO-GD/D		NO-GD		STANDARD		NO-GD/D		NO-GD	
	LAS	kt/s	LAS	kt/s	LAS	kt/s	LAS	kt/s	LAS	kt/s	LAS	kt/s
Afrikaans	82.72	3.3	71.67[--]	8.4	82.42[-]	4.0	82.55	3.0	70.59[--]	7.7	82.96[+]	3.8
Anc Greek	56.85	3.5	50.27[--]	8.9	56.63[-]	4.3	58.97	2.9	51.36[--]	7.8	58.48[-]	3.8
Arabic	77.46	3.1	70.69[--]	7.7	77.87[+]	3.7	76.77	3.0	70.4[--]	7.4	77.5[++]	3.7
Basque	74.26	3.6	68.13[--]	9.0	74.05[-]	4.4	73.98	3.2	67.31[--]	8.4	72.44	3.8
Belarusian	70.12	2.4	61.43[--]	5.8	67.73[-]	2.9	69.75	2.4	62.81[--]	5.6	70.33[+]	2.9
Bulgarian	88.42	3.4	77.88[--]	8.4	88.24[-]	4.1	87.95	3.2	77.41[--]	8.2	87.98[+]	4.2
Catalan	87.57	3.4	76.79[--]	8.9	87.5[-]	4.2	87.01	3.1	76.48[--]	8.4	87.06[+]	3.9
Chinese	79.23	3.2	64.66[--]	8.3	79.2[-]	4.0	78.26	3.2	62.74[--]	8.0	78.8[+]	4.0
Coptic	78.68	1.9	71.32[--]	4.9	76.0[--]	2.3	77.25	1.3	70.08[--]	3.1	77.44[+]	1.5
Croatian	81.23	3.2	72.11[--]	7.8	81.4[+]	3.8	80.63	3.0	70.54[--]	7.6	81.39[++]	3.6
Czech	85.74	3.5	78.1[--]	8.3	86.09[++]	4.2	85.55	3.4	77.9[--]	7.9	85.42[-]	4.2
Danish	80.93	3.1	70.54[--]	7.3	81.28[+]	3.7	79.79	2.9	65.4[--]	7.1	79.55[-]	3.6
Dutch	78.67	3.3	66.82[--]	8.4	79.41[+]	4.1	77.02	3.1	64.83[--]	7.8	78.15[++]	3.8
English	84.16	3.6	72.68[--]	8.8	84.42[+]	4.4	83.19	3.6	72.76[--]	8.7	84.09[++]	4.4
Estonian	81.57	3.1	72.63[--]	7.6	81.74[+]	3.8	80.65	2.9	72.68[--]	6.6	81.06[+]	3.7
Finnish	81.25	3.3	69.08[--]	8.0	82.08[++]	4.1	81.47	3.3	69.36[--]	7.8	80.4	3.9
French	84.65	3.0	73.15[--]	7.2	84.83[+]	3.5	83.54	2.7	72.31[--]	6.8	83.27[-]	3.5
Galician	80.51	3.5	68.82[--]	8.5	80.29[-]	4.2	79.85	3.3	69.25[--]	8.3	80.01[+]	4.2
German	79.86	3.3	72.3[--]	8.1	79.67[-]	4.1	78.52	3.1	70.69[--]	8.2	77.65[--]	3.4
Gothic	74.57	3.2	66.19[--]	8.0	74.18[-]	3.8	72.92	2.7	65.92[--]	7.6	73.19[+]	3.4
Greek	84.71	3.1	77.53[--]	7.8	85.07[+]	3.7	84.13	3.0	76.54[--]	7.5	84.21[+]	3.8
Hebrew	82.16	3.2	67.9[--]	7.9	82.63[+]	3.8	81.87	3.1	68.77[--]	7.6	82.06[+]	4.0
Hindi	90.8	3.5	81.8[--]	8.8	90.69[-]	4.3	90.46	3.2	80.5[--]	8.3	90.01[--]	4.0
Hungarian	73.34	3.1	66.39[--]	7.0	73.14[-]	3.5	72.33	2.9	66.88[--]	6.8	73.36[++]	3.1
Indonesian	79.47	2.9	62.58[--]	7.3	79.3[-]	3.5	78.86	2.8	63.62[--]	7.1	79.07[+]	3.5
Irish	60.07	2.8	52.66[--]	7.4	59.94[-]	3.5	61.82	2.8	54.28[--]	7.0	60.3[--]	3.4
Italian	89.21	2.9	78.16[--]	7.2	89.33[+]	3.3	88.34	2.9	78.13[--]	7.0	88.81[++]	3.6
Japanese	92.16	3.3	74.2[--]	8.6	92.19[+]	4.1	91.95	3.3	74.09[--]	9.0	91.91[-]	4.2
Kazakh	22.78	3.4	16.1[--]	8.9	27.41[++]	4.3	29.32	3.4	20.47[--]	8.7	33.0[++]	4.1
Korean	60.84	3.5	46.27[--]	8.9	60.13[-]	4.4	60.46	3.5	47.63[--]	8.8	57.98[--]	4.3
Latin	43.31	3.3	41.33[--]	7.8	44.16[++]	3.9	47.11	2.6	45.33[--]	7.1	46.54[-]	3.4
Latvian	75.14	3.4	64.88[--]	8.3	75.36[+]	4.1	74.73	3.3	65.11[--]	8.1	75.55[++]	4.1
Lithuanian	42.74	1.5	40.75[-]	3.5	42.64[-]	1.8	46.79	1.4	38.21[--]	3.4	43.4[--]	1.8
Marathi	66.02	1.7	61.89[--]	4.4	62.14[--]	2.1	65.05	1.7	59.95[--]	4.2	66.26[+]	2.2
Old Church Slavonic	78.33	3.3	71.07[--]	8.4	78.97[++]	4.1	79.48	3.0	69.65[--]	8.3	79.76[+]	3.8
Persian	82.1	3.1	66.16[--]	7.6	81.1[--]	3.8	80.79	3.0	65.35[--]	7.3	81.08[+]	3.8
Polish	90.92	3.5	83.03[--]	8.8	90.9[-]	4.3	90.49	3.5	83.46[--]	8.7	90.29[-]	4.4
Portuguese	86.27	3.1	74.09[--]	8.3	86.58[+]	4.0	83.87	2.7	71.84[--]	7.0	85.23[++]	3.6
Romanian	82.12	3.3	68.89[--]	8.2	81.73[-]	4.1	80.92	3.3	68.82[--]	7.9	81.05[+]	4.1
Russian	79.47	3.0	70.0[--]	7.5	79.14[-]	3.7	78.55	2.9	68.63[--]	7.4	77.62[--]	3.7
Serbian	84.9	3.3	76.57[--]	8.4	85.17[+]	4.0	85.8	3.2	76.04[--]	7.7	85.64[-]	4.0
Slovak	85.54	3.2	76.44[--]	7.8	85.45[-]	4.0	84.96	3.2	77.72[--]	8.2	84.25[--]	3.9
Slovenian	88.73	3.2	78.06[--]	7.3	88.74[+]	3.8	89.35	3.0	77.67[--]	7.1	88.31[--]	3.7
Spanish	85.16	2.8	71.78[--]	6.7	83.75[--]	3.5	84.32	2.7	71.78[--]	7.2	82.96[--]	3.5
Swedish	83.73	3.4	71.21[--]	8.6	83.63[-]	4.2	84.37	3.4	69.96[--]	8.5	83.78[--]	4.3
(Sw) Sign Language	23.4	1.1	25.53[+]	2.5	22.7[-]	1.3	10.64	0.9	23.05[++]	2.4	21.99[++]	1.2
Tamil	69.18	2.0	66.47[--]	4.8	69.58[+]	2.4	71.04	1.7	67.77[--]	4.7	71.09[+]	2.4
Telugu	75.17	1.5	74.76[-]	3.1	74.48[-]	1.6	74.2	1.4	75.45[+]	3.0	75.03[++]	1.6
Turkish	59.51	3.2	53.47[--]	7.4	59.29[-]	3.9	60.32	3.0	53.14[--]	7.7	59.35[-]	3.8
Ukrainian	81.29	3.2	71.95[--]	7.9	81.71[+]	3.8	81.8	3.0	69.82[--]	7.6	81.19[--]	3.9
Urdu	83.12	3.3	71.84[--]	8.5	83.03[-]	4.1	81.29	2.9	69.42[--]	7.9	80.93[-]	3.4
Vietnamese	64.73	3.4	54.71[--]	9.0	64.39[-]	4.3	64.35	3.5	55.51[--]	8.8	63.71[-]	4.3
AVERAGE	75.67	3.0	66.42	7.5	75.57	3.7	75.29	2.8	66.07	7.2	75.44	3.6

Table 2: Performance for the (1) de facto standard, (2) NO-GD/D and (3) NO-GD set of features, when used to train oracles with the ARC-STANDARD and SWAP algorithms. Red cells indicate a significant loss (--) with respect to the baseline, the yellow ones a non-significant gain(+)/loss (-) and the green ones a significant gain (++).

| | STANDARD | | ARC-STANDARD NO GD | | | | | | | | |
| | | | size -10% | | size -20% | | size -30% | | size -40% | | size -50% | |
Treebank	LAS	kt/s	LAS	kt/s	LAS	kt/s	LAS	kt/s	LAS	kt/s	LAS	kt/s
Afrikaans	82.72	3.3	82.66[-]	4.1	82.64[-]	4.4	82.72	4.3	82.5[-]	4.6	83.11[+]	4.5
Anc Greek	56.85	3.5	57.03[+]	4.4	56.52[-]	4.6	56.56[-]	4.6	56.24[--]	4.8	56.87[+]	4.8
Arabic	77.46	3.1	77.24[--]	3.8	76.55[--]	4.0	77.97[++]	4.0	77.18[-]	4.2	77.41[-]	4.7
Basque	74.26	3.6	74.78[++]	4.5	74.05[-]	4.7	74.12[-]	4.7	73.8[-]	4.9	74.21[-]	4.9
Belarusian	70.12	2.4	68.67[-]	2.9	68.74[-]	3.0	68.02[--]	3.0	69.18[-]	3.1	66.86[--]	3.3
Bulgarian	88.42	3.4	87.62[--]	4.2	87.95[-]	4.5	87.58[--]	4.4	87.9[--]	4.6	87.53[--]	4.6
Catalan	87.57	3.4	86.77[--]	4.3	87.63[+]	4.7	87.22[--]	4.6	87.28[--]	4.8	87.35[--]	4.7
Chinese	79.23	3.2	79.0[-]	4.1	79.31[+]	4.3	79.15[-]	4.3	79.13[-]	4.5	78.8[-]	4.4
Coptic	78.68	1.9	76.58[-]	2.4	78.68[+]	2.5	79.73[+]	2.5	77.25[-]	2.6	75.62[--]	2.5
Croatian	81.23	3.2	80.76[-]	3.9	81.44[+]	4.1	81.2[-]	4.0	81.58[+]	4.2	80.5[--]	4.3
Czech	85.74	3.5	85.98[++]	4.3	85.88[++]	4.5	86.01[++]	4.4	86.02[++]	4.6	85.39[--]	4.9
Danish	80.93	3.1	81.02[+]	3.8	80.68[-]	4.0	80.61[--]	4.0	80.83[-]	4.2	80.81[-]	4.4
Dutch	78.67	3.3	78.63[-]	4.2	78.63[-]	4.4	78.87[+]	4.4	78.13[-]	4.6	79.36[++]	4.6
English	84.16	3.6	84.09[-]	4.5	83.91[-]	4.7	84.49[+]	4.7	84.35[+]	4.9	83.78[-]	4.5
Estonian	81.57	3.1	82.2[+]	3.9	81.55[-]	4.0	81.9[+]	4.0	81.05[-]	4.2	81.48[-]	4.5
Finnish	81.25	3.3	81.37[+]	4.2	81.8[+]	4.4	81.52[+]	4.3	81.71[+]	4.5	81.03[-]	4.6
French	84.65	3.0	84.88[+]	3.6	85.18[+]	3.8	84.74[+]	3.8	84.51[-]	3.9	85.19[+]	4.3
Galician	80.51	3.5	79.67[--]	4.3	80.24[-]	4.5	79.88[--]	4.4	80.36[-]	4.7	80.59[+]	4.8
German	79.86	3.3	79.0[--]	4.2	79.54[-]	4.4	79.65[-]	4.4	79.54[-]	4.6	79.38[-]	4.4
Gothic	74.57	3.2	74.77[+]	3.9	74.63[+]	4.2	73.75[--]	4.1	73.96[--]	4.3	73.93[-]	4.5
Greek	84.71	3.1	84.87[+]	3.7	84.45[-]	4.0	84.61[-]	3.9	84.18[--]	4.1	85.21[+]	4.5
Hebrew	82.16	3.2	81.94[-]	3.8	82.13[-]	4.1	81.83[-]	4.0	81.42[-]	4.2	81.67[-]	4.4
Hindi	90.8	3.5	90.92[+]	4.4	90.66[-]	4.7	90.46[--]	4.6	90.73[-]	4.8	90.42[--]	4.8
Hungarian	73.34	3.1	72.78[-]	3.5	73.02[-]	3.7	72.73[-]	3.7	72.6[-]	3.9	72.85[-]	4.2
Indonesian	79.47	2.9	78.81[--]	3.5	79.07[-]	3.7	79.23[-]	3.7	79.31[-]	3.9	79.1[--]	4.0
Irish	60.07	2.8	59.17[--]	3.5	59.72[-]	3.7	57.94[--]	3.7	58.6[--]	3.9	57.55[--]	3.8
Italian	89.21	2.9	89.34[+]	3.3	89.16[-]	3.5	88.33[--]	3.5	89.16[-]	3.6	89.57[+]	3.8
Japanese	92.16	3.3	92.14[-]	4.3	91.95[-]	4.4	91.97[-]	4.4	92.27[+]	4.6	91.86[-]	4.7
Kazakh	22.78	3.4	26.79[++]	4.5	24.82[++]	4.8	24.22[++]	4.7	20.17[--]	4.9	23.64[++]	4.7
Korean	60.84	3.5	58.97[--]	4.5	58.8[--]	4.6	59.89[-]	4.7	59.85[--]	4.8	59.37[--]	4.9
Latin	43.31	3.3	43.59[++]	4.0	43.45[++]	4.2	42.19[--]	4.2	43.84[+]	4.4	40.22[--]	4.5
Latvian	75.14	3.4	75.83[++]	4.2	75.23[+]	4.5	75.26[+]	4.4	74.85[-]	4.7	75.1[-]	4.6
Lithuanian	42.74	1.5	44.06[+]	1.8	44.43[+]	1.9	40.75[-]	1.8	41.98[-]	1.9	40.94[-]	2.0
Marathi	66.02	1.7	64.32[-]	2.2	65.53[-]	2.3	64.81[-]	2.3	62.86[-]	2.3	63.11[-]	2.4
Old Church Slavonic	78.33	3.3	78.86[+]	4.2	79.01[++]	4.5	78.81[++]	4.4	78.55[+]	4.6	78.86[++]	4.5
Persian	82.1	3.1	81.95[-]	3.9	82.23[+]	4.1	82.3[+]	4.1	82.12[+]	4.2	82.63[+]	4.3
Polish	90.92	3.5	90.87[-]	4.4	90.34[--]	4.7	90.65[-]	4.7	90.44[-]	4.9	90.02[--]	4.7
Portuguese	86.27	3.1	86.47[+]	4.0	86.5[+]	4.3	86.72[+]	4.2	86.02[-]	4.5	86.53[+]	4.2
Romanian	82.12	3.3	81.71[-]	4.2	80.47[--]	4.3	81.28[--]	4.4	81.13[--]	4.5	81.55[-]	4.6
Russian	79.47	3.0	79.49[+]	3.7	79.28[-]	3.9	79.1[-]	3.9	79.4[-]	4.0	79.21[-]	4.0
Serbian	84.9	3.3	85.15[+]	4.1	85.81[++]	4.4	85.16[+]	4.3	85.02[+]	4.5	85.71[++]	4.4
Slovak	85.54	3.2	85.07[--]	4.1	85.52[-]	4.4	85.02[-]	4.3	84.49[--]	4.5	85.06[--]	4.5
Slovenian	88.73	3.2	88.6[-]	3.9	88.63[-]	4.1	88.59[-]	4.0	88.46[-]	4.2	88.43[-]	4.4
Spanish	85.16	2.8	85.1[-]	3.6	84.58[--]	3.8	84.63[-]	3.7	84.47[--]	3.9	84.93[-]	4.1
Swedish	83.73	3.4	84.22[++]	4.3	83.91[+]	4.6	84.0[+]	4.5	82.73[--]	4.8	83.51[-]	4.6
(Sw) Sign Language	23.4	1.1	24.47[+]	1.4	27.3[+]	1.4	24.82[+]	1.4	24.11[+]	1.5	22.7[-]	1.4
Tamil	69.18	2.0	69.83[+]	2.4	69.28[+]	2.5	68.58[-]	2.5	70.04[+]	2.6	70.14[++]	2.7
Telugu	75.17	1.5	75.73[+]	1.7	75.73[+]	1.7	74.48[-]	1.7	73.65[-]	1.7	74.06[-]	1.9
Turkish	59.51	3.2	60.49[++]	4.0	59.74[+]	4.1	59.53[+]	4.0	59.6[+]	4.3	59.64[+]	4.5
Ukrainian	81.29	3.2	82.05[++]	3.9	81.61[+]	4.1	81.79[+]	4.0	82.08[++]	4.2	81.46[+]	4.2
Urdu	83.12	3.3	83.79[++]	4.1	83.41[+]	4.4	83.65[++]	4.3	83.68[++]	4.6	83.48[+]	4.5
Vietnamese	64.73	3.4	63.73[--]	4.4	63.5[--]	4.7	64.32[-]	4.6	64.7[-]	4.9	63.96[--]	4.8
AVERAGE	75.67	3.0	75.65	3.8	75.67	3.9	75.45	3.9	75.29	4.1	75.22	4.2

Table 3: ARC-STANDARD baseline configuration versus different runs with the NO-GD feature set and embedding size reduction from 10% to 50%. See Table 2 for color scheme definition.

| | STANDARD | | NO-GD | | | | | STANDARD | | NO-GD | | | |
| | | | size -10% | | size -50% | | | | | size -10% | | size -50% | |
Treebank	LAS	kt/s	LAS	kt/s	LAS	kt/s	Treebank	LAS	kt/s	LAS	kt/s	LAS	kt/s
Afrikaans	82.55	3.0	83.19[+]	3.9	80.55[--]	4.2	Anc Greek	58.97	2.9	59.04[+]	3.6	60.3[++]	3.8
Arabic	76.77	3.0	76.8[+]	3.8	76.71[-]	4.1	Basque	73.98	3.2	73.74[-]	4.2	72.48[--]	4.3
Belarusian	69.75	2.4	69.54[-]	2.9	68.52[-]	3.2	Bulgarian	87.95	3.2	87.06[--]	4.2	87.73[-]	4.9
Catalan	87.01	3.1	87.16[+]	3.9	86.8[-]	4.6	Chinese	78.26	3.2	79.76[++]	4.1	78.19[-]	4.6
Coptic	77.25	1.3	78.01[+]	1.7	76.29[-]	1.5	Croatian	80.63	3.0	81.28[+]	4.0	81.37[++]	4.1
Czech	85.55	3.4	83.49[--]	4.3	84.97[--]	4.7	Danish	79.79	2.9	78.79[--]	3.7	78.55[--]	4.0
Dutch	77.02	3.1	77.93[+]	3.9	77.53[+]	4.3	English	83.19	3.6	83.61[+]	4.5	83.92[++]	4.9
Estonian	80.65	2.9	80.01[-]	3.7	80.72[+]	4.1	Finnish	81.47	3.3	80.98[--]	4.1	81.25[-]	4.4
French	83.54	2.7	82.53[--]	3.5	83.78[+]	3.9	Galician	79.85	3.3	80.44[++]	4.4	80.01[+]	4.8
German	78.52	3.1	77.53[--]	3.5	77.6[--]	4.2	Gothic	72.92	2.7	72.96[+]	3.5	71.43[--]	3.8
Greek	84.13	3.0	83.91[-]	3.9	84.11[-]	4.4	Hebrew	81.87	3.1	82.07[+]	4.0	82.41[+]	4.5
Hindi	90.46	3.2	89.86[--]	4.0	89.58[--]	4.4	Hungarian	72.33	2.9	73.77[++]	3.7	72.8[+]	3.3
Indonesian	78.86	2.8	79.0[+]	3.6	79.19[+]	3.9	Irish	61.82	2.8	60.67[--]	3.5	60.88[--]	3.9
Italian	88.34	2.9	88.39[+]	3.4	88.51[+]	4.0	Japanese	91.95	3.3	92.02[+]	4.3	91.91[-]	4.7
Kazakh	29.32	3.4	29.64[++]	4.3	29.77[+]	4.8	Korean	60.46	3.5	59.66[--]	4.4	58.75[--]	5.1
Latin	47.11	2.6	45.05[--]	3.3	44.3[--]	3.6	Latvian	74.73	3.3	75.05[+]	4.2	75.05[+]	4.8
Lithuanian	46.79	1.4	44.72[-]	1.8	44.91[-]	1.9	Marathi	65.05	1.7	64.81[-]	2.2	65.53[+]	2.4
Old Church Slavonic	79.48	3.0	80.07[+]	3.9	77.62[--]	4.4	Persian	80.79	3.0	81.54[+]	3.7	80.84[+]	4.3
Polish	90.49	3.5	90.49	4.4	90.17[-]	4.9	Portuguese	83.87	2.7	83.09[-]	2.9	84.41[+]	3.6
Romanian	80.92	3.3	80.08[--]	4.1	80.1[--]	4.5	Russian	78.55	2.9	77.78[--]	3.7	77.75[--]	4.1
Serbian	85.8	3.2	85.02[--]	4.1	85.24[-]	4.5	Slovak	84.96	3.2	85.25[+]	3.9	84.27[--]	4.4
Slovenian	89.35	3.0	88.85[--]	3.6	88.88[--]	4.2	Spanish	84.32	2.7	83.84[-]	3.6	83.28[--]	3.7
Swedish	84.37	3.4	82.8[--]	4.3	83.72[--]	4.8	(Sw) Sign Language	10.64	0.9	21.28[++]	1.2	17.73[++]	1.2
Tamil	71.04	1.7	70.54[-]	3.2	70.79[-]	2.6	Telugu	74.2	1.4	75.17[++]	1.7	73.79[-]	1.7
Turkish	60.32	3.0	59.71[-]	3.9	58.45[--]	4.3	Ukrainian	81.8	3.0	80.66[--]	4.0	80.86[--]	4.4
Urdu	81.29	2.9	81.42[+]	3.7	82.3[++]	4.0	Vietnamese	64.35	3.5	64.32[-]	4.4	64.67[+]	5.0

Table 4: SWAP baseline configuration versus different runs with the NO-GD feature set and embedding size reduction by a factor of 0.1 and 0.5. The average LAS/speed for the baseline is 75.29/2.8, for the NO-GD feature set with embedding reduction by a factor of 0.1 is 75.27/3.6, and with embedding reduction by a factor of 0.5 75.02/4.0. See Table 2 for color scheme definition.

number of features (§5.2), an additional speed improvement is expected, as less features need to be collected. But broadly speaking, the speed obtained by skipping half of the features should be in line with that obtained by reducing the size of the embeddings of the original features by a factor of 0.5.

For a practical point of view, in this work we relied on `keras` (Chollet et al., 2015). With respect to the part reported in §5.2, the experiments went as expected. Taking as examples the results for the ARC-STANDARD algorithm, using no *grand-daughter* features implies to diminish the dimension of the input vector from 1860 dimensions to 1420, a reduction of ∼23%. The average thousands of tokens parsed per second of the *de facto standard* features was 3.0 and the average obtained without *grand-daughter* features was 3.7, a gain of ∼20%. If we also skip *daughter* features and reduce the size of the input vector by ∼71%, the speed increased by a factor of 2.5. Similar tendencies were observed with respect to the SWAP algorithm. When reducing the size of the embeddings (§5.3), the obtained speed-ups were however lower than those expected in theory. In this sense, an alternative implementation or a use of a differ-

ent framework could lead to reduce these times to values closer to the theoretical expectation.

Trying other neural architectures is also of high interest, but this is left as an open question for future research. In particular, in the popular BIST-based parsers (Kiperwasser and Goldberg, 2016; de Lhoneux et al., 2017; Vilares and Gómez-Rodríguez, 2017), the input is first processed by a bidirectional LSTM (Hochreiter and Schmidhuber, 1997) that computes an embedding for each token, taking into account its left and right context. These embeddings are then used to extract the features for transition-based algorithms, including the head of different elements and their leftmost/rightmost children. Those features are then fed to a feed-forward network, similar to the one evaluated in this work. Thus, the results of this work might be of future interest for this type of parsers too, as the output of the LSTM can be seen as improved and better contextualized word embeddings.

6 Conclusion

We explored whether it is possible to reduce the number and size of embedded features assumed as *de facto standard* by feed-forward network transition-based dependency parsers. The aim was to train efficient and light parsers for a vast amount of languages showing a rich variety of structures and morphologies.

To test the hypothesis we used a multilingual testbed: the Universal Dependencies v2.1. The study considered two transition-based algorithms to train the oracles: a stack-based ARC-STANDARD and its non-projective version, by adding the SWAP operation. We first evaluated three sets of features, clustered according to their extraction costs: (1) the *de facto standard* features that usually are fed as input to feedforward parsers and consider *daughter* and *grand-daughter* features, (2) a *no grand-daughter* feature set and (3) a *no grand-daughter/daughter* feature set. For the majority of the treebanks we found that the feature set (2) did not cause a significant loss, both for the stack-based ARC-STANDARD and the SWAP algorithms. We then took that set of features and reduced the size of the embeddings used to represent each feature, up to a factor of 0.5. The experiments also show that for both the ARC-STANDARD and the SWAP algorithms these reductions did not cause, in general terms, a significant loss. As a result, we obtained a set of lighter and faster transition-based parsers that achieve a better *accuracy vs bandwidth* ratio than the original ones. It was observed that these improvements were not restricted to a particular language family or specific morphology.

As future work, it would be interesting to try alternative experiments to see whether reducing the size of embeddings works the same for words as for other features. Also, the results are compatible with existent optimizations and can be used together to obtain further speed-ups. Related to this, quantized word vectors (Lam, 2018) can save memory and be used to outperform traditional embeddings.

Acknowledgments

We would like to thank the anonymous reviewers for their useful suggestions and detailed comments. This work has received funding from the European Research Council (ERC), under the European Union's Horizon 2020 research and innovation programme (FASTPARSE, grant agreement No 714150), from the TELEPARES-UDC project (FFI2014-51978-C2-2-R) and the ANSWER-ASAP project (TIN2017-85160-C2-1-R) from MINECO, and from Xunta de Galicia (ED431B 2017/01). We gratefully acknowledge NVIDIA Corporation for the donation of a GTX Titan X GPU.

References

Daniel Andor, Chris Alberti, David Weiss, Aliaksei Severyn, Alessandro Presta, Kuzman Ganchev, Slav Petrov, and Michael Collins. 2016. Globally normalized transition-based neural networks. In *Proceedings of the 54th Annual Meeting of the Association for Computational Linguistics (Volume 1: Long Papers)*, pages 2442–2452, Berlin, Germany. Association for Computational Linguistics.

Miguel Ballesteros and Joakim Nivre. 2012. Maltoptimizer: A system for maltparser optimization. In *LREC*, pages 2757–2763.

Yevgeni Berzak, Yan Huang, Andrei Barbu, Anna Korhonen, and Boris Katz. 2016. Anchoring and agreement in syntactic annotations. In *Proceedings of the 2016 Conference on Empirical Methods in Natural Language Processing*, pages 2215–2224, Austin, Texas. Association for Computational Linguistics.

Bernd Bohnet. 2010. Very high accuracy and fast dependency parsing is not a contradiction. In *Proceedings of the 23rd International Conference on Computational Linguistics*, COLING '10, pages 89–97, Stroudsburg, PA, USA. Association for Computational Linguistics.

Jan A. Botha, Emily Pitler, Ji Ma, Anton Bakalov, Alex Salcianu, David Weiss, Ryan McDonald, and Slav Petrov. 2017. Natural language processing with small feed-forward networks. In *Proceedings of the 2017 Conference on Empirical Methods in Natural Language Processing*, pages 2879–2885. Association for Computational Linguistics.

Sabine Buchholz and Erwin Marsi. 2006. CoNLL-X shared task on multilingual dependency parsing. In *Proceedings of the Tenth Conference on Computational Natural Language Learning*, pages 149–164. Association for Computational Linguistics.

Danqi Chen and Christopher Manning. 2014. A fast and accurate dependency parser using neural networks. In *Proceedings of the 2014 conference on empirical methods in natural language processing (EMNLP)*, pages 740–750.

François Chollet et al. 2015. Keras. https://github.com/keras-team/keras.

Michael A Covington. 2001. A fundamental algorithm for dependency parsing. In *Proceedings of the 39th annual ACM southeast conference*, pages 95–102. Citeseer.

Jacob Devlin, Rabih Zbib, Zhongqiang Huang, Thomas Lamar, Richard Schwartz, and John Makhoul. 2014.

Fast and robust neural network joint models for statistical machine translation. In *Proceedings of the 52nd Annual Meeting of the Association for Computational Linguistics (Volume 1: Long Papers)*, volume 1, pages 1370–1380.

Timothy Dozat and Christopher D. Manning. 2017. Deep biaffine attention for neural dependency parsing. In *Proceedings of the 5th International Conference on Learning Representations*.

Daniel Fernández-González and Carlos Gómez-Rodríguez. 2018. Non-projective dependency parsing with non-local transitions. In *Proceedings of the 2018 Conference of the North American Chapter of the Association for Computational Linguistics: Human Language Technologies, Volume 2 (Short Papers)*, pages 693–700. Association for Computational Linguistics.

Xavier Glorot and Yoshua Bengio. 2010. Understanding the difficulty of training deep feedforward neural networks. In *Proceedings of the Thirteenth International Conference on Artificial Intelligence and Statistics*, pages 249–256.

Carlos Gómez-Rodríguez, Iago Alonso-Alonso, and David Vilares. 2017. How important is syntactic parsing accuracy? an empirical evaluation on rule-based sentiment analysis. *Artificial Intelligence Review*.

Carlos Gómez-Rodríguez and Joakim Nivre. 2010. A transition-based parser for 2-planar dependency structures. In *Proceedings of the 48th Annual Meeting of the Association for Computational Linguistics*, pages 1492–1501. Association for Computational Linguistics.

Sepp Hochreiter and Jürgen Schmidhuber. 1997. Long short-term memory. *Neural computation*, 9(8):1735–1780.

Liang Huang, Wenbin Jiang, and Qun Liu. 2009. Bilingually-constrained (monolingual) shift-reduce parsing. In *Proceedings of the 2009 Conference on Empirical Methods in Natural Language Processing: Volume 3-Volume 3*, pages 1222–1231. Association for Computational Linguistics.

Eliyahu Kiperwasser and Yoav Goldberg. 2016. Simple and accurate dependency parsing using bidirectional LSTM feature representations. *Transactions of the Association for Computational Linguistics*, 4:313–327.

Marco Kuhlmann, Carlos Gómez-Rodríguez, and Giorgio Satta. 2011. Dynamic programming algorithms for transition-based dependency parsers. In *Proceedings of the 49th Annual Meeting of the Association for Computational Linguistics: Human Language Technologies-Volume 1*, pages 673–682. Association for Computational Linguistics.

M. Lam. 2018. Word2Bits - Quantized Word Vectors. *ArXiv e-prints*.

Miryam de Lhoneux, Yan Shao, Ali Basirat, Eliyahu Kiperwasser, Sara Stymne, Yoav Goldberg, and Joakim Nivre. 2017. From raw text to universal dependencies-look, no tags! *Proceedings of the CoNLL 2017 Shared Task: Multilingual Parsing from Raw Text to Universal Dependencies*, pages 207–217.

Mitchell P Marcus, Mary Ann Marcinkiewicz, and Beatrice Santorini. 1993. Building a large annotated corpus of English: The Penn treebank. *Computational linguistics*, 19(2):313–330.

Ryan McDonald, Fernando Pereira, Kiril Ribarov, and Jan Hajič. 2005. Non-projective dependency parsing using spanning tree algorithms. In *Proceedings of the conference on Human Language Technology and Empirical Methods in Natural Language Processing*, pages 523–530. Association for Computational Linguistics.

Joakim Nivre. 2004. Incrementality in deterministic dependency parsing. In *Proceedings of the Workshop on Incremental Parsing: Bringing Engineering and Cognition Together*, IncrementParsing '04, pages 50–57, Stroudsburg, PA, USA. Association for Computational Linguistics.

Joakim Nivre. 2008. Algorithms for deterministic incremental dependency parsing. *Computational Linguistics*, 34(4):513–553.

Joakim Nivre. 2009. Non-projective dependency parsing in expected linear time. In *Proceedings of the Joint Conference of the 47th Annual Meeting of the ACL and the 4th International Joint Conference on Natural Language Processing of the AFNLP: Volume 1-Volume 1*, pages 351–359. Association for Computational Linguistics.

Joakim Nivre and Johan Hall. 2010. A quick guide to MaltParser optimization. *http://maltparser. org/guides/opt/quick-opt.pdf*.

Joakim Nivre, Johan Hall, Jens Nilsson, Atanas Chanev, Gülşen Eryigit, Sandra Kübler, Svetoslav Marinov, and Erwin Marsi. 2007. Maltparser: A language-independent system for data-driven dependency parsing. *Natural Language Engineering*, 13(2):95–135.

Joakim Nivre et al. 2017. Universal dependencies 2.1. LINDAT/CLARIN digital library at the Institute of Formal and Applied Linguistics (ÚFAL), Faculty of Mathematics and Physics, Charles University.

Peng Qi and Christopher D. Manning. 2017. Arc-swift: A novel transition system for dependency parsing. In *Proceedings of the 55th Annual Meeting of the Association for Computational Linguistics (Volume 2: Short Papers)*, pages 110–117, Vancouver, Canada. Association for Computational Linguistics.

Mohammad Sadegh Rasooli and Joel Tetreault. 2015. Yara parser: A fast and accurate dependency parser. *arXiv preprint arXiv:1503.06733*.

Tianze Shi, Liang Huang, and Lillian Lee. 2017. Fast(er) exact decoding and global training for transition-based dependency parsing via a minimal feature set. In *Proceedings of the 2017 Conference on Empirical Methods in Natural Language Processing*, pages 12–23. Association for Computational Linguistics.

Milan Straka, Jan Hajic, Jana Straková, and Jan Hajic jr. 2015. Parsing universal dependency treebanks using neural networks and search-based oracle. In *International Workshop on Treebanks and Linguistic Theories (TLT14)*, pages 208–220.

Ivan Titov and James Henderson. 2007. Fast and robust multilingual dependency parsing with a generative latent variable model. In *Proc. of the CoNLL shared task. Joint Conf. on Empirical Methods in Natural Language Processing and Computational Natural Language Learning (EMNLP-CoNLL)*, Prague, Czech Republic.

Andrei Vlad Vacariu. 2017. *A high-throughput dependency parser*. Ph.D. thesis, Applied Sciences: School of Computing Science, Simon Fraser University.

David Vilares and Carlos Gómez-Rodríguez. 2017. A non-projective greedy dependency parser with bidirectional LSTMs. *Proceedings of the CoNLL 2017 Shared Task: Multilingual Parsing from Raw Text to Universal Dependencies*, pages 152–162.

Alexander Volokh. 2013. *Performance-Oriented Dependency Parsing*. Doctoral dissertation, Saarland University, Saarbrücken, Germany.

Naiwen Xue, Fei Xia, Fu-Dong Chiou, and Marta Palmer. 2005. The Penn Chinese Treebank: Phrase structure annotation of a large corpus. *Natural language engineering*, 11(2):207–238.

Yue Zhang and Joakim Nivre. 2011. Transition-based dependency parsing with rich non-local features. In *Proceedings of the 49th Annual Meeting of the Association for Computational Linguistics: Human Language Technologies: short papers-Volume 2*, pages 188–193. Association for Computational Linguistics.

Extended and Enhanced Polish Dependency Bank
in Universal Dependencies Format

Alina Wróblewska

Institute of Computer Science
Polish Academy of Sciences
ul. Jana Kazimierza 5
01-248 Warsaw, Poland
`alina@ipipan.waw.pl`

Abstract

The paper presents the largest Polish Dependency Bank in Universal Dependencies format – PDBUD – with 22K trees and 352K tokens. PDBUD builds on its previous version, i.e. the Polish UD treebank (PL-SZ), and contains all 8K PL-SZ trees. The PL-SZ trees are checked and possibly corrected in the current edition of PDBUD. Further 14K trees are automatically converted from a new version of Polish Dependency Bank. The PDBUD trees are expanded with the enhanced edges encoding the shared dependents and the shared governors of the coordinated conjuncts and with the semantic roles of some dependents. The conducted evaluation experiments show that PDBUD is large enough for training a high-quality graph-based dependency parser for Polish.

1 Introduction

Natural language processing (NLP) is nowadays dominated by machine learning methods, especially deep learning methods. Data-driven NLP tools not only perform more accurately than rule-based tools, but are also easier to develop. The shift towards machine learning methods is also visible in syntactic parsing, especially dependency parsing. The vast majority of the contemporary dependency parsing systems (e.g. Nivre et al., 2006; Bohnet, 2010; Dozat et al., 2017; Straka and Straková, 2017) take advantage of machine learning methods. Based on training data, parsers learn to analyse sentences and to predict the most appropriate dependency structures of these sentences. Even if various learning methods were applied to data-driven dependency parsing (e.g. Jiang et al., 2016), the best results so far are given by the supervised methods (cf. Zeman et al., 2017). Supervised dependency parsers trained on correctly annotated data achieve high parsing performance even for languages with rich morphology and relatively free word order, such as Polish.

The supervised learning methods require gold-standard training data, whose creation is a time-consuming and expensive process. Nevertheless, dependency treebanks have been created for many languages, in particular within the Universal Dependencies initiative (UD, Nivre et al., 2016). The UD leaders aim at developing a cross-linguistically consistent tree annotation schema and at building a large multilingual collection of dependency treebanks annotated according to this schema.

Polish is also represented in the Universal Dependencies collection. There are two Polish treebanks in UD: the Polish UD treebank (PL-SZ) converted from *Składnica zależnościowa*[1] and the LFG enhanced UD treebank (PL-LFG) converted from a corpus of the Polish LFG structures.[2] PL-SZ contains more than 8K sentences with 10.1 tokens per sentence on average. PL-LFG is larger and contains more than 17K sentences, but the average number of tokens per sentence is only 7.6.[3]

This paper presents the largest Polish Dependency Bank in Universal Dependencies format – PDBUD[4] – with 22K trees and 352K tokens (hence 15.8 tokens per sentence on average). PDBUD builds on its previous version, i.e. the Polish UD treebank (PL-SZ), and contains all 8K PL-SZ trees. The PL-SZ trees are checked and possibly corrected in the current edition of

---

[1] *Składnica zależnościowa* was converted to the UD format by Zeman et al. (2014).

[2] LFG structures were converted by A. Przepiórkowski and A. Patejuk.

[3] A detailed comparison of PL-SZ and PL-LFG is presented on `http://universaldependencies.org/treebanks/pl-comparison.html`.

[4] PDBUD is publicly available on `http://zil.ipipan.waw.pl/PDB`.

Proceedings of the Second Workshop on Universal Dependencies (UDW 2018), pages 173–182
Brussels, Belgium, November 1, 2018. ©2018 Association for Computational Linguistics

PDBUD. Further 14K trees are automatically converted from a new version of Polish Dependency Bank (PDB, see Section 2). Polish sentences underlying the additional PDB trees contain problematic linguistic phenomena whose conversion requires some modifications of the UD annotation schema (see Section 3). Furthermore, the PDBUD trees are expanded with the enhanced edges encoding the shared dependents and the shared governors of the coordinated conjuncts (see Section 4) and with the semantic roles of some dependents (see Section 5). Finally, we conduct some evaluation experiments. The evaluation results show that PDBUD is large enough for training a high-quality graph-based dependency parser for Polish (see Section 6).

2 Polish Dependency Bank

2.1 PDB

The first Polish dependency treebank – *Składnica zależnościowa* (Wróblewska, 2012) – was a collection of about 8K trees which were automatically converted from Polish constituent trees of *Składnica frazowa* (Woliński et al., 2011). All sentences of *Składnica* were derived from Polish National Corpus (Przepiórkowski et al., 2012). The annotated sentences are rather short with 10.2 tokens per sentence on average and corresponding trees are relatively simple (there is only 289 non-projective trees,[5] i.e. 3.5% of all trees).

This first version of Polish dependency treebank was enlarged with 4K trees (Wróblewska, 2014). The additional trees resulted from the projection of English dependency structures on Polish parallel sentences from *Europarl* (Koehn, 2005), *DGT-Translation Memory* (Steinberger et al., 2012), OPUS (Tiedemann, 2012) and *Pelcra Parallel Corpus* (Pęzik et al., 2011). The additional sentences with the average length of 15.9 tokens per sentence were longer than the sentences from

Składnica. The projection-based trees were also more complex and 235 of them are non-projective (i.e. 5.9% of all added trees). The entire set of *Składnica* trees and the projection-based trees is called Polish Dependency Bank (PDB).

PDB is still being developed at the Institute of Computer Science PAS. The current version of PDB is enlarged with a suite of 10K sentences annotated with the dependency trees. The additional sentences are relatively complex (20.5 tokens per sentence on average) and come from Polish National Corpus (Przepiórkowski et al., 2012), Polish CDSCorpus[6] (Wróblewska and Krasnowska-Kieraś, 2017), and literature. There are 1388 non-projective trees in this set (i.e. 13.9% of 10K trees). Besides enlarging PDB, the development consists in correcting the previous PDB trees. The *Składnica* trees and the projection-based trees are manually checked and corrected if necessary.

The current version of PDB consists of more than 22K trees with 15.8 tokens per sentence on average (see Table 1). There are 1912 non-projective trees in PDB (i.e. 8.61% of all trees).

	PDB	PDBUD
# sentences		22,208
# tokens		351,715
# tokens per sentence		15.84
# dependency types	28	31 (48)*
% non-projective edges	1.76	1.75
% non-projective trees	8.61	8.03
% enhanced edges	n/a	4.96
% enhanced graphs	n/a	41.58

Table 1: Statistics of Polish Dependency Bank (PDB) and its UD conversion (PDBUD). *There are 31 universal dependency types in PDBUD and 48 universal types with the Polish-specific subtypes.

2.2 PDBUD

The PDB trees are automatically converted to the UD trees according to the guidelines of Universal Dependencies v2[7] and the resulting set is called PDBUD (i.e. Polish Dependency Bank in Universal Dependencies format). PDBUD contains all trees of the Polish UD treebank (PL-

---

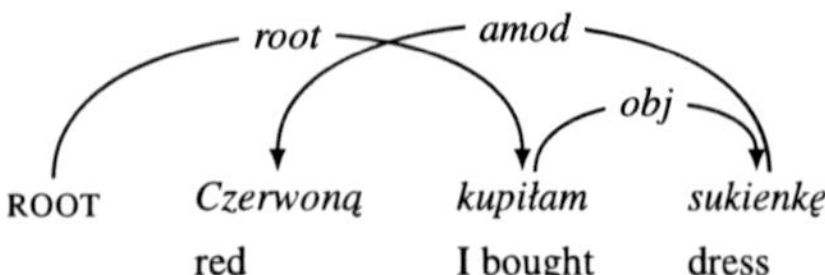

SZ), which are possibly corrected. The size of PDBUD is exactly the same as the size of PDB, i.e. 22K trees and 351K tokens (see Table 1). 1783 of the PDBUD trees are non-projective, i.e. 8.03% of all trees. There are 17K enhanced edges (4.96% of all edges) in PDBUD and 41.6% of the PDBUD graphs have at least one enhanced edge.

The converted PDBUD trees are largely consistent with the PL-SZ trees. While converting, we try to preserve the universality principle of UD, but some necessary modifications are essential. The PL-SZ trees are rather simple and the sentences underlying this data set do not contain some linguistic phenomena, e.g. ellipsis, comparative constructions, directed speech, interpolations and comments, nominative noun phrases used in the vocative function, and many others. Therefore, the repertoire of the UD relation subtypes and language-specific features is slightly extended in PDBUD to cover these phenomena (see Section 3). Furthermore, in contrast to the PL-SZ trees, the PDBUD graphs contain enhanced edges encoding shared dependents or shared governors of coordinated elements (see Section 4). Finally, some semantic labels are added that goes beyond the standard annotation scheme of Universal Dependencies (see Section 5).

3 Corrections and extensions

Plenty of errors are corrected in the original *Składnica* trees (and the projection-based trees) and thus they are not transferred to these PDBUD trees, which correspond to the PL-SZ trees. The errors in the *Składnica* trees were predominantly caused by the inadequate automatic conversion of the phrase-structure trees into the dependency trees, particularly by the erroneous labelling. Defective part-of-speech tags, morphological features, lemmas, dependency relations and their labels are manually corrected by highly qualified linguists. The correction issues do not fall within the scope of this paper. The conversion issues and extension suggestions are described in the following sections.

3.1 Comparative constructions

Comparative constructions are distinguished in the PDB trees and thus they are also marked in PDBUD. According to Bondaruk (1998), there are two types of comparative constructions in Polish: *comparatives of equality* marked with e.g. *tak ... jak* ('as ... as'), *taki ... jaki* ('just like'), and *com-

paratives of inequality marked with NIŻ ('than').[8] All markers introducing comparative constructions, e.g. JAK, NIŻ, JAKBY, NICZYM, are converted as the subordinate conjunctions SCONJ with the feature ConjType=Cmpr.[9] Comparative constructions are annotated with the following dependencies (see Figure 1): the comparative marker is labelled mark and it depends on the main element of the comparative construction labelled obl:cmpr (a new UD subtype).

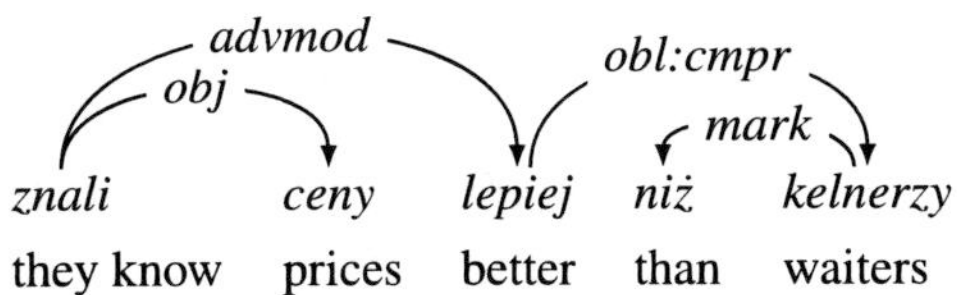

Figure 1: The PDBUD tree of [...] *znali ceny potraw lepiej niż kelnerzy* ('they know the prices of dishes better than the waiters') with the comparative construction.

3.2 Constructions with JAKO

The lexeme JAKO is one of the uninflectable Polish parts of speech. It causes considerable difficulties and is heterogeneously analysed as a preposition, a coordinating conjunction, a subordinating conjunction, or an adverb in the traditional Polish linguistics. According to the concept of the bi-functional subordinating conjunction JAKO (Wróblewska and Wieczorek, 2018), we convert all examples of JAKO as SCONJ with the feature ConjType=Pred (i.e. a predicative conjunction – a new Polish-specific feature). The subordinating conjunction JAKO, which is labelled mark, can be governed by the head of any constituent phrase (e.g. a nominal, prepositional, or verbal phrase) which is, in turn, governed by the sentence predicate subcategorising another phrase of the same type (see Figure 2). There is an identification relation between the sub-

---

[8] Comparatives of inequality are sometimes introduced by the comparative forms of adjectives or adverbs (marked in PDBUD with the feature Degree=Cmp). However, comparatives of inequality can also be introduced by non-comparative adjectives (e.g. *inny* 'other'), adverbs (e.g. *inaczej* 'in another way', *przeciwnie* 'on the contrary'), or even the verb *woleć* 'to prefer'.

[9] Cmp is the value of Degree in UD and comp stands either for the oblique complement obl:comp in French or for the object of comparison nmod:comp in Uyghur. We therefore decide to introduce a new value Cmpr/cmpr to indicate comparative constructions.

categorised argument and the phrase introduced by JAKO (hence the bi-functional subordinating conjunction) which could be marked with an enhanced edge.

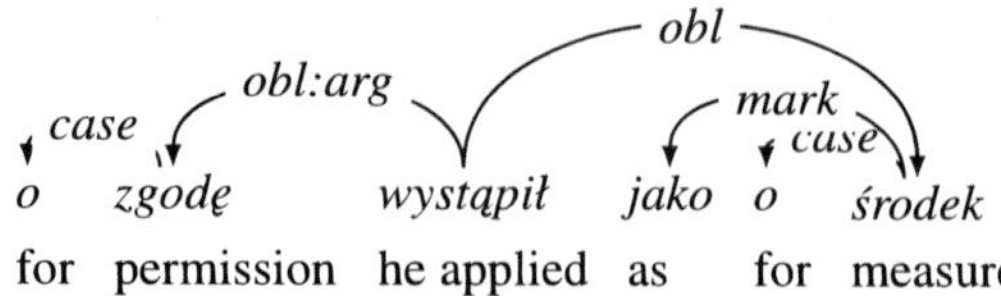

Figure 2: The PDBUD tree of the sentence *O zgodę taką wystąpił jako o środek zapobiegawczy* ('He applied for such permission as a precautionary measure') with JAKO.

3.3 Mobile inflection

The mobile inflections (marked as aglt in the Polish tagset, e.g. *-em* in *odwołałem* 'I$_{Mask}$ recalled' or *-ś* in *zrobiłabyś* 'you$_{Fem}$ would do') are the enclitics which substitute auxiliary verbs in the past perfect constructions. We convert them as AUX with Aspect, Number, and Person features, similar to PL-SZ. The repertoire of the morphological features of the mobile inflections is enriched with Clitic=Yes and its Variant – either Long (e.g. *-em* in *odwołałem* 'I$_{Mask}$ recalled') or Short (e.g. *-m* in *odwołałam* 'I$_{Fem}$ recalled'). The mobile inflections are marked with the further features VerbForm=Fin and Mood=Ind in the PL-SZ trees, but as they are not the proper finite verbs, these features seem to be incorrect and are not included in PDBUD. A mobile inflection is the special case of an auxiliary verb. Therefore, the relation between the mobile inflection and its governing participle is labelled with a special subtype aux:clitic (a new UD subtype).

3.4 Conditional particle

The conditional particle BY, e.g. *-by-* in *zrobiłabyś* ('you$_{Fem}$ would do'), is annotated in PL-SZ as an auxiliary AUX with the features Aspect=Imp, Mood=Cnd and VerbForm=Fin, and with the lemma BYĆ ('to be'). It is a particle which doesn't bear any grammatical features in Polish (cf. Przepiórkowski et al., 2012). Since it is not any verb form, it cannot be annotated with Aspect, Mood and VerbForm features which are reserved for verbs. Furthermore, its lemma form is BY and not BYĆ. The conditional particle BY is converted as PART in PDBUD. The relation between this particle and its governor is labelled with aux:cnd (a new UD subtype).

3.5 Other morphosyntactic extensions

We propose some morphosyntactic extensions of the schema which was used to annotate the PL-SZ trees. Some of these extensions are already defined in the UD guidelines, but they were not applied in PL-SZ. Other extensions are newly defined.

ADP There is only one postposition in Polish – TEMU ('ago'), which is converted in PDBUD as the adposition ADP with the feature AdpType=Post. In PL-SZ, the postposition TEMU was wrongly assigned the feature AdpType=Prep, which is reserved for prepositions.

CCONJ We convert the conjunctions PLUS and MINUS as the coordinating conjunction CCONJ with the feature ConjType=Oper (a mathematical operator). There was not any conjunction of this kind in PL-SZ.

Digits Digits (NumForm=Digit) and roman numbers (NumForm=Roman), which are distinguished in PDB, are converted as follows:

- ordinal numbers: the adjectives ADJ with the feature NumType=Ord and other standard features of the adjectives,

- cardinal numbers: the numerals NUM with the feature NumType=Card and other standard features of the numerals,

- other numbers: the tag X.

PUNCT Some features of the punctuation marks are specified:

- PunctSide with the values Initial or Final,

- PunctType with one of the following values: Brck (bracket), Colo (colon), Comm (comma), Dash, Elip (elipsis), Slsh (slash), Blsh (backslash), etc.

Note that Elip, Slsh and Blsh are the newly defined PunctType values.

SYM There are some symbols, e.g. %, §, $, +, $\leq$, and emojis, e.g. :-), :), in the PDB trees which are converted as the symbols SYM in PDBUD. Emojis are always labelled with the function discourse:emo in PDBUD (a new UD subtype).

VERB The impersonal verb forms[10] are converted as the adjectives ADJ with the feature Case in PL-SZ. In the Polish linguistics however, the impersonals are considered verb forms which cannot be conjugated by the grammatical case. Therefore, we convert them as the verbs VERB with the following features: Aspect (Perfective or Imperfective), Mood=Ind, Person=0, Tense=Past, VerbForm=Fin, and Voice=Act.

X The foreign words are converted as X tags with the feature Foreign=Yes. Abbreviations are also annotated as X tags with the features Abbr=Yes and Pun=Yes if the abbreviation requires a full stop (e.g. *art.* 'article'), or Pun=No if it doesn't (e.g. *cm* 'centimetre').

3.6 Additional relation subtypes

We also propose to extend the inventory of the UD relation subtypes with some additional subtypes listed in the alphabetical order below.[11]

acl:attrib A Polish clause can modify a noun phrase, even if it is not a proper relative clause, e.g. [...] *jest jedynie przejawem* [...] *prawa przyciągania seksualnego: owad nieomylnie trafia do pragnącej zapylenia rośliny.* ('[it] is just a sign of the law of sexual attraction: an insect infallibly goes to a plant that wants to be pollinated.') – the clause *owad nieomylnie trafia* [...] modifies the noun *prawa* ('of the law'). The relation subtype acl:attrib (adverbial clause modifier of a noun)[12] is therefore introduced to cover constructions of this type.

advmod:arg It is possible in Polish that an adverbial is subcategorised by the verb, e.g. *lepiej* ('better') is subcategorised by the infinitive *mieć* ('to have') in *Wiem, że możemy mieć lepiej* ('I know that our situation/conditions will improve', lit. 'I know that we can have better'). The relations between adverbials with the argument status and governing verbs are labelled with the subtype advmod:arg (an adverbial with the argument status) in PDBUD.

advmod:neg The relation between the negation particle NIE ('not') and its governor is labelled with advmod:neg.

aux:imp The relation between the imperative particle NIECH ('let's') and its governor is labelled with aux:imp.

ccomp:obj The PDB direct objects are these verb arguments which are shifted into the grammatical subjects in the passive sentences. Not only noun objects but also clausal objects undergo this shift, e.g. *Przewidział, że inflacja będzie spadać* ('He predicted that inflation would go down') and its passive version *Że inflacja będzie spadać zostało przewidziane* ('It was foreseen that inflation would go down', lit. 'That inflation would go down was foreseen'). In order to convert the clausal objects, the subtype ccomp:obj is proposed. It is worth considering whether it is not a better solution to introduce a new UD type cobj in analogy to csubj.

discourse:intj Interjections, e.g. *cześć* ('hello'), *Och* ('Oh'), *Okay*, are labelled with the function discourse:intj.

nmod:arg Noun complements of various parts of speech, except for verbs, are labelled with the function nmod:arg (noun complement), e.g. *środowiska* in *ochrona*_{NOUN} *środowiska*_{NOUN}[13] ('environmental protection'), *dzieci* in *korytarz pełen*_{ADJ} *dzieci*_{NOUN} ('a corridor full of children').

nmod:subj Polish allows the grammatical subject realised as a prepositional phrase, e.g. *do*_{ADP} *2 lat więzienia* in *Grozi mu do 2 lat więzienia* ('He faces up to two years in prison', lit. 'Up to two years in prison threatens him') or an adverbial phrase, e.g. *Rzadko*_{ADV} in *Rzadko nie znaczy*

---

[10]Impersonal verb forms are annotated with the tag imps in PDB.

[11]The list of all dependency labels used in PDBUD is as follows (the new dependency labels are underlined): <u>acl:attrib</u>, acl:relcl, advcl, advmod, <u>advmod:arg</u>, <u>advmod:neg</u>, amod, appos, aux, <u>aux:clitic</u> (see Section 3.3), <u>aux:cnd</u> (see Section 3.4), <u>aux:imp</u>, aux:pass, case, cc, cc:preconj, ccomp, <u>ccomp:obj</u>, conj, cop, csubj, det, <u>discourse:emo</u> (see Section 3.5), discourse:intj, expl:impers, fixed, flat, iobj, list, mark, nmod, <u>nmod:arg</u>, nmod:subj, nsubj, nsubj:pass, nummod, obj, obl, <u>obl:agent</u>, <u>obl:arg</u>, obl:cmpr (see Section 3.1), orphan, parataxis, <u>parataxis:insert</u>, parataxis:obj, punct, root, vocative, xcomp.

[12]We considered labelling this relation with the function advcl. However, "an adverbial clause modifier is a clause which modifies a verb or other predicate" (see the UD guidelines http://universaldependencies.org/u/dep/advcl.html). Therefore, we decided not to use the label advcl for an adverbial clause modifier of a noun. Alternatively, this relation could be labelled with parataxis.

[13]*Ochrona* ('a protection') is a deverbal noun that is derived from the verb *chronić* ('to protect') subcategorising an object.

wcale ('It's rare, nevertheless still occurs', lit. 'Rarely does not mean at all'). The relation between a prepositional or adverbial subject and its governing verb is labelled with the subtype nmod:subj. We realise that this subtype is not the best solution. Alternatively, an adverbial subject could be labelled advmod:arg and a prepositional subject could be labelled obl:arg, but then we lose information about their subject function. We also consider introducing two additional subtypes – advmod:subj and obl:subj, but they are extremely confusing.[14]

4   Enhanced graphs

The PDBUD graphs contain the enhanced edges encoding the dependents shared by the conjuncts in coordinate structures (see Figure 3) and the shared governors of the coordinated elements (see Figure 4).

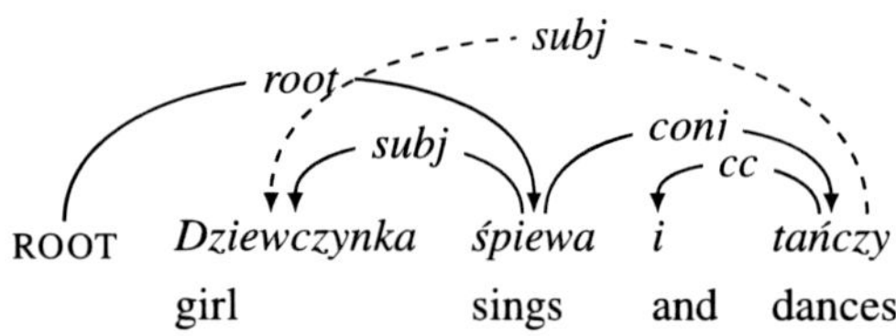

Figure 3: The PDBUD graph of the sentence *Dziewczynka śpiewa i tańczy* ('A girl sings and dances') with the shared subject. The enhanced edge is marked with the dashed arrow.

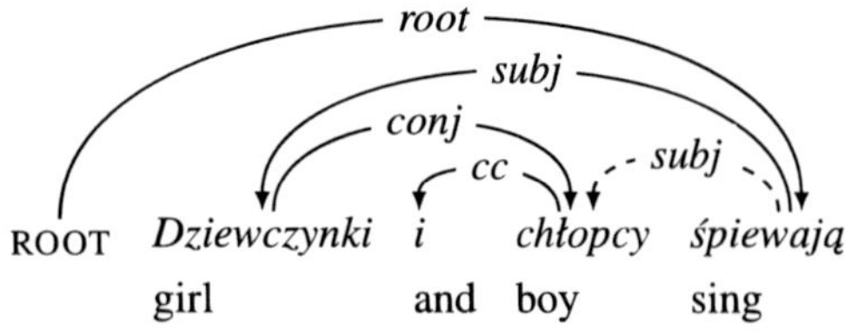

Figure 4: The PDBUD graph of *Dziewczynki i chłopcy śpiewają* ('Girls and boys are singing') with the shared governor of the coordinated subject. The enhanced edge is marked with the dashed arrow.

In the PDB trees, all coordinated elements depend on a conjunction and the relations between the conjunction and these elements are labelled with a technical dependency type – conjunct. A dependent shared by all conjuncts also depends on the conjunction, but this relation is labelled with the grammatical function of the shared dependent, e.g. subj, obj. The conversion of the PDB trees into the enhanced PDBUD graphs is thus a straightforward process. There are only enhanced edges involved in the coordination constructions in PDBUD, but they are numerous, i.e. more than 41% of all PDBUD trees contain at least one enhanced edge (see Table 1).

5   Semantic labels

The UD format is extended by adding some semantic labels in the 11th column. There are 28 semantic labels corresponding to some selected *frame elements* of FrameNet (Fillmore and Baker, 2009; Ruppenhofer et al., 2010). In addition to the common semantic roles: THEME, RECIPIENT/BENEFICIARY, RESULT, there are roles related to

- place: SOURCE, GOAL, PLACE, PATH,

- time: TIME, DURATION, STARTING_POINT, END_POINT, FREQUENCY/ITERATION,

- some other roles: ATTITUDE, CAUSE/EXPLANATION/REASON, CIRCUMSTANCES/OTHER, CONCESSIVE, CONDITION, CO-PARTICIPANT, DEGREE, EVENT_DESCRIPTION, INSTRUMENT, MANNER, PURPOSE, REPLACEE, ROLE, STIMULUS, SUPERSET, and TITLE.

The additional semantic labels extend the semantic meaning of indirect objects (iobj), oblique nominals (obl)[15], adverbial clause modifiers (advcl), some adverbial modifiers (advmod), some noun modifiers (nmod), etc.

6   Evaluation

6.1   Dependency parsing systems

Various contemporary dependency parsing systems are tested in our evaluation experiments. All of the tested systems allow dependency parsing, but only some of them allow part-of-speech tagging, morphological analysis and lemmatisation. We test transition-based parsers (i.e. MaltParser, UDPipe, and the transition-based version of BIST

---

[14]One of the reviewers of the paper suggests to use the label subj. It would be an ideal solution. However, the function subj does not belong to the repertoire of the UD functions.

[15]obl:arg is not semantically specified in PDBUD.

system	architecture	classifier	parsing	tagging	lemmatisation
MaltParser (Nivre et al., 2006)	trans	LR	yes	no	no
MATE parser (Bohnet, 2010)	graph	perceptron	yes	no	no
BIST parser (Kiperwasser and Goldberg, 2016)	trans/graph	biLSTM	yes	no	no
Stanford parser (Dozat et al., 2017)	graph	biLSTM	yes	yes	no
UDPipe (Straka and Straková, 2017)	trans	1-layer NN	yes	yes	yes

Table 2: Properties of the dependency parsing systems tested in our experiments. Explanation: trans – a transition-based parser, graph – a graph-based parser, LR – a linear classifier based on logistic regression, 1-layer NN – a non-linear classifier based on 1-layer neural network, biLSTM – Bidirectional Long-Short Term Memory network.

parser) as well as graph-based parsers (i.e. MATE parser, Stanford parser, and the graph-based version of BIST parser). The properties of the tested dependency parsing systems are summarised in Table 2.

6.2 Data split

PDBUD is divided into three parts – training, test and development data sets. The procedure of assigning dependency trees to particular data sets is generally random, but there is one constraint on the dividing procedure – the *Składnica* trees, and thus also the PL-SZ trees, are not included in the test set.[16] Since sentences underlying the *Składnica* trees are generally shorter than the remaining sentences, the average number of tokens per sentence is significantly higher in the test set than in two other sets. The statistics of the particular data sets is given in Table 3.

	PDBUD		
	train	test	dev
# sentences	17770	2219	2219
# tokens per sentence	15.4	20.2	15.1
# non-projective trees	1310	302	172
% non-projective trees	7.4	13.6	7.7
# enhanced graphs	7147	1181	855
% enhanced graphs	40.2	53.2	38.5

Table 3: Statistics of the training (train), test (test), and development (dev) data sets of PDBUD.

6.3 Evaluation methodology

We apply the evaluation measures defined for the purpose of CoNLL 2018 shared task on Multilingual Parsing from Raw Text to Universal Dependencies.[17] The proposed metrics, i.e. LAS, UAS, CLAS, MLAS, BLEX, evaluate the different prediction aspects.

Two evaluation scenarios are proposed: 1) testing the quality of dependency parsing of Polish, and 2) testing the quality of morphosyntactic prediction of dependency trees, i.e. part-of-speech tagging, lemmatisation, and dependency parsing of Polish. For the purpose of our evaluation, we use the script[18] of CoNLL 2018 shared task.

6.4 Results

6.4.1 Evaluation of dependency parsing

Stanford parser is the best performing parser on Polish data (see Table 4). The second best parser – MATE parser – performs surprisingly well. Even if it doesn't have any neural component, it outperforms not only the graph-based neural parser BIST (87.06 LAS vs. 84.88 LAS), but also all transition-based parsers. It is also worth mentioning that the worst graph-based parser – BIST parser – performs slightly better than its transition-based version, which achieves LAS of 84.79% and is the best of all transition-based parsers. It follows that the graph-based parsers are generally better suited for parsing Polish than the transition-based parsers.

---

[16]PDBUD is used in the shared task on dependency parsing of Polish – PolEval 2018 (http://poleval.pl). The organisers of this shared task decided not to use the PL-SZ trees, which have been publicly available for some time, for validation of the participating systems. Therefore, the PL-SZ trees are not part of the PDBUD test set.

[17]http://universaldependencies.org/conll18/evaluation.html

[18]http://universaldependencies.org/conll18/conll18_ud_eval.py
In order to evaluate the dependency parsers in the first evaluation scenario, the script conll18_ud_eval.py is slightly modified, i.e. some conditions (e.g. single-root property) are disregarded.

System	UAS	LAS
MaltParser	79.73	74.57
BIST transition-based	87.91	84.79
UDPipe	86.23	83.41
MATE parser	89.49	87.06
BIST graph-based	87.97	84.88
Stanford parser	**92.41**	**90.03**

Table 4: Parsers are tested on the sentences with the gold-standard tokens, lemmas, and part-of-speech tags.

System	UAS	LAS	CLAS	MLAS	BLEX
Stanford	**91.33**	**88.04**	**85.48**	n/a	n/a
UDPipe	83.32	78.93	75.22	**64.33**	**71.17**

Table 6: The quality (F1 scores) of predicting unlabelled dependency trees (UAS), labelled dependency trees (LAS), governors and dependency relation types of content words (CLAS), governors, dependency relation types, universal part-of-speech tags and morphological features of content words (MLAS), governors, dependency relation types and lemmas of content words (BLEX).

6.4.2 Evaluation of morphosyntactic prediction of dependency trees

Two systems – Stanford system and UDPipe – are tested in the task of morphosyntactic prediction of dependency trees. These systems predict universal part-of-speech tags (UPOS) as well as language-specific tags (XPOS). Stanford system outperforms UDPipe in part-of-speech tagging (see Table 5). Only UDPipe predicts morphological features (UFEATS) and lemmas (LEMMA).

System	UPOS	XPOS	UFEATS	LEMMA
Stanford	**97.87**	**92.45**	n/a	n/a
UDPipe	96.81	86.05	**88.02**	**95.61**

Table 5: The quality (F1 scores) of predicting universal part-of-speech tags (UPOS), Polish-specific tags (XPOS), morphological features (UFEATS), and lemmas (LEMMA).

Stanford parser significantly outperforms UDPipe in predicting labelled dependency trees (LAS) and in predicting governors and dependency relation types of content words (CLAS), see Table 6. Since Stanford system doesn't predict morphological features and lemmas, we cannot compare MLAS and BLEX scores.

6.4.3 Summary

We carried out two evaluation experiments on PDBUD data. The results of these experiments show that the graph-based parsers, even the parsers without any neural component, are better suited for parsing Polish than the transition-based parsing systems. The best results in parsing Polish data without preceding morphosyntactic analysis are achieved with Stanford parser, i.e. 88.04 LAS. These results are slightly lower than those reported in Dozat et al. (2017), i.e.

90.32 LAS. The possible reason for this is that our test data contains the dependency trees of the longer sentences and thus there is more room for making mistakes. If Stanford parser operates on the PDBUD sentences with the gold-standard part-of-speech tags, it performs better, i.e. 90.03 LAS.

7 Conclusions and future work

We presented PDBUD – the largest Polish dependency bank with 22K dependency trees in Universal Dependencies format. PDBUD contains the corrected trees of the Polish UD treebank (PL-SZ) and 14K dependency trees automatically converted from Polish Dependency Bank. The PDBUD trees are expanded with the enhanced edges encoding the shared dependents and the shared governors of the coordinated conjuncts and with the semantic roles of some dependents. Our evaluation experiments showed that PDBUD is large enough for training a high-quality graph-based dependency parser for Polish.

We did our best to maintain consistency with the UD guidelines while building PDBUD. However, some of our annotation decisions could be arguable and should be discussed again in the context of the universality assumptions of Universal Dependencies.

There is plenty of elliptical constructions in Polish. Some of them are labelled with the function orphan in PDBUD. In our future works, we plan to add empty nodes representing the elided elements to the PDBUD trees. Furthermore, we are going to create a Polish version of Parallel Universal Dependency treebank.

PDBUD data were already used in the shared task on automatic identification of verbal multiword expressions (LAW-MWE-CxG-2018)[19] and are currently used in the shared task on dependency parsing of Polish (PolEval 2018).[20] This is a confirmation of the fact that PDBUD is of very high quality. Therefore, in the future we would like to replace the Polish UD treebank PL-SZ with its corrected, extended and enhanced version – PDBUD.

Acknowledgments

We would like to thank the anonymous reviewers for their valuable comments that we will undoubtedly take into consideration before publishing the final version of our data set.

The research presented in this paper was founded by SONATA 8 grant no 2014/15/D/HS2/03486 from the National Science Centre Poland and by the Polish Ministry of Science and Higher Education as part of the investment in the CLARIN-PL research infrastructure.

References

Bernd Bohnet. 2010. Very High Accuracy and Fast Dependency Parsing is not a Contradiction. In *Proceedings of the 23rd International Conference on Computational Linguistics*, COLING 2010, pages 89–97.

Anna Bondaruk. 1998. *Comparison in English and Polish Adjectives: A Syntactic Study*, volume 6 of *PASE Studies and Monographs*. Folium, Lublin.

Timothy Dozat, Peng Qi, and Christopher D. Manning. 2017. Stanford's Graph-based Neural Dependency Parser at the CoNLL 2017 Shared Task. In *Proceedings of the CoNLL 2017 Shared Task: Multilingual Parsing from Raw Text to Universal Dependencies*, pages 20–30. Association for Computational Linguistics.

Charles J. Fillmore and Collin Baker. 2009. A Frames Approach to Semantic Analysis. In Bernd Heine and Heiko Narrog, editors, *The Oxford Handbook of Linguistic Analysis*, pages 313–340. Oxford University Press.

Yong Jiang, Wenjuan Han, and Kewei Tu. 2016. Unsupervised neural dependency parsing. In *Proceedings of the 2016 Conference on Empirical Methods in Natural Language Processing*, pages 763–771, Austin, Texas. Association for Computational Linguistics.

Eliyahu Kiperwasser and Yoav Goldberg. 2016. Simple and Accurate Dependency Parsing Using Bidirectional LSTM Feature Representations. *Transactions of the Association for Computational Linguistics*, 4:313–327.

Philipp Koehn. 2005. Europarl: A Parallel Corpus for Statistical Machine Translation. In *Proceedings of the 10th Machine Translation Summit Conference*, pages 79–86.

Joakim Nivre, Johan Hall, and Jens Nilsson. 2006. MaltParser: A Data-Driven Parser-Generator for Dependency Parsing. In *Proceedings of the Fifth International Conference on Language Resources and Evaluation*, LREC'06, pages 2216–2219.

Joakim Nivre, Marie-Catherine de Marneffe, Filip Ginter, Yoav Goldberg, Jan Hajič, Christopher D. Manning, Ryan T. McDonald, Slav Petrov, Sampo Pyysalo, Natalia Silveira, Reut Tsarfaty, and Daniel Zeman. 2016. Universal Dependencies v1: A Multilingual Treebank Collection. In *Proceedings of the Tenth International Conference on Language Resources and Evaluation LREC 2016*, pages 1659–1666.

Piotr Pęzik, Maciej Ogrodniczuk, and Adam Przepiórkowski. 2011. Parallel and spoken corpora in an open repository of Polish language resources. In *Proceedings of the 5th Language & Technology Conference: Human Language Technologies as a Challenge for Computer Science and Linguistics*, pages 511–515.

Adam Przepiórkowski, Mirosław Bańko, Rafał L. Górski, and Barbara Lewandowska-Tomaszczyk, editors. 2012. *Narodowy Korpus Języka Polskiego*. Wydawnictwo Naukowe PWN, Warsaw.

Josef Ruppenhofer, Michael Ellsworth, Miriam R. L. Petruck, Christopher R. Johnson, and Jan Scheffczyk. 2010. *FrameNet II: Extended Theory and Practice*. International Computer Science Institute, Berkeley, California.

Ralf Steinberger, Andreas Eisele, Szymon Klocek, Spyridon Pilos, and Patrick Schlüter. 2012. DGT-TM: A freely Available Translation Memory in 22 Languages. In *Proceedings of the 8th International Conference on Language Resources and Evaluation*, pages 454–459.

Milan Straka and Jana Straková. 2017. Tokenizing, POS Tagging, Lemmatizing and Parsing UD 2.0 with UDPipe. In *Proceedings of the CoNLL 2017 Shared Task: Multilingual Parsing from Raw Text to Universal Dependencies*, pages 88–99, Vancouver, Canada. Association for Computational Linguistics.

Jörg Tiedemann. 2012. Parallel Data, Tools and Interfaces in OPUS. In *Proceedings of the 8th International Conference on Language Resources and Evaluation*, pages 2214–2218.

---

[19]`http://multiword.sourceforge.net/PHITE.php?sitesig=CONF&page=CONF_04_LAW-MWE-CxG_2018___lb__COLING__rb__&subpage=CONF_40_Shared_Task`

[20]`http://poleval.pl`

Marcin Woliński, Katarzyna Głowińska, and Marek Świdziński. 2011. A preliminary version of Składnica treebank of Polish. In *Proceedings of the 5th Language & Technology Conference: Human Language Technologies as a Challenge for Computer Science and Linguistics*, pages 299–303, Poznań, Poland.

Alina Wróblewska. 2012. Polish Dependency Bank. *Linguistic Issues in Language Technology*, 7(1):1–15.

Alina Wróblewska. 2014. *Polish Dependency Parser Trained on an Automatically Induced Dependency Bank*. Ph.D. dissertation, Institute of Computer Science, Polish Academy of Sciences, Warsaw.

Alina Wróblewska and Katarzyna Krasnowska-Kieraś. 2017. Polish evaluation dataset for compositional distributional semantics models. In *Proceedings of the 55th Annual Meeting of the Association for Computational Linguistics (Volume 1: Long Papers)*, pages 784–792, Vancouver, Canada. Association for Computational Linguistics.

Alina Wróblewska and Aleksandra Wieczorek. 2018. Status składniowy *jako* we współczesnej polszczyźnie. *Język Polski*, to appear.

Daniel Zeman, Ondřej Dušek, David Mareček, Martin Popel, Loganathan Ramasamy, Jan Štěpánek, Zdeněk Žabokrtský, and Jan Hajič. 2014. HamleDT: Harmonized Multi-Language Dependency Treebank. *Language Resources and Evaluation*, 48(4):601–637.

Daniel Zeman, Martin Popel, Milan Straka, Jan Hajič, Joakim Nivre, Filip Ginter, Juhani Luotolahti, Sampo Pyysalo, Slav Petrov, Martin Potthast, Francis Tyers, Elena Badmaeva, Memduh Gökırmak, Anna Nedoluzhko, Silvie Cinková, Jan Hajič jr., Jaroslava Hlaváčová, Václava Kettnerová, Zdenka Urešová, Jenna Kanerva, Stina Ojala, Anna Missilä, Christopher D. Manning, Sebastian Schuster, Siva Reddy, Dima Taji, Nizar Habash, Herman Leung, Marie-Catherine de Marneffe, Manuela Sanguinetti, Maria Simi, Hiroshi Kanayama, Valeria dePaiva, Kira Droganova, Héctor Martínez Alonso, Çağrı Çöltekin, Umut Sulubacak, Hans Uszkoreit, Vivien Macketanz, Aljoscha Burchardt, Kim Harris, Katrin Marheinecke, Georg Rehm, Tolga Kayadelen, Mohammed Attia, Ali Elkahky, Zhuoran Yu, Emily Pitler, Saran Lertpradit, Michael Mandl, Jesse Kirchner, Hector Fernandez Alcalde, Jana Strnadová, Esha Banerjee, Ruli Manurung, Antonio Stella, Atsuko Shimada, Sookyoung Kwak, Gustavo Mendonça, Tatiana Lando, Rattima Nitisaroj, and Josie Li. 2017. CoNLL 2017 Shared Task: Multilingual Parsing from Raw Text to Universal Dependencies. In *Proceedings of the CoNLL 2017 Shared Task: Multilingual Parsing from Raw Text to Universal Dependencies*, pages 1–19. Association for Computational Linguistics.

Approximate Dynamic Oracle for Dependency Parsing with Reinforcement Learning

Xiang Yu, Ngoc Thang Vu, and **Jonas Kuhn**
Institut für Maschinelle Sprachverarbeitung
Universität Stuttgart
{xiangyu,thangvu,jonas}@ims.uni-stuttgart.de

Abstract

We present a general approach with reinforcement learning (RL) to approximate dynamic oracles for transition systems where exact dynamic oracles are difficult to derive. We treat oracle parsing as a reinforcement learning problem, design the reward function inspired by the classical dynamic oracle, and use Deep Q-Learning (DQN) techniques to train the oracle with gold trees as features. The combination of a priori knowledge and data-driven methods enables an efficient dynamic oracle, which improves the parser performance over static oracles in several transition systems.

1 Introduction

Greedy transition-based dependency parsers trained with static oracles are very efficient but suffer from the error propagation problem. Goldberg and Nivre (2012, 2013) laid the foundation of dynamic oracles to train the parser with imitation learning methods to alleviate the problem. However, efficient dynamic oracles have mostly been designed for *arc-decomposable* transition systems which are usually projective. Gómez-Rodríguez et al. (2014) designed a non-projective dynamic oracle but runs in $O(n^8)$. Gómez-Rodríguez and Fernández-González (2015) proposed an efficient dynamic oracle for the non-projective Covington system (Covington, 2001; Nivre, 2008), but the system itself has quadratic worst-case complexity.

Instead of designing the oracles, Straka et al. (2015) applied the imitation learning approach (Daumé et al., 2009) by rolling out with the parser to estimate the cost of each action. Le and Fokkens (2017) took the reinforcement learning approach (Maes et al., 2009) by directly optimizing the parser towards the reward (i.e., the correct arcs) instead of the the correct action, thus no oracle is required. Both approaches circumvent the difficulty in designing the oracle cost function by us-

ing the parser to (1) explore the cost of each action, and (2) explore erroneous states to alleviate error propagation.

However, letting the parser explore for both purposes is inefficient and difficult to converge. For this reason, we propose to separate the two types of exploration: (1) the oracle explores the action space to learn the action cost with reinforcement learning, and (2) the parser explores the state space to learn from the oracle with imitation learning.

The objective of the oracle is to prevent further structure errors given a potentially erroneous state. We design the reward function to approximately reflect the number of unreachable gold arcs caused by the action, and let the model learn the actual cost from data. We use DQN (Mnih et al., 2013) with several extensions to train an Approximate Dynamic Oracle (ADO), which uses the gold tree as features and estimates the cost of each action in terms of potential attachment errors. We then use the oracle to train a parser with imitation learning methods following Goldberg and Nivre (2013).

A major difference between our ADO and the search-based or RL-based parser is that our oracle uses the gold tree as features in contrast to the lexical features of the parser, which results in a much simpler model solving a much simpler task. Furthermore, we only need to train one oracle for all treebanks, which is much more efficient.

We experiment with several transition systems, and show that training the parser with ADO performs better than training with static oracles in most cases, and on a par with the exact dynamic oracle if available. We also conduct an analysis of the oracle's robustness against error propagation for further investigation and improvement.

Our work provides an initial attempt to combine the advantages of reinforcement learning and imitation learning for structured prediction in the case of dependency parsing.

Proceedings of the Second Workshop on Universal Dependencies (UDW 2018), pages 183–191
Brussels, Belgium, November 1, 2018. ©2018 Association for Computational Linguistics

2 Approximate Dynamic Oracle

We treat oracle parsing as a deterministic Markov Decision Process (Maes et al., 2009), where a state corresponds to a parsing configuration with the gold tree known. The tokens are represented only by their positions in the stack or buffer, i.e., without lexical information. Unlike normal parsing, the initial state for the oracle can be any possible state in the entire state space, and the objective of the oracle is to minimize further structure errors, which we incorporate into the reward function.

2.1 Transition Systems and Reward Function

We define a unified reward function for the four transition systems that we experiment with: Arc-Standard (Yamada and Matsumoto, 2003; Nivre, 2004), Attardi's system with gap-degree of 1 (Attardi, 2006; Kuhlmann and Nivre, 2006), Arc-Standard with the *swap* transition (Nivre, 2009), and Arc-Hybrid (Kuhlmann et al., 2011). We denote them as STANDARD, ATTARDI, SWAP, and HYBRID, respectively. We formalize the actions in these systems in Appendix A.

The reward function approximates the *arc reachability* property as in Goldberg and Nivre (2013). Concretely, when an arc of head-dependent pair $\langle h, d \rangle$ is introduced, there are two cases of unreachable arcs: (1) if a pending token h' ($h' \neq h$) is the gold head of d, then $\langle h', d \rangle$ is unreachable; (2) if a pending token d' whose gold head is d, then $\langle d, d' \rangle$ is unreachable. If an attachment action does not immediately introduce unreachable arcs, we consider it *correct*.

The main reward for an attachment action is the negative count of immediate unreachable arcs it introduces, which sums up to the total attachment errors in the global view. We also incorporate some heuristics in the reward function, so that the *swap* action and non-projective (Attardi) attachments are slightly discouraged. Finally, we give a positive reward to a correct attachment to prevent the oracle from unnecessarily postponing attachment decisions. The exact reward values are modestly tuned in the preliminary experiments, and the reward function is defined as follows:

$$
r = \begin{cases}
-0.5, & \text{if action is } swap \\
0, & \text{if action is } shift \\
-n, & \text{if } n \text{ unreachable arcs are introduced} \\
0.5, & \text{if attachment is correct but non-projective} \\
1, & \text{if attachment is correct and projective}
\end{cases}
$$

Although we only define the reward function for the four transition systems here, it can be easily extended for other systems by following the general principle: (1) reflect the number of unreachable arcs; (2) identify the unreachable arcs as early as possible; (3) reward correct attachment; (4) add system-specific heuristics.

Also note that the present reward function is not necessarily optimal. E.g., in the HYBRID system, a *shift* could also cause an unreachable arc, which is considered in the exact dynamic oracle by Goldberg and Nivre (2013), while the ADO can only observe the loss in later steps. We intentionally do not incorporate this knowledge into the reward function in order to demonstrate that the ADO is able to learn from delayed feedback information, which is necessary in most systems other than HYBRID. We elaborate on the comparison to the exact dynamic oracle in Section 4.

2.2 Feature Extraction and DQN Model

In contrast to the rich lexicalized features for the parser, we use a very simple feature set for the oracle. We use binary features to indicate the position of the gold head of the first 10 tokens in the stack and in the buffer. We also encode whether the gold head is already lost and whether the token has collected all its *pending* gold dependents. Additionally, we encode the 5 previous actions leading to this state, as well as all valid actions in this state.

We use the Deep Q-Network (DQN) to model the oracle, where the input is the aforementioned binary features from a state, and the output is the estimated values for each action in this state. The training objective of the basic DQN is to minimize the expected Temporal Difference (TD) loss:

$$
L_{TD} = \mathbb{E}_{s,a \sim \pi}[(r + \gamma \max_{a'} Q(a'|s') - Q(a|s))^2]
$$

where π is the policy given the value function Q, which assigns a score for each action, s is the current state, a is the performed action, r is the reward, γ is the discount factor, s' is the next state, and a' is the optimal action in state s'.

We apply several techniques to improve the stability of the DQN, including the averaged DQN (Anschel et al., 2016) to reduce variance, the dueling network (Wang et al., 2016) to decouple the estimation of state value and action value, and prioritized experience replay (Schaul et al., 2015) to increase the efficiency of samples.

2.3 Sampling Oracle Training Instances

Our goal is learning to handle erroneous states, so we need to sample such instances during training. Concretely, for every state in the sampling process, apart from following the ε-greedy policy (i.e., select random action with ε probability), we fork the path with certain probability by taking a valid random action to simulate the mistake by the parser. We treat each forked path as a new episode starting from the state after the forking action. Also, to increase sample efficiency, we only take the first N states in each episode, as illustrated in Figure 1.

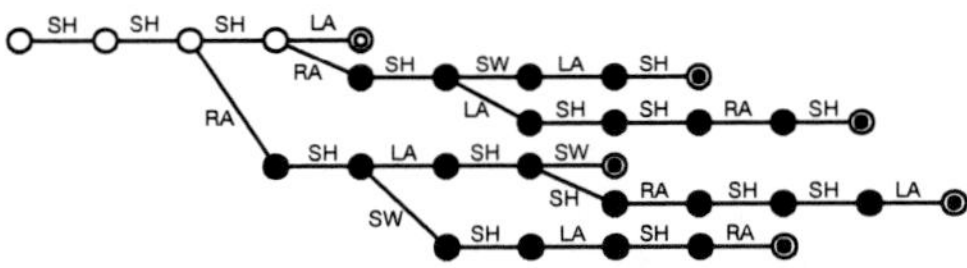

Figure 1: An illustration of the sampled episodes with $N = 5$, where light nodes represent the original path, dark nodes represent the forked paths, and double circles represent the end of the sampled path.

2.4 Cost-Sensitive Parser Training

Since the DQN estimates the cost for each action, we can thus apply cost-sensitive training with multi-margin loss (Edunov et al., 2017) for the parser instead of negative log-likelihood or hinge loss. Concretely, we enforce the margin of the parser scores between the correct action and every other action to be larger than the difference between the oracle scores of these two actions:

$$L = \sum_{a \in A} \max(0, P(a|s) - P(a^*|s) + Q(a^*|s) - Q(a|s))$$

where A is the set of valid actions, $P(\cdot|s)$ is the parser score, $Q(\cdot|s)$ is the oracle score, and a^* is the optimal action according to the oracle.

Cost-sensitive training is similar to the *non-deterministic* oracle (Goldberg and Nivre, 2013), since actions with similar oracle scores need to maintain a smaller margin, thus allowing spurious ambiguity. On the other hand, it also penalizes the actions with larger cost more heavily, thus focusing the training on the more important actions.

3 Experiments

3.1 Data and Settings

We conduct our experiments on the 55 big treebanks from the CoNLL 2017 shared task (Zeman et al., 2017), referred to by their treebank codes, e.g., `grc` for Ancient Greek. For easier replicability, we use the predicted segmentation, part-of-speech tags and morphological features by UDPipe (Straka et al., 2016), provided in the shared task, and evaluate on Labeled Attachment Score (LAS) with the official evaluation script. We also provide the parsing results by UDPipe as a baseline, which incorporates the search-based oracle for non-projective parsing (Straka et al., 2015).

We implement the parser architecture with bidirectional LSTM following Kiperwasser and Goldberg (2016) with the minimal feature set, namely three tokens in the stack and one token in the buffer. For each token, we compose character-based representations with convolutional neural networks following Yu and Vu (2017), and concatenate them with randomly initialized embeddings of the word form, universal POS tag, and morphological features. All hyperparameters of the parser and the oracle are listed in Appendix B.[1]

We compare training the parser with ADOs to static oracles in the four transition systems STANDARD, ATTARDI, SWAP, and HYBRID. Additionally, we implement the exact dynamic oracle (EDO) for HYBRID as the upper bound. For each system, we only use the portion of training data where all oracles can parse, e.g., for STANDARD and HYBRID, we only train on projective trees.

We did preliminary experiments on the ADOs in three settings: (1) $O_{\texttt{all}}$ is trained only on the non-projective trees from all training treebanks (ca. 133,000 sentences); (2) $O_{\texttt{ind}}$ is trained on the individual treebank as used for training the parser; and (3) $O_{\texttt{tune}}$ is based on $O_{\texttt{all}}$, but fine-tuned interactively during the parser training by letting the parser initiate the forked episodes. Results show that three versions have very close performance, we thus choose the simplest one $O_{\texttt{all}}$ to report and analyze, since in this setting only one oracle is needed for training on all treebanks.

3.2 Oracle Recovery Test

Before using the oracle to train the parser, we first test the oracle's ability to control the mistakes. In this test, we use a parser trained with the static oracle to parse the development set, and starting from the parsing step 0, 10, 20, 30, 40, and 50, we let the ADO fork the path and parse until the end. We

---

[1]The parser and the oracle are available at `http://www.ims.uni-stuttgart.de/institut/mitarbeiter/xiangyu/index.en.html`.

use the error rate of the oracle averaged over the aforementioned starting steps as the measurement for the oracle's robustness against error propagation: the smaller the rate, the more robust the oracle. Note that we identify the errors only when the incorrect arcs are produced, but they could be already inevitable due to previous actions, which means some of the parser's mistakes are attributed to the oracle, resulting in a more conservative estimation of the oracle's recovery ability.

Figure 2a and 2b show the average error rate for each treebank and its relation to the percentage of non-projective arcs in the projective STANDARD and the non-projective SWAP systems. Generally, the error rate correlates with the percentage of the non-projective arcs. However, even in the most difficult case (i.e., grc with over 17% non-projective arcs), the oracle only introduces 5% errors in the non-projective system, which is much lower than the parser's error rate of over 40%. The higher error rates in the projective system is due to the fact that the number of errors is at least the number of non-projective arcs. Figure 2c and 2d show the oracles' error recovery performance in the most difficult case grc. The error curves of the oracles in the non-projective systems are very flat, while in the STANDARD system, the errors of the oracle starting from step 0 is only slightly higher than the number of non-projective arcs (the dotted line), which is the lower bound of errors. These results all confirm that the ADO is able to find actions to minimize further errors given any potentially erroneous state.

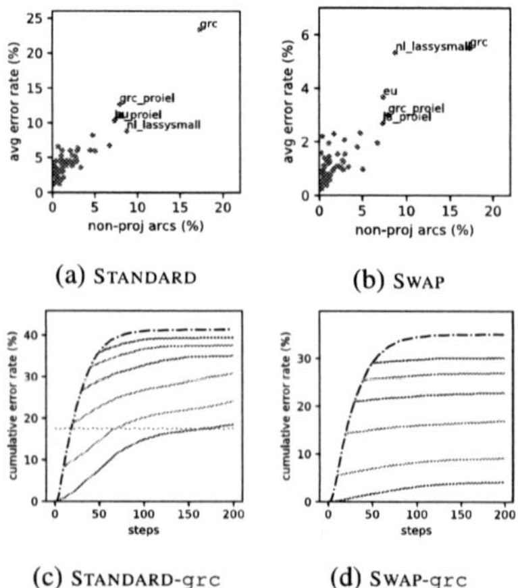

(a) STANDARD   (b) SWAP

(c) STANDARD-grc   (d) SWAP-grc

Figure 2: Results of the oracle recovery test, where (a) and (b) are average error rates across treebanks, (c) and (d) are cumulative error rates for grc.

3.3 Final Results

		UDPipe	STANDARD static	STANDARD ADO	ATTARDI static	ATTARDI ADO	SWAP static	SWAP ADO	HYBRID static	HYBRID ADO	HYBRID EDO
most non- proj	grc	56.04	51.49	51.94	59.02	60.21	58.59	60.87	50.40	52.46	52.74
	nl_las.	78.15	73.07	73.57	79.17	81.88	79.67	81.48	72.29	73.45	73.08
	grc_pro.	65.22	63.85	63.96	68.30	67.79	67.01	67.52	64.26	64.75	64.41
least non- proj	ja	72.21	73.03	73.07	73.12	72.99	73.16	73.26	72.91	73.39	73.34
	gl	77.31	77.19	77.47	77.34	77.63	77.28	77.39	77.27	77.50	77.49
	zh	57.40	57.99	58.56	58.69	58.86	57.83	59.19	57.99	57.83	58.57
most data	cs	82.87	84.32	84.04	84.99	84.72	84.90	84.14	84.34	84.29	84.24
	ru_syn.	86.76	88.09	87.32	88.78	88.09	88.64	87.83	88.05	88.20	88.22
	cs_cac	82.46	83.61	83.57	83.65	83.68	83.64	84.40	82.94	83.52	83.69
least data	cs_cltt	71.64	71.36	73.65	74.04	74.93	73.81	74.23	70.54	72.32	72.25
	hu	64.30	62.91	65.08	65.75	67.02	64.79	66.69	63.65	64.34	63.39
	en_par.	73.64	74.10	74.04	73.74	74.80	73.87	74.65	73.74	73.88	73.22
	AVG	73.04	73.59	73.92	74.66	74.99	74.50	75.01	73.47	73.68	73.74

Table 1: LAS on the selected test sets, where green cells mark ADO outperforming the static oracle and red cells otherwise. Average is calculated over all 55 test set.

In the final experiment, we compare the performance of the parser trained by the ADOs against the static oracle or the EDO if available. Table 1 shows the LAS of 12 representative treebanks, while the full results are shown in Appendix C. In the selection, we include treebanks with the highest percentage of non-projective arcs (grc, nl_lassysmall, grc_proiel), almost only projective trees (ja, gl, zh), the most training data (cs, ru_syntagrus, cs_cac), and the least training data (cs_cltt, hu, en_partut).

Out of the 55 treebanks, the ADO is beneficial in 41, 40, 41, and 35 treebanks for the four systems, and on average outperforms the static baseline by 0.33%, 0.33%, 0.51%, 0.21%, respectively. While considering the treebank characteristics, training with ADOs is beneficial in most cases irrespective of the projectiveness of the treebank. It works especially well for small treebanks, but not as well for very large treebanks. The reason could be that the error propagation problem is not as severe when the parsing accuracy is high, which correlates with the training data size.

In HYBRID, the benefit of the ADO and EDO is very close, they outperform the static baseline by 0.21% and 0.27%, which means that the ADO approximates the upper bound EDO quite well.

Note that we train the parsers only on projective trees in projective systems to ensure a fair comparison. However, the ADO is able to guide the parser even on non-projective trees, and the resulting parsers in STANDARD outperform the baseline by 1.24% on average (see Appendix C), almost bridging the performance gap between projective and non-projective systems.

4 Comparing to Exact Dynamic Oracle

The purpose of the ADO is to approximate the dynamic oracle in the transition systems where an exact dynamic oracle is unavailable or inefficient. However, it could demonstrate how well the approximation is when compared to the EDO, which serves as an upper bound. Therefore, we compare our ADO to the EDO (Goldberg and Nivre, 2013) in the HYBRID system.

First, we compare the reward function of the ADO (see Section 2.1) to the cost function of the EDO, which is: (1) for an attachment action that introduces an arc $\langle h, d \rangle$, the cost is the number of reachable dependents of d plus whether d is still reachable to its gold head h' ($h' \neq h$); and (2) for *shift*, the cost is the number of reachable dependents of d in the stack plus whether the gold head of d is in the stack except for the top item.

The general ideas of both oracles are very similar, namely to punish an action by the number of unreachable arcs it introduces. However, the definitions of reachability are slightly different.

Reachable arcs in the ADO are defined more loosely: as long as the head and dependent of an arc are pending in the stack or buffer, it is considered reachable, thus the reward (cost) of *shift* is always zero. However, in the HYBRID system, an arc of two tokens in the stack could be unreachable (e.g. $\langle s_0, s_1 \rangle$), thus the cost of *shift* in the EDO could be non-zero.

Note that both oracles punish each incorrect attachment exactly once, and the different definitions of reachability only affect the time when an incorrect attachment is punished, namely when the correct attachment is deemed unreachable. Generally, the ADO's reward function delays the punishment for many actions, and dealing with delayed reward signal is exactly the motivation of RL algorithms (Sutton and Barto, 1998).

The DQN model in the ADO bridges the lack of prior knowledge in the definitions of reachability by estimating not only the immediate reward of an action, but also the discounted future rewards. Take the HYBRID system for example. Although the immediate reward of a *shift* is zero, the ADO could learn a more accurate cost in its value estimation if the action eventually causes an unreachable arc. Moreover, in a system where the *exact* reachability is difficult to determine, the ADO estimates the *expected* reachability based on the training data.

We then empirically compare the behavior of the ADO with the EDO, in which we use a parser trained with the static oracle to parse the development set of a treebank, and for each state along the transition sequence produced by the parser we consult the ADO and the EDO. Since the EDO gives a set of optimal actions, we check whether the ADO's action is in the set.

On average, the ADO differs from the EDO (i.e., making suboptimal actions) only in 0.53% of all cases. Among the states where the ADO makes suboptimal actions, more than 90% has the pattern shown in Figure 3, where the gold head of s_1 is s_0 but it is already impossible to make the correct attachment for it, therefore the correct action is to make a *left-arc* to ensure that s_0 is attached correctly. However, the ADO does not realize that s_1 is already lost and estimates that a *left-arc* attachment would incur a negative reward, and is thus inclined to make a "harmless" shift, which would actually cause another lost token s_0 in the future. This type of mistakes happens about 30% of the time when this pattern occurs, and further investigation is needed to eliminate them.

$$[\ \dots \ s_1 \ s_0 \ ]_\sigma \ [\ b_0 \ \dots \ ]_\beta$$

Figure 3: A typical pattern where the ADO makes a mistake.

5 Conclusion

In this paper, we propose to train efficient approximate dynamic oracles with reinforcement learning methods. We tackle the problem of non-decomposable structure loss by letting the oracle learn the action loss from incremental immediate rewards, and act as a proxy for the structure loss to train the parser. We demonstrate that training with a single treebank-universal ADO generally improves the parsing performance over training with static oracle in several transition systems, we also show the ADO's comparable performance to an exact dynamic oracle.

Furthermore, the general idea in this work could be extended to other structured prediction tasks such as graph parsing, by training a better-informed oracle to transform structure costs into action costs, which gives the learning agent more accurate objective while staying in the realm of imitation learning to ensure training efficiency.

References

Oron Anschel, Nir Baram, and Nahum Shimkin. 2016. Averaged-dqn: Variance reduction and stabilization for deep reinforcement learning. *arXiv preprint arXiv:1611.01929*.

Giuseppe Attardi. 2006. Experiments with a multilanguage non-projective dependency parser. In *Proceedings of the Tenth Conference on Computational Natural Language Learning*, pages 166–170. Association for Computational Linguistics.

Michael A Covington. 2001. A fundamental algorithm for dependency parsing. In *Proceedings of the 39th annual ACM southeast conference*, pages 95–102. Citeseer.

Hal Daumé, John Langford, and Daniel Marcu. 2009. Search-based structured prediction. *Machine learning*, 75(3):297–325.

Sergey Edunov, Myle Ott, Michael Auli, David Grangier, and Marc'Aurelio Ranzato. 2017. Classical structured prediction losses for sequence to sequence learning. *arXiv preprint arXiv:1711.04956*.

Yoav Goldberg and Joakim Nivre. 2012. A dynamic oracle for arc-eager dependency parsing. *Proceedings of COLING 2012*, pages 959–976.

Yoav Goldberg and Joakim Nivre. 2013. Training deterministic parsers with non-deterministic oracles. *Transactions of the Association of Computational Linguistics*, 1:403–414.

Carlos Gómez-Rodríguez and Daniel Fernández-González. 2015. An efficient dynamic oracle for unrestricted non-projective parsing. In *Proceedings of the 53rd Annual Meeting of the Association for Computational Linguistics and the 7th International Joint Conference on Natural Language Processing (Volume 2: Short Papers)*, volume 2, pages 256–261.

Carlos Gómez-Rodríguez, Francesco Sartorio, and Giorgio Satta. 2014. A polynomial-time dynamic oracle for non-projective dependency parsing. In *Proceedings of the 2014 Conference on Empirical Methods in Natural Language Processing (EMNLP)*, pages 917–927.

Eliyahu Kiperwasser and Yoav Goldberg. 2016. Simple and accurate dependency parsing using bidirectional lstm feature representations. *Transactions of the Association for Computational Linguistics*, 4:313–327.

Marco Kuhlmann, Carlos Gómez-Rodríguez, and Giorgio Satta. 2011. Dynamic programming algorithms for transition-based dependency parsers. In *Proceedings of the 49th Annual Meeting of the Association for Computational Linguistics: Human Language Technologies-Volume 1*, pages 673–682. Association for Computational Linguistics.

Marco Kuhlmann and Joakim Nivre. 2006. Mildly non-projective dependency structures. In *Proceedings of the COLING/ACL 2006 Main Conference Poster Sessions*, pages 507–514.

Minh Le and Antske Fokkens. 2017. Tackling error propagation through reinforcement learning: A case of greedy dependency parsing. In *Proceedings of the 15th Conference of the European Chapter of the Association for Computational Linguistics: Volume 1, Long Papers*, volume 1, pages 677–687.

Francis Maes, Ludovic Denoyer, and Patrick Gallinari. 2009. Structured prediction with reinforcement learning. *Machine learning*, 77(2-3):271.

Volodymyr Mnih, Koray Kavukcuoglu, David Silver, Alex Graves, Ioannis Antonoglou, Daan Wierstra, and Martin Riedmiller. 2013. Playing atari with deep reinforcement learning. *arXiv preprint arXiv:1312.5602*.

Graham Neubig, Chris Dyer, Yoav Goldberg, Austin Matthews, Waleed Ammar, Antonios Anastasopoulos, Miguel Ballesteros, David Chiang, Daniel Clothiaux, Trevor Cohn, Kevin Duh, Manaal Faruqui, Cynthia Gan, Dan Garrette, Yangfeng Ji, Lingpeng Kong, Adhiguna Kuncoro, Gaurav Kumar, Chaitanya Malaviya, Paul Michel, Yusuke Oda, Matthew Richardson, Naomi Saphra, Swabha Swayamdipta, and Pengcheng Yin. 2017. Dynet: The dynamic neural network toolkit. *arXiv preprint arXiv:1701.03980*.

Joakim Nivre. 2004. Incrementality in deterministic dependency parsing. In *Proceedings of the Workshop on Incremental Parsing: Bringing Engineering and Cognition Together*, pages 50–57. Association for Computational Linguistics.

Joakim Nivre. 2008. Algorithms for deterministic incremental dependency parsing. *Computational Linguistics*, 34(4):513–553.

Joakim Nivre. 2009. Non-projective dependency parsing in expected linear time. In *Proceedings of the Joint Conference of the 47th Annual Meeting of the ACL and the 4th International Joint Conference on Natural Language Processing of the AFNLP: Volume 1-Volume 1*, pages 351–359. Association for Computational Linguistics.

Tom Schaul, John Quan, Ioannis Antonoglou, and David Silver. 2015. Prioritized experience replay. *arXiv preprint arXiv:1511.05952*.

Milan Straka, Jan Hajic, and Jana Straková. 2016. Udpipe: Trainable pipeline for processing conll-u files performing tokenization, morphological analysis, pos tagging and parsing. In *LREC*.

Milan Straka, Jan Hajic, Jana Straková, and Jan Hajic jr. 2015. Parsing universal dependency treebanks using neural networks and search-based oracle. In *International Workshop on Treebanks and Linguistic Theories (TLT14)*, pages 208–220.

Richard S Sutton and Andrew G Barto. 1998. *Reinforcement learning: An introduction*, volume 1. MIT press Cambridge.

Ziyu Wang, Tom Schaul, Matteo Hessel, Hado Hasselt, Marc Lanctot, and Nando Freitas. 2016. Dueling network architectures for deep reinforcement learning. In *International Conference on Machine Learning*, pages 1995–2003.

Hiroyasu Yamada and Yuji Matsumoto. 2003. Statistical dependency analysis with support vector machines. In *Proceedings of IWPT*, volume 3, pages 195–206. Nancy, France.

Xiang Yu and Ngoc Thang Vu. 2017. Character composition model with convolutional neural networks for dependency parsing on morphologically rich languages. In *Proceedings of the 55th Annual Meeting of the Association for Computational Linguistics (Volume 2: Short Papers)*, volume 2, pages 672–678.

Daniel Zeman, Martin Popel, Milan Straka, Jan Hajic, Joakim Nivre, Filip Ginter, Juhani Luotolahti, Sampo Pyysalo, Slav Petrov, Martin Potthast, Francis Tyers, Elena Badmaeva, Memduh Gokirmak, Anna Nedoluzhko, Silvie Cinkova, Jan Hajic jr., Jaroslava Hlavacova, Václava Kettnerová, Zdenka Uresova, Jenna Kanerva, Stina Ojala, Anna Missilä, Christopher D. Manning, Sebastian Schuster, Siva Reddy, Dima Taji, Nizar Habash, Herman Leung, Marie-Catherine de Marneffe, Manuela Sanguinetti, Maria Simi, Hiroshi Kanayama, Valeria dePaiva, Kira Droganova, Héctor Martínez Alonso, Çağr Çöltekin, Umut Sulubacak, Hans Uszkoreit, Vivien Macketanz, Aljoscha Burchardt, Kim Harris, Katrin Marheinecke, Georg Rehm, Tolga Kayadelen, Mohammed Attia, Ali Elkahky, Zhuoran Yu, Emily Pitler, Saran Lertpradit, Michael Mandl, Jesse Kirchner, Hector Fernandez Alcalde, Jana Strnadová, Esha Banerjee, Ruli Manurung, Antonio Stella, Atsuko Shimada, Sookyoung Kwak, Gustavo Mendonca, Tatiana Lando, Rattima Nitisaroj, and Josie Li. 2017. Conll 2017 shared task: Multilingual parsing from raw text to universal dependencies. In *Proceedings of the CoNLL 2017 Shared Task: Multilingual Parsing from Raw Text to Universal Dependencies*, pages 1–19, Vancouver, Canada. Association for Computational Linguistics.

A   Transition Systems

Table 2 provides a unified view of the the actions in the four transition systems: *shift* and *right* are shared by all four systems; *left* is shared by all but the HYBRID system, which uses *left-hybrid* instead; *left-2* and *right-2* are defined only in the ATTARDI system; and *swap* is defined only in the SWAP system.

For all systems, the initial states are identical: the stack contains only the root, the buffer contains all other tokens, and the set of arcs is empty. The terminal states are also identical: the stack contains only the root, the buffer is empty, and the set of arcs is the created dependency tree.

Action	Before		After
shift	$(\sigma, j \mid \beta, A)$	$\rightarrow$	$(\sigma \mid j, \beta, A)$
left	$(\sigma \mid i \mid j, \beta, A)$	$\rightarrow$	$(\sigma \mid j, \beta, A \cup \{\langle j,i \rangle\})$
right	$(\sigma \mid i \mid j, \beta, A)$	$\rightarrow$	$(\sigma \mid i, \beta, A \cup \{\langle i,j \rangle\})$
left-2	$(\sigma \mid i \mid j \mid k, \beta, A)$	$\rightarrow$	$(\sigma \mid j \mid k, \beta, A \cup \{\langle k,i \rangle\})$
right-2	$(\sigma \mid i \mid j \mid k, \beta, A)$	$\rightarrow$	$(\sigma \mid i \mid j, \beta, A \cup \{\langle i,k \rangle\})$
left-hybrid	$(\sigma \mid i, j \mid \beta, A)$	$\rightarrow$	$(\sigma, j \mid \beta, A \cup \{\langle j,i \rangle\})$
swap	$(\sigma \mid i \mid j, \beta, A)$	$\rightarrow$	$(\sigma \mid j, i \mid \beta, A)$

Table 2: The actions defined in the four transition systems, where σ denotes the stack, β denotes the buffer, and A denotes the set of created arcs.

B   Architecture and Hyperparameters

The parser takes characters, word form, universal POS tag and morphological features of each word as input. The character composition model follows Yu and Vu (2017), which takes 4 convolutional filters with width of 3, 5, 7, and 9, each filter has dimension of 32, adding to a 128-dimensional word representation. The randomly initialized word embeddings are also 128-dimensional, the POS tag and morphological features are both 32-dimensional. The concatenated word representations are then fed into a bidirectional LSTM with 128 hidden units to capture the contextual information in the sentence. The contextualized word representations of the top 3 tokens in the stack and the first token in the buffer are concatenated and fed into two layers of 256 hidden units with the ReLU activation, and the output are the scores for each action. The argmax of the scores are then further concatenated with the last hidden layer, and outputs the scores for the labels if the predicted action introduces an arc. In this way, the prediction of action and label are decoupled, and they are learned separately.

The oracle (DQN) takes the binary features described in Section 2.2 as input, which is fed into a layer of 128 hidden units. It then forks into two channels to calculate the value for the state and the actions separately, then they are aggregated as the estimated state-action value, as in Wang et al. (2016). In the DQN training, we use discount factor $\gamma = 0.9$, for the proportional prioritized experience replay, we select $\alpha = 0.9$, $\beta = 0.5$.

Both the parser and the oracle are trained with maximum 50000 mini-batches and early-stop on the development set. In every step, the parser trains on mini-batches of 10 sentences, and the oracle generates samples from 5 sentences into the replay memory, and trains on mini-batches of 1000 samples. While generating the samples for the oracle, we fork each state by a random valid action with a probability of 0.05, and we take at most 5 forked episodes for each sentence, with the maximum episode length $N = 20$.

C   Full Results

The results for all 55 treebanks are shown in Table 3.

	UDPipe	STANDARD			SWAP		ATTARDI		HYBRID		
		static	ADO	ADO*	static	ADO	static	ADO	static	ADO	EDO
ar	65.30	66.75	66.75	66.75	67.34	67.34	67.15	67.15	67.14	67.14	67.14
bg	83.64	84.14	84.54	84.48	84.19	84.64	83.95	84.46	84.31	84.31	84.31
ca	85.39	86.08	86.08	86.08	86.62	86.62	86.54	86.54	86.09	86.09	86.15
cs	82.87	84.32	84.32	84.47	84.99	84.99	84.90	84.90	84.34	84.34	84.34
cs_cac	82.46	83.61	83.61	84.48	83.65	83.68	83.64	84.40	82.94	83.52	83.69
cs_cltt	71.64	71.36	73.65	75.15	74.04	74.93	73.81	74.23	70.54	72.32	72.25
cu	62.76	63.81	64.16	65.94	66.47	66.92	66.37	67.09	63.85	64.39	64.69
da	73.38	73.55	74.73	75.50	74.51	75.00	74.51	75.30	73.45	73.45	74.36
de	69.11	71.93	71.94	72.87	73.26	73.26	73.03	73.03	71.72	71.80	71.96
el	79.26	79.47	79.99	80.27	80.15	80.84	79.96	80.64	79.04	79.04	79.20
en	75.84	75.99	76.37	76.76	76.37	76.65	76.32	76.63	75.82	76.31	76.19
en_lines	72.94	72.52	72.76	73.56	74.12	74.27	74.08	74.57	73.20	73.20	73.20
en_partut	73.64	74.10	74.10	74.56	73.74	74.80	73.87	74.65	73.74	73.88	73.74
es	81.47	82.79	82.79	82.79	82.76	82.76	82.49	82.49	82.85	82.85	82.85
es_ancora	83.78	84.83	84.85	85.33	85.56	85.56	85.66	85.66	85.34	85.34	85.34
et	58.79	58.77	59.34	59.47	59.10	60.84	58.93	61.12	59.11	59.11	59.11
eu	69.15	68.91	69.54	71.27	71.44	72.72	70.63	72.64	68.55	68.95	68.72
fa	79.24	79.73	79.76	80.47	80.47	80.47	79.67	79.87	80.20	80.20	80.20
fi	73.75	74.34	74.57	74.90	74.53	74.70	74.48	75.20	73.96	73.96	74.33
fi_ftb	74.03	75.58	75.86	76.10	75.93	76.03	75.18	75.18	75.41	75.41	75.42
fr	80.75	81.42	81.44	81.42	81.88	81.88	81.21	81.98	81.25	81.25	81.25
fr_sequoia	79.98	80.90	80.90	81.52	81.64	81.76	81.37	81.37	80.56	80.58	80.67
gl	77.31	77.19	77.47	77.96	77.34	77.63	77.28	77.39	77.27	77.50	77.49
got	59.81	59.81	60.61	62.05	61.26	61.97	60.94	62.53	59.09	60.78	60.14
grc	56.04	51.49	51.94	58.13	59.02	60.21	58.59	60.87	50.40	52.46	52.74
grc_proiel	65.22	63.85	63.96	67.40	68.30	68.30	67.01	67.52	64.26	64.75	64.41
he	57.23	57.95	58.30	59.01	58.02	58.72	58.18	58.41	57.82	58.02	58.06
hi	86.77	87.48	87.48	88.06	88.22	88.22	88.08	88.08	87.53	87.53	87.56
hr	77.18	77.19	77.98	78.23	78.45	78.63	77.64	77.96	77.26	77.45	77.70
hu	64.30	62.91	65.08	65.59	65.75	67.02	64.79	66.69	63.65	64.34	63.65
id	74.61	74.85	74.85	74.85	74.42	74.42	74.79	74.79	74.17	74.50	74.48
it	85.28	85.76	86.06	85.91	86.33	86.33	86.18	86.18	86.24	86.24	86.24
ja	72.21	73.03	73.07	73.06	73.12	73.12	73.16	73.26	72.91	73.39	73.34
ko	59.09	72.48	74.07	75.09	73.98	74.61	73.97	74.70	72.25	73.40	72.85
la_ittb	76.98	77.80	77.80	80.56	81.27	81.35	82.33	82.33	77.05	77.56	77.61
la_proiel	57.54	56.15	56.85	60.00	58.67	59.38	59.18	60.80	55.92	57.01	57.58
lv	59.95	60.04	61.39	61.53	60.62	60.66	60.32	60.96	59.76	60.34	60.05
nl	68.90	69.69	70.47	71.53	71.77	72.03	70.50	71.87	69.42	69.83	69.90
nl_lassysmall	78.15	73.07	73.57	78.82	79.17	81.88	79.67	81.48	72.29	73.45	73.08
no_bokmaal	83.27	84.07	84.50	84.56	84.47	84.68	84.15	84.82	83.92	83.92	84.04
no_nynorsk	81.56	82.41	82.45	83.46	82.64	82.99	82.64	82.91	81.74	82.47	82.32
pl	78.78	80.25	80.41	80.61	80.28	80.34	79.84	80.14	79.26	80.20	79.95
pt	82.11	82.33	82.33	82.83	82.49	82.73	82.92	83.07	81.77	82.03	81.93
pt_br	85.36	86.11	86.40	86.30	86.17	86.17	85.98	86.28	86.01	86.21	86.17
ro	79.88	80.06	80.21	80.45	79.96	80.37	80.41	80.41	79.59	79.66	79.73
ru	74.03	74.66	74.66	75.26	75.07	75.78	74.62	75.60	74.68	74.68	75.15
ru_syntagrus	86.76	88.09	88.09	88.09	88.78	88.78	88.64	88.64	88.05	88.20	88.22
sk	72.75	73.73	73.99	75.84	74.27	74.75	74.28	75.58	74.09	74.26	74.51
sl	81.15	81.26	81.97	83.13	82.94	83.32	82.61	83.65	81.85	81.86	81.94
sv	76.73	77.24	77.70	78.39	77.86	78.25	78.03	78.54	77.70	78.24	77.70
sv_lines	74.29	74.28	74.64	75.49	74.32	75.22	74.01	75.36	73.40	73.80	74.00
tr	53.19	53.97	54.82	55.38	54.20	55.38	54.53	55.18	54.32	54.56	54.32
ur	76.69	77.16	77.16	77.25	77.40	77.83	77.89	77.92	77.16	77.16	77.16
vi	37.47	38.32	39.09	39.10	38.38	38.85	38.50	39.68	38.36	38.67	38.80
zh	57.40	57.99	58.56	58.65	58.69	58.86	57.83	59.19	57.99	57.99	58.57
AVG	73.04	73.59	73.92	74.83	74.66	74.99	74.50	75.01	73.47	73.68	73.74

Table 3: LAS on the 55 test sets, where green cells mark ADO outperforming the static oracle and red cells for the opposite. The column ADO* indicate the parsers trained on both projective and non-projective trees. Average is calculated over all 55 test set.

The Coptic Universal Dependency Treebank

Amir Zeldes and **Mitchell Abrams**
Department of Linguistics, Georgetown University
{amir.zeldes,mja284}@georgetown.edu

Abstract

This paper presents the Coptic Universal Dependency Treebank, the first dependency treebank within the Egyptian subfamily of the Afro-Asiatic languages. We discuss the composition of the corpus, challenges in adapting the UD annotation scheme to existing conventions for annotating Coptic, and evaluate inter-annotator agreement on UD annotation for the language. Some specific constructions are taken as a starting point for discussing several more general UD annotation guidelines, in particular for appositions, ambiguous passivization, incorporation and object-doubling.

1 Introduction

The Coptic language represents the last phase of the Ancient Egyptian phylum of the Afro-Asiatic language family, forming part of the longest continuously documented human language on Earth. Despite its high value for historical, comparative and typological linguistics, as well as its cultural importance as the heritage language of Copts in Egypt and in the diaspora, digital resources for the study of Coptic have only recently become available, while syntactically annotated data did not exist until the beginning of the present project. This paper presents the first treebank of Coptic, constructed within the UD framework and currently encompassing over 20,000 tokens. In this section we give a brief overview of some pertinent facts of Coptic grammar, before moving on to describing how these are encoded in our corpus.

Unlike earlier forms of Ancient Egyptian, which were written in hieroglyphs or hieratic script throughout the first three millennia BCE, Coptic was written starting in the early first millenium CE using a variant of the Greek alphabet, with several added letters for Egyptian sounds absent from Greek. Figure 1 shows the script, which was originally written without spaces (the Greek loan word ⲯⲩⲭⲏ 'psyche' is visible at the top left). Manuscript damage, also shown in the figure, represents a frequent challenge to annotation efforts (see Section 7).

Figure 1: Excerpt from a papyrus letter by Besa, Abbot of the White Monastery in the 5th century, showing text without spaces and a lacuna. Image: Österreichische Nationalbibliothek, http://digital.onb.ac.at/rep/access/open/10099409.

Modern conventions separate Coptic text into multi-word units known as bound groups (Layton, 2011, 19-20) using spaces, based on the presence of one stressed lexical item in each group. This leads to multiple units being spelled together which would normally receive separate tokens and part of speech tags in annotated corpora. Similarly to languages such as Arabic, Amharic, or Hebrew, simple examples include noun phrases or prepositional phrases spelled together, as in (1), or clitic possessors spelled together with nouns, as in (2).[1]

(1)   ϩⲙ-ⲡ-ⲣⲁⲛ hm-p-ran 'in-the-name'

(2)   ⲡⲣⲛⲧ⸗ⲕ   rnt=k   'name-your (SG.M)'

However, Coptic fusional morphology can be much more complex than in Semitic languages, for several reasons. Developing from a morphologically rich synthetic language through an analytic phase in Late Egyptian, Coptic has fusional morphology and is usually seen as an agglutinative

---

[1]We follow common Egyptological practice in separating lexical items within bound groups by '-' and clitic pronouns by '='.

Proceedings of the Second Workshop on Universal Dependencies (UDW 2018), pages 192–201
Brussels, Belgium, November 1, 2018. ©2018 Association for Computational Linguistics

or even polysynthetic language (Loprieno, 1995, 51). Similarly to inflection in Hausa, auxiliaries and clitics attach to verbs as in (3), and unlike in Semitic languages, compounds are spelled together and do not allow intervening articles. The language also exhibits frequent verb-object incorporation, complicating word segmentation for tokenization (see Grossman 2014), as in the complex verb shown in (4). Such complex verbs can be embedded in word formation processes, leading to nominalizations such as (5).

(3) ⲁ-ϥ-ϩⲱⲧⲃ   ⲙ-ⲡ-ⲣⲙⲛⲕⲏⲙⲉ
     a-f-hōtb   m-p-rmnkēme
     PST-3.SG.M-kill ACC-the-Egyptian
     'he killed the Egyptian'

(4) ϩⲉⲧⲃ-ⲯⲧⲭⲏ
     hetb-psychē
     kill-soul
     '(to) soul-kill' (incorporated)

(5) ⲙⲛⲧ-ⲣⲉϥ-ϩⲉⲧⲃ-ⲯⲧⲭⲏ
     mnt-ref-hetb-psychē
     ness-er-kill-soul
     'soul-killing' (lit. 'soul-kill-er-ness')

Finally, some auxiliaries, such as the optative in (6) may either fuse with and even circumfix adjacent pronouns as in (7), or in some cases exhibit 'zero' forms for pronouns, as in (8).

(6) ⲉⲣⲉ-ⲡ-ⲣⲱⲙⲉ   ⲥⲱⲧⲙ   ⲉⲡⲟ≠ⲕ
     ere-p-rōme   sōtm   ero=k
     OPT-the-man hear   to-you.2SG.M
     'may the man hear you'

(7) ⲉ-ϥ-ⲉ-ⲥⲱⲧⲙ   ⲉⲡⲟ≠ⲕ
     e-f-e-sōtm   ero=k
     OPT-3.SG.M-OPT-hear to-you.2SG.M
     'may he hear you' (circumfix auxiliary)

(8) ⲉⲣⲉ-ⲥⲱⲧⲙ   ⲉⲡⲟ≠ϥ
     ere-sōtm   ero=f
     OPT+2.SG.F-hear to-him.3.SG.M
     'may you hear him' (SG.F subj, fused)

Representing these discontinuous and null phenomena within the UD framework is difficult in the first instance because of their intrinsic complexity (for example, UD prohibits null pronoun nodes, even in enhanced dependencies), but is further complicated by the use of existing standards in Coptic tokenization and tagging, which we present next.

2 Previous work

Of the vast literary, documentary and epigraphic material available in Coptic, print editions have focused on a small subset of early literature in the Sahidic dialect of Upper Egypt, the most prominent of six major dialects (see Shisha-Halevy 1986), which is also considered to be the classical form of the language. While all examples in this paper come from Sahidic sources, we believe that the analyses will generalize well to other dialects, which we intend to approach in the future.

Sizable digital corpora, which have only recently become available in machine readable formats (see Schroeder and Zeldes 2016 on the Coptic Scriptorium project and `http://marcion.sourceforge.net/`, which provides transcriptions of multiple out of copyright editions) have generally followed the same path of starting with classic Sahidic authors. Other targeted projects have focused on translations from Greek, and especially the Bible, e.g. the Digital Edition of the Coptic Old Testament in Göttingen (Behlmer and Feder, 2017), but also tracking Greek influence in Coptic in general (Almond et al., 2013). Finally Some other projects are advancing the availability of documentary, mostly papyrus materials as well (notably `http://papyri.info/`), which are as yet only digitized in small quantities.

Although there is a plan to build a constituent treebank of hieroglyphic Ancient Egyptian (Polis and Rosmorduc, 2013), it is as yet unavailable. The UD Coptic Dependency Treebank represents the first dependency treebank for the entire Egyptian language family as well as the only publicly available treebank for Coptic in particular, and for any phase of Egyptian in general.

As a basis for the Coptic Treebank, we selected data from Coptic Scriptorium (available at `http://copticscriptorium.org/`; see the next section for the specific genres and texts), for two main reasons: 1. the data is freely available under a Creative Commons license, facilitating its re-annotation and distribution; and 2. the data is already tokenized and POS tagged, using a native Coptic POS tagging scheme. Using the Coptic Scriptorium (CS) corpora therefore substantially reduces the required annotation effort, but imposes certain constraints on the segmentation and tagging schemes chosen, which will be presented in Section 4.

source	genre	documents	tokens	sents
translated				
Apophthegmata Patrum	hagiography	1–6, 18–19, 23–26	1,318	62
Gospel of Mark	Bible (narrative)	Chapters 1–6	7,087	248
1 Corinthians	Bible (epistle)	Chapters 1–6	3,571	124
original				
Shenoute, Discourses 4	sermons	Not Because a Fox Barks	2,553	97
Shenoute, Canons 3	sermons	Abraham our Father (XL93-94)	579	26
		Acephalous 22 (YA421-28)	1,703	43
Letters of Besa	letters	Letters 13, 15, 25	1,981	93
Martyrdom of Victor	martyrdom	Chapters 1–6	1,985	88
total			20,777	781

Table 1: Texts and genres in UD Coptic.

3 Texts

The selection of texts for the Coptic Treebank was meant to satisfy four criteria:

1. Data should be freely available

2. A range of different genres should be covered

3. Text types should be chosen which are interesting to users

4. Data should resemble likely targets for automatic parsing using the treebank for training

A dilemma in realizing 3. is that typical UD users interested in computational linguistics, corpus linguistics and language typology may have different interests than Coptologists: the former may prefer texts which resemble other treebank texts or are even available in other languages, such as the Bible, while the latter may be most interested in classic Coptic literature by prominent authors such as Shenoute of Artipe, archmandrite of the White Monastery in the 3rd–4th centuries.

To balance these needs, we decided to include both translated Biblical material and original Coptic works, with a view to allowing comparisons with other languages for which Bible treebanks are available, as well as studies of untranslated Coptic syntax. Table 1 shows the selection of texts currently available in the corpus.

4 Segmentation

While all digital corpora of Coptic referenced in Section 2 separate bound groups, for treebanking purposes we require a more fine grained tokenization. The only tokenization for which NLP tools

are available is the one used in the Coptic Scriptorium project, though automatic segmentation accuracy is currently around 94.5% (Feder et al., 2018), meaning that working with data that is already gold-segmented is highly desirable. As a result, the Coptic Treebank inherits some segmentation guidelines, which will be discussed below.[2]

To represent Coptic segmentation correctly, at least three levels of granularity are required: at the highest level, bound groups, which are spelled together, can be regarded as a purely orthographic device, similar to fused spellings of clitics in English, but much more common. To represent these in the CoNLL-U format, we use multi-tokens and the property SpaceAfter=No on non final tokens, as shown in Table 2 for the two bound groups 'in|his|deeds of|soul-killing', which contains the deverbal incorporated noun from (5). This practice corresponds to the same guideline used in Semitic languages, such as Arabic or Hebrew, which use multi-tokens to represent multiword units with a single lexical stress. The second level of granularity corresponds to POS-tag bearing units, which correspond to CoNLL-U tokens.

Finally, for units below the POS tag level, such as components of incorporated 'soul-killing', we

---

[2]Compatibility with existing resources will motivate several annotation guidelines below; following reviewer comments we suggest this is in keeping with Manning's Law: it offers satisfactory linguistic analysis (rule 1, evidenced by use in existing linguistic studies), allows for consistent human annotation (rule 3, see Section 4 on agreement), and forms a standard comprehensible to and used by non-linguist annotators (rule 5). We also attempt to follow rule 2 in adhering to decisions in other languages to allow for typological comparison where possible. Finally, we have reason to believe the present scheme works well for parsing and downstream NLP tasks (rule 6), though evaluating these is outside the scope of this paper.

text= ... ϩⲛⲛⲉϥϩⲃⲏⲩⲉ ⲙⲙⲛⲧⲣⲉϥϩⲉⲧⲃⲯⲩⲭⲏ
transc=... hn|nef|hbēue m|mnt-ref-hetb-psuxē
gloss= ... in|his|deeds of|ness-er-kill-soul

...

12-14	ϩⲛⲛⲉϥϩⲃⲏⲩⲉ	-	-	-	-	-	-	-	-
12	ϩⲛ	in	ADP	PREP	_	14	case	_	Orig=ϩⲛ̄|SpaceAfter=No
13	ⲛⲉϥ	his	DET	PPOS	...	14	det	_	SpaceAfter=No
14	ϩⲃⲏⲩⲉ	deeds	NOUN	N	_	9	obl	_	_
15-16	ⲙⲙⲛⲧⲣⲉϥϩⲉⲧⲃⲯⲩⲭⲏ	_	-	-	-	-	-	-	-
15	ⲙ	of	ADP	PREP	_	16	case	_	Orig=ⲙ̄|SpaceAfter=No
16	ⲙⲛⲧⲣⲉϥϩⲉⲧⲃⲯⲩⲭⲏ	soul-killing	NOUN	N	_	14	nmod	_	Morphs=ⲙⲛⲧ-ⲣⲉϥ-ϩⲉⲧⲃ-ⲯⲩⲭⲏ

Table 2: Segmentation in CoNLL-U format for a sentence fragment. The lemma column has been filled with glosses for convenience, and features in column 6 have been omitted for space.

use the MISC column to reproduce the morphological segmentation of complex items, as shown in the final column in the example, using hyphens as morpheme separators. Although we considered using sub-tokens to represent incorporation, and using the *compound* relation, we decided against this in order to maintain parity with CS tokens and segmentation practices, and to match up with the practice in Hebrew and Arabic, which use sub-tokens for constituents of bound groups (and not for smaller units, e.g. portmanteau compounds in both languages[3]). This also allows us to benefit from existing POS tagging software to feed automatic parsing. At the same time, because we have a morphological analysis of complex tokens in the tagged source corpora, we retain this information in the MISC column, and a version of the data instantiating the components as tokens could be produced fully automatically if needed. The MISC column is also used to hold an attribute *Orig* with original forms of tokens as spelled in the source manuscripts, which often deviate from standard spellings or contain added optional diacritics (the word form column is always normalized). As a result the data can be used to train automatic normalization tools.

A further complication arises in the case of fused auxiliaries and pronouns, as in the cases from examples (7) and (8). Here too, a solution splitting the fused form into three tokens would be conceivable, in order to represent the circumfix auxiliaries. However, CS guidelines do not tokenize such units apart, instead using portmanteau tags such as AOPT_PPER (optative auxiliary, fused with personal pronoun), and a lemma joining the lemmas of both units via an underscore. A

potential pitfall of splitting these units is that, if we consider a form such as *e-f-e* to consist of three tokens, there is a chance that automatic taggers and parsers will tag one of the two 'e' vowels correctly as an auxiliary, but not the other, leading to an incoherent analysis.[4] The token *efe*, by contrast, will always receive a single tag, and since the form is unambiguous, it will always be correct. While we would not prioritize ease of tagging over an adequate linguistic analysis, we feel that, coupled with the desire to maintain parity with larger corpora, Manning's Law favors this analysis, which is unambiguous, deterministic and easy to convert into a different form if necessary using the native XPOS tags.

We therefore decided to retain CS tokenization practices with regard to fused forms, both in order to benefit from existing NLP tools and to retain parity with the un-treebanked source corpora, which contain a variety of additional non-linguistic annotations. In order to adhere to strict UPOS and UD dependency relations, we have opted to always tag such cases by reference to the argument pronoun, i.e. a form such as 'efe' is tagged as *PRON* and labeled *nsubj*, not *AUX/aux*. The native CS XPOS tag nevertheless uses the portmanteau notation, and the MISC field includes a segmented form, which can be converted into a subtoken representation if desired.

---

[3]e.g. Hebrew רמזור *ramzor* 'stop-light' (a portmanteau, lit. 'light-cue'), which is left unsegmented as a single token. We thank an anonymous reviewer for providing this example.

[4]The form *e* in Coptic is highly polysemous: it can stand for the preposition meaning 'to', a relativizer, an adverbial subordinating conjunction, a focus marker, the second person singular feminine (in some inflections), and more. One reviewer has asked whether contemporary taggers are actually susceptible to such errors, and the answer in our experience has been positive, probably because 'e' and 'f' are among the most common Coptic tokens. Additionally, due to null forms associated with the 2.SG.F subject (cf. (8) for example) and UD's policy against null subject nodes, fused forms become unavoidable.

5 POS tags

Coptic Scriptorium offers two tagsets with different levels of granularity: CS Fine and CS Coarse, distinguishing 44 and 23 tags respectively. Due to the possibility of a number of portmanteau tags in fusional cases, the CS Fine tagset effectively included 15 additional distinct labels arising from the cross-product of fusable parts-of-speech.

Table 3 gives the mapping between CS tags and UPOS, but excluding portmanteau tags. In all cases of portmanteau tags, we adopt the strategy outlined in the previous section, of giving content words priority over function words, and more specifically, of preferring arguments over fused auxiliaries.

Coptic auxiliaries fall into two main syntactic classes: main clause auxiliaries (e.g. past tense, CS *APST*) and subordinating auxiliaries (e.g. precursive, *APREC*, which roughly means 'after [VERB]ing, ...'. The tag A* in Table 3 stands for any main clause auxiliary (12 CS Fine tags), while subordinating auxiliary tags are listed separately, all corresponding to *SCONJ* in UPOS. The entry P* stands for four pronoun tags mapped to *PRON*, and V* stands for all CS verbal tags.

CS	UPOS	CS	UPOS
A*	AUX	FUT	AUX
ACAUS	VERB	IMOD	ADV
ACOND	SCONJ	N	NOUN
ADV	ADV		ADJ
ALIM	SCONJ	NEG	ADV
APREC	SCONJ	NPROP	PROPN
ART	DET	NUM	NUM
CCIRC	SCONJ	PDEM	DET
CCOND	SCONJ	P*	PRON
CFOC	PART	PPOS	DET
CONJ	CCONJ	PREP	ADP
COP	PRON	PTC	PART
CPRET	AUX	PUNCT	PUNCT
CREL	SCONJ	UNKNOWN	X
EXIST	VERB	V*	VERB
FM	X		

Table 3: Mapping of CS Fine tags to UPOS.

A point worth noting is that although the CS tags are generally more fine grained than UPOS, no CS tag maps unambiguously to UPOS *ADJ*. This is because true adjectives are extremely rare in Coptic, limited to about a dozen items, which can appear immediately following a noun they describe. For almost all attributive modification, Coptic uses an 'of'-PP, i.e. a 'wise man' is simply a 'man of wisdom'. Due to the fact that true adjectives are so rare in Coptic (all are archaisms left over from Late Egyptian), and the fact that some can also be used in the 'of' construction as though they were nouns, the CS tagset does not reserve a POS tag for them. However for the handful of items that do occur as adjectival modifiers (post-nominal, not mediated by 'of'), we use the *amod* relation and UPOS *ADJ* based on the relation.

Additionally, some CS tags provide morphological information that would otherwise be lost in UPOS, but can be represented in UD features (CoNLL-U column 6), which are outlined in the next section.

6 Morphological features

Morphological features are automatically added to the corpus using DepEdit,[5] a freely available Python library for manipulating dependency data in the CoNLL-U format (see Peng and Zeldes 2008). Some of the morphological feature categories are trivial to assign based on word forms, such as gendered and numbered article forms, or pronoun types.

However there are also some features that can be derived from native POS tags, such as mood and polarity: the imperative CS tag *VIMP* can be used to feed the UD `Mood=Imp` feature, and some auxiliaries are inherently negative, feeding the `Polarity=Neg` feature. For example, Coptic distinguishes some tenses with paired negative and positive auxiliaries (e.g. CS tags *APST* and *ANEGPST* for positive and negative past tense). Some tensed auxiliaries are exclusively negative, such as the perfective negative conjugation (CS *ANY*, cf. Loprieno 1995, 221), which roughly translates into a clause modified by 'not yet' which has no morphologically positive counterpart. All forms of such auxiliaries are automatically flagged as `Polarity=Neg` based on CS tags.

Finally, Coptic possessive determiners indicate gender and number for both the possessor and possessed, as in languages such as French or German, and therefore we use the 'layered feature' facility in the CoNLL-U format, distinguishing `Gender` and `Number` from `Gender[psor]` and `Number[psor]` for possessor features, as in (9), which shows a masculine singular noun possessed by an article agreeing with these features, but also marking a third person singular feminine possessor.

---

[5] `https://corpling.uis.georgetown.edu/depedit/`

(9) пес-ні
pes-ēi
her-house (house = Masc. Sg.)
```
Gender=Masc|Gender[psor]=Fem|
Number=Sing|Number[psor]=Sing|
Person=3|Poss=Yes|PronType=Prs
```
'her house'

7 Dependencies

7.1 Absent relations

UD Coptic uses all UD relations, with the exception of *expl* and *clf*, since the language does not have expletive pronouns or classifiers. Among the recommended and frequently used subtypes, we do not use the *:pass* subtypes (i.e. *nsubj:pass* and *aux:pass*) due to the ambiguous nature of Coptic passives. While there is a morphological form, the 'stative' (CS tag *VSTAT*) which can express a stative passive for transitive verbs, as in (10), the same form simply means persisting in a state for intransitive verbs, as in (11).

(10) п-ні кнт
p-ēi kēt
the-house build.VSTAT
'the house is built'

(11) п-ллоот голб
p-moou holk^j
the-water sweet.VSTAT
'the water is sweet[6]'

In both cases, the sense is not actional. For the actional passive more directly translating the English passive, Coptic uses an ambiguous 3rd person plural, as in (12). When an oblique agent is supplied which conflicts in agreement with the non-referential 3rd person plural, it is possible to distinguish active plural from the passive, as shown in (13).

(12) а-т-готб-ч
a-u-hotb-f
PST-3.PL-kill-3.SG.M
'they killed him/he was killed'

(13) а-т-готб-ч   гітп-те-чнлле
a-u-hotb-f   hitn-te-shime
PST-3.PL-kill-3.SG.M by-the-woman
'he was killed by the woman'
(lit. 'they killed him by the woman')

However since cases like (13) are rare, we have

opted not to distinguish passives, annotating 3rd person plural verbs uniformly with regular dependent *nsubj* and *aux* children (i.e. active syntax).

7.2 Other problematic constructions

During the annotation process, we encountered several problems and special constructions highlighting the complications of adapting the UD annotation scheme to Coptic. One difficulty was handling lacunae in the data: since we wanted to include some major literary texts in their entirety which are only attested in damaged manuscripts, we were not able to select only texts with complete sentences, and we also expect parsers trained on our data to be applied to damaged text. In cases where the damaged words can be reconstructed with high confidence (usually meaning that at least their POS tag can be assigned), words are attached as usual. For more incomprehensible or very fragmentary phrases, especially those tagged as CS *UNKNOWN* (UPOS: *X*), we attach all tokens to the root as *dep*. For linguistically interpretable scribal errors, by contrast, we use the *reparandum* label, using the general UD guidelines for disfluency annotation.

As an example of a more linguistic issue with Coptic annotation, we consider the case of appositions that are non-adjacent, as the current UD guidelines define appositional modifiers as "immediately following the first noun that serves to define, modify, name, or describe that noun".[7] This definition assumes that appositions are adjacent, with nothing intervening between two nominals. However, this is problematic for some Coptic constructions where enclitic particles, mostly borrowed from Greek such as ае 'but, and', must appear in the second position in the sentence (immediately following the first stressed word), breaking up two appositional nominals, as shown in (14).

(14) п-рро ае аіокантіаnoc а-ч-гроketе
p-rro **de** Dioklētianos   a-f-hrokeue
the-king **but** Diocletian   PST-3SGM-amble
'but the Emperor Diocletian went about'

Since the very same two nominals would be considered an apposition if the particle did not occur, and since the particle is always a clause-level dependent that invariably appears in second position, we decided to analyze this construction as *appos*.[8]

---

[6]Many words translated as adjectives in English are verbs in Coptic: the intransitive infinitive *hlok^j* means 'become sweet', and the corresponding stative *holk^j* means 'be sweet'. Morphologically both are verbal forms in Coptic.

[7]http://universaldependencies.org/u/dep/appos.html, accessed 2018-07-10.

[8]An anonymous reviewer has suggested creating a sub-

Further difficulties in applying UD guidelines to Coptic arise in handling direct objects. Coptic exhibits a regular alternation or differential object marking depending on tense/aspect distinctions. In the durative tenses (Layton, 2011, 233–250), including indicative present, future and imperfect, objects are usually mediated by the preposition ⲛ- *n-* 'of' (or before pronouns, taking the form ⲙⲙⲟ⸗ *mmo=*), as in (15), whereas in other tenses featuring an auxiliary before the subject, objects are enclitic, appearing directly after the verb without a preposition (this is known as Stern-Jernstedt's Rule, Jernstedt 1927), as shown earlier in (12).

(15)   ⲥⲉ-ϩⲱⲧⲃ ⲙⲙⲟ-ϥ
        se-hōtb   mmo=f
        3.PL-kill   ACC-3.SG.M
        'they are killing him'

The fact that these object positions are semantically identical has led us to analyze both constructions as *obj*. This has the uncomfortable result of the same preposition *n-* sometimes acting as an adnominal modifier marker (*nmod*, in a literal 'of'-PP), and sometimes as an accusative case marker, similarly to the analysis of the differential object marking preposition *et* in the UD Hebrew treebank (only used with definite objects). The advantage is that it is easier to use the corpus to extract all object arguments of a certain verb, or to identify all cases of transitive verbs in general. As a criterion for objecthood, we use the possibility of the Stern-Jernstedt alternation: this criterion is more easily decidable than other tests which have been advocated, such as passivization (Zeman, 2017), since passives are not always reliably identifiable in Coptic (see above), though if passivizability is taken as a criterion (cf. Przepiórkowski and Patejuk 2018) then objects mediated by the prepositional case marker are in fact equally passivizable as well.

A further complication in Coptic direct objects arises from the fact that object clauses can co-occur with correlate pronouns in the main clause, as shown in Figure 2. In adopting the analysis in the figure we followed the practice found in

most UD treebanks, tolerating *obj* and coreferential *ccomp* for one verb, despite some misgivings.[9]

Although this analysis conforms to the practice in other treebanks, we are still considering alternatives, such as marking the pronoun in the matrix clause as *expl*, or using *dislocated* for the clause. However these solutions also lead to odd splits, whereby a pronoun could be expletive if the object clause was mentioned, but an object if the clause is fully pronominalized (i.e. when only a pronoun is used). Using *dislocated* is also counter-intuitive, since the clause is not actually out of place: it is in its expected position (not topicalized or unusually postponed). Finally some have proposed marking either the nominal argument or the clause as oblique (Przepiórkowski and Patejuk, 2018), but this seems odd too, since each construction in isolation looks like a core object.

8 Evaluation

In this section we evaluate the application of the UD annotation scheme to Coptic by conducting an inter-annotator agreement experiment using three pairs of annotators. We report label scores (LS) using Cohen's Kappa and % unlabeled attachment score (UAS) with and without punctuation.

The annotators include two pairs of BA students with three semesters of Coptic but no experience with corpus annotation or dependencies, and a third pair consisting of one MA student with two semesters of Coptic but substantial experience annotating English (and some Coptic) dependencies, and one professor proficient in Coptic and dependency annotation (these are also the co-authors of the present paper, and will be referred to as the 'Expert' group below).[10] For the undergraduate students, labeled group A and B, we conducted

---

type for these cases, e.g. *appos:disjoint*. While this would certainly be possible, such cases are overall rare, making such a label potentially very sparse. Conversely, it is fairly easy to locate such cases based on the dependency graph if needed, and from a linguistic perspective, there is nothing unusual about such appositions – the unusual construction is more properly the particle invariably appearing in second position.

[9]We take this to be a still open point, which we are looking forward to discussing: The current UD guidelines explicitly rule out multiple *obj* relations, but do not specifically refer to *obj* + *ccomp*, which Przepiórkowski and Patejuk (2018) take to be equivalent. Other UD literature has been ambivalent about ruling out multiple *obj* dependents in general (Zeman, 2017, 290). In practice, we have seen UD treebanks in multiple languages allow *obj* + *ccomp*, such as UD German-GSD, UD English-EWT, the UD French treebanks and others. German cases in particular seem to mirror the construction above, e.g. *Ich finde es wirklich toll, dass es Euch jetzt gibt!*, lit. "I find **it**$_{obj}$ really cool, that you **exist**$_{ccomp}$ now!".

[10]An anonymous reviewer has inquired whether the developers of the annotation scheme also taught the annotators Coptic, thereby facilitating higher than expected agreement. This was actually not the case: the BA students studied Coptic at the Hebrew University of Jerusalem, apart from the authors, and the MA student studied Coptic independently using a textbook.

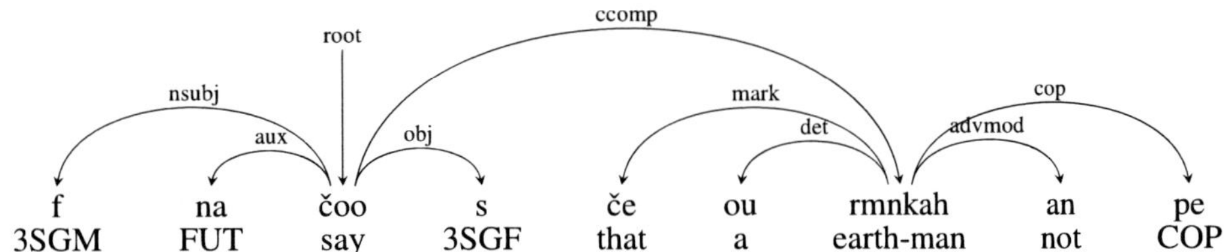

Figure 2: Analysis of a doubled object clause construction: *He would say (it) that he is not an earthly man.*

annotators	tokens	UAS (% agreement)		LS (kappa)	
		punctuation	no punctuation	punctuation	no punctuation
Group A: Pre-Adjud.	276	81.1%	79.0%	0.78	0.75
Group A: Post-Adjud.	319	87.7%	86.5%	0.88	0.86
Group B: Pre-Adjud.	287	84.3%	82.9%	0.79	0.76
Group B: Post-Adjud.	297	86.5%	84.6%	0.81	0.79
Expert	703	96.0%	95.8%	0.93	0.92

Table 4: Agreement Scores. 'no punctuation' denotes scores with punctuation removed from evaluation

two experiments: a pre-adjudication round and a post-adjudication round. In pre-adjudication, annotators only read the online UD Coptic guidelines without any prior annotation experience. Afterwards, student annotators discussed points of disagreement with the professor and adjudicated their sentences, before proceeding to the post-adjudication round, in which we expected annotators to fare better. Annotators had unlimited time to complete the task and the text in all rounds was a portion of *the Martyrdom of St. Victor*, which was presented together with a standard literary translation. As an annotation interface, we used the Arborator (Gerdes, 2013).

Table 4 compares the results of the three pairs of annotators. All results are divided into two sections: with and without punctuation.[11] Results are further separated into pre-adjudication and post-adjudication for the two undergraduate groups.

As shown, the expert annotator scores and the student annotator scores after post-adjudication exhibit relatively high levels of agreement. Within the label score (LS) category, expert annotators scored $k = 0.92$ without punctuation and 0.93 with punctuation, both of which can be considered very good agreement. Post-adjudication, group B produced a label score (LS) of 0.81, while group A scored 0.88. Both of these scores can

be interpreted as strong agreement, and noticeably higher than scores between 0.75–0.79, which were achieved solely by reading the guidelines and without previous annotation experience.

Unlabeled attachment scores (UAS) also shows good results. Expert annotators achieve 95.8% without punctuation and 96.0% with, and the student groups have reasonable post-adjudication agreement scores as high as 86.5% and 87.7%, respectively. We observed notable improvements from pre-adjudication to post-adjudication from the student groups. This shows that annotation accuracy on this task can improve after experience and discussing common annotation errors.

The fact that annotators are non-native speakers with limited experience with the language likely affects the inter-annotator agreement results and makes this a challenging task relative to evaluations in other languages, such as English. Berzak et al. (2016) report an agreement experiment on English dependencies with a UAS score of 97.16% and an LS score of 96.3%, conducted on section 23 of the Wall Street Journal corpus (Marcus et al., 1993). Although the labeled score is evaluated as % agreement rather than kappa, these results likely outperform our scores. However in a more challenging task of annotating English tweets, Liu et al. (2018) report a UAS score of 88.8% and LS score of 84.3%, showing that quality can vary substantially across text types.[12]

---

[11] Scores that include punctuation are based on punctuation attachment to the root, but Udapi (Popel et al., 2017) is used to automatically attach punctuation according to UD guidelines for the final adjudicated gold version.

[12] We do not mean to imply that Coptic data is similar to

Bamman et al. (2009) report results from a dependency annotation experiment on Ancient Greek with an attachment score of 87.4% and a label score of 85.3%. While this experiment wasn't within the UD framework, it offers comparable agreement scores with respect to non-native speaker annotation. The scores presented in their study are close to the attachment scores from our undergraduate student annotator pairs, though admittedly Coptic and Greek are typologically very distant. Scores from other African languages are scarce, but Seyoum et al. (2018) report a kappa score of 0.488 for agreement on UD relations for the morphologically rich language Amharic. This score is interpreted as moderate agreement and is substantially lower than our label scores.

We conducted an error analysis to find common areas of disagreement. While some errors can be attributed to simple, non-systematic mistakes, many high frequency errors are the result of complicated constructions or alternative interpretations of the text, which is at times not trivial to translate. The majority of disagreements for the expert annotators pertained to coordination scope (which is often ambiguous in the translation); confusion over labeling objects (*obj*) and obliques (*obl*), often due to annotating more closely to the source language or the available translation's interpretation; and whether an item has an (*obl*) relation to a verb or an (*nmod*) relation to its dependent noun in constructions that are close to light-verb constructions, but not entirely lexicalized. Coordination proved challenging for longer ambiguous sentences where, as non-native speakers, we relied on our own interpretation of the text for parsing. Confusion over labeling items as *obj* and *obl* can also be attributed to similar syntactic environments where objects and obliques are both mediated by the preposition ⲛ- *n-* 'of'.

9 Conclusion

In this paper we presented the Coptic Universal Dependency Treebank, the first treebank in the UD project from the Egyptian phylum of the Afro-Asiatic language family, and the first Coptic treebank in general. Our evaluation shows that UD guidelines can be applied to Coptic consistently, with rising accuracy based on annotator experience. We are currently expanding the treebank

______
tweets, but rather point out the variability in UD agreement scores depending on context.

and aim to reach a size allowing for the training of robust parsers and evaluating parsing results on Coptic in future shared tasks.

The discussion has also shown that there are a number of challenges in adapting the UD scheme for Coptic, some of which are shared with other languages: in particular, we advocate a less strict interpretation of adjacency constraints for the *appos* relation, which would also be needed for languages such as Classical Greek, and raise issues with the consistent encoding of pronominal/clausal double object constructions, as well as differential object marking and the handling of ambiguous passivization. We look forward to discussing these issues with the UD community.

Acknowledgments

This work is funded by the National Endowment for the Humanities (NEH) and the German Research Foundation (DFG) (grants HG-229371 and HAA-261271). Special thanks are due to Elizabeth Davidson for work on annotating multiple documents in the treebank, as well as to Israel Avrahamy, Asael Benyami, Yinon Kahan and Oran Szachter for annotating sections of the Martyrdom of Victor. We also thank the anonymous reviewers for helpful comments on previous versions of this paper.

References

Mathew Almond, Joost Hagen, Katrin John, Tonio Sebastian Richter, and Vincent Walter. 2013. Kontaktinduzierter Sprachwandel des Ägyptisch-Koptischen: Lehnwort-Lexikographie im Projekt Database and Dictionary of Greek Loanwords in Coptic (DDGLC). In *Perspektiven einer corpusbasierten historischen Linguistik und Philologie*, pages 283–315, Berlin. BBAW.

David Bamman, Francesco Mambrini, and Gregory Crane. 2009. An ownership model of annotation: The Ancient Greek dependency treebank. In *Proceedings of the Eighth International Workshop on Treebanks and Linguistic Theories (TLT 8)*, pages 5–15, Groningen.

Heike Behlmer and Frank Feder. 2017. The complete digital edition and translation of the Coptic Sahidic Old Testament. A new research project at the Göttingen Academy of Sciences and Humanities. *Early Christianity*, 8:97–107.

Yevgeni Berzak, Yan Huang, Andrei Barbu, Anna Korhonen, and Boris Katz. 2016. Anchoring and agreement in syntactic annotations. In *Proceedings of EMNLP 2016*, pages 2215–2224, Austin, TX.

Frank Feder, Maxim Kupreyev, Emma Manning, Caroline T. Schroeder, and Amir Zeldes. 2018. A linked Coptic dictionary online. In *Proceedings of LaTeCH 2018 - The 11th SIGHUM Workshop at COLING2018*, pages 12–21, Santa Fe, NM.

Kim Gerdes. 2013. Collaborative dependency annotation. In *Proceedings of the Second International Conference on Dependency Linguistics (DepLing 2013)*, pages 88–97, Prague.

Eitan Grossman. 2014. Transitivity and valency in contact: The case of Coptic. In *47th Annual Meeting of the Societas Linguistica Europaea*, Poznań, Poland.

Peter V. Jernstedt. 1927. Das koptische Praesens und die Anknüpfungsarten des näheren Objekts. *Doklady Akademii Nauk SSSR*, 1927:69–74.

Bentley Layton. 2011. *A Coptic Grammar*, third edition, revised and expanded edition. Porta linguarum orientalium 20. Harrassowitz, Wiesbaden.

Yijia Liu, Yi Zhu, Wanxiang Che, Bing Qin, Nathan Schneider, and Noah A. Smith. 2018. Parsing tweets into Universal Dependencies. In *Proceedings of NAACL-HLT 2018*, pages 965–975.

Antonio Loprieno. 1995. *Ancient Egyptian. A Linguistic Introduction*. Cambridge University Press, Cambridge.

Mitchell P. Marcus, Beatrice Santorini, and Mary Ann Marcinkiewicz. 1993. Building a large annotated corpus of English: The Penn Treebank. *Special Issue on Using Large Corpora, Computational Linguistics*, 19(2):313–330.

Siyao Peng and Amir Zeldes. 2008. All roads lead to UD: Converting Stanford and Penn parses to English Universal Dependencies with multilayer annotations. In *Proceedings of the Joint Workshop on Linguistic Annotation, Multiword Expressions and Constructions (LAW-MWE-CxG-2018)*, pages 167–177, Santa Fe, NM.

Stéphane Polis and Serge Rosmorduc. 2013. Building a construction-based treebank of Late Egyptian: The syntactic layer in Ramses. In Stéphane Polis & Jean Winand, editor, *Texts, Languages & Information Technology in Egyptology. Selected papers from the meeting of the Computer Working Group of the International Association of Egyptologists*, pages 45–59. Presses Universitaires de Liège.

Martin Popel, Zdenek Zabokrtský, and Martin Vojtek. 2017. Udapi: Universal API for Universal Dependencies. In *Universal Dependencies Workshop at NoDaLiDa 2017*, pages 96–101.

Adam Przepiórkowski and Agnieszka Patejuk. 2018. Arguments and adjuncts in Universal Dependencies. In *Proceedings of COLING2018*, pages 3837–3852, Santa Fe, NM.

Caroline T. Schroeder and Amir Zeldes. 2016. Raiders of the lost corpus. *Digital Humanities Quarterly*, 10(2).

Binyam Ephrem Seyoum, Yusuke Miyao, and Baye Yimam Mekonnen. 2018. Universal Dependencies for Amharic. In *Proceedings of LREC 2018*, pages 2216–2222, Miyazaki, Japan.

Ariel Shisha-Halevy. 1986. *Coptic Grammatical Categories. Structural Studies in the Syntax of Shenoutean Sahidic*. Pontificum Institutum Biblicum, Rome.

Dan Zeman. 2017. Core arguments in Universal Dependencies. In *Proceedings of the Fourth International Conference on Dependency Linguistics (Depling 2017)*, pages 287–296, Pisa, Italy.

Author Index

Øvrelid, Lilja, 18
Çöltekin, Çağrı, 8

Abrams, Mitchell, 192
Agić, Željko, 151
Alzetta, Chiara, 1
Angulo, Candy, 151
Asahara, Masayuki, 75, 117

Bentz, Christian, 8
Berdicevskis, Aleksandrs, 8
Blokland, Rogier, 126
Bouma, Gosse, 18

Cecchini, Flavio Massimiliano, 27
Choi, Jinho D., 75
Cotterell, Ryan, 91

Dell'Orletta, Felice, 1
Demberg, Vera, 8
Dobrovoljc, Kaja, 37
Droganova, Kira, 47
Dyer, William, 55

Ego Aguirre, Renzo, 151
Ehret, Katharina, 8

Gómez-Rodríguez, Carlos, 162
Gerdes, Kim, 66
Ginter, Filip, 47, 102
Guillaume, Bruno, 66

Hajic, Jan, 18
Han, Jiyoon, 108
Han, Na-Rae, 75
Haug, Dag, 18
Hulden, Mans, 91
Hwang, Jena D., 75

Kahane, Sylvain, 66
Kanayama, Hiroshi, 75
Kanerva, Jenna, 47, 102
Kim, Hansaem, 108
Kuhn, Jonas, 183

Lacroix, Ophélie, 85

Lim, KyungTae, 126
Lupyan, Gary, 8

Marongiu, Paola, 27, 102
Martinc, Matej, 37
Martynova, Aleksandra, 144
Matsumoto, Yuji, 75
McCarthy, Arya D., 91
Miller, John, 151
Miyao, Yusuke, 75
Montemagni, Simonetta, 1, 102

Nivre, Joakim, 18, 102
Noh, Youngbin, 108

Oh, Tae Hwan, 108
Omura, Mai, 117
Oncevay, Arturo, 151

Partanen, Niko, 126
Passarotti, Marco, 27
Perrier, Guy, 66
Poibeau, Thierry, 126

Rama, Taraka, 8
Rießler, Michael, 126
Ross, Daniel, 8

Sade, Shoval, 133
Schuster, Sebastian, 102
Seker, Amit, 133
Sheyanova, Mariya, 144
Silfverberg, Miikka, 91
Simi, Maria, 1, 102
Solberg, Per Erik, 18
Stepachev, Pavel, 144

Thompson, Bill, 8
Tsarfaty, Reut, 133
Tyers, Francis, 144

Vásquez, Alonso, 151
Venturi, Giulia, 1
Vilares, David, 162
Villanueva, Claudia, 151
Vinogorodskiy, Konstantin, 144

von Prince, Kilu, 8
Vu, Ngoc Thang, 183

Wróblewska, Alina, 173

Yan, Chunxiao, 8
Yarowsky, David, 91
Yu, Xiang, 183

Zariquiey, Roberto, 151
Zeldes, Amir, 192
Zeman, Daniel, 27, 47

Association for Computational Linguistics
209 N. Eighth Street
Stroudsburg, Pennsylvania 18360

ISBN 978-1-5108-7428-2